NORMS AND THE LAW

This book contains perspectives of world-renowned scholars from the fields of law, economics, and political science about the relationship between law and norms. The authors take different approaches by using a wide variety of perspectives from law, legal history, neoclassical economics, new institutional economics, game theory, political science, cognitive science, and philosophy. The essays examine the relationship between norms and the law in four different contexts. Part One consists of essays that use the perspectives of cognitive science and behavioral economics to analyze norms that influence the law. In Part Two, the authors use three different types of common property to examine cooperative norms. Part Three contains essays that deal with the constraints imposed by norms on the judiciary. Finally, Part Four examines the influence formal law has on norms.

John N. Drobak earned Bachelor of Science degrees in electrical engineering and management science from the Massachusetts Institute of Technology and a law degree from Stanford University. He joined the law faculty at Washington University in 1979, where he served as Associate Dean from 1986 to 1990, and now holds appointments as the George Alexander Madill Professor of Law in the School of Law and also in the Department of Economics in Arts and Sciences. He is the director of the Center for Interdisciplinary Studies in the School of Law, a fellow in the Center in Political Economy in Arts and Sciences, and former co-director of the Business, Law, and Economics Center in the John M. Olin School of Business. In his pro bono work, he consulted with Vaclav Klaus, then Finance Minister of Czechoslovakia and now President of the Czech Republic, in connection with Czechoslovakia's voucher privatization of large government enterprises and with the Republic of Georgia in connection with the drafting of a new constitution.

Norms and the Law

Edited by

JOHN N. DROBAK
Washington University School of Law

CAMBRIDGE
UNIVERSITY PRESS

CAMBRIDGE UNIVERSITY PRESS
Cambridge, New York, Melbourne, Madrid, Cape Town, Singapore, São Paulo

Cambridge University Press
32 Avenue of the Americas, New York, NY 10013-2473, USA

www.cambridge.org
Information on this title: www.cambridge.org/9780521862257

© Cambridge Universtiy Press 2006

First published 2006

Printed in the United States of America

A catalog record for this publication is available from the British Library.

Library of Congress Cataloging in Publication Data

Norms and the law / edited by John N. Drobak.
    p.   cm.
Includes bibliographical references and index.
ISBN-13: 978-0-521-86225-7 (hardback)
ISBN-10: 0-521-86225-6 (hardback)
ISBN-13: 978-0-521-68079-0 (pbk.)
ISBN-10: 0-521-68079-4 (pbk.)
1. Law – Social aspects.   2. Social norms.   I. Drobak, John N.   II. Title.
K370.N67   2006
340′.115 – dc22   2006001220

ISBN-13   978-0-521-86225-7 hardback
ISBN-10   0-521-86225-6 hardback

ISBN-13   978-0-521-68079-0 paperback
ISBN-10   0-521-68079-4 paperback

Contents

Contributors

Kathryn Abrams, Herma Hill Kay Distinguished Professor, University of California at Berkeley School of Law

Juan-Camilo Cárdenas, Facultad de Economia-CEDE, Universidad de Los Andes, Bogota, Columbia

Harry T. Edwards, Circuit Judge and Chief Judge Emeritus, United States Court of Appeals for the District of Columbia Circuit

Robert C. Ellickson, Walter E. Meyer Professor of Property and Urban Law, Yale Law School

John Ferejohn, Carolyn S. G. Munro Professor of Political Science, Stanford University, and Visiting Professor of Law and Politics, New York University School of Law

Lawrence M. Friedman, Marion Rice Kirkwood Professor, Stanford Law School

Larry D. Kramer, Richard E. Lang Professor of Law and Dean, Stanford Law School

Lawrence Lessig, C. Wendell and Edith Carlsmith Professor of Law, Stanford Law School

Douglass C. North, Spencer T. Olin Professor in Arts and Science, Washington University

Elinor Ostrom, Arthur F. Bentley Professor of Political Science, Indiana University

Amartya Sen, Lamont University Professor and Professor of Economics and Philosophy, Harvard University

Lynn A. Stout, Professor, University of California at Los Angeles School of Law

Cass R. Sunstein, Karl N. Llewellyn Distinguished Service Professor of Jurisprudence, University of Chicago, Law School and Department of Political Science

Acknowledgments

The essays in this book were initially presented at the inaugural conference of the Center for Interdisciplinary Studies at the Washington University School of Law. This book would not have been possible without the sponsorship and financial support of the Center. Linda McClain, who coordinated the conference for the Center, was instrumental to the success of that program. I am indebted to Hannah Fleener, a 2006 graduate of the Washington University School of Law, for her editorial assistance and to Jane Bettlach and Beverly Owens for their preparation of the manuscript. I appreciate the advice of Gary Libecap and an anonymous referee who reviewed the manuscript and the support of John Berger, my editor at the Cambridge University Press. Finally, I want to thank the authors of the essays in this book for their hard work, patience, and creativity. They are the ones who gave life to this book.

John N. Drobak

Introduction

John N. Drobak

Norms guide human conduct and social interaction as much as formal legal rules. The new institutional economics, premised on institutions as the "rules of the game" that structure social and economic systems, defines institutions to include informal rules, like norms, religious precepts and codes of conduct, and formal rules, like statutes and the common law.[1] In this sense, norms and law work in parallel to influence society.

Norms and law also have an impact on each other. Sometimes the law can be a strong influence on a change in norms, by forcing a change in conduct that gradually becomes accepted throughout society or by inducing a change in the perceptions about the propriety of certain conduct. Changes in social norms regarding the use of seat belts and smoking in public places are examples of this. Of course, the law can rarely change norms, even over decades, without the concomitant influence of education, propaganda, peer pressure, and other similar forms of social persuasion. The influence in the other direction, however, is much stronger because much of the law reflects society's values and norms.

A country's formal law grows out of its culture and society, as emphasized by scholars as different as F. A. Hayek and Lawrence Friedman.[2] The prevailing views of a society act as a constraint on both judge-made and statutory law because social norms influence judges and legislators alike. To the extent that law reflects society, enforcement costs are lower as citizens are more willing to follow the law. Similarly, if social norms promote adherence to contractual obligations and fairness in business dealings, there will be less need to resort

---

[1] See DOUGLASS C. NORTH, INSTITUTIONS, INSTITUTIONAL CHANGE AND ECONOMIC PERFORMANCE (1990).

[2] See 1 FRIEDRICH A. HAYEK, LAW, LEGISLATION AND LIBERTY 72–93 (1973); Lawrence M. Friedman, *Judging the Judges: Some Remarks on the Way Judges Think and the Way Judges Act*, this volume, *infra* p. 139.

to judicial enforcement of contractual and business obligations. Not only will
the legal system operate more efficiently, the economy will be more likely to
grow. As Douglass C. North has written, "Strong moral and ethical codes of
a society are the cement of social stability which makes an economic system
viable."[3]

Norms influence people to comply with the law even when doing so would
work against their own self interests. It is understandable that people will accept
a loss in a business transaction in order to establish a reputation that will bring
them more business in the future. But people comply with legal rules that
cause losses even if there is no possibility of a long-term gain. The question of
a society's support for and acceptance of the rule of law is part of the broader
question of how do groups overcome collective action problems or, to quote
Robert Putnam, how does a society create "social capital . . . that can improve
the efficiency of society by facilitating coordinated actions."[4] In economic
terms, it is the same as asking how to minimize free-riding; in game-theoretic
terms, it is asking how to induce people to cooperate rather than to defect.
Examining why people follow the rule of law is the same as trying to understand
why people cooperate. The answer lies in the norms that induce this type of
behavior.

Over the past few years, legal scholars have begun to devote more attention
to the importance of norms in analyzing legal issues.[5] The essays in this book
examine the relationship between norms and the law in four different contexts.
Part One consists of three essays, by Lynn Stout, Cass Sunstein, and Douglass
North, that use the perspectives of cognitive science and behavioral economics
to analyze norms that influence the law. The three essays in Part Two, by Robert
Ellickson, Lawrence Lessig, and Elinor Ostrom and Juan-Camilo Cárdenas,
use three different types of common property to examine cooperative norms.
Part Three contains four essays, by Lawrence Friedman, John Ferejohn and
Larry Kramer, Kathryn Abrams, and Harry T. Edwards, that deal with the
constraints imposed by norms on the judiciary. Finally, in Part Four, Amartya
Sen examines the influence formal law has on norms.

Part One begins with the essay "Social Norms and Other-Regarding Preferences" in which Lynn Stout examines the assumption of self-interest in the
rational choice model. While many contemporary critiques of rational choice
theory have focused on the assumption of rationality, few have examined

---

[3] Douglass C. North, Structure and Change in Economic History 47 (1981).
[4] Robert D. Putnam, Making Democracy Work: Civic Traditions in Modern Italy 167 (1993).
[5] *See* Lynn A. Stout, *Social Norms and Other-Regarding Preferences*, this volume, *infra* p. 13.

self-interest. Professor Stout argues that the tendency to act in an other-regarding fashion (to sacrifice in order to help or harm others) is far more pervasive, powerful, and important than generally recognized. In support of this claim, she reviews the extensive empirical evidence that has been accumulated over the past four decades on human behavior in social dilemma games, ultimatum games, and dictator games. This evidence establishes that in the right circumstances, experimental subjects routinely behave as if they care about costs and benefits to others. Moreover, the subjects' decisions to reveal other-regarding preferences appear driven primarily not by their own payoffs but by social context – that is, their perceptions of what others believe, what others expect, and how others are likely to behave.

Professor Stout then considers how understanding socially-contingent, other-regarding behavior may offer insights into the nature and workings of social norms. In particular, she uses the phenomenon of other-regarding preferences to examine questions that are crucial to understanding the role of norms in maintaining societies and countries. These include the questions of what sorts of behavior are most likely to solidify into norms, why people follow norms, and how policymakers can best use norms to change behavior. In her chapter, Professor Stout also surveys the broad scope of the legal scholarship on law and norms and lays a foundation for the consideration of norms in the rest of this book.

Cass Sunstein uses Chapter 2, "Damages, Norms, and Punishment," to analyze group decisionmaking in the context of jury deliberation. His survey of the evaluation of personal injury cases by thousands of people showed that all kinds of demographic groups displayed considerable agreement in how they ranked and rated the cases. This finding led Professor Sunstein to conclude that the social norms that govern moral outrage and intended punishment are widely shared. This cohesion breaks down, however, in the evaluation of the dollar amount of damage awards. A study of about 3,000 people put into 6-person juries showed that deliberation made the lower punishment ratings decrease when compared to the median of predeliberation judgments of individuals, while deliberation made the higher punishment ratings increase and drove up damage awards. The difference was so dramatic that in 27 percent of the cases the dollar value was as high as, or higher than, the highest individual predeliberation judgment.

To find an explanation for these consistent differences between individual and group decisionmaking, Professor Sunstein turned to notions of "group polarization" and "rhetorical asymmetry." He finds additional support for his conclusions in two studies of the effects of group deliberation on social norms, one involving the medical norm of protecting patients and the other the norm in favor of altruism. Then, Professor Sunstein examines the issue of punitive damages and asks whether the social norms at work in jury deliberation are consistent with optimal deterrence. Professor Sunstein ends his chapter with some tentative suggestions about how to deal with the cognitive problems faced by jurors and how to bring coherence to jury decisionmaking.

In Chapter 3, "Cognitive Science and the Study of the 'Rules of the Game' in a World of Uncertainty," Douglass North explains how economics, law, and social science in general should deal with the problem of uncertainty. He begins by departing from the rationality assumption and looks to Frederick Hayek for an alternative theory, based on the idea that the mind develops systems of classifications, theories, and belief systems to help the understanding of the external world. Assessing the effect of new policies, whether economic, legal, or social, can be quite difficult as a result of the feedback created by the consequences of the new policies. Not only might the feedback be imperfect, it might be so antithetical to the belief systems of the policymakers that they will be unwilling to recognize the true information provided by the feedback. Professor North uses the collapse of the Soviet Union to illustrate this.

Professor North then examines this feedback process in a world of uncertainty. He asks whether our social world is ergodic, that is, whether there is an underlying unity that would permit us to develop theories to explain the social world, just as scientists believe there is an underlying unity in the physical world that justifies the quest for explanatory and predictive theories in the physical sciences. If our social world is ergodic, social scientists are engaged in productive enterprises in their quest for underlying theories and policymakers have a chance at being effective. If the world is nonergodic, however, the work of social scientists and policymakers becomes much more difficult. It is this kind of dynamic world, without fundamental underlying structures, that makes research in cognitive science so important. Professor North concludes by explaining his belief that the study of the brain and its connections to the mind hold the greatest promise for dealing with a world of uncertainty.

Part Two uses three different types of "commons" – households, cyberspace, and natural resources – to examine cooperative norms and their relationship to laws that regulate common property. In Chapter 4, "Norms of the Household," Robert Ellickson defines a household to mean a private space where two or more people regularly share shelter and meals, including such social arrangements as a family sharing a home, students sharing an apartment, and unrelated adults living together in a house. Professor Ellickson limits his analysis to living arrangements in which the participants have the power to exit, as well as the power to control entry by newcomers. In the tradition of the "liberal commons" in which privilege of exit is a central feature, he refers to these arrangements as liberal households. Professor Ellickson uses economics to elucidate some of the central aspects of a household: distinguishing between those who supply capital to the household from those who supply labor; noting that a household living arrangement generates "household surplus" from the increased utility of living together; and analyzing who has the better claim to the surplus in different situations. He also analogizes to ownership and control rights of corporations, as well as using game theory to analyze the interaction among the members of the household. Professor Ellickson emphasizes that trust among the members of a household is the most important source of cooperation, but he also cites other interrelated sources of social control in a household. Norms sometimes are very important to the household, both in the form of internalized ethical norms and diffused enforced social norms. Contracts can be important, especially oral informal ones, as can be organizational rules for the household. Finally, Professor Ellickson notes the role of formal legal rules that govern household relations.

In his examination of the household, Professor Ellickson raises the question of whether the contribution of capital to a household bestows certain control powers or increases the risk of opportunistic behavior, as in a business firm. He also explores whether the threat of exit from the household can be used to gain a greater share of the household surplus or greater power to control the household. Finally, Professor Ellickson's analysis also raises the question of the importance of various procedural and decisionmaking rules within the household, such as acting by consensus or through a majority rule.

Lawrence Lessig views cyberspace as a commons in Chapter 5 because it is a resource that may be used simultaneously by millions of people without the need to obtain the permission of anyone else. In fact, Professor Lessig believes that the essence of the Internet was the decision to not allow anyone the power to control access. This took place through an unusual combination of property rights regimes. The bottom layer of the Internet is a physical layer made up of wires and computers, and wires linking computers, that are all owned. The middle layer is a logical layer made up of the protocols that make the Internet run. This layer is the commons, owned by no one and purposely open to all. The top, content, layer is both free and controlled. Much of the material accessible over the Internet is free to the user but controlled by someone who creates the webpage. It is the middle, logical layer that makes the Internet a commons. The creators of the Internet designed the protocols of that layer to permit anyone to have access to the Internet. The norm underlying the creation of the Internet was to make it free and open to all, unlike any other communications network. It was, as Professor Lessig puts it, the norm of "open code."

The commons feature of the Internet has led to extraordinary creativity as great as humankind has ever seen, not just innovation in technological matters but also innovation in human interaction and in cultural growth. This prompts Professor Lessig to ask how "an environment where property is only imperfectly protected" led to such an explosion in creativity and innovation. With tremendous profits available for businesses involved with the Internet, there is great pressure to diminish the commons and place more and more of all layers of the Internet under private control. This harm to the commons would, in turn, harm creativity and innovation. Professor Lessig identifies some of the principal threats to the Internet commons and questions how we can preserve the commons against those threats.

In Chapter 6, Elinor Ostrom and Juan-Camilo Cárdenas explain cooperative behavior through a framework that focuses on information gathering and learning for the building of norms that help reduce the tragedy of the commons. The authors note that experimental research still provides evidence of substantial variation in the levels of cooperation within the exact same treatment, a variation that cannot be totally explained by the laboratory setting or the rules induced by the experimenter. They point out that the differences may emerge from elements that the subjects bring into the lab from their own experience, values, group composition, or background. To reach those elements, Professors Ostrom and Cárdenas develop a framework of four layers of different kinds of information that individuals use when facing a collective-action dilemma. Two of the layers involve "systemic" variables that are difficult to control for in a laboratory setting. Consequently, the authors designed an experiment to study cooperation among the inhabitants of three different villages in Colombia, with the participants bringing to the game backgrounds and relationships that enabled the authors to analyze the two systemic layers. This enabled them to test their framework by comparing the experimental results from a laboratory setting with the results from their field experiments.

One of the norms that has now been widely discussed in the literature on collective action is reciprocity as a key engine for cooperation. Through the experimental data from the field, they show how reciprocal behavior in participants can, for the case of self-governed institutions such as face-to-face communication, help to reinforce group-oriented strategies in a game. On the other hand, negative reciprocity can act against the interests of the group within an institutional environment in which agents face imperfectly monitored regulations that are enforced by external authorities.

Professors Ostrom and Cárdenas conclude that their model provides "some initial guidance" in organizing the various factors relevant to cooperative behavior, but also raises questions about the importance of the information layers in different circumstances. The authors believe that some aspects of their model are poorly understood and understudied, such as the cross-effects between the layers and the characteristics of a game that prompt individuals to switch on and off different information layers. Their model also raises questions about the importance of contract law and enforcement since strong and well-enforced contractual rights make it unnecessary to use some of the information layers. From a broader perspective, the importance of the characteristics and experiences of individuals to the outcome of games raises doubt about the ability of transplanting legal systems from one country to another, where the culture, norms, and history of the two countries differ.

Part Three contains four essays that examine the influence of norms on the judiciary. Lawrence Friedman's essay in Chapter 7, "Judging the Judges: Some Remarks on the Way Judges Think and the Way Judges Act," investigates the popular conception of judges as impartial, independent, and autonomous decisionmakers. He does this by recognizing that judges are products of their contemporary society, of its culture and norms. Thus, Professor Friedman believes that the "framework of norms and values and ideas floating about in society" has a powerful impact on judicial rulings. Noting that judges invariably view themselves as free from social influences, Professor Friedman considers why that is and suggests that the process of judicial decisionmaking may explain this difference between perceptions and reality.

Professor Friedman's essay raises the question of the degree of social influences on judges. How much does it vary from judge to judge and from era to era? He also inquires whether there are systematic differences in judicial decisionmaking that can be attributed to race, gender, or ethnicity. Without a doubt, judges behave differently than legislators in making the law, but Professor Friedman seeks a better understanding of those differences in the context of the similar social influences on both groups.

In Chapter 8, "Judicial Independence in a Democracy: Institutionalizing Judicial Restraint," John Ferejohn and Larry Kramer focus on judicial independence, one of the characteristics examined by Professor Friedman. They do so from the premise that unbridled independence undermines democratic values and so our system of government tries to balance both. This is done through substantial protection of individual judges from political influence and from pressure by the other branches of government, while the judiciary as an institution is dependent upon (and so threatened by) political forces and other governmental actors. Professor Ferejohn and Dean Kramer review the numerous ways Congress and the President constrain the judiciary through such things as the appointment process, impeachment, budgets, executive enforcement of judicial decisions, and Congressional control over jurisdiction. They also examine the ways the judiciary minimizes conflict with the other branches through mechanisms for correcting individual judges when they ignore or erroneously apply prevailing law and through doctrines for removing cases from the purview of the judiciary, such as limits on jurisdiction and justiciability. These doctrines of self-restraint are equivalent to a judicial norm that has developed and become embedded since *Marbury v. Madison,* itself a case in which the ruling was designed to avoid conflict with the President.

Professor Ferejohn and Dean Kramer raise the issue of the proper balance between judicial independence and judicial accountability or, to put it another way, between the rule of law and democratic values. Their essay also asks the important question of why the branches of government avoid deep conflict with each other. Congress could do much more to limit the judiciary, through budgetary limitation, shrinking jurisdiction, or even impeachment, but Congress does not. The Supreme Court could expand its power by cutting back on its justiciability restraints, but it does not. This essay asks why this equilibrium between the branches of government continues to persist.

In Chapter 9, "Black Judges and Ascriptive Group Identification," Kathryn Abrams also considers an issue raised by Professor Friedman, that is, whether race affects judicial decisionmaking. Professor Abrams contrasts judicial impartiality from judicial "interdependence," which she defines as a judge's connection or affiliation with an identifiable group within the larger population. Using African-American judges as her study group, she examines empirical studies and judicial narratives to determine whether racial affinity has any effect on judicial conduct. The empirical studies found that the race of the judge made no significant difference in decisionmaking, except for sentencing in criminal cases. The narratives indicated the strongest effects took place outside the adjudicative process, with many African-American judges expressing an obligation to help other African-Americans in civic and social matters.

If it is true that African-American judges rule differently than other judges in criminal cases, Professor Abrams asks whether that means that African-American judges have been able to overcome barriers, including unconscious ones, to fair treatment of Blacks, rather than demonstrating greater partiality to members of their own race. She wonders whether interdependence may actually increase objectivity in some cases. Professor Abrams ends her essay by identifying a research agenda that would lead to a better understanding of the patterns and tentative conclusions she describes.

Harry T. Edwards adds another dimension to the analysis in Chapter 10, "Judicial Norms: A Judge's Perspective." He agrees with the assessment of Professor Ferejohn and Dean Kramer that the judiciary maintains its independence through self-restraint, but adds that the relationship between the branches of government is dynamic. Judge Edwards believes that the executive and legislative branches need to develop, over time, the habit of enforcing judicial judgments, which when reinforced, over time, by judicial self-restraint, will lead to the real independence of the judiciary. Judge Edwards also adds the importance of collegiality among the judges on a court to the development of judicial self-restraint. He believes that judges will better understand their limited role in governance if they view themselves as part of a collective enterprise. Citing examples from his experience as Chief Judge of the D.C. Circuit Court of Appeals, Judge Edwards agrees with the concern for administrative obstruction of the judiciary raised by Professor Ferejohn and Dean Kramer, but he believes that administrative obstruction does not impede the decisional independence of the judiciary.

Not surprisingly, Judge Edwards disagrees with Professor Friedman's assessment of the social and cultural constraints on judicial decisionmaking. Judge Edwards does believe that judges are "significantly constrained," but by discernible legal principles, not by social norms or contemporary views. The stark disagreement between these two authors may result from a focus on different kinds of court cases or from different temporal perspectives of society's influence, although it may reflect a genuine disagreement over the influences on judicial decisionmaking. Finally, as an African-American who has served as a judge for decades, Judge Edwards is an ideal commentator who supports the thesis of Professor Abrams. To those who would ask why we should care about racial diversity on the federal bench if race is largely irrelevant to judicial decisionmaking, Judge Edwards's thoughtful answer may surprise some readers.

The book ends in Chapter 11 with an essay by Amartya Sen, "Normative Evaluation and Legal Analogues," in which he reverses the focus of the other authors. Rather than examining the influence norms have on the law, he concentrates on formal law's effect on norms and rights. Professor Sen explains the importance of natural human rights in structuring a wide domain of human conduct, even though these rights are not part of the formal law. There is a long history of the distinction between human rights and legal rights, which Professor Sen illustrates by contrasting the views of Tom Paine and Mary Wollstonecraft with those of Jeremy Bentham. Professor Sen also emphasizes the harm that can result to basic human rights, such as freedom from poverty, by the view that rights not formalized into law are somehow subordinate or inferior to legal rights. An even greater danger, according to Professor Sen, stems from the excessive influence of legal thinking on moral and political reasoning. The wide-spread acceptance of the legal contract as the proper analogy for contemporary philosophical investigation is harmful because a contractarian model rigidly confines analysis and forecloses alternative perspectives. This is especially the case, Professor Sen believes, for issues involving global justice. Consequently, he argues for an alternative mode of analysis based on Adam Smith's "impartial spectator."

In considering the relationship between law and rights, Professor Sen argues that many rights should not be enacted into formal law. His analysis raises two important questions that are relevant to many of the other essays in the book – which rights should be formalized into law and which should be left as custom or norms; and how should we determine that boundary between formal law and moral rights and duties? Many of the authors provide their own answers to Professor Sen's questions, albeit implicitly in some cases.

As you read this book, you will see the different styles and approaches of the authors as they examine the relationship between norms and the law in a variety of contexts. These differences reflect the wide range of academic disciplines used in the essays – including law, legal history, neoclassical economics, new institutional economics, experimental economics, game theory, political science, cognitive science, and philosophy. This blend of perspectives from so many disciplines is one of the special attributes of this book.

PART ONE

RATIONALITY AND NORMS

1 Social Norms and Other-Regarding Preferences

Lynn A. Stout

Several months ago I returned home from an out-of-town business trip. By the time the taxi made the trip from the airport to my house it was dark. The driver told me the fare was $16, and I fumbled in my wallet and pulled out what I thought was a $20 bill. I gave the bill to the driver and told him to keep the change. There came a moment of silence. Then the driver said, "You just gave me a $50 bill."

In the early 1980s, when I was taking graduate level courses in economics and in law, my instructors taught me that events like this generally did not occur, and if they did, I ought not pay attention because such behavior was uncommon and unpredictable. Instead, I was taught that the best way to model human behavior was to assume that people always behaved like *homo economicus* – that they were both perfectly rational and perfectly selfish creatures. Both I and my instructors knew, of course, that real people did not always behave this way. But departures from rational selfishness were presumed to be rare, capricious, and not worth trying to consider.

Times change, and these days even scholars who are sympathetic to rational choice – I fit myself into that category – have begun to question the wisdom of always assuming that people behave in a rational and selfish manner.[1] This trend is especially obvious in the legal literature. In the last few years legal scholars have published a flurry of articles investigating how human choices are distorted by overconfidence, framing effects, anchoring effects, availability biases, and similar deficiencies of human cognition.[2]

[1] Rational choice analysis has both normative and positive aspects. From a normative perspective, rational choice analysis usually assumes a goal of maximizing social welfare, interpreted either as maximizing aggregate utility or maximizing aggregate wealth. This essay embraces the normative goal of rational choice while questioning its positive assumptions and especially the assumption that human behavior is driven by selfishness.

[2] See, e.g., Jon D. Hanson & Douglas A. Kysar, *Taking Behavioralism Seriously: The Problem of Market Manipulation*, 74 N.Y.U. L. REV. 630 (1999); Christine Jolls, Cass R. Sunstein &

There is a curious imbalance to this new "behavioral law and economics" literature, however. Contemporary challenges to the rational selfishness model of human behavior tend to focus more on the first adjective – the assumption of rationality – than on the second – the assumption of selfishness. In this essay I reverse that emphasis. Instead of examining the myriad ways in which human beings act illogically, I focus on the many ways in which we act as if we care about the costs borne and the benefits enjoyed by others.

I shall refer to this phenomenon as *other-regarding preferences*. It is important to understand that in adopting this phrase, I am employing the word "preferences" in its most narrow and technical economic sense. In other words, I am describing *behavior* rather than *motivation*. I make no attempt to determine what might subjectively inspire one person to look out for another's interests. Pride, guilt, love, or religious piety may be responsible, or something else entirely. The point is that people sometimes *do* behave as if they care about costs and benefits to others. When they do, they have (in the economist's parlance) "revealed a preference" for taking account of others' welfare.[3]

I focus on the phenomenon of other-regarding preferences for two reasons. First, I am a bit of an optimist. To an optimist, the currently popular task of cataloging people's various cognitive deficiencies can be a bit depressing, as it often leads to the conclusion that someone who is left to make her own choices will use this freedom to shoot herself in the foot. The natural implication is that people are flighty, neurotic, and weak-minded, and these deficiencies must be either remedied or compensated for to maximize social welfare.

In contrast, the phenomenon of other-regarding preferences casts a much more flattering light on human nature. This is because other-regarding preferences have tremendous potential to make people *better off*. As an economist would put it, other-regarding preferences can be efficient.

The potential efficiency of other-regarding preferences lies in their capacity to address a basic problem in economics. This is the problem of inefficient "externalities." Externalities occur whenever people make choices that ignore

---

Richard Thaler, *A Behavioral Approach to Law and Economics*, 50 STAN. L. REV. 1471 (1998); Russell Korobkin, *Bounded Rationality, Standard Form Contracts, and Unconscionability*, 70 U. CHI. L. REV. 1203 (2003); Russell B. Korobkin & Thomas S. Ulen, *Law and Behavioral Science: Removing the Rationality Assumption from Law and Economics*, 88 CAL. L. REV. 1051 (2000); Symposium, *Empirical Legal Realism: A New Social Scientific Assessment of Law and Human Behavior*, 97 NW. U. L. REV. 1075 (2003).

[3] As this discussion suggests, this essay is not offering a cognitive model of other-regarding behavior. Although such a model would be extremely useful, social scientists are not in agreement about what motivates other-regarding behavior. Instead, this essay adopts a simple behavioral approach that treats the human actor as a "black box" whose inner workings are unobservable. We can only observe the inputs that go into the box and the behavior that comes out. As will be seen, even this simple approach offers a variety of useful insights.

costs and benefits to others: for example, whenever a smoker lights up in a restaurant or a *homo economicus* out for a stroll by a river ignores the cries of a drowning child. Someone who cares about others' welfare will think twice before imposing costs on or withholding benefits from those around them. As a result, other-regarding preferences can "internalize" what would otherwise be external costs and benefits, allowing us to achieve better outcomes, in terms of both individual and aggregate social welfare, than we can through selfishness alone.

I have a second reason for wanting to draw attention to the phenomenon of other-regarding preferences, however. In brief, other-regarding preferences may be far more common and important than generally recognized. Extensive empirical evidence suggests that people often behave as if they are keeping at least one eye on others' welfare. Moreover, far from being rare or mercurial, this tendency towards other-regarding behavior is pervasive, powerful, and to a great degree predictable. That observation in turn suggests that a solid understanding of the phenomenon of other-regarding preferences is essential to a solid understanding of the behavior of both individuals and societies.

In illustration, I will explore the role other-regarding preferences may play in creating and enforcing social norms. As noted earlier, legal scholars have become intrigued by behavioral approaches to the law. This enthusiasm has been matched, however, by their increasing fascination with the phenomenon that is the subject of this volume – the phenomenon of social "norms." Over the past decade legal scholars have published a host of articles, symposia, and books addressing how norms regulate behavior and how they interact with legal rules in the process.[4]

Even a cursory review of this literature quickly reveals a puzzle, however. There is substantial difference of opinion in the legal literature about how norms work and even what norms are. A general consensus holds that norms are rules of behavior that people follow for some reason *other than* the fear of legal sanction. Beyond this area of agreement, norms scholars disagree significantly in their views of how norms should be defined and why people follow norms-based rules.[5]

---

[4] *See, e.g.*, Robert C. Ellickson, Order Without Law: How Neighbors Settle Disputes (1991); Eric A. Posner, Law and Social Norms (2000); Richard H. McAdams, *The Origin, Development, and Regulation of Social Norms*, 96 Mich. L. Rev. 338, 343–46 (1997); Symposium, *Law, Economics, and Norms*, 144 U. Pa. L. Rev. 1643 (1996); Symposium, *The Legal Construction of Norms*, 86 Va. L. Rev. 1577 (2002); Symposium, *Norms and Corporate Law*, 149 U. Pa. L. Rev. 1607 (2001); Symposium, *Social Norms, Social Meaning, and the Economic Analysis of Law*, 27 J. Legal Stud. 537 (1998).
[5] Robert C. Ellickson, *The Evolution of Social Norms: A Perspective from the Legal Academy*, in Social Norms 35, 36 (Michael Hechter & Karl-Dieter Opp eds., 2001).

This essay addresses the norms puzzle by suggesting that there may be an important linkage between these two emerging areas of scholarship (behavioral analysis of law and the study of social norms). In particular, it argues that the phenomenon of other-regarding preferences offers important insights into what norms are, how norms work, and what sorts of norms are most likely to emerge under what circumstances. But before we explore how other-regarding behavior sheds light on social norms, we must first address an antecedent question: do revealed other-regarding preferences exist?

I. EMPIRICAL EVIDENCE OF OTHER-REGARDING PREFERENCES

Everyday life is full of anecdotal evidence of other-regarding behavior. Travelers leave tips in restaurants they do not expect to visit again; strangers on the street offer directions to the lost; cab drivers stop passengers from paying mistakenly high tips. Yet anecdotal evidence alone may not suffice to convince a dedicated skeptic that people are not purely selfish. The reason has to do with the fact that contemporary life is usually arranged so that other-regarding behavior is also consistent with, if perhaps not fully explained by, observable external incentives.[6]

Suppose, for example, that I walk down the street and no one mugs me. (I have performed this experiment successfully on many occasions and in many locations.) One possible explanation for this result is that most people would prefer not to harm me just to get the contents of my wallet. However, it also is possible that I have not been mugged because most people fear that if they did mug me they would be arrested and thrown into jail. It is also possible that would-be muggers worry that if they attacked me I would harm *them* (unlikely, but not entirely out of the question). Finally, perhaps my fellow pedestrians have been deterred from mugging me by the concern that they might be observed by others who know them and who would carry news of their misbehavior back to their neighborhoods, sullying their reputations.

---

[6] Other-regarding behavior is often consistent with legal incentives because a variety of legal rules, including many rules of criminal, tort, and contract law, are designed to promote other-regarding behavior. Similarly, many of the acts of altruism we observe in daily life involve people who are acquainted with each other or who operate in the same community. As a result it is difficult to rule out the possibility that apparently other-regarding behavior observed "in the field" is in fact motivated entirely by concern for future consequences in the form of legal sanctions, reciprocal interactions, or reputational loss.

In daily life it is hard to rule out external forces entirely as reasons for good behavior. For example, I once recounted the story of the cab driver to a colleague. He suggested, with a straight face, that perhaps the cab driver corrected my mistake and told me I had given him a $50 bill because the driver suspected me of being a plainclothes officer sent out by the taxi-regulating authorities.[7] This seemed quite unlikely to me. Nevertheless I could not disprove his hypothesis. To convince such a cynic one needs more than anecdotal evidence.

Luckily, there is much more than anecdotal evidence available. A full review of the social sciences literature on other-regarding behavior lies well beyond the scope of this essay. (Indeed, it might make a nice multi-volume treatise.) Instead I focus on a particular kind of evidence that ought to persuade even the dedicated cynic. This is evidence that has emerged from several decades of experiments in which social scientists have placed human subjects into situations quite consciously designed to make their self-interest, as measured by their external rewards and punishments, conflict with the interests of others.

In particular, I focus on three broad categories of experiments commonly known as *social dilemma* games, *ultimatum* games, and *dictator* games. As will be seen, these experimental games force subjects to choose between strategies that maximize their own payoffs, and strategies that help or harm others. As will also be seen, the results of these experiments establish conclusively that other-regarding revealed preferences exist. They also offer considerable insight *when* and *why* other-regarding preferences appear.

A. *Social Dilemma Games and Altruism*

Let us begin with one of the best-known experimental games to demonstrate other-regarding preferences, the *social dilemma* game. As its name suggests, the social dilemma game is based on the familiar prisoner's dilemma of game theory. However, where the archetypal prisoner's dilemma involves only two people, social dilemma games can be played by more (sometimes quite a few more) than two players. As in a prisoner's dilemma, each subject in the game is allowed to choose between a "cooperation" strategy or a noncooperative "defection" strategy. As in the prisoner's dilemma, an individual player always maximizes her personal payoff by defecting, no matter what the other players

---

[7] The cabdriver offered a different explanation. When I complimented him on his honesty he replied, "I have to live with myself." Although this statement clearly suggests some internal enforcement mechanism, the point is that it *is* internal.

choose to do. As in the prisoner's dilemma, however, the group gets the greatest aggregate payoff when all its members choose to cooperate.

A typical example of a social dilemma is the "contribution game." A group of players – say, four individuals – is assembled. Each player is given an initial monetary "stake" of some amount, perhaps $20. The players are then asked to choose between either keeping all the cash they have been given for themselves, or contributing some or all of it a common "investment pool." The players are told that any money contributed to the pool will be doubled and then distributed back to the players in equal amounts, whether or not they chose to contribute to the pool. A moment's thought quickly reveals that the best strategy for the individual player is to keep the $20 and hope to receive as well one-fourth of any amount that ends up in the common pool. The relentless pursuit of self-interest, however, ultimately leaves both the group and its individual members worse off. If each player keeps selfishly keeps all his or her $20 stake, each ends up with $20. If each contributes the entire $20, each receives $40 back.

This example demonstrates how social dilemmas are structured so that no rational selfish player would ever choose to cooperate. What do real people do?

Over the past four decades social scientists have reported the results of count-less studies testing how real people behave when asked to play a single social dilemma game with strangers.[8] Rational choice theory predicts that there is a zero percent probability that a subject in such a "one-shot" game would choose to cooperate. Defection is always the dominant strategy for *homo economicus*. Yet when *homo sapiens* play social dilemma games, experimenters observe cooperation rates averaging about 50 percent.[9]

What does this finding tell us? Most obviously, that other-regarding prefer-ences exist and indeed are common. The subject in a social dilemma game who chooses to cooperate is choosing an option that quite plainly serves the group's interest more than her own.[10] There are several lay terms available to

[8] *See, e.g.*, David Sally, *Conversation and Cooperation in Social Dilemmas: A Meta-Analysis of Experiments from 1958 to 1992*, 7 RATIONALITY & SOC'Y 58 (1995) (summarizing over 100 studies done between 1958 and 1992); Robyn M. Dawes & Richard H. Thaler, *Anomalies: Coopera-tion*, 2 J. ECON. PERSP. 187 (1988) (summarizing studies); Robyn M. Dawes et al., *Coopera-tion for the Benefit of Us – Not Me, or My Conscience*, in BEYOND SELF-INTEREST 97–110 (Jane J. Mansbridge ed., 1990) (summarizing studies); Toshio Yamagishi, *The Structural Goal/ Expectation Theory of Cooperation in Social Dilemmas*, 3 ADVANCES IN GROUP PROCESSES 51 (1986) (summarizing studies).

[9] *See* Sally, *supra* note 8, at 62 (finding mean cooperation rate of 47.4 in sample of 130 studies).

[10] Again, the claim that cooperation does not "serve" the player's interest refers to external payoffs and not to any internal rewards that might motivate cooperation. Guilt, sympathy, ego, or

describe this type of other-regarding preference, including kindness, consideration, generosity, sympathy, and (more generally) altruism.

B. *Ultimatum Games and Spite*

Altruism is not the only type of other-regarding preference we find in experimental subjects, however. Social dilemmas demonstrate that people sometimes sacrifice their own payoffs to help others. It turns out they also sometimes sacrifice their own payoffs to harm others.

This phenomenon can be observed in the results of a second experimental game known as the *ultimatum game*. The typical ultimatum game involves two players. The first player, who is called the "proposer," is given a stake of money (say, $20). The proposer is then told that she can offer to give any portion of the $20 that she chooses – all, a lot, a little, or nothing – to the second player. The second player, who is called the "responder," then has a choice of his own. The responder can choose to accept the proposer's offer. In this case the $20 stake will be divided between the two players exactly as the proposer suggests. The responder can also choose to reject the proposer's offer. If the responder rejects the offer, both players get nothing.

It is clear what *homo economicus* would do in an ultimatum game. A *homo economicus* proposer would offer the minimum amount of money possible short of offering nothing (one penny), and a *homo economicus* responder would accept this minimal amount. It is also clear from the experimental results that real people don't play ultimatum games this way. When people play ultimatum games, the proposer usually offers the responder a substantial portion of the stake, often half.[11] And – this is even more interesting – if the proposer does *not* do this, the responder frequently responds by rejecting the offer.[12]

Revenge is sweet. But in an ultimatum game, it is not costless. When a responder in an ultimatum game rejects any positive offer, he loses an opportunity to make himself better off (as measured by external payoffs) than he was before. Why does he choose to do this? The explanation that immediately comes to mind is that the responder wants to punish the proposer. If the altruism

---

religious piety may all lead a player to conclude she is psychologically better off (happier, less conflicted) if she cooperates. Whatever the internal mechanism, subjects who cooperate in a social dilemma can be said to "reveal a preference for" (to *act as if* they care about) serving others' welfare.

[11] *See generally* Colin Camerer & Richard H. Thaler, *Anomalies: Ultimatums, Dictators and Manners*, 9 J. ECON. PERSP. 209 (1995) (summarizing studies); Martin A. Nowak et al., *Fairness Versus Reason in the Ultimatum Game*, 289 SCI. 1773 (2000) (same).

[12] Camerer & Thaler, *supra* note 11, at 210 ("offers of less than 20 percent are frequently rejected").

seen in social dilemma games is the light side of other-regarding preferences, ultimatum games give us a glimpse of the dark side. Responders who reject offers that they perceive to be "too low" are displaying a willingness to incur a personal sacrifice not to help another but to *harm* her. Synonyms for this form of other-regarding behavior include malevolence, antipathy, vengefulness, and spite.

C. *Dictator Games and Second-Order Effects*

As noted above, ultimatum games demonstrate that other-regarding preferences can take the form of a willingness to sacrifice to harm others as well as a willingness to sacrifice to help them. But ultimatum games teach us something else as well.

To see what, we need to compare the behavior observed in ultimatum games with that observed in a similar but slightly different sort of game called the *dictator game*. Just as in the typical ultimatum game, there are two players in the typical dictator game. Just as the proposer in an ultimatum game is given an initial stake of money and invited to propose a distribution rule, one of the two players in a dictator game is given an initial stake and asked to divide that money between herself and the second player. However, a dictator game differs from an ultimatum game in an important respect. In a dictator game, the second player is not given any choice or any right to veto the first player's division of the loot. (This is why the first player is now called a "dictator.") The second player gets what the dictator is willing to give up, no more and no less.

Interestingly, most subjects asked to fill the role of the dictator in a dictator game choose to give the other player at least some portion of their initial stake.[13] Thus most subjects who play the dictator display at least some degree of altruism. However, while dictators in dictator games usually share their wealth, on average they do not share *as much* of their initial stake as proposers in ultimatum games do. Offers in dictator games tend to be smaller than offers in ultimatum games.[14]

This finding is significant. It suggests that in addition to being influenced by the sort of altruistic preferences we see in social dilemmas, dictator games, and ultimatum games alike, proposers in ultimatum games are subject to a second influence that increases their willingness to share their stakes. This second, additional influence seems to be a fear that a responder in an ultimatum game

---

[13] Camerer & Thaler, *supra* note 11, at 213.   [14] *Id.*

might react to a low offer by spitefully choosing to reject the offer. In other words, proposers in ultimatum games fear responders' vengeance.

This is an interesting observation, for it suggests not only that people have other-regarding preferences, but also that they know that *other* people have other-regarding preferences. That possibility in turn suggests that other-regarding preferences influence human behavior on at least two levels.

At the first level, other-regarding preferences can cause some people to make sacrifices either to help or to harm others around them. In other words, people who have other-regarding preferences will behave differently than they would if they were purely selfish.

At the second level, the knowledge that some people have other-regarding preferences will lead *other people* to alter their behavior in reliance upon this possibility – even if those others are themselves are purely selfish. For example, suppose Mary is purely selfish, like *homo economicus*. She still might choose to deliberately make herself vulnerable to John if she expects John to behave altruistically. This sort of reliance behavior might be called "rational trust." Similarly, a selfish Mary might avoid taking advantage of John's vulnerability if she believes that if she were to exploit John, John would be willing to incur a personal cost just to spitefully punish her. This might be called "rational fear of vengeance."

D. *Determinants of Other-Regarding Preferences in Experimental Games*

At this point it is possible to summarize at least three important lessons to be learned from social dilemma games, ultimatum games, and dictator games. These lessons are: (1) people sometimes reveal other-regarding preferences; (2) other-regarding preferences come in both positive (altruistic) and negative (vengeful) flavors; and (3) other-regarding preferences can have both first- and second-order effects on human behavior.

These are interesting lessons, especially to those weaned on the *homo economicus* model of human behavior. Alone, however, their usefulness remains limited. To predict human behavior – more, to influence human behavior – we need to know other things as well. Most obviously, we need to know *when* people are likely to reveal other-regarding preferences.

Let us return again to the 50 percent cooperation rate typically observed in many social dilemma experiments. This 50 percent cooperation rate result supports the claim that people can behave in an other-regarding fashion. But it also supports the claim that people can behave selfishly. After all, if people were purely altruistic, we would observe 100 percent cooperation rates.

What can explain why some people cooperate but others don't, or why the same person may cooperate at one time and not at another? What determines when we are altruistic, when we are spiteful, and when, like Rhett Butler, we don't give a damn?

Answers to these questions are available. Over the past four decades social scientists have published the results of literally hundreds of studies of human behavior in social dilemmas, ultimatum games, and dictator games.[15] These studies have produced a wealth of evidence on who is likely to behave in an other-regarding fashion and under what circumstances they are most likely to do this. Taken as a whole, the evidence strongly supports the following proposition: *whether or not people behave in an other-regarding fashion is determined largely by social context, tempered – but only tempered – by considerations of personal cost.*

1. The Role of Social Variables

One of the most consistent and striking findings that has emerged from the experimental literature is that human behavior in social dilemma, ultimatum, and dictator games appears largely driven by what might be called "social" variables. In other words, the subjects' decisions whether or not to behave in an other-regarding fashion in these games appear largely determined by their perceptions of how their behavior will affect others; their perceptions of what others expect and desire of them; their perceptions of how others are themselves likely to behave; and their perceptions of the nature of their relationships with others.

Homo economicus, of course, would be indifferent to such considerations unless they somehow altered his own payoffs. Real people seem exquisitely sensitive to social cues. Recall the 50 percent average cooperation rate commonly observed in one-shot social dilemma experiments. This average figure obscures an important reality: cooperation rates in social dilemma experiments can vary widely and appear to be highly manipulable. By altering particular variables, experimenters have been able to reliably elicit cooperation rates from different groups of subjects that range *from a low of 5 percent to more than 95 percent.*[16] (To appreciate what a truly astonishing degree of range this is, simply recall that the payoff function in a social dilemma is structured so that a rationally selfish player would *always* defect.)

What types of social variables have proven important in determining cooperation rates in social dilemma games? Researchers have found that cooperation

---

[15] *See* authorities cited *supra* notes 8, 11.   [16] Sally, *supra* note 8, at 62.

rates can be raised by allowing the players to speak with each other;[17] by promoting or discouraging a sense of group identity among the players;[18] and by increasing the benefits of cooperation to one's fellow players (that is, the size of the loss to the group if a self-interested strategy is chosen).[19] In this essay, however, I want to highlight in particular two social variables that appear especially important, in a statistical sense, to determining the incidence of other-regarding behavior in experimental games. These variables are (1) instructions from authority and (2) whether subjects believe that their fellow players will behave in an other-regarding fashion.

Studies have consistently found that subjects in a social dilemma game tend to do what the experimenter instructs them to do. If the experimenter says "cooperate," they cooperate; if the experimenter says "defect," they defect.[20] This behavior is puzzling from a rational choice perspective, because the experimenter's instructions do not alter the objective payoffs in the game. Nevertheless, people are so sensitive to directions from authority that they change their behavior in response to mere *hints* about what the experimenter desires. In one experiment, for example, subjects playing a social dilemma game were told that they were playing the "Community Game." The experimenters observed a cooperation rate of 60 percent. When a group of similar subjects was told they were playing the "Wall Street Game," the cooperation rate dropped to 30 percent.[21]

A second social variable that appears to have an especially strong impact on other-regarding behavior in experimental games is whether or not a player perceives the other players in the game as other-regarding. This pattern is obvious in the case of the ultimatum game, where the perception that a proponent is too "selfish" (self-regarding) often triggers other-regarding spiteful behavior from the responder.[22] But social dilemma studies also demonstrate the importance

---

[17] *Id.* at 78.

[18] If experimental subjects are divided into subgroups and then asked to play a social dilemma game with members of another subgroup, cooperation rates fall below those observed when the experimenter makes no attempt to foment any subgroup identity. *Id.* at 78. *See also* Camerer & Thaler, *supra* note 11, at 213–14 (reporting study finding that the size of the offers made by dictators in dictator games gets smaller as "social distance" between dictator and recipient increases).

[19] Sally, *supra* note 8, at 79.   [20] *Id.* at 78.

[21] *See* Lee Ross & Andrew Ward, *Naive Realism in Everyday Life: Implications for Social Conflict and Misunderstanding, in* VALUES AND KNOWLEDGE 103, 106–07 (T. Brown et al. eds., 1996). Similar results have been observed in dictator games, where dictators make larger offers when they are instructed to "divide" their stakes than when the experimenters use the "language of exchange." *See* Camerer & Thaler, *supra* note 11, at 213.

[22] Interestingly, responders are more likely to accept a small offer they believe was generated by a computer than a small offer they think came from a human proposer. Camerer & Thaler, *supra* note 11, at 214–15.

of others' choices in triggering one's own other-regarding behavior: subjects who believe that their fellow players are likely to cooperate are far more likely to cooperate themselves.[23] This second result is particularly good evidence of how social factors can outweigh selfish economic concerns in determining other-regarding behavior, because a belief that other players in a social dilemma game will cooperate *increases* the perceived economic return from defecting oneself. Nevertheless, subjects who expect other players to behave altruistically are themselves more likely to choose altruism.

2. The Role of Economic Variables
The previous section explores how social cues play critical roles in eliciting other-regarding behavior. This does not mean, however, that economic payoffs are irrelevant. To the contrary, a second significant finding that emerges from the experimental literature is that other-regarding preferences depend not only on social context, but also on personal economic payoffs. People are more likely to indulge in altruism and spite when it doesn't cost too much to do so.

This is not, of course, the same thing as saying that people are purely self-regarding: *any* degree of cooperation in a social dilemma, and *any* significant sharing in an ultimatum or dictator game, is inconsistent with the *homo economicus* model. But the observation that people are capable of both benevolence and malice does not mean that they are indifferent to costs associated with these behaviors. When people indulge in altruism or spite, they keep one eye on self-interest in doing so.

This phenomenon is perhaps most clearly observable in social dilemma games, where studies have found that as the personal cost associated with cooperating in a social dilemma rises (that is, as the expected gains from defecting increase), cooperation rates tend to decline.[24] Similarly, and as noted earlier, if a proposer offers a relatively larger share in a dictator game, the likelihood that the responder will spitefully reject it decreases.[25] Such results suggest that the supply of other-regarding behavior is, in a sense, "downward-sloping."

---

[23] *See* Scott T. Allison & Norbert L. Kerr, *Group Correspondence Biases and the Provision of Public Goods*, 66 J. PERSONALITY & SOC. PSYCHOL. 688 (1994) ("[n]umerous studies have reported that individuals are more likely to cooperate when they expect other group members to cooperate than when they expect others to defect"); Yamagishi, *supra* note 8, at 64–65 (discussing experimental findings that "expectations about other members' behavior is one of the most important individual factors affecting members' decisions in social dilemmas").

[24] *See, e.g.,* Sally, *supra* note 8, at 75 (finding in regression analysis of over 100 social dilemma studies that doubling the reward from defecting decreased average cooperation rates by as much as 16 percent).

[25] This is not quite as good evidence of the influence of personal cost, because a larger offer might also lead a responder to conclude a proposer is acting "fairly" and that spite is not called for.

The higher the personal cost associated with other-regarding behavior, the less likely a person will indulge in it. People are more likely to act altruistically when altruism is inexpensive, and more likely to act spitefully when spite is cheap.[26]

E. *On the Efficiency of Other-Regarding Preferences*

The observation that other-regarding behavior depends on both social context and personal cost leads to an interesting conclusion. In brief: *most people seem to have at least two personalities or revealed preference functions.*[27] The first might be described as our "self regarding" personality. When our self-regarding personality dominates, we seek to maximize our personal payoffs without any apparent regard for how our behavior affects others. Most people, however, have a second, more "other-regarding" personality. When our other-regarding personality dominates we take account of how our conduct affects others, at least to some extent. Like the Roman god Janus, we all wear two faces. Which we choose to present to the world in any particular situation is determined by social context, tempered by considerations of personal cost.

From a purely intellectual standpoint this is surely an intriguing perspective on human nature. It may also be of tremendous practical consequence. This is because our human capacity to adopt other-regarding preferences may be of vital importance in promoting the welfare of both individuals and societies.

To understand why, take a moment to imagine a world in which everyone was in fact perfectly selfish. In economic terms, *homo economicus* is utterly indifferent to the external costs and benefits that flow from her actions. She plots her course through life with complete indifference to the wake she leaves behind her, ignoring both injuries she inflicts on others and blessings she declines to bestow. Unencumbered by pity or remorse, she will lie, cheat, steal, neglect duties, break promises, even murder, whenever a cold calculation of

---

[26] This observation naturally raises the question: if people are only likely to reveal other-regarding preferences when this is not too personally costly, how can other-regarding preferences produce significant social gains? The answer has two parts. First, other-regarding acts that are relatively inexpensive to the actor can provide much larger gains to the beneficiary of the actor's kindness. Consider the low costs and high benefits of giving directions to a lost stranger, or throwing a life preserver to a drowning swimmer. Second, small acts of other-regarding behavior, when added up over many individuals and many social interactions, can produce great aggregate social gains.

[27] One might argue that it is equally accurate to say we have a single revealed preference function that responds to both social context and personal costs. This essay employs the image of two preference functions, however, to highlight the fact that preferences seem endogenous and not fixed and exogenous as the *homo economicus* model predicts.

cost and benefits leads her to conclude it will make her better off. Not to put too fine a point on it, *homo economicus* is a sociopath.

Of course, there are a variety of tools available to "internalize" externalities and to encourage even sociopaths to avoid harming others and instead to provide benefits. These tools include the legal sanctions imposed by a coercive state; the prospect of personal profit from voluntary exchange in the market; the threat of retaliation in repeated dealings; and reputational concerns (at least in smaller communities where people know, or know of, each other).

But are such external forces, alone, enough to always control the depredations of *homo economicus*? The answer to this question must be "no." This is especially true in developed economies characterized by large populations, free migration, complex production, specialized investment, anonymous exchange, and a high degree of uncertainty – in other words, in economies like our own.

The reason has to do with the fact that external incentives, alone, can only influence the behavior of a rational selfish actor if two criteria are met. First, her behavior must be observed by others. Second, someone or something must be both willing and able to reward her good behavior and to punish her bad behavior – and to reward or punish sufficiently. Even a moment's reflection quickly suggests myriad circumstances in modern life where one or the other criterion won't be met. On any given day, the average person is presented with a number of unplanned opportunities to inflict external costs and withhold benefits without fear of detection or effective punishment (e.g., littering, breaking promises, jumping queues, shirking at work). With a bit of forethought, a purely selfish person could identify many more, and more profitable, opportunities (e.g., burglary, fraud, contract breach, the manufacture of illegal drugs, murder for hire). The end result is that external incentives, alone, are often insufficient to motivate a purely selfish actor to take full account of the external costs and benefits of her conduct.

So we come to the economic role played other-regarding preferences. To the extent that people adopt other-regarding preference functions, they will be motivated to benefit others even when they receive no obvious reward for doing so, and to refrain from harming others even when they would suffer no likely punishment. *Other-regarding preferences can "internalize" externalities* – without any need for time-consuming contract negotiation and drafting, for expensive monitoring, or for costly enforcement measures. In short, other-regarding preferences are often efficient.

This may explain why we have evolved a capacity for them. Evolutionary theorists have long argued that, for a variety of reasons, a capacity for altruism can prove adaptive in social species.[28] Cooperation that seems "irrational" from the perspective of an individual organism can still evolve if it bene-fits the individual's family, or potential exchange partners, or, in some cases, fellow members of the individual's tribe or group. For similar reasons, other-regarding behavior may play an evolutionary role not only in the evolution of social organisms, but in the evolution of social *institutions* that promote cooperation within a group in a fashion that allows that group to thrive at the expense of other groups whose institutions do not encourage cooperative behavior.[29]

Law, of course, is a social institution. I have written elsewhere on how the experimental evidence on other-regarding preferences may offer insights into a variety of important questions about how and why law works.[30] In this essay, however, I would like to focus on how other-regarding preferences may shed light on a second form of social institution – social norms.

II. OTHER-REGARDING PREFERENCES AND THE LITERATURE OF LAW AND SOCIAL NORMS

Sociologists have long incorporated the concept of norms into their analyses of human behavior. More recently, however, the idea of norms has come to the attention of the legal academy as well.[31] Over the past fifteen years a number of prominent legal scholars – including but not limited to Lisa Bernstein, Robert Cooter, Robert Ellickson, Dan Kahan, Richard McAdams, Eric Posner, and

---

[28] *See, e.g.,* CHARLES DARWIN, THE DESCENT OF MAN, AND SELECTION IN RELATION TO SEX 166 (1871); RICHARD DAWKINS, THE SELFISH GENE (1976); ELLIOTT SOBER & DAVID SLOAN WILSON, UNTO OTHERS: THE EVOLUTION AND PSYCHOLOGY OF UNSELFISH BEHAVIOR (1998); ROBERT WRIGHT, THE MORAL ANIMAL: THE NEW SCIENCE OF EVOLUTIONARY PSYCHOLOGY 313–379 (1994); Jack Hirshleifer, *There Are Many Evolutionary Pathways to Cooperation,* 1 J. BIOECONOMICS 73–93 (1999).

[29] *See, e.g.,* GENETIC AND CULTURAL EVOLUTION OF COOPERATION (Peter Hammerstein ed., 2003); ROBERT BOYD & PETER J. RICHERSON, CULTURE AND THE EVOLUTIONARY PROCESS (1985).

[30] *See, e.g.,* Margaret M. Blair & Lynn A. Stout, *Trust, Trustworthiness, and the Behavioral Foundations of Corporate Law,* 149 U. PA. L. REV. 1735 (2001); Lynn A. Stout, *Judges As Altruistic Hierarchs,* 43 WM. & MARY L. REV. 1605 (2002); Lynn A. Stout, *On The Proper Motives of Corporate Directors (Or, Why You Don't Want to Invite* Homo Economicus *to Join Your Board),* 28 DEL. J. CORP. L. 1 (2003).

[31] *See* Ellickson, *supra* note 5, at 35 (describing "boomlet" of interest in norms among legal scholars); Richard H. McAdams, *Signaling Discount Rates: Law, Norms, and Economic Methodology,* 110 YALE L. J. 625, 626 (2001) (same). *See, e.g.,* sources cited *supra* note 4, *infra* note 32.

Cass Sunstein – have published articles or books examining how social norms interact with formal law in regulating human behavior.[32]

Legal scholars who write about social norms often disagree in their exact definitions of what norms are. There seems a general consensus, however, that norms are rules of behavior that are enforced not by courts but by other forces.[33] For example, in the United States there are norms prescribing that one ought to wear shoes in the office and ask permission before smoking in another's house. People perceive such norms as serious constraints on day-to-day behavior. This is true even though it is extremely unlikely that a decision to take off one's shoes at work or light up at a dinner party would trigger a criminal investigation or a civil suit for damages.

Why then do people follow norms? Sometimes legal scholars who write on the subject of norms suggest that under the right circumstances a norm can become "internalized," so that people obey it even when they would suffer no adverse consequences if they did not.[34] There is an interesting pattern to the way legal scholars tend to talk about social norms, however. In brief, many if not most rely heavily on the idea that norms are followed not primarily because they are internalized, but because someone who violates a norm can expect to suffer a range of external but nonlegal sanctions, including loss of reputation as well as raised eyebrows, disparaging remarks, and other social "punishments." In other words, much of the new norms scholarship continues to rely, implicitly or explicitly, on the *homo economicus* model of human behavior.[35]

I believe the emerging literature on law and social norms is important and offers a variety of useful insights to legal scholars. I also believe, however, that we can understand how and why norms work far better if we adopt a model of human behavior that acknowledges and incorporates the reality of socially-contingent, other-regarding preferences. To illustrate, this essay briefly explores how the phenomenon of other-regarding preferences sheds light on three important questions that have been raised in the norms literature.

---

[32] *See* ELLICKSON, *supra* note 4; POSNER, *supra* note 4; Lisa Bernstein, *Opting Out of the Legal System: Extralegal Contractual Relations in the Diamond Industry*, 21 J. LEGAL STUD. 115 (1992); Robert D. Cooter, *Decentralized Law for A Complex Economy: The Structural Approach to Adjudicating the New Law Merchant*, 144 U. PA. L. REV. 1643 (1996); Dan M. Kahan, *Social Influence, Social Meaning, and Deterrence*, 83 VA. L. REV. 349 (1997); Richard McAdams, *supra* note 4; Eric A. Posner, *Law, Economics, and Inefficient Norms*, 144 U. PA. L. REV. 1697 (1996); Cass R. Sunstein, *Social Norms and Social Roles*, 96 COLUM. L. REV. 903 (1996).

[33] Ellickson, *supra* note 5, at 35.

[34] *See, e.g., id.* at 36; Robert Cooter, *Models of Morality in Law and Economics: Self-Control and Self-Improvement for the "Bad Man" of Holmes*, 78 B.U. L. REV. 903 (1998).

[35] Ellickson, *supra* note 5, at 36 ("the new norms scholars all hew to a rational-choice model of human behavior").

These questions are (1) *what* sorts of norms are most likely to emerge in a society; (2) *why* are norms followed; and (3) *how* can policymakers and other norms "entrepreneurs" deliberately employ social norms to change human behavior.

A. *Other-Regarding Preferences and the Evolution of Norms*

One of the most interesting questions posed by the idea of social norms is the question of why particular norms emerge in particular societies. A related question is why some sorts of norms are more likely than others to prove "sticky" (i.e., more likely to be internalized and followed even when external incentives are missing). These questions are, of course, of critical importance in understanding the value of norms as constraints on human behavior. After all, if norms evolve randomly – that is, if any form of behavior is just as likely to become and to remain a norm as any other – why should we conclude that norms provide a social benefit? Indeed, isn't it just as likely that they could impose social costs?[36]

The empirical evidence on other-regarding behavior gives us reason to suspect that norms do *not* evolve randomly, however. To understand why, let us stop to consider some of the norms we observe in our own society. Many of these norms do indeed seem somewhat arbitrary and fatuous (e.g., the norm that adult males ought to wear ties at work, or that lawn grass ought to be mowed two inches high). These types of norms tend to vary from time to time and from place to place. In some cultures men wear ties; in others, togas or kilts. But there is an important subcategory of norms that are far more universal and that are seen in most societies. Examples include the norm of abiding by the law even when authorities are absent; the norm of keeping one's commitments to others; and, more generally, the norm of treating others as you would like them to treat you.

It should be obvious what these "deeper" norms have in common. They are all significantly *other-regarding*.[37] The behavioral literature offers an explanation for this tendency. Other-regarding rules of conduct are especially likely to be socially "codified" into norms, and especially likely to prove sticky, because

---

[36] *See generally* Posner, *Law, Economics, and Inefficient Norms, supra* note 32. It should be noted that norms that encourage behavior that would not necessarily be efficient in isolation may nevertheless promote social welfare if they provide a "focal point" for coordinating behavior, and coordination is itself efficient. *See generally* Richard H. McAdams, *A Focal Point Theory of Expressive Law*, 86 VA. L. REV. 1649 (2000).

[37] By this I mean that someone who violates the norm imposes a cost on another above and beyond any offense that other may take from the mere knowledge that the norm was not followed.

human beings are predisposed to other-regarding behavior. Thus an employee who is working late at the office one night might readily choose to violate a dress norm by loosening his tie or taking off his shoes. He is far less likely to help himself to the office supplies.

The notion that people may be particularly inclined to adopt, and then to internalize, other-regarding norms sheds light on an important and ongoing debate in the norms literature: the debate over whether we should expect norms to favor efficient or inefficient behaviors. As the necktie demonstrates, inefficient norms can develop and persist. Nevertheless, a number of scholars have argued that efficient norms are more likely to survive, and that as a result norms tend to evolve in the long run to favor efficient behaviors.[38] The experimental evidence on other-regarding preferences lends support to this view by suggesting why "sticky," other-regarding norms have staying power.

It also suggests why other-regarding norms may be more likely to arise in the first place. Robert Ellickson has suggested that norms tend to support efficient behaviors because people have an innate preference for utilitarian (welfare-improving) norms.[39] The empirical evidence on human behavior in experimental games provides support for Ellickson's thesis. When the social conditions are right – when a respected authority tells us we ought to look out for others, when we believe those others are also other-regarding – we in fact behave like intuitive utilitarians, and take account of others' welfare as well as our own.[40] That observation in turn suggests that people are likely to recognize and prefer social norms that promote utilitarian behavior.

B. *Other-Regarding Preferences and the Enforcement of Social Norms*

Let us now consider the question of why people obey norms. As the discussion above suggests, one reason why people may obey other-regarding norms is because they internalize them, at least when social and economic conditions are favorable. The experimental evidence on other-regarding behavior has more interesting insights to offer, however, into why people obey norms. In particular, it sheds light on the otherwise puzzling phenomenon of "third-party norms enforcement."

[38] *See* Posner, *Law, Economics, and Inefficient Norms, supra* note 32, at 1697–98 (discussing debate).
[39] Ellickson, *supra* note 5, at 38–39.
[40] *See supra* text accompanying note 19 (noting that the likelihood of altruism increases as the benefit to beneficiary increases) and notes 24–25 (noting that the likelihood of altruism decreases as the cost of altruistic behavior to the altruist increases).

Contemporary norms scholars frequently emphasize the role that bystanders play in enforcing norms by punishing norm-breakers with social sanctions such as dirty looks, disparaging remarks, ostracism, and the like.[41] I suspect this emphasis springs from a desire to keep the study of norms within the parameters of rational choice analysis. After all, if bystanders commonly employ social sanctions against norms-breakers, even *homo economicus* might be tempted to adhere to norms of behavior in order to avoid such punishments

Closer inspection reveals, however, that the idea of third-party enforcement poses some problems for rational choice analysis. For example, one can see why *homo economicus* would want to avoid social sanctions that take the form of others refusing to do business with her. But why should she care if her behavior provokes raised eyebrows? Even more troubling is the notion that third-party bystanders are willing to expend significant personal resources to enforce norms. After all, rude stares and disparaging remarks can provoke conflict. Conflict is costly. Why should a third-party norms enforcer be willing to incur that cost when the benefits of her vigilance are shared by the larger society?[42]

Norms scholars have offered some possible explanations. For example, Richard McAdams has argued that people value being esteemed by others, and that third-party norm enforcers can bestow or withhold esteem at no personal cost.[43] Similarly, Eric Posner has suggested that third-party norms enforcers are motivated by the desire to signal to potential exchange partners that they are trustworthy "good types" to deal with.[44] It should be noted that both explanations seem in tension with rational choice. Why would a purely selfish person care about others' opinions? And why would someone whose sole motivation is to impress others ever enforce a norm absent an audience of potential exchange partners?[45]

---

[41] *See, e.g.*, Bernstein, *supra* note 32, at 116 (discussing importance of reputational concerns in ensuring compliance with industry norms), Cooter, *supra* note 32, at 1665, 1668–69 (suggesting third-party enforcement is important in explaining emergence of norms); Posner, *Law, Economics, and Inefficient Norms, supra* note 32, at 1699 ("a norm is like a law, except that a private person sanctions the violator of a norm, whereas a state actor sanctions the violator of a law"); Sunstein, *supra* note 32, at 915 (discussing norms as enforced through social sanctions).

[42] *See* Geoffrey P. Miller & Lori S. Singer, Norm Enforcement in a Noncooperative Setting (1999) (unpublished manuscript, on file with author) (discussing numerous accounts of instances where third parties employed social sanctions against strangers to enforce handicapped parking rules at significant personal cost, including threat of injury).

[43] See McAdams, *supra* note 4.   [44] See POSNER, *supra* note 4, at 18.

[45] Indeed, even if there were an audience, it is unclear why they would accept the enforcement action as a signal of good character rather than assuming that a "bad type" is strategically pretending to be a "good type."

The phenomenon of other-regarding preferences suggests another, simpler explanation for third-party norms enforcement. In brief, this behavior reflects other-regarding preferences in the form of spite. The argument goes as follows. As noted earlier, altruistic behavior can be adaptive if it allows social organisms to benefit their kin, potential exchange partners, or fellow group members. Similarly, spiteful third-party norms enforcement can be adaptive if it benefits the enforcer's kin, exchange partners, or fellow group members. Thus people who obey other-regarding norms may perceive individuals who violate these norms as selfish recalcitrants whose noncooperation threatens the welfare of others whom the norm enforcer cares about. This perceived threat triggers other-regarding spite that makes a bystander willing to incur the personal cost associated with punishing a norms-breaker through dirty looks, disparaging remarks, and confrontations.

Such vengeful "shaming" may not be pretty to watch. But it is, quite possibly, efficient. By increasing the cost of selfish behavior, social sanctions decrease the relative cost of obeying norms of altruism. As we have seen, when the cost of altruistic behavior declines, the supply increases. Thus third-party norms enforcement serves economic efficiency by discouraging would-be sinners from straying.

C. *Other-Regarding Preferences and the Manipulation of Social Norms*

So we turn to the third and final question: what does the behavioral evidence on other-regarding preferences tell policymakers and other "norms entrepreneurs" about how they can deliberately employ norms to control behavior?

Perhaps the most obvious and important lesson to be drawn from the evidence is that *social context matters*. People can be motivated to adopt other-regarding norms, to follow norms even when they have no external incentives to do so, and to enforce norms against others even when this involves a personal cost. But they can only be motivated to do these things when the social conditions are favorable.

When are the conditions favorable? The experimental evidence reviewed in Part One suggests some obvious possibilities. As noted earlier, subjects in experimental games are much more likely to behave in an other-regarding fashion if the experimenter tells them they should. This intimates that other-regarding norms are more likely to be adopted and followed when people believe they enjoy the support of a respected authority. Courts and legislatures, obviously, can play the role of such an authority. The natural implication is that courts and legislatures can change or support norms through their pronouncements of what people "ought" to do, and so influence behavior *without actually imposing legal sanctions*. In other words (as many scholars have suggested) law can change behavior through its "expressive function."[46] Conversely, when a social norm is *not* supported by the law (or by some other respected authority, such as a religious institution), it will likely prove far more ephemeral.

Similarly, if we want people to conform to other-regarding norms, the experimental evidence suggests that it is important to promote a perception that others in society are also conforming to those norms. This observation lends additional support to the "broken windows" school of law enforcement, which posits that when individuals in society observe evidence that others are committing crimes, they are more likely to commit crimes themselves.[47] Commentators who support the broken windows thesis sometimes argue that visible signs of disorder encourage crime because they send a signal that the police are either unwilling or unable to enforce the law, making criminal behavior seem more appealing by reducing the perceived probability of apprehension and punishment.[48] The experimental evidence on other-regarding behavior suggests a second explanation: visible crime encourages self-regarding behavior because it signals that *others* are being selfish. Conversely, focusing enforcement efforts on such highly-visible but minor "quality of life" crimes as loitering or defacing property may be an effective strategy for deterring more serious crimes because it encourages altruistic, law-abiding behavior by sending the social message that others are altruistically law-abiding.

It is important for the norm entrepreneur to bear in mind, however, that while social context may be vitally important, it is not the sole determinant of other-regarding behavior. Personal cost is a factor too. Thus social norms may work best at promoting other-regarding behavior when obeying (or enforcing) the norm is not too burdensome. Put differently, norms may be a highly efficient means of inducing individuals to make small contributions to others' welfare – small contributions that over time add up to large aggregate effects. But we cannot ask norms to bear too much weight. When compliance with other-regarding norms becomes too costly, compliance falters.

---

[46] *See, e.g.,* Robert Cooter, *Expressive Law and Economics,* 27 J. LEGAL STUD. 585 (1998); Dan M. Kahan, *What Do Alternative Sanctions Mean?,* 63 U. CHI. L. REV. 591 (1996); Lawrence Lessig, *The Regulation of Social Meaning,* 62 U. CHI. L. REV. 943 (1995); Cass R. Sunstein, *On the Expressive Function of Law,* 144 U. PA. L. REV. 2021 (1996).

[47] *See generally* Kahan, *supra* note 32 (discussing theory).

[48] *See, e.g., id.* at 357.

III. CONCLUSION

Rational choice analysis offers a wide variety of important insights into the behavior of both individuals and societies. At the same time, rational choice falls short in its attempt to explain a number of patterns of conduct we observe in daily life. One such pattern is adherence to social norms.

This essay argues that we can make far more sense of the idea of norms if we abandon the *homo economicus* model in favor of a behavioral model that recognizes an important reality of human nature: the reality of socially contingent, other-regarding preferences. Extensive empirical evidence supports the claim that most people shift freely between self-regarding and other-regarding modes of behavior, depending on their perceptions of social context and relative personal cost. This phenomenon is neither rare nor capricious. To the contrary, it is endemic and predictable. As a result it will often be of vital importance to a sound understanding of many social phenomena, including norms.

I would like to close by returning to the case of the other-regarding cab driver. In the months following this incident I have had occasion to think about it quite a bit. More importantly, I have had occasion to think about it in light of the extensive evidence social scientists have amassed on human behavior in social dilemma games, ultimatum games, and dictator games. That literature has led me to two conclusions.

First, I should not have been as surprised as I was by the driver's altruistic behavior in correcting my mistake. As I observed to him at the time, there are many taxi drivers out there who would not have felt compelled to warn me about accidentally giving an enormous tip. But there are many who would have.

Second, I have concluded that although I should be grateful to the driver for telling me that I had handed him a $50 bill, the driver should not be the sole object of my gratitude. Certainly he is a fine fellow. But I am grateful as well for the social context that promoted his kind and considerate act. I am grateful that some respected authority at some time – his boss, his religious leader, his mother – taught him that it was morally wrong, even in a nakedly commercial transaction, to take advantage of someone else's clear mistake. I also am grateful that I clearly communicated my own altruistic intent to give him a good tip. Through this behavior I signaled my own intent to behave in an other-regarding fashion.

Finally, I am grateful that I didn't give him a $100 bill.

2 Damages, Norms, and Punishment

Cass R. Sunstein

How do people make judgments about appropriate punishment? How do they translate their moral judgments into more tangible penalties? What is the effect of group discussion? And what does all this have to do with social norms?

In this essay I attempt to make some progress on these questions. I do by outlining some of the key results of a series of experimental studies conducted with Daniel Kahneman and David Schkade, and by elaborating, in my own terms, on the implications of those studies.[1] Among other things, we find that the process of group discussion dramatically changes individual views, most fundamentally by making people move toward higher dollar awards. In other words, groups often go to extremes.[2] The point has large implications for the role of norms in deliberation and the effect of deliberation in altering norms. We also find that people's judgments about cases, viewed one at a time, are very different from their judgments about cases seen together. Making one-shot decisions, people produce patterns that they themselves regard as arbitrary and senseless. The point has large implications for the aspiration to coherence within the legal system.

---

[1] This chapter draws on joint work with Daniel Kahneman and David Schkade, who deserve the credit for what is worthwhile here, and who deserve no blame for what is not. Interested readers might consult the papers from which I draw: Daniel Kahneman et al., *Shared Outrage and Erratic Awards: The Psychology of Punitive Damages*, 16 J. RISK & UNCERTAINTY 9 (1998); David Schkade et al., *Deliberating About Dollars: The Severity Shift*, 100 COLUM. L. REV. 1139 (2000); Cass R. Sunstein et al., *Assessing Punitive Damages*, 107 YALE L. J. 2071 (1988); Cass R. Sunstein et al., *Do People Want Optimal Deterrence?*, 29 J. LEGAL STUD. 237 (2000); Cass R. Sunstein et al., *Predictably Incoherent Judgments*, 54 STAN. L. REV. 1153 (2002). Many of these papers are collected in CASS R. SUNSTEIN ET AL., PUNITIVE DAMAGES: HOW JURIES DECIDE (2002).

[2] The point is discussed in more detail in CASS R. SUNSTEIN, WHY SOCIETIES NEED DISSENT (2003).

More particularly, our principal findings are as follows:

- In making moral judgments about personal injury cases, people's judgments are both predictable and widely shared. The judgments of one group of six people, or twelve people, nicely predict the judgments of other groups of six people, or twelve people.
- In making punitive damage awards for personal injury cases, people's judgments are highly unpredictable and far from shared. People do not have a clear sense of the meaning of different points along the dollar scale. Hence dollar judgments of one group of six people, or twelve people, do not well predict the dollar judgments of other groups of six people, or twelve people.
- As compared with the median of predeliberation judgments, the effect of deliberation is to *increase* dollar awards, often quite substantially. Group discussions have the remarkable effect of raising group members' judgments about appropriate punishment.
- People care about deterrence, but they do not think in terms of *optimal* deterrence. People are intuitive retributivists, and they reject some of the most common and central understandings in economic and utilitarian theory.
- People's judgments about cases in isolation are systematically different from their judgments about cases taken together. The consequence of the system of "one at a time" judgments is to produce a pattern of outcomes that seems incoherent to the very people who make those judgments.

Now for some details. For purposes of the present discussion, I speak broadly and in qualitative terms; readers interested in numbers and statistical analysis might consult the papers from which I draw.

I. STEADY NORMS, UNSTEADY AWARDS

Suppose that people are asked to rank a set of personal injury cases, or libel cases, or cases involving sexual harassment or damage to the environment. Suppose too that people are asked to rate those cases, in terms of appropriate punishment, on a bounded numerical scale – say, 0 to 8, where 0 means "punished not at all," and 4 means "punished moderately," and 8 means "punished extremely severely." Will people agree? Will the decision of one group of six or twelve provide good predictions about what other groups of six or twelve will do? The answer will depend on whether the social norms that govern moral outrage and intended punishment are widely shared. If they are shared, we should not expect sharp divergences in terms of both ranking and rating.

A. *Remarkably Shared Judgments*

Undertaking a series of studies of citizen judgments, we have found that at least in some domains, the relevant norms are indeed widely shared. In personal injury cases, the judgment of any particular group of six is highly likely to provide a good prediction of the judgment of any other group of six. In this sense, a "moral judgment" jury is indeed able to serve as the conscience of the community.[3]

Indeed it is possible to go further. Members of different demographic groups show considerable agreement about how to rank and rate personal injuries cases. We asked thousands of people to rank and rate cases. We also elicited information about the demographic characteristics of all of those people. As a result, it is possible, with the help of the computer, to put individuals together, so as to assemble all-male juries, all-female juries, all-white juries, all–African-American juries, all-poor juries, all-rich juries, all-educated juries, all–less-educated juries, and so forth. Creating "statistical juries" in this way, we found no substantial disagreement, in terms of rating or ranking, within any group. In personal injuries cases, people simply agree.

Subsequent work has broadened this finding, showing that people agree on how to rank tax violations, environmental violations, and occupational safety and health violations. From this evidence, it seems reasonable to hypothesize that in a wide range of domains, people will agree how to rank and rate cases. The moral norms within a heterogeneous culture are, to that extent, widely shared, and strikingly so. Now this does not mean that people will agree on how to rank cases from different categories (a point to which I will return). Nor does it mean that small groups will always agree on how to do the ranking. But it does mean that within a category, agreement is the exception, not the rule.

B. *Remarkably Erratic Dollar Awards*

What about dollars? Do the broadly shared norms also produce regularity in jury verdicts? One of our central findings is that it does not.

With respect to dollars, both individuals and jury-size groups are all over the map. Even when moral rankings are shared – as they generally are – dollar awards are extremely variable. A group that awards a "5," for defendant's misconduct, might give a dollar award of $500,000, or $2 million, or $10 million. A group that awards a "7" might award $1 million, or $10 million,

[3] Cass R. Sunstein et al., *Assessing Punitive Damages*, 107 YALE L. J. 2071 (1988).

or $100 million. In fact there is so much noise in the dollar awards that differences cannot be connected with demographic characteristics. It is not as if one group – whites, for example – gives predictably different awards from another – say, African-Americans or Hispanics. We cannot show systematic differences between young and old, men and women, well-educated and less-educated. The real problem is that dollar awards are quite unruly, from one individual to another and from one small group to another.

What accounts for this? Why do people share moral judgments but diverge on dollar awards? The best answer is that the effort to "map" moral judgments onto dollars is an exercise in "scaling without a modulus." In psychology, it is well known that serious problems will emerge when people are asked to engage in a rating exercise on a scale that is bounded at the bottom but not at the top and when they are not given a "modulus" by which to make sense of various points along the scale. For example, when people are asked to rate the brightness of lights or the loudness of noises, they will not be able to agree if no modulus is supplied and if the scale lacks an upper bound. But once a modulus is supplied, agreement is substantially improved. Or if the scale is given an upper bound, and if verbal descriptions accompany some of the relevant points, people will come into accord with one another.

The upshot is that much of the observed variability with punitive damage awards – and in all likelihood with other damage awards too – does not come from differences in social norms. It comes from variable, and inevitably somewhat arbitrary, "moduli" selected by individual jurors and judges. If the legal system wants to reduce the problem of different treatment of the similarly situated, it would do well to begin by appreciating this aspect of the problem. The point applies to many legal problems, including criminal sentences, pain and suffering awards, administrative penalties, and damages for libel, sexual harassment, and intentional infliction of emotional distress. In all of these areas, the existence of variability might well have little to do with diverse norms. Even when norms are widely shared, the unbounded dollar scale is a recipe for arbitrariness and unpredictability.

II. WHAT DO GROUPS DO? THE EFFECTS OF DELIBERATION

The discussion thus far been coy about a key question: whether the studies involved deliberating juries, or mere individuals placed, by computer, into small groups, with individual views being somehow "pooled" to create a verdict. The coyness stems from the fact that our initial study did indeed involve merely individual judgments, unaccompanied by deliberation and statistical pooling, creating what might be called "statistical juries" – whose verdict, as we reported it, consisted of the view of the median juror. We chose the median juror on the ground that this seemed to be the most plausible estimate of what the jury itself would do. But in a subsequent study, involving about 3000 people, we tested this hypothesis – and found that it was wrong.[4] What we found does not falsify the findings just described; on the contrary, it reinforces them. But it also says a great deal about the effects of deliberation and the role of social norms in that process.

In brief, we tested the effects of deliberation on both punitive intentions and dollar judgments. To test the effects of deliberation on punitive intentions, we asked people to record their individual judgments privately, on a bounded scale, and then we asked them to join six-member groups to generate unanimous "punishment verdicts." To test the effects of deliberation on dollar judgments, we also asked people to record their private judgment, predeliberation, and then to join six-member groups to produce unanimous dollar awards. Juries produced both punishment verdicts and dollar verdicts; half entered punishment verdicts first, and half entered dollar awards first. Only a small number of the 500 juries "hung."

Two findings are especially important. First, deliberation made the *lower* punishment ratings *decrease*, when compared to the median of predeliberation judgments of individuals, while deliberation made the *higher* punishments ratings *increase*, when compared to that same median. Hence deliberation produced a remarkably robust "leniency shift" with low punishment ratings and an equally robust "severity shift" with high punishment ratings. Second, *dollar awards of groups were systematically higher than the median of individual group members* – so much so that in 27 percent of the cases, the dollar verdict was as high as, or higher than, that of the highest individual judgment, predeliberation. With respect to dollars, deliberation produced a systematic "severity shift," apparently as a result of the interaction of deliberation and social norms.

How can this pattern be explained?

A. *Group Polarization*

With respect to punishment ratings, the answer lies in the phenomenon of group polarization – a pervasive process by which group members end up

---

[4] David Schkade et al., *Deliberating About Dollars: The Severity Shift*, 100 Columb. L. Rev. 1139 (2000).

in a more extreme position in line with the predeliberation tendencies of group members.[5] It is now well-known that if a group has a defined median position – if, for example, people in the group tend to think that global warming is a serious problem, or that gun control is bad idea – members will shift toward a more extreme version of what they already think. Critics of gun control, talking with one another, will end up more critical of gun control. Those fearful of global warming will, as a result of group discussion, end up more fearful of global warming. The basic finding has been made on many topics and in many nations.

In my view, there are large lessons here about the formation of social norms and attitudes, and in particular about the role of groups in forming the norms and views of group members. A homogeneous group might well lead members in quite extreme directions. After speaking with one another, like-minded people are apt to end up thinking what they thought before, but much more so. (Perhaps we can find some of the well-springs of extremism and even terrorism in this process; like-minded people, beginning with certain norms, are likely to end up with an exaggerated version of these norms as a result of frequent interactions.) A heterogeneous group is far less likely to have this effect.

What explains group polarization? Why does deliberation drive low punishment ratings down and move high punishment ratings up? There appear to be two answers. The first involves the exchange of information within the group. In a group whose members initially favor a high punishment rating, group members will make many arguments that support high ratings, and relatively few arguments the other way. Speaking purely descriptively, the group's "argument pool" will be skewed in the direction of severity. Group members, listening to the various arguments, will naturally move in that direction. As with punishment ratings, so too with much else: feminism, global warming, capital punishment, affirmative action, and so forth. The initial dispositions of group members will determine the proportion of arguments in the various directions. And individuals will respond, quite rationally, to what they have heard, thus moving in the direction suggested by the dominant tendency. Because of how information flows within a group, both beliefs and norms can be rendered more extreme.

The second explanation involves social influences. Most people want to be, and to be perceived in, a certain way. If you are in a group that wants to punish someone severely, you might find it uncomfortable to be urging relative leniency. To protect your reputation, and perhaps even your self-conception,

[5] *See* SUNSTEIN, WHY SOCIETIES NEED DISSENT, *supra* note 2, for details.

you might move, if you move at all, in the most favored direction. Those who want to think of themselves as tough on corporate wrongdoing might well shift toward more severe punishment if they find that most people within the group are inclined in favor of severity.

To be sure, some hardy souls will not move at all, simply because they do not care about how others perceive them. And those who are self-identified contrarians might deliberately move in the opposite direction, rejecting the dominant view just because it is the dominant view. But what we observed, and what is universally observed, is that most of those who move tend to go in the group's preferred direction – and that as a result, the group will be more extreme than its members before deliberation began.

B. *Rhetorical Asymmetry and Social Norms*

Group polarization seems to explain two of our findings: the leniency shift with low punishment ratings and the severity shift with high punishment ratings. But nothing said thus far provides an adequate account of what was observed with dollar awards. Here we found a general increase in verdicts. To be sure, groups whose predeliberation median was low tended to see a smaller increase than groups whose predeliberation median was high. But dollar awards increased quite generally. Unlike in the context of punishment ratings, there was no "switchpoint" along which some went up and some went down. Why is this?

Some clue, I think, is provided by two fascinating studies of the effects of group deliberation on social norms. It has been found that as compared with individuals, groups of doctors are more likely to engage in heroic measures to save patients.[6] The norm in favor of protecting patients, even at great cost, appears to intensify in teams. It has also been found that as compared with individuals, groups are more likely to divide sums of money equally with strangers.[7] The norm in favor of altruism and generosity also grows in groups.

Perhaps these results can be understood to exemplify unusual forms of group polarization, with the initial tendency – to save the patient, to be fair – being amplified as a result of discussion in both instances. This is certainly possible. But a more specific explanation would suggest that in these domains,

---

[6] *See* Caryn Christenson & Ann Abbott, *Team Medical Decision Making, in* DECISION MAKING IN HEALTH CARE 267, 273–76 (Gretchen Chapman & Frank Sonnenberg eds., 2000).

[7] Timothy Cason & Vai-Lam Mui, *A Laboratory Study of Group Polarisation in the Team Dictator Game*, 107 ECON. J.1465 (1997).

existing social norms generate a kind of *rhetorical asymmetry* between the two opposing positions. When a rhetorical asymmetry is in place, one side has an automatic upper-hand in an argument. One side is likely to win, simply because in light of existing norms, that side has a rhetorical advantage. Doctors who seek more in the way of heroic measures are more likely to win an argument with those who seek less. Group members who seek more fairness are likely, at least in the relevant settings, to prevail over those who seek more selfishness.

It is important to see that rhetorical asymmetry can operate in many domains, and that all this is a function of social norms. In one group, those who favor stiffer penalties for drug offenders might have an automatic advantage – so that any discussion will move the group toward stiffer penalties. In another group, the opposite might be true, so that the effect of the discussion will be to produce greater leniency. It is undoubtedly easy to come up with a long list of groups showing a rhetorical asymmetry in one direction or another. Social norms in favor of protecting the environment, expressing patriotism, acting courteously, refraining from racist jokes, or speaking respectfully of political leaders are likely to be formed and intensified as a result of rhetorical asymmetry; and the nature and extent of the asymmetry will vary from one group to another.

With respect to punitive damage awards, we hypothesize that especially in light of the difficulty of using the scale of dollars, *those who favor higher dollar punishments for corporate wrongdoing are in a much better rhetorical position than those who favor lower ones.* The arguments on behalf of the higher awards are simply more intuitive, at least in the abstract. In fact we conducted a simple follow-up study, asking participants to list arguments for higher and lower awards (knowing nothing about the particular case), and then asking which set of arguments was easier to make. Far more people said that the higher award was easier to support than the lower one.

There are general implications here about the *effect* of social norms on group discussion and also about the *production* of social norms through group discussion. It seems clear that preexisting norms can push people in predictable directions, and also that these very movements can help create new norms, or at least stronger versions of the preexisting ones. In an "iterated polarization game," or an "iterated rhetorical asymmetry game," very significant shifts are to be expected. Perhaps the point helps to account for political movements, for religious and ethnic strife, for feuds, and even for violent behavior.[8]

---

[8] On the latter, see the treatment in DONALD HOROWITZ, THE DEADLY ETHNIC RIOT (2000).

III. RETRIBUTION AND DETERRENCE

On the economic theory of punishment, the state's goal, when imposing penalties, is to ensure optimal deterrence. To increase deterrence, the law might increase the severity of punishment, or instead increase the likelihood of punishment. A government that lacks substantial enforcement resources might impose high penalties, thinking that it will produce the right deterrent "signal" in light of the fact that many people will escape punishment altogether. A government that has sufficient resources might impose a lower penalty, but enforce the law against all or almost all violators.

In the context of punitive damages, all this leads to a simple theory: the purpose of such damages is to make up for the shortfall in enforcement. If injured people are 100 percent likely to receive compensation, there is no need for punitive damages. If injured people are 50 percent likely to receive compensation, those who bring suit should receive a punitive award that is twice the amount of the compensatory award. The simple exercise in multiplication will ensure optimal deterrence.

But there is a large question whether social norms and the theory of optimal deterrence can fit together. Do people want optimal deterrence? Do they accept or reject the economic theory of punishment?

We attempted to cast light on this question through two experiments.[9] In the first, we gave people cases of wrongdoing, arguably calling for punitive damages, and also provided people with explicit information about the probability of detection. Different people saw the same case, with only one difference: varying probability of detection. People were asked about the amount of punitive damages that they would choose to award. Our goal was to see if people would impose higher punishments when the probability of detection was low. Economic theory argues that they should; the question is whether social norms accord with economic theory.

In the second experiment, we asked people to evaluate judicial and executive decisions to *reduce* penalties when the probability of detection was high, and to *increase* penalties when the probability of detection was low. We wanted people to say whether they approved or disapproved of varying the penalty with the probability of detection.

Our findings were simple and straightforward. The first experiment found that varying the probability of detection had no effect on punitive awards. Even when people's attention was explicitly directed to the probability of detection, people were indifferent to it. People's decisions about appropriate

---

[9] Cass R. Sunstein et al., *Do People Want Optimal Deterrence?*, 29 J. LEGAL STUD. 237 (2000).

punishment were unaffected by seeing a high or low probability of detection. The second experiment found that strong majorities of respondents rejected judicial decisions to reduce penalties because of high probability of detection – and also rejected executive decisions to increase penalties because of low probability of detection. In other words, people did not approve of an approach to punishment that would make the level of punishment vary with the probability of detection. What apparently concerned them was the extent of the wrongdoing and the right degree of moral outrage – not optimal deterrence.

The most general conclusion is that social norms do not coexist comfortably with optimal deterrence theory. People are intuitive retributivists. They come to the social role of juror with moral intuitions inconsistent with the economic theory of deterrence. Widely-held social norms are flatly inconsistent with that theory. Of course this finding does not show that the economic theory is wrong. But it does suggest that those who want to use that theory will have a great deal of work to do if they seek to convince ordinary people that the theory is the right one.

IV. COHERENCE, CATEGORIES, AND CONTEXT

I have suggested that people have a fairly easy time rating and ranking cases within a single category. Hence they share judgments about the outrageousness of a defendant's conduct in a personal injury case. But do people share judgments about how to compare a personal injury case with a libel case? Can people compare cases across categories? Probably most important: what would they think of the pattern that they produce if, as is usual, they tend to decide cases one at a time?

We do not have full answers to these questions, but suggestive evidence has started to emerge. The simplest point is that when people are trying to rank cases from different categories, they have far more difficulty, in the sense that they are unsure exactly what to do.[10] This lack of certainty translates into a stunning lack of consensus. People agree much more on how to rank cases *within* a category than how to rank cases *across* categories. (I put to one side the evident difficulties in deciding what counts as a "category.") It is easy to design experiments in which people will simply disagree about whether, for example, a comparatively serious tax violation is worse, or less bad, than a lawless act that harms the environment. Hence the social norms that govern

---

[10] Cass R. Sunstein et al., *Predictably Incoherent Judgments,* 54 STAN. L. REV. 1153 (2002).

cross-category comparisons are not as widely shared as the social norms that govern within-category comparisons.

Perhaps this is not big news. A more striking finding is that people's judgments about cases, taken one at a time, are very different from their judgments about the same cases taken in the context of a problem from another category. For example, we asked people to assess a case involving personal injury on a bounded scale and also on a dollar scale. We also asked people to assess a case involving financial injury on a bounded scale and on a dollar scale. When the two cases are judged in isolation, the financial injury case receives a more severe rating and a higher dollar award. But when the two cases are seen together, there is a significant *judgment reversal*, in which people try to ensure that the financial award is not much higher, and for many respondents is lower, than the personal injury award. People's decisions about the two cases are very different, depending on whether they see the case alone or in the context of a case from another category.

We observed exactly the same kind of shift for judgments about two problems calling for government regulation and expenditures: skin cancer among the elderly and protection of coral reefs. Looking at the two cases in isolation, people will pay more to protect coral reefs, and register more satisfaction from doing that. But looking at the two cases together, people will be quite disturbed at this pattern, and will generally want to pay more to protect elderly people from cancer. Here too there is a significant shift in judgment. It follows that if people see cases one at a time, they will produce patterns that they themselves will deem implausible and incoherent.

Is this a problem? And what accounts for the switch? Consider a tentative account.[11] When people see a case in isolation, they naturally "normalize" it by comparing it to a set of comparison cases that it readily calls up. If you are asked, is a German Shepherd big or small, you are likely to respond that it is big; if you are asked, is a Volkswagon Bug big or small, you are likely to respond that it is small. But people are well-aware that a German Shepherd is smaller that a Volkswagon Bug. People answer as they do because a German Shepherd is compared with dogs, whereas a Volkswagon Bug is compared with cars. So far, so good; in these cases, everyone knows what everyone else means. We easily normalize judgments about size, and the normalization is mutually understood. (Michael Jordan, standing about 6′ 6″, was a medium-sized basketball player!)

In the context of legally relevant moral judgments, something similar happens, but it is far from innocuous. When evaluating a case involving financial

---

[11] *See id.* for more details.

injury, people apparently "normalize" the defendant's conduct by comparing it with conduct in other cases from the same category. They do not easily or naturally compare that defendant's conduct with conduct from other categories. Because of the natural comparison set, people are likely to be quite outraged by the misconduct if it is far worse than the comparison cases that spring naturally to mind. The same kind of thing happens with the problem of skin cancer among the elderly. People compare that problem with other similar problems – and conclude that it is not so serious, within the category of health-related or cancer-related problems. So too with personal injury cases (normalized against other personal injury cases) and problems involving damage to coral reefs (normalized against other cases of ecological harm). So too, perhaps, with the operation of social norms in general, in which people can become extremely outraged by conduct that would not seem so bad if compared to cases from other categories.

When a case from another category is introduced, this natural process of comparison is disrupted. Rather than comparing a skin cancer case with other cancers or other human health risks, people see that it must be compared with ecological problems, which (in most people's view) have a lesser claim to public resources. Rather than comparing a financial injury case to other cases of business misconduct, people now compare it to a personal injury case, which (in most people's view) involves more serious wrongdoing. As a result of the wider viewscreen, judgments shift, often dramatically. Outside of law, people might become indignant on hearing of a case of academic plagiarism; but if they compared plagiarism to assault, rape, and murder, their indignation would undoubtedly diminish.

Because so much of law operates "one case at a time," I believe that this uncovers a serious problem with current practice in many legal domains. The problem is that when people assess cases in isolation, their viewscreen is narrow, indeed limited to the category to which the case belongs, and as a result, people produce a pattern of outcomes that makes no sense by their own light. In other words, the overall set of outcomes is one that people would not endorse if they were only to see it as a whole. Their considered judgments reflect the very pattern that they have produced, because of a predictable feature of human cognition. The result is a form of incoherence. And indeed, the pattern of punitive damage awards in the real world seems to be afflicted by just that incoherence. We can find similar incoherence not only in jury verdicts, but also in administrative fines and in criminal sentencing, where no serious effort has been made to ensure that the overall pattern of outcomes makes the slightest sense.

V. CONCLUSION

In this chapter I have attempted to cast some light on the relationship among social norms, punitive intuitions, group deliberation, coherence, and several other issues in law and legal theory. We have seen that diverse people rank and rate cases within a single category in a similar way; that they produce erratic dollar awards largely because of the difficulty of using a dollar scale; that with respect to moral judgments, discussion moves people toward a more extreme point in line with their initial predisposition; that with respect to dollars, discussion systematically increases awards; that existing norms fit poorly with optimal deterrence theory; and that one-shot judgments produce patterns that people would reject, if only they were to see them.

These are descriptive points. It is far from clear what, if anything, should be done by way of legal reform. But it would be reasonable to conclude that a system of one-shot judgments by juries, scaling in the dark and offered no comparison cases, is not likely to be a sensible way to produce civil fines. Arbitrariness and incoherence are almost inevitable. In the abstract, a more guided and disciplined approach, allowing a degree of rationalization, would seem to be far superior.

Of course I cannot defend such an approach in this space; those who provide guidance and discipline will undoubtedly have problems of their own, not least because they can be out of touch with prevailing social norms. But with an understanding of the problems discussed here, perhaps we can make better sense of some of the largest movements in twentieth-century law, which consisted precisely in an effort to replace one-shot jury decisions with institutions that are accountable and subject to prevailing norms, but also able to overcome serious cognitive problems faced by isolated individuals and groups.[12] In this view, the proper response to the problems I have identified here consists of better institutional design. It would not be at all surprising if the twenty-first century saw bolder movements in the same general direction.

---

[12] For example, *see* PRICE FISHBACK & SHAWN KANTOR, A PRELUDE TO THE WELFARE STATE: THE ORIGINS OF WORKERS' COMPENSATION (2000).

3 Cognitive Science and the Study of the "Rules of the Game" in a World of Uncertainty

Douglass C. North

The subject of this chapter is cognitive science, economics, and law, and some issues and problems confronting their interaction. The fundamental problems that face societies, economies, polities – and indeed the law – result from a world of ubiquitous uncertainty. Considered here is the nature of that uncertainty, its interaction with economics and legal systems, and its implications for our understanding the world and improving the human condition.

It will be useful to begin with some definitions. Economics is about how people make choices in a world of scarcity. A legal system is part of the institutional framework that structures human interaction. And uncertainty, using the Frank Knight definition, is a condition in which we cannot make a probability distribution of outcomes.[1] Or, going to Lord Keynes's definition, it is a condition which does not allow us even to know what possible outcomes could occur.[2]

The approach of economics to uncertainty is that it is an unusual condition. Because most economists agree that it is impossible to theorize in the face of uncertainty, they assert that what we really face is risk. According to Knight, risk does allow a probability distribution of outcomes and, therefore, we can theorize about it. If, as economists typically assume, risk rather than uncertainty is the usual state of affairs, then humans can act rationally in the pursuit of their objectives of improving the economic human condition and reducing scarcity.

The rationality assumption has served economists well for a limited range of issues. Specifically, it works well when people are thoroughly informed, when they are motivated, and when the problems are simple. We typically use the

---

[1] FRANK H. KNIGHT, RISK, UNCERTAINTY AND PROFIT 197–232 (1921).
[2] *Quoted in* Paul Davidson, *Is Probability Theory Relevant for Uncertainty? A Post Keynesian Perspective*, 5 J. ECON. PERSP. 129, 131 (1991).

rationality assumption, for example, in modeling competitive markets: here the players do not have to worry about price; they simply worry about quantity because the price is set by competitive conditions.

When we move beyond the rationality assumption, we move into a world that economists do not deal with properly and adequately, but that gradually is becoming a central concern of economics. How do we deal with uncertainty? Specifically, how do we make choices under conditions of uncertainty? In order to understand how we make choices, we must look at how the brain and the mind interpret the environment. We begin by briefly exploring the way a pioneering economist dealt with the issue.

More than 85 years ago, before cognitive science became fashionable or, indeed, was even of concern, Frederick Hayek wrote an early draft of *The Sensory Order*, a book about cognitive science, which was published in 1952 but written in 1920.[3] For Hayek, beliefs are a construction of the mind as interpreted by the senses. We do not reproduce reality; rather, we construct systems of classifications to interpret the external environment. As Hayek wrote in *The Sensory Order*,

> perception is thus always an interpretation, the placing of something into one or several classes of objects. The qualities which we attribute to the experienced object are, strictly speaking, not properties of that object at all, but a set of relations by which our nervous system classifies them. Or, to put it differently, all we know about the world is of the nature of theories, and all experience can do is change these theories.[4]

Hayek conceived of the semipermanent network of connections among nerve fibers as mapping the classification process. Given that structure, the mind models the immediate environment. A reinterpretation of reality occurs when the prevailing model, or maps, produce unanticipated results, forcing a reclassification. However, such reclassification is constrained by deep-seated tacit rules that determine the flexibility of the mind to adjust. For Hayek, the mind is inseparably connected with the environment:

> [T]he apparatus by means of which we learn about the external world is of itself the product of a kind of experience. It is shaped by the conditions prevailing in the environment in which we live, and it represents a kind of generic reproduction of the relations between the elements of this environment which

---

[3] F. A. Hayek, The Sensory Order: An Inquiry into the Foundations of Theoretical Psychology (1952).
[4] *Id.* at 143.

we have experienced in the past, and we interpret any new event in the environment in the light of that experience.[5]

It follows that experiences that have shaped the mental classifications in the mind can and frequently will lead to misinterpretations of the problems confronting the individual.

Hayek maintained that the classification of the stimuli performed by our senses will be based on a system of acquired connections that reproduce in a partial and imperfect manner the relationships existing in the external environment. The model of the physical world that is thus formed would give us only a very distorted reproduction of the relationships existing in that world. And the classifications of these events by our senses would often prove to be false, that is, give rise to expectations that will not be borne out by the events.

Hayek's views in *The Sensory Order* have survived very well as cognitive science has come to be a major field of inquiry and one that is rapidly becoming integrated with social science analysis. Two points about Hayek's description should be emphasized. The first is the subjective nature of the external environment. Our minds do not reproduce reality; rather they attempt to interpret the very complex relationships in what are always theories. We may know all the facts and numbers possible about a particular set of events, but to order them and to explain them requires theory, and that theory, obviously, is a construction of the mind.

This does not mean that all results are subjective. Obviously, what we try to do is to test the theories we have against the evidence so that we can arrive at rough, very rough, estimates of the reliability of such theories. But it does mean that all the theories we have are subjective; they are always imperfect, they are always incomplete, and frequently – very frequently, because there seldom is a chance to provide unambiguous tests – they misdirect us and lead us in wrong directions.

The second of Hayek's points to be emphasized is equally important: there is an intimate connection between the mind and the external environment. Much exciting research has been done recently in cognitive science on the way the mind interprets the artifactual structure of the external world in order to account for the human command over our complex environment. The importance of this connection between the mind and the environment can be illustrated as follows. There is growing attention to policy matters that would improve performance in third-world countries, but advisors typically, and mistakenly, think that simply introducing into third-world countries the laws and

[5] *Id.* at 165.

rules that appear to work in developed countries will get the same result. But clearly the artifactual environments of developed and of third-world countries are different. The complex structure of technology, institutions, organizations, language – both oral and written – differs from one society to the next. Making choices, therefore, is a complex process and clearly deviates a great deal from the standard rationality assumption that assumes people are perfectly informed and motivated and have relatively simple problems to resolve.

This aspect of the failures of economics was well documented by two psychologists, Daniel Kahneman and Amos Tversky.[6] They carefully demonstrated that human beings' behavior is not perfectly rational, in the sense of consistent logical ordering of the way in which they solve problems. That is not the subject here, although it is an important one and, indeed, Dan McFadden, who won a Nobel Prize in 2000, recently wrote an essay in which he resurrected Kahneman and Tversky and argued that economists should be concerned about the behavioral assumptions they use.[7]

Here we concentrate on the macro issues of making choices in the world of dynamic change. That is not only the world of economic history and economic development; it is in fact much more than that. Dynamic change and uncertainty as defined here are characteristic of everyday aspects of our environment and making choices in that environment. That is, we continually are confronting new and novel problems. To the degree that problems are new and novel, they pose real dilemmas with respect to the way in which the mind, which has constructed classifications and orderings through neural networks, can interpret them in a consistent and effective way.

That raises the crucial issue of whether the world we are living in is an ergodic or a nonergodic world. Paul Samuelson has argued that economics is only a science if the world is ergodic.[8] In an ergodic world there is a basic underlying structure, a basic underlying unity, such that even though we may face problems that are different in kind, we can, as physicists and chemists and geneticists do, go back to fundamentals and build our theory up from its basic underlying structure. Physical sciences have made impressive strides in constructing new theories about new problems by such reductionist methods.

If the world is ergodic, then deep down economists should be able to have a body of theory that they can rely on and resort to when they want to understand new problems. But if it is nonergodic, there is not any fundamental underlying

---

[6] Amos Tversky & Daniel Kahneman, *Rational Choice and the Framing of Decisions, in* RATIONAL CHOICE (Robin Hogarth & Melvin Reder eds., 1987).

[7] Daniel McFadden, *Economic Choices*, 91 AM. ECON. REV. 351 (2001).

[8] Paul A. Samuelson, *Classical and Neoclassical Theory, in* MONETARY THEORY (Robert W. Clower ed., 1969).

structure that we can rely on. If the world is nonergodic, we must ask some profound and very disturbing questions. For example, as we attempt to make policy with respect to a particular problem, we need to ask, "Is the theory we derived from experience in modeling the world in the past applicable to new and future problems or is it not?"

In many respects, economists have been fortunate and have, indeed, developed a body of theory in microeconomics which has proven to be quite resilient in being able to deal with novel problems. Certainly micro theory has been a powerful tool of analysis, and, in that sense, gives some confidence with respect to some aspects of our being able to apply it over and over again.

But, what about macro theory? We know what happened to the long-term capital investment firm of two Nobel prize winners a few years ago; although their theory was founded on very good empirical work that they had done, which still has lasting value in understanding the nature of risk in certain kinds of markets, it failed them because the failure of the Russian bond market was a new development which was not built into the models they had from the past.

Just how far can we go in understanding the world? Can we develop effective theories of how economies evolved through time? Many economists, including among them Kenneth Arrow, say you cannot theorize in the face of real uncertainty.[9] But, we do it all the time. Religions, obviously, are theorizing in the face of uncertainty. And indeed, all kinds of secular theories, like Marxism, are theorizing in the face of uncertainty.

The rise and fall of the Soviet Union is an example of the problems we confront in dealing with uncertainty. The Soviet Union was founded on the basis of theory – beliefs – that originated with Marx and Engels and continued under Lenin. After Lenin occupied the Winter Palace and managed to gain power, those beliefs were translated into an institutional structure that defined the way in which the Soviet system evolved. The problem was, however, that while Marx and Engels had talked about capitalism and property rights, they never specified what a socialist system should look like or what institutional framework was needed. Consequently, when we look at the Soviet Union in the 1920s, we observe a fascinating search on the part of Bukharin, Lenin, Stalin, and Trotsky. Then what does the system look like after Trotsky gets thrown out, Lenin dies, and Bukharin gets done in by Stalin? Stalin makes the first five-year plan, in 1928. From then on there is an orthodoxy with respect to the institutional structure that is developed, built on some archaic and ancient

[9] Kenneth Arrow, *Alternative Approaches to the Theory of Choice in Risk-Taking Situations*, 19 ECONOMETRICA 404 (1951).

views about economies of scale and so on. The system can be envisioned as a giant factory that produced the Soviet Union of the 1930s. World War II was a terrible disaster for the Soviet Union. Nevertheless, in spite of all the problems (like those of agriculture, which never succeeded), a superpower emerged by the 1950s and 1960s. In those times the world was half socialist or communist, and communism was the wave of the future. However, by the mid-1970s, the Soviet Union began to fall apart. By the early 1980s, indeed, the rate of growth of its economy by any measure had slowed almost to a halt. In Oslo in 1982 some members of the Communist Party declared that, in fact, the transaction sector in the Soviet economy had become so alarmingly large that the economy could no longer grow.[10] By 1985, with the end of the Brezhnev era, Gorbachev tried to improve conditions with *perestroika*, but his efforts were a disaster, eventually leading to the demise of the Soviet Union. That demise in 1991 was extraordinary because it was the first time in all of history that a world power collapsed under its own internal weight without any external, or at least obviously external, force leading to that collapse.

Please notice each part of this story. This is a story about the perceptions of reality held by human beings. Those perceptions of reality are translated into beliefs. The beliefs, in turn, are translated into institutions, which are the structures that humans impose in an attempt to understand human interaction. These institutions then lead, as new problems evolve, to policies to modify the institutional framework, which in turn leads to a revision of reality because we are changing the way the game is played. This is a continuous process, characteristic of the human condition for at least the last ten thousand years.

The key part of the issue – and this gets us back to the world being ergodic or nonergodic – is whether, in fact, the feedback we get from enacting policies is such that we understand what the consequences of those policies really are. If we got perfect feedback and the world stayed constant, we would assume over time that if we enacted policies that did not work, the feedback would tell us they did not work and we could correct the policies, modify our beliefs, and again revise the policies. We would continue this process until, in fact, there was an identification between the beliefs we held, the theories we formed, and, indeed, the outcome. But rather than a constant world with perfect feedback, what if we have a world of dynamic change? Then, in fact, do we ever catch up with the new and novel problems we are facing?

Actually, if we consider in greater detail what happened in the Soviet Union during the Brezhnev era, we observe that there were two failures of feedback.

---

[10] A personal observation made in the course of my delivering a paper to Norwegian economists, some of whom were members of the Communist Party.

One of them is that the information about the failures of the Soviet Union – as in agriculture, for example – never could penetrate the top echelon of Soviet leaders. The second problem is that such information was antithetical to fundamental Marxist tenets about the nature of property. It was widely known in the late 1970s, although not officially admitted, that the one acre private plots in Uzbekistan made up one percent of the arable land and produced about twenty percent of total Soviet agricultural output.

The effectiveness of the feedback process is very important. Feedback may be and frequently is very imperfect – we simply do not know the consequences of many of the policies we pursue. In addition, feedback may be so antithetical to the belief system we have inherited that we are not willing to accept modifications or alterations in that system. That tension between novel situations, new developments, and the degree to which the mind is willing to accept alterations in the way the game is played is one of the fundamental interests of cognitive science.

Obviously, whether it is an ergodic or a nonergodic world plays a critical part in our success in theorizing about the world. If in fact the world is nonergodic, if we have novelty in the way the world is changing because we face new situations and novel problems that humans never have experienced before, then it is much more difficult, perhaps impossible, to be able to theorize about it. We are asking the mind in the face of a novel situation to interpret that situation and come up with profoundly new conclusions about it. We are asking a great deal, because we typically think of the mind – to use connectionist theory in cognitive science – as having patterned-based reasoning. With the neural networks having evolved in a certain pattern structure, the mind, when it faces new evidence, new information from the senses, sees what understanding it can make out of it from the patterns that exist. But if the new information is so novel, so far away from anything that the mind has had before, the mind is going to have grave difficulty in being able to deal with the problem and achieve an effective solution.

A number of implications can be drawn from a nonergodic world. First of all, throughout most of history, we have gotten it wrong. This in an odd thing to say at a time when the world has incredibly higher standards of living and income than at any time in the past, and when the United States has unequaled prosperity and relatively low unemployment. All of that makes us look like we know what we are doing.

But there are at least three ways that we get it wrong. The first is very simple. We do not understand reality very well. If it is a nonergodic world, that is a phenomenon very likely to happen. Second, even if we could understand reality pretty well, the belief system that we evolved could be wrong because it does not accept changes in reality. The persistence of fundamentalist religions in the face of anomalies and inconsistent evidence illustrates this. Third, the only way we can change things is by changing the formal rules of the game. But, in fact, three factors determine the institutional framework of a society: formal rules; informal norms of behavior, conventions, and codes of conduct; and their enforcement characteristics. If all we can change are the formal rules, and not the other factors that also shape the performance characteristics, then we are going to get unforeseen and undesirable results. When Latin American countries became independent in the early nineteenth century, they adopted for the most part much of the United States Constitution but with radically different results. The distinguishing factors were in the informal norms and the enforcement characteristics – and that made all the difference. So, even though we might understand the world around us, and even though we might have a good sense of evolved beliefs, we have an imperfect ability to undertake and make the needed changes. This conclusion applies not only to third-world countries but to developed nations like the United States. Consequently, the implication is that getting it wrong is not just common, but is very likely to be the usual case.

A second implication is an old theme Hayek used a long time ago: in order to have the best chances of success and survival in a world of uncertainty, we must maximize the choice set of the players. Hayek argued for the kind of set that allowed for a variety of choices in society all the time. In the face of uncertainty, we are more likely to get it right if we have a variety of choices than if we have only a single way of doing things. The history of the command and control economy of the Soviet Union, compared to the adaptive efficiency of the American economy over the last century, illustrates dramatically Hayek's conclusion.

A third implication, and the one that is at the heart of the contents of this chapter, is that the most important frontier in the social and cognitive sciences is understanding how human beings learn. This entails a deeper understanding than we currently have about both the mind and the brain. It requires us to integrate into our analysis not only the interplay between the mind and the external environment that people such as Edwin Hutchins emphasize,[11] but also the connections between the mind and the brain. One of the things we have been learning from recent brain research is the very complex way that the brain actually implements and alters the way we perceive the world.

This complex connection between brain and mind has been noticeably promoted by recent studies based on brain scans showing which parts of the

---

[11] EDWIN HUTCHINS, COGNITION IN THE WILD (1995).

brain operate as we make choices and decisions in different contexts. It is also a part of the recent work attempting to show the complex relationships between feelings inside the body and the mind's interpretation of the external world. We have a long way to go to fully understand the economic and social world, but perhaps the most promise will come from cognitive science – down the road it may provide us with better understanding of the world around us. It is not going to provide us with a sure thing. It is not going to explain whether we will get it right in the future all the time. If the story here about a nonergodic world is correct, we will not. But, I think that it will mean that we can do better.

PART TWO

NORMS OF THE COMMONS

4   Norms of the Household

Robert C. Ellickson

Scholars of the commons typically have compared the merits of ownership of a pasture (or similar resource) by a single individual with its ownership by dozens of villagers.[1] This stylized bifurcation neglects the reality that many pastures and other resources are owned and occupied exclusively by members of a multiperson household – an institution situated somewhere between the individual and the village.[2] This chapter investigates this intermediate organization, including the rules that household members implicitly adopt to govern their affairs.

Households are ancient human institutions and have had Promethean influence. The rules that our ancestors developed to resolve problems arising around their hearths have provided templates for solutions to other small-scale problems of interpersonal coordination. It is within the household that most children first learn how to recognize and deal with the problems posed by common property, collective enterprise, and intrafamily dependence. A deeper understanding of the household therefore can shed light on more complex institutions.

The members of a multiperson household can be defined as the customary users of a space where two or more persons regularly share shelter and meals. Because many individuals spend over half their time at home, the household is a prime site for economic production, leisure activity, and intimate social

---

[1] See, e.g., Garrett Hardin, *The Tragedy of the Commons*, 162 SCI. 1243 (1968).

[2] See Robert C. Ellickson, *Property in Land*, 102 YALE L. J. 1315, 1394–97 (1993) [hereinafter Ellickson, *Property in Land*]. See also ELINOR OSTROM, GOVERNING THE COMMONS: THE EVOLUTION OF INSTITUTIONS OF COLLECTIVE ACTION 13–28 (1990) (urging a more pluralistic view of possible solutions to the challenge of the commons).

I thank Henry Hansmann, Robert Pollak, Roberta Romano, Reva Siegel, and an anonymous reviewer for their counsel, and John Eisenberg for research assistance.

interactions. In the United States, estimates of the value of within-household production have run from 24 percent to 60 percent of GDP – that is, to trillions of dollars per year.[3]

At the outset, it is important to distinguish the household from two closely related, but conceptually distinguishable, social molecules: marriage and the "family." As mentioned, *household* denotes an enterprise conducted on a particular piece of real estate. *Marriage*, by contrast, denotes a legal relationship between two people – one that need not involve cohabitation. Indeed, in the United States 6 percent of married persons do not live with their spouses.[4] In addition, when a married couple does cohabit, some core marital property rules govern assets other than the shared household space itself – for example, children, financial investments, and the spouses' aggregate human capital. In this chapter I generally ignore these much discussed issues and focus instead on the property rights and governance mechanisms associated with a household's physical domain.[5]

Similarly, *family* denotes a kinship relationship, but not necessarily the sharing of a physical space. Family members commonly engage in informal social insurance and intergenerational wealth transmission. Like spouses, however, family members need not cohabit and cohabitants need not be kin. In the United States in 1998, there were 5.3 million multiperson households whose occupants consisted entirely of unrelated individuals.[6] Included in this rich array of minicommonses were the households of unmarried heterosexual couples, gay and lesbian partners, Platonic housemates, and residents of communes and other intentional communities.

Despite its undeniable significance, the household as such has received little systematic analysis. To be sure, countless social historians, demographers, and sociologists have described home life in specific settings, and theorists as early as Aristotle recognized the centrality of the household in social

---

[3] For reviews of the literature, see EUSTON QUAH, ECONOMICS AND HOME PRODUCTION: THEORY AND MEASUREMENT 80–89 (1993); Oli Hawrylyshyn, *The Value of Household Services: A Survey of Empirical Estimates*, 22 REV. INCOME & WEALTH 101 (1976). Most estimates fall in the lower part of the range described.

[4] In 1998, 110.6 million married Americans were living with their spouses, but 7.3 million were not. U.S. CENSUS BUREAU, STATISTICAL ABSTRACT OF THE UNITED STATES: 1999, at 60 (1999) [hereinafter 1999 STATISTICAL ABSTRACT].

[5] On the law and economics of the marriage relationship itself, *see, e.g.*, Elizabeth S. Scott, *Social Norms and the Legal Regulation of Marriage*, 86 VA. L. REV. 1901 (2000); Amy L. Wax, *Bargaining in the Shadow of the Market: Is There a Future for Egalitarian Marriage?*, 84 VA. L. REV. 509 (1998).

[6] 1999 STATISTICAL ABSTRACT, *supra* note 4, at 60. The number of these households increased almost fivefold from 1.1 million in 1970. *Id.*

organization.[7] Property scholars and practitioners of the new institutional economics, however, have largely ignored this basic institution.

The aim of this chapter is to stimulate scholarly interest in the theory of household organization. The central theme is that the tools of transaction-cost economics promise to be particularly fruitful in this domain. Transaction-cost considerations, I assert, tend to keep households small and kinship-based, owned by providers of capital (not by providers of labor), and governed according to unwritten norms and customs (not written contracts and laws).

I. THE ECONOMY OF A LIBERAL HOUSEHOLD

Households vary in the goods and services they produce. By definition, a household must provide both shelter and meals to its occupants. Particularly in a family household, occupants also are likely to provide emotional and medical care, child training, entertainment, and other intimate services.

A. *Participants and Flows within the Household*

There are three basic participants in a household's economy: owners, occupants, and outsiders. (Note that a single individual may play more than one of these roles, e.g., an occupant may also be an owner.) Each type of participant provides some inputs into household production and shares in the resulting output. Owners supply either at-risk capital (equity) or tangible assets, in particular, unencumbered real estate. (A later portion of this chapter explains why these contributions usually entitle them to the powers associated with "owners.") Occupants supply most household labor. A household also may import goods and services – for example, lawn mowing – by means of contracts with outsiders. Using these various inputs, a household generates goods and services. It distributes most of these to occupants, but may export some products to outsiders, and may trade some services with casual guests invited in to share meals or accommodations. Residual outflows go to owners.

The rules of a household – which mainly take the form of informal norms[8] – determine what it produces, how particular owners and occupants

---

[7] In Book I of *The Politics*, Aristotle analyzes the household (*oikos*), which he sees as the basic building block of larger social institutions – first, the village, and, beyond that, the city (*polis*). ARISTOTLE, THE POLITICS 8–12 (Ernest Barker trans., R. F. Stalley rev., 1995). Although *oikos* is the etymological root of *economics*, mid–twentieth-century economists devoted little attention to "home economics." Gary Becker and Robert Pollak, both of whose work is cited later in this chapter, helped overcome this tradition of neglect.

[8] *See infra* text accompanying notes 63–112.

share in the flows of inputs and outputs, and how much the household trades with outsiders. A household's rules also include procedures for making decisions on all these fronts.

B. *Liberal and Illiberal Households: On Freedom of Exit*

I restrict my analysis to the liberal household, the form that best honors the ideal of individual self-determination long central in American law. A household is "liberal" when each of its members (that is, occupants and owners) individually have the power to exit from the arrangement and collectively have the power to control the entry of new occupants and owners.[9] Key legal rules, supported by social norms, assure these rights. Legal prohibitions on slavery and kidnapping help assure an occupant's freedom to decamp from a household.[10] An owner can unilaterally withdraw his capital over the objection of others by invoking his legal power to partition jointly owned property.[11] To enable the self-determination of existing household members, a liberal society must empower a household to reject an unwanted person who seeks to be taken in as either an occupant or owner.[12] Although there are exceptions, most nonfamily households in the United States – ordinary roommate situations, for example – comfortably fit this ideal type. Over the course of recent centuries, moreover, households in most developed nations generally have become more liberal.[13]

It is important to recognize, however, that even in the United States today many households are not entirely, or in some cases even remotely, liberal. First,

---

[9] I owe the term to WILLIAM JAMES BOOTH, HOUSEHOLDS: ON THE MORAL ARCHITECTURE OF THE ECONOMY 95–176 (1993). Dagan and Heller place protection of the privilege of exit at the center of their vision of a normatively attractive regime that they call the "liberal commons." *See* Hanoch Dagan & Michael A. Heller, *The Liberal Commons*, 110 YALE L. J. 549, 567–77 (2001).

[10] In a liberal society, a court would not order specific performance of a promise to remain in a household, but might conceivably award damages for breach of a contractual commitment to reside there.

[11] *See* WILLIAM B. STOEBUCK ET AL., THE LAW OF PROPERTY §§ 5.11–5.13 (3d ed. 2000).

[12] *See, e.g.*, the federal Fair Housing Act, 42 U.S.C. § 3603(b)(2) (2000) (exempting from coverage of Act (except for its advertising provisions) "rooms or units in dwellings containing living quarters occupied or intended to be occupied by no more than four families living independently of each other, if the owner actually maintains and occupies one of such living quarters as his residence"). *Cf.* U.S. CONST. amend. III, limiting the quartering of troops in "houses"; Thomas W. Merrill, *Property and the Right to Exclude*, 77 NEB. L. REV. 730 (1998) (on landowners' rights to exclude); Seana Valentine Shiffrin, *What Is Really Wrong with Compelled Association?*, 99 NW. U. L. REV. 839 (2005) (on associations' rights to exclude).

[13] *See* MARY ANN GLENDON, THE NEW FAMILY AND THE NEW PROPERTY 11–13, 41–46 (1981) (endorsing Henry Maine's notion of a broad historical trend toward the freeing of the individual from immutable blood and marriage obligations).

exit is never costless. Any occupant who leaves a household must incur moving expenses, the transaction costs of winding up intra-household claims, and the sacrifice of any household-specific human capital. In total, these costs may be small, as is likely when a graduating senior departs from a room in a college dormitory. In middle age, when ties are deeper and knowledge of household operations has become more specialized, exit is more costly.

Second, exit is not invariably available.[14] For example, residents of jails, mental institutions, and other group quarters may not be free to leave.[15] Minor children and incompetent adults are under the control of others. Social norms may shackle a competent adult, for example, one who remains in a nuclear household only on account of the social stigma that exit would trigger. A spouse also may decide against exiting out of fear of a violent response by the abandoned mate.

Liberal households have been even less common in other times and places. In the Soviet Union, where urban housing was notoriously scarce, the authorities often randomly assigned unrelated families to share communal housing units (the notorious *komunalkas*).[16] In many societies, parents still arrange their children's marriages (and, as the usual practical result, their children's households). Three millennia ago, the Homeric household portrayed in the Odyssey took the form of a large (around 30-member) extended-family household hierarchically governed by a *pater familias*.[17] Most slaves – whether chattel or debt – traditionally have resided in households. Indeed, in *The Politics*, Aristotle devotes much of his pioneering discussion of the household to rationalizations for slavery.[18]

---

[14] Although entry into a liberal household usually is voluntary, it need not be. For example, as a result of a will or the application of a statute governing intestate succession, several persons who never would have sought the arrangement may find themselves to be co-owners of a household. For descriptions of how the traditional reliance of African Americans on intestate succession led to fractionated ownership of rural lands in the South, see Dagan & Heller, *supra* note 9, at 551, 603–09; Thomas W. Mitchell, *From Reconstruction to Deconstruction: Undermining Black Landownership, Political Independence, and Community Through Partition Sales of Tenancies in Common*, 95 Nw. U. L. Rev. 505, 517–23 (2001).

[15] The U.S. Census Bureau uses *group quarters* to denote the residences of persons in dormitories, jails, nursing homes, military barracks and the like. 1999 Statistical Abstract, *supra* note 4, at 6. In 1990, just under 3% of the United States population lived in group quarters. U.S.Census Bureau, Statistical Abstract of the United States: 1996, at 67 (1996) [hereinafter 1996 Statistical Abstract]. Of these, 3.3 million were "institutionalized" in nursing homes, prisons, mental health facilities, and so on. *Id.*

[16] On *komunalkas*, see Michael A. Heller, *The Tragedy of the Anticommons: Property in the Transition from Marx to Markets*, 111 Harv. L. Rev. 621, 650–58 (1998).

[17] For discussion of the Homeric household, see Booth, *supra* note 9, at 15–34.

[18] See Aristotle, *supra* note 7, at 7–37. On the Hellenic household, see Booth, *supra* note 9, at 34–93.

C. *Distribution of Surplus Within a Liberal Household*

1. Household Surplus

The internal social and economic exchanges within a household typically enable its members to obtain more utility than they would enjoy if they were to live and own alone. This increment in utility is the *household surplus*.[19] A particular household's surplus is enhanced by efficiencies of scale and scope that its members are able to exploit, especially ones that take advantage of their affective ties.

A household setting is rife with possibilities for an opportunist. A bad apple can abuse the common space, pilfer personal property, neglect household duties, and divulge secrets about the personal lives of housemates. The magnitude of a household's aggregate surplus depends in part on its ability to develop internal substantive and procedural rules that serve to control these sorts of potential abuses. A household's substantive rules determine both the duties that individual owners and occupants owe to one another and also the entitlements that they each have to a share of the household's output. Procedural rules, by contrast, determine how household members make decisions.[20]

All else equal, household members prefer to shape their rules so as to reduce the transaction costs of their interactions. A key means to this end is to develop – or, better yet, start with – a high level of trust. Because trusting housemates incur lower transaction costs than untrusting ones do, they have more surplus to share. Trust is the expectation that another person will act cooperatively, instead of opportunistically, in a situation where both options are available.[21] The presence of trust helps enable occupants of a household readily to arrange for productive activities that are extremely difficult to monitor, for example, infant and toddler care. Trust also facilitates the process of gift exchange, the source of many of the household's advantages as an economic unit.[22]

The trust factor helps explain why most households are kinship-based. As Robert Pollak ably explains, family ties help foster trustfulness for a number of reasons.[23] First, biologists hypothesize the existence of an evolved altruism

---

[19] I coin this phrase as an extension of the notion of a "marital surplus," a concept used in some law-and-economics work on the family. *See, e.g.,* Wax, *supra* note 5, at 529–31.

[20] The last section of this chapter addresses these household rules in more detail. See *infra* text accompanying notes 98–112.

[21] For a review of social-scientific definitions of trust, see Erik Luna, *Transparent Policing*, 85 Iowa L. Rev. 1107, 1159 n.205 (2000). On the general topic, see, e.g., James S. Coleman, Foundations of Social Theory 91–116 (1990).

[22] *See infra* text accompanying notes 34–41.

[23] *See* Robert A. Pollak, *A Transaction Cost Approach to Families and Households*, 23 J. Econ. Literature 581, 585–88 (1985). Pollak also notes some disadvantages of kinship-based

toward kin – that is, the persons whose gene pool one shares.[24] Second, expulsion from a kinship network is particularly costly because that network is irreplaceable. Because of its uniqueness, the kinship game is a long-term game played until death, and the long shadow of its future helps induce cooperative play at present. Third and relatedly, information about one's kin is apt to be unusually complete, a reality that tends to deter a person from acting in a way that would tarnish his reputation with kin. Fourth and finally, in most societies prevailing social norms support loyalty to kin.[25]

2. The Distribution of Surplus among Household Members

Until a generation ago, economists modeled the family household as if all members had identical preferences. Paul Samuelson supposed that household members were cohesive enough to resolve all issues by consensus. Gary Becker hypothesized the existence of an altruistic dictator who served as the household head and whose decisions would thwart opportunism by any household member. More recently, however, economists have begun to apply game-theoretic models that assume that household members may battle over shares of household production.[26] This conception is more consistent with the rational-choice approach that is dominant in economics, and also with observations of actual households.[27]

In game-theoretic terms, a member's utility level in the event of exit establishes that member's "threat point."[28] A liberal household, to deter exit by a valued member, must allocate to that person enough household surplus to make it more advantageous for that person to stay than to leave. In many households, however, particularly ones based on kinship, there is likely to be enough

households. The multiplex nature of kinship ties poses risks that conflict will be imported into the household from an external strand of the kinship relationship, for example, a sibling rivalry. Members who are added to a household mainly for kinship reasons are not likely to possess the labor skills the household most needs, and may make the household expand beyond its most efficient size. *See id.* at 587–88.

[24] *See generally* GARY S. BECKER, A TREATISE ON THE FAMILY 277–306 (enlarged ed. 1991) (discussing altruism within the family).

[25] These same four factors explain the predominance of households containing closely related kin (e.g., parents and children), as opposed to more distantly related ones (e.g., second cousins).

[26] Noncooperative game theory stresses the risk that household members may become stuck at some suboptimal equilibrium. Cooperative game theory assumes that they will maximize total surplus, but wrangle over how to distribute it among themselves.

[27] For a valuable review of the intellectual trends described in this paragraph, see Shelly Lundberg & Robert A. Pollak, *Bargaining and Distribution in Marriage*, 10 J. ECON. PERSP. 139 (1996). Wax, *supra* note 5, provides a tour-de-force of the legal and social scientific literature on bargaining between marriage partners.

[28] *See* Lundberg & Pollak, *supra* note 27, at 146–49.

surplus to accomplish this result for all members. If there is an excess of surplus, how can the members be expected to divide it up? Game theory suggests that a member's prospective bargaining power within a household turns on the effects that the exit of that member would have on all involved.[29] Those effects depend both on the uniqueness of the contributions of the various members to the generation of the household surplus and on current household policies governing the distribution of that surplus. The power of a member within a household is positively associated with the irreplaceable contributions that member currently makes to the welfare of the other members.

As a member's opportunities on the outside improve, his threat of exit becomes more credible. Recognizing this reality, the other members may reallocate prospective shares of household surplus to reduce the likelihood that the threat will be carried out. In colonial Andover, Massachusetts, for example, as young men had increasingly good opportunities to the west, fathers had to grant their youngest sons land to dissuade them from migrating.[30] It is widely believed that a husband is likely to obtain a majority of the surplus from a marriage because he usually has greater opportunities to remarry after divorce, a reality that makes his threat of exit more credible than his wife's threat.[31] A wife, however, may be able to increase her power within a household either by increasing her conferrals of irreplaceable services within it or by improving the quality of her opportunities outside it.

Changes in law and social norms can alter threat points by changing both opportunity sets and the transaction costs of exit. Enhancement of women's employment opportunities outside the home serves to boost women's power within the home. Legal reforms that make it easier for a co-owner to partition property, or a spouse to divorce, ease exit and thereby strengthen the bargaining position of those with comparatively good opportunities on the outside.[32]

---

[29] In some contexts, however, a threat of uncooperative action within a household might be more potent than a threat to exit from it.

[30] *See* Pollak, *supra* note 23, at 603–04 (drawing this example from PHILIP J. GREVEN, FOUR GENERATIONS (1970)).

[31] *See, e.g.*, Wax, *supra* note 5, at 547–51.

[32] If transactions costs were zero, the strongest version of the Coase Theorem would imply that easing rules of divorce would not increase the incidence of divorce. For example, if it were efficient for a disgruntled wife to remain married, her husband could bargain with her to waive her legal entitlement to exit. *See* BECKER, *supra* note 24, at 331–34 (making this argument and offering data to support it). In practice, however, the Coase Theorem's invariance proposition is implausible in this context for a number of familiar reasons. First, shifting an entitlement may have wealth effects. Second, because of bilateral monopolies and emotional overlays in a household setting, transaction costs may be high even though few are involved. Third, there is the familiar asymmetry between willingness to pay and willingness to receive, which tends to

Housemates, perhaps especially in nonfamily settings, commonly have a strong mutual commitment to equality among themselves, a stance that tends to mute their attentiveness to small differences in their individual threat points. Equality, apart from whatever independent value it may have, has the instrumental merit of fostering cooperative group outcomes.[33]

D. *The Central Role of Gift Exchange in a Household Economy*

When hiring, say, food preparation services from an outsider, a household typically engages in a simultaneous bilateral exchange. For example, housemates likely would pay cash on delivery to a home deliverer of hot pizza. What is striking about most internal household economies, however, is the relative absence of explicit bilateral exchanges, especially ones involving transfers of money. A live-in servant who provides cooking services of course may have explicit contract rights to receive room, board, and wages. But everyday experience suggests that it is vanishingly rare for a household consisting only of kin to pay wages to an adult occupant for performing specific tasks such as cooking meals, mowing the lawn, or protesting the house's property tax assessment.[34] In most households, especially small ones, most acts of household labor are unilaterally initiated and delivered as gifts.[35] Although housemates occasionally may discuss how to share household chores, the terms of much of this coordination are likely to be unspoken.[36]

As just discussed, however, a household economy based on gift exchange is unlikely to endure unless it succeeds in delivering to all members some

make entitlements stick where they are allocated. For evidence contrary to Becker's, *see* Martin Zelder, *The Economic Analysis of the Effect of No-Fault Divorce Law on the Divorce Rate*, 16 HARV. J. L. PUB. POL'Y 241 (1993) (finding that enactment of a no-fault divorce statute increases the rate of divorce).

[33] This is a staple of sociological theory. *See, e.g.*, DONALD BLACK, THE BEHAVIOR OF LAW 11–36 (1976). Transaction-cost economics supports the same proposition. Equality among decision-makers enhances their homogeneity and thus reduces their decision-making costs. *See* HENRY HANSMANN, THE OWNERSHIP OF ENTERPRISE 39–44 (1996).

[34] Some parents do pay children to perform household chores, perhaps partly to prepare them for work experiences outside the household.

[35] *Cf.* ROBERT C. ELLICKSON, ORDER WITHOUT LAW: HOW NEIGHBORS SETTLE DISPUTES 61– 62, 78, 234–36 (1991) [hereinafter ELLICKSON, ORDER WITHOUT LAW] (describing preference of neighbors in rural Shasta County, California, to use in-kind gifts, not money, to compensate one another). The term *gift* is potentially misleading because it connotes only the delivery of a positive reinforcement. The sanctions informally administered by housemates in fact include both carrots (such as returned favors) and sticks (such as the withholding of customary services).

[36] For elaboration, *see infra* text accompanying notes 81–97.

share of the household surplus. Each member therefore is likely to keep a rough mental account of who has contributed and received what.[37] (In a family household, of course, many gifts, especially ones from parents to children, may be given altruistically, with little expectation of future repayment.) In a successful household, explicit reference to perceived imbalances in internal gift exchange may be regarded as inappropriate because they signal a lack of trust. Nevertheless, a member who is receiving too little from the household economy eventually can be expected to respond through escalating self-help measures. As his grievances deepen, his informal remedies may progress from gentle reminders, to forceful protests, to conspicuous refusals to perform customary duties, to threats of exit, and finally to actual exodus from the household.[38] The ready availability of this graduated panoply of responses helps to deter opportunistic behavior by other household members.

Why are the transactions within household economies so rarely commodified?[39] The first and main reason is that gift exchange is administratively cheaper than a system of explicit bilateral contracts. Household members confident that their gift exchange system will be mutually advantageous are able to avoid the hassle of negotiating and enforcing agreements over particular contributions. How much is sweeping out the garage worth? How well was the job done? These sorts of questions may arise in a household based on gift exchange because members may find it desirable to keep rough mental accounts. But the transaction costs of keeping those accounts are far less than the costs of bargaining out in advance the terms of a garage-cleaning deal and later administering that contract. In a household where members generally trust one another and where all members receive some share of the surplus, a garage cleaning may be initiated unilaterally, without any prior negotiation among housemates.

A second reason bilateral transactions are disfavored within households is that the buying and selling of services typically is a less enjoyable *process* than exchanging services as gifts. Money, the handiest medium for bilateral exchange, symbolizes a lack of intimacy. A well-socialized dinner guest arrives bearing the gift of a bottle of wine, not proffering a twenty-dollar bill. Both law and social norms permit gifts of babies and sexual favors, but are hostile to their sale.[40] By engaging in daily gift exchanges, household members not only

---

[37] *Cf.* ELLICKSON, ORDER WITHOUT LAW, *supra* note 35, at 55–56 (discussing mental accounting of interneighbor debts).

[38] *Cf. id.* at 56–64 (on neighbors' application of escalating self-help sanctions to control deviants).

[39] While avoidance of cash payments for labor also may reduce income-tax liabilities, the prevalence of gift exchange in households predated the advent of the income tax.

[40] *See* Margaret Jane Radin, *Market-Inalienability*, 100 HARV. L. REV. 1849 (1987).

reduce their transaction costs and signal their mutual trust, but also experience the warm glow of intimacy.[41]

II. THE GOVERNANCE OF HOUSEHOLDS: WHY OWNERSHIP TYPICALLY IS BESTOWED ON PROVIDERS OF EQUITY CAPITAL

The operation of a household requires the combination of inputs of both labor and capital to produce the goods and services that occupants (mainly) consume. A household thus is an economic enterprise. Who "owns" it? If asked this question, the occupants of a single-family house probably would respond by mentioning the names of the grantees listed in the most recent deed conveying the house. Logically the next question to put to them would be: what contribution did those persons make that led them to having been listed as the grantees? The occupants typically would answer that the grantees had provided the equity capital – that is, the funds used to defray the portion of the purchase price not financed by means of debt capital provided by mortgage lenders with fixed claims.[42] After acquiring title, these same "owners" also are likely to be the persons who provide additional infusions of equity, either to cover deficits incurred in household operations or to finance improvements to the premises.[43] As this section explains, in return for these equity inputs, owners tend to be granted both the power to make key household decisions and the right to reap any beneficial financial consequences of those decisions. In short, contributors of equity capital typically have roles in households similar to their central roles in business firms.

A. *Basic Concepts in the Theory of Ownership*

The theory of the organization of enterprise can readily be extended to the household sector. According to this theory, the owner of a firm possesses two

---

[41] See ELLICKSON, ORDER WITHOUT LAW, *supra* note 35, at 234–35. Some feminist scholars who favor monetary compensation for household work are sensitive to this consideration. *See, e.g.,* SUSAN MOLLER OKIN, JUSTICE, GENDER, AND THE FAMILY 180–81 (1989) (advocating that each spouse receive half of any paycheck received for work outside the household, but opposing cash compensation for particular household tasks).

[42] There are exceptions of course. In particular, a loving spouse may provide all the equity for a house purchase but, as a gift, provide that both spouses take title in equal shares.

[43] The donee of a dwelling conveyed as a gift initially puts up no equity, but can be expected to make later cash infusions. In an instance where an owner has been exceptionally passive, the doctrine of adverse possession may confer title to a household premises on long-time occupants, including ones who previously had not contributed capital. Once adverse possessors obtain title, however, they similarly are likely to become capital providers.

key entitlements: the power to make residual control decisions and the right to receive residual financial flows.[44] What are these entitlements, and why do they tend to be tied together in both business enterprises and domestic households?

1. Residual Control Decisions

Household ownership is a form of land ownership. In a society with a private property system, a private landowner has broad powers to decide three basic sorts of issues: (1) who can enter and remain on the premises; (2) how the premises are to be used and developed; and (3) under what circumstances the premises are to be transferred to another owner.[45] Within a given household, some decisions about the exercise of these basic powers may already be settled – that is, controlled by law, binding social norms, or contract. Because law, norms, and contracts invariably are incomplete, however, many decisions about the use of a household commons remain up for grabs. These are the residual control decisions. The owners of a household have the ultimate power to decide these open questions.

There are, of course, limitations on the powers of the owners of a household. First, an owner may choose not to enjoy the entitlements of ownership, but instead to trade or give them away. The possibility of these sorts of transfers complicates empirical analysis of the locus of power within households, especially nuclear family households infused with altruism. Second, the theory of ownership suggests that the residual powers of the owners of a household will be limited in scope – that is, only cover the management of the physical premises and not extend to aspects of the lives of occupants that would not affect the residual value of the premises. Third, legal rules may regulate owners' powers to control occupants. For example, statutes may limit self-help evictions by owners.

2. Residual Financial Flows

Members of a household may provide funds to the enterprise and also share in monetary outflows. Entitlements to these financial flows may be governed by contracts, external norms, or laws. For instance, a lease might specify an occupant's obligation to pay rent to the owners; a mortgage, the owners' obligation to lenders;[46] and a labor contract, the rights and duties of a domestic

---

[44] For a lucid formulation of these notions, see PAUL MILGROM & JOHN ROBERTS, ECONOMICS, ORGANIZATION AND MANAGEMENT 289–90 (1992).

[45] *See* Ellickson, *Property in Land, supra* note 2, at 1362–63.

[46] Like a bondholder of a business corporation, a mortgagee may use covenants and security interests to protect itself against household policies that would jeopardize repayment of the

worker. As in a business firm, the residual financial flows in a household are the ones that remain unallocated after all the contracts, norms, and laws governing inflows and outflows have been honored. The value of owners' "equity" in the household is the discounted present value of these residuals. In most instances, ownership of a household has positive market value. The value might be negative, however, if the household premises were to be burdened with excessive mortgage debt, unfavorable leases, or confiscatory property taxes.

3. Ownership: An Amalgamation of Control and Financial Residuals

The owner of a household, like the owner of any enterprise, typically has *both* the power to make residual control decisions *and* the right to receive residual financial flows.[47] Scholars of enterprise argue that this pairing of control powers with financial stakes sharpens incentives for prudent management.[48] To illustrate, suppose that the roof of a household's dwelling had begun to leak, an eventuality not covered by contract among the housemates. If the owners of the household had residual control powers, they could decide how to repair the roof and also how to pay for it out of household assets. If the roof repair would increase the discounted present value of future occupancy of the space by an amount greater than the repair would cost, the owners' residual would become more valuable. If the roof repair would not be cost-effective, on the other hand, the value of the residual would drop. Someone who bears the financial consequences of a decision is likely to deliberate more carefully than someone who does not bear those consequences. For this reason it would be

---

debt. A basic strategy of many mortgage lenders is to ensure that the equity owners have stakes sufficiently large to deter them from pursuing overly risky projects. Absent government-subsidized mortgage insurance, the combined loan-to-value ratios of first and second mortgages therefore rarely exceed 90%. Otherwise, as loan-to-value ratios escalate, junior mortgage lenders (and their insurers) have to be increasingly active in monitoring the behavior of mortgagors. *See also infra* text accompanying notes 56–59.

[47] Additional complexities arise when the ownership of a household premises is divided among owners of present and future interests. For instance, three co-tenants might lease a unit in an apartment building from a landlord who retains ownership of the reversion – the interest that becomes possessory at the end of the leasehold. To simplify the exposition, I restrict my analysis to ownership of a currently possessory interest – in this instance, to the lease held by the three co-tenants. Subject to contractual and legal constraints designed to protect the landlord from tenant opportunism ("waste" is the pertinent legal term), the three tenants in fact have residual control rights and residual financial claims during the term of the leasehold. For example, if they could make a profit by subleasing one of the bedrooms to a fourth person who had not signed the primary lease, their ownership of the lease would give them the residual control powers to determine how they would split that surplus.

[48] Theorists of business organization agree that it generally is efficient to bestow residual rights of control on the residual claimant. *See, e.g.*, HANSMANN, *supra* note 33, at 11–12; MILGROM & ROBERTS, *supra* note 44, at 289–93.

wise for housemates to delegate the decision on the roof repair to the party with the residual financial claim – that is, to the owner.

B. *Why Suppliers of a Household's Risk Capital Tend to End up as Its Owners*

Bestowing on the owner of a household both residual control powers and residual financial claims thus tends to improve the quality of household decisions. This proposition, however, leaves open the issue of which of the parties involved in a household should serve as its owner.

1. The Various Patrons Who Might Own a Household

Like any enterprise, a household is associated with a variety of "patrons" (to borrow a term from Henry Hansmann).[49] A household's chief patrons are its occupants, its providers of equity capital, its lenders of debt capital, and the other outsiders with whom it trades. Those jointly involved in an enterprise have an interest in allocating ownership rights to the patron that values ownership rights the most.[50] This assignment reduces the costs of obtaining whatever factor of production that particular patron provides to the household. More importantly, allocating ownership to the most efficient owner reduces the total transaction costs of governing the enterprise. If not granted ownership rights, the supplier of the factor in question would insist on being protected with contractual guarantees that would be both costly to draft and cumbersome to administer. Selecting a governance system for a household thus is a positive-sum game: all patrons, including nonowners, can benefit from an arrangement that maximizes household surplus by reducing total governance costs.[51]

Of the various patrons of a household, outside suppliers and customers are the least plausible candidates to serve as owners. Because they usually are not knowledgeable about household conditions, they are poorly qualified to make residual control decisions. In addition, unlike providers of capital, they typically

---

[49] Hansmann uses "patron" to describe any party who transacts with a business firm. HANSMANN, *supra* note 33, at 12.

[50] Splitting ownership rights among two or more types of patrons generally is inadvisable. For example, if suppliers of both labor and capital were to share the ownership of a household, transaction costs would escalate because both the number and the heterogeneity of the decision-makers would increase. *See infra* text accompanying notes 53–55. *But cf.* MARGARET M. BLAIR, OWNERSHIP AND CONTROL: RETHINKING CORPORATE GOVERNANCE FOR THE TWENTY-FIRST CENTURY 238–74 (1995) (arguing that an employee with firm-specific human capital merits sharing in the ownership of a corporation).

[51] In Hansmann's terms, this is the "lowest-cost assignment of ownership." *See* HANSMANN, *supra* note 33, at 21–22.

can protect themselves by means of simple express contracts. For instance, a disgruntled provider of ephemeral services can resort to the self-help measure of refusing additional service, and a provider of a durable good or permanent physical improvement can insist on being paid in advance.

Occupants, however, are facially plausible candidates to serve as the owners of a household. Unlike outsiders, occupants typically do have detailed knowledge of the enterprise because they provide most household labor and consume most household production. If occupants indeed were to own a household, they conceivably could raise all the capital they needed through either loans or retained earnings.[52]

2. The Advantages of Conferring Ownership on a Household's Contributors of Risk Capital

In practice, a household's patrons typically arrange to confer ownership on its suppliers of equity capital, not on its occupants.[53] (In situations where household workers live on the premises but household financiers do not, this approach tends to lead to a separation of ownership from control – a homespun version of a problem commonly encountered in the business context.[54]) Why this pattern? The literature on the ownership of enterprise offers four reasons, presented here in order of increasing complexity and weightiness:

a. *Equity Investors in Households Tend to Be Few in Number and Relatively Unchanging.* The providers of a household's equity capital are likely to be less numerous than its occupants. Available data indicate that the owners of, say, a single-family house rarely exceed two in number, while the number of occupants commonly is greater than that. A study in Iowa in 1954–64, for example, found that in over 95 percent of real estate transfers to persons, the deed named either a single individual or a married couple as the grantee.[55] Decisions tend

---

[52] Scholars of business organization have analyzed the analogous possibility of a worker-owned business firm that borrows all needed capital. *See, e.g.,* HANSMANN, *supra* note 33, at 75–77.

[53] A young adult who wishes to acquire a home knows that the key step is to marshal enough money for a down payment (as opposed, say, to acquiring labor skills with an eye later to trading labor services for a share of household ownership).

[54] A classic expression of this problem in the corporate context is ADOLPH BERLE & GARDINER MEANS, THE MODERN CORPORATION AND PRIVATE PROPERTY (1932). *See also* Michael C. Jensen & William H. Meckling, *Theory of the Firm: Managerial Behavior, Agency Costs, and Ownership Structure,* 3 J. FIN. ECON. 305 (1976).

[55] About 40% of the deeds named single grantees, and about 55% named only a husband and wife. Computed from data presented in N. William Hines, *Real Property Joint Tenancies: Law, Fact, and Fancy,* 51 IOWA L. REV. 582, 607, 617 (1966). *See also* Evelyn Alicia Lewis, *Struggling with Quicksand: The Ins and Outs of Cotenant Possession, Value Liability and a Call for Default Rule Reform,* 1994 WIS. L. REV. 331, 398 n.204 (citing other studies of incidence of co-ownership).

to be made faster when fewer have to agree. By empowering its equity contributors to govern, a household can keep decision costs down without forgoing the economies of scale in household production and consumption that may be achievable when occupants are numerous.

The equity investors in a household also are likely to turn over less frequently than its occupants. If an occupant's ownership rights were contingent on continued occupancy, an occupant about to depart would take a short-sighted view of household decisions. This problem of limited time-horizons would be eliminated if departing occupants could transfer their ownership rights to successors (or sell them back to the other occupants). That solution, however, would increase occupants' transaction costs of entering and exiting a household. A revolving door of owners also would confuse and confound vendees, mortgage lenders, tax collectors, and other outsiders who need assurances about the state of the current title to a household premises. By adding to transaction costs, occupant ownership thus would disadvantage all of a household's patrons.

b. *Owners of Capital Tend to Be Superior Risk Bearers.* A supplier of capital typically can bear risk better than can a consumer or a supplier of labor. In particular, a person can diversify a holding of financial capital more easily than his own human capital. The occupants of a household therefore commonly are poor candidates to bear the downside risks of household operations, as they would if they were to serve as its residual claimants.

c. *The Interests of Suppliers of Capital Are More Homogeneous than the Interests of Occupants.* Hansmann has stressed the transaction-cost advantages to conferring ownership on persons whose interests are homogeneous. The interests of suppliers of equity capital to a household typically are more homogeneous than are the interests of the household's occupants (whether in their capacities as consumers, suppliers of labor, or both). Equity investors who own a dwelling, for example, would have similar financial stakes in any roof repair project that might be undertaken. This would reduce their decisionmaking costs.

A roof repair project, by contrast, would affect occupants in different ways. The construction activity might inconvenience some occupants more than others. Or the occupants of some bedrooms might obtain special benefits from the repair. If occupants controlled the decision over whether to replace the roof, these differences could complicate their discussions.

In addition, homogeneity of ownership interests facilitates the calculation of shares of ownership. Capital contributions are especially easy to value.

Although some account may have to be made of the time at which a contributor provided capital, figuring out the shares of a household's equity capital is likely to require no more than simple mathematical calculations. This is not true in the case of labor or consumer interests. If occupants were to apply a simple rule such as one-occupant/one-share, they would fail to correlate shares with either contributions made or interests at stake.

d. *Because Suppliers of Risk Capital Are the Patrons Most Vulnerable to Opportunism, They Value Rights of Control More than Others Do.* Suppliers of capital to a household have reason to be especially apprehensive of exploitation. In a liberal society, a household worker who feels abused typically can exit with most personal human capital in tow.[56] Suppliers of risk capital, by contrast, turn over a long-lived asset that opportunistic household managers can expropriate and expose to unduly high risks. Oliver Williamson has argued that providers of risk capital to a business firm typically cannot readily negotiate adequately protective contractual provisions from the firm's other patrons.[57] In light of this special vulnerability, the patrons of a household enterprise similarly are likely to conclude that their cost-minimizing approach is to give ownership rights to suppliers of risk capital.

Suppose, for example, that occupants owned a household and had previously raised all needed capital by means of mortgage loans from outsiders. To finance a prospective roof repair, these owner-occupants might turn to a bank. Because the owners would not have invested any equity capital in their house, the bank likely would be highly skittish about making the loan. Because prior lenders to the household would have senior liens on household assets, the bank would have little or no security if the owners were either to squander the loan proceeds on a foolish repair project or divert the sum to another purpose.[58] The bank, of course, could take defensive measures. It might make its own appraisal of the cost-effectiveness of the proposed roof repair project, condition the disbursement of loan installments on the submission of evidence of actual repair work, and so on. Those precautions, however, would give rise to redundant transaction costs. Not only would the owners of the household have to appraise the merits of a proposed roof repair, but so would their lender.

---

[56] Just as an industrial worker may have firm-specific human capital (*see* BLAIR, *supra* note 50, at 238–74), a household worker may have household-specific human capital. To that extent, an occupant may indeed be vulnerable to opportunism by others.

[57] *See* Oliver Williamson, *Corporate Governance*, 93 YALE L. J. 1197, 1210 (1984).

[58] Especially if not personally liable for the debt, the residual claimant of an enterprise that is fully leveraged may be tempted to invest in an overly-risky project because the owner reaps all gains if the project is successful but bears none of the losses if it fails.

By contrast, if the owners of the household were to have an equity stake that would be jeopardized if the household were to waste the funds, the bank would not need to monitor the situation so closely.[59]

For all these reasons, in a typical household the least-cost approach is to confer ownership on providers of risk capital. Indeed, this approach usually is so much the best that household members are unlikely even to consider other alternatives. Utopians – such as Plato and B. F. Skinner – of course have imagined other arrangements.[60] A utopia typically is conceived as a place where dozens or even hundreds of unrelated adults share meals and reside in collectively governed housing.[61] In practice, intentional communities that experiment with occupant ownership tend to succumb within a few years to some form of creeping capitalism.[62] The capitalist-controlled household, by contrast, is an ownership form with proven capacity to endure. Whatever the social environment, it offers inherent transactional advantages that generally have enabled it to outlast more idealistic forms of domestic organization.

III. NORMS FOR A HOUSEHOLD IN MIDGAME

Even in an informal setting like a home, individuals who repeatedly interact develop rules for their interactions. Often unarticulated, these household rules are the stuff of everyday life. In prior work I assert that the overall system of social control is an amalgam of rules emanating from five interrelated sources: personal ethics (including internalized norms), contracts, diffusely enforced social norms, organizational rules, and law.[63] In any arena of social control the

---

[59] On the agency costs of 100% debt financing in the corporate context, see HANSMANN., *supra* note 33, at 53–56; ROBERTA ROMANO, FOUNDATIONS OF CORPORATE LAW 119–120 (1993) (noting, at 120, that "we do not see 100 percent debt-financed firms").

[60] Plato proposed that Guardians share dwellings, storehouses, wives, and a modest food allotment. PLATO, THE REPUBLIC, bk. 3, 416d–e, bk. 4, 419–420c. Skinner envisioned nearly 1,000 persons sharing a common eating room, and dwelling in "personal rooms" located within a complex of buildings governed by a six-person "Board of Planners." B. F. SKINNER, WALDEN TWO 18–20, 40–44, 48 (Macmillan 1976) (1948).

[61] See generally FRANK E. MANUEL & FRITZIE MANUEL, UTOPIAN THOUGHT IN THE WESTERN WORLD (1979).

[62] See BENJAMIN ZABLOCKI, ALIENATION AND CHARISMA: A STUDY OF CONTEMPORARY AMERICAN COMMUNES 76–77, 148–51 (1980); Ellickson, *Property in Land*, *supra* note 2, at 1359–60.

[63] See ELLICKSON, ORDER WITHOUT LAW, *supra* note 35, at 123–36. Commonly the agent that makes a rule also is the agent that enforces it; for example, state bureaucracies enforce law (that is, state-made rules), and an individual enforces his own personal ethics on himself. But hybrid systems of social control also are common. For example, housemates might use an express contract to create rules, and then rely on another controlling agent – perhaps external gossip networks, or the state – to enforce that contract. *See id.*

first-order decisions for participants involve the selection of controlling agents: in the setting at hand, from what sources are rules to be found? And who is to enforce them?

As Lisa Bernstein has demonstrated in another context, participants may prefer different rulemakers during midgame than they do during endgame.[64] In midgame, when a household is generating and distributing enough surplus to satisfy all occupants and owners, members anticipate that their relationships will continue. Under these conditions, household members are likely to rely more on rules of their own making than on external rules. Endgame commences when members have come to anticipate that some or all of them are about to exit from the arrangement. In endgame, external rules become increasingly important. The discussion that follows, however, addresses only the rules of a household in midgame.

A. *Sources of Midgame Rules*

1. Potential External Sources of Household Rules

To some degree, members of a household may follow rules that outsiders have devised for domestic affairs. In particular, members may look either to the legal system or to ambient social norms (that is, the general practices of other households in salient social environments).

a. *The Peripheral Role of the Legal System.* Traditionally, legal scholars have assumed that individuals in most contexts look primarily to the legal system to determine their entitlements. In recent years, however, scholars increasingly have come to recognize that this legal-centralist perspective can be highly misleading. To be sure, the legal system does help ensure the basic liberal entitlements that underpin interactions among household members.[65] But when a dispute over some day-to-day affair arises within an ongoing household, its members are highly unlikely to look to the legal system for either rules or enforcement actions.

---

[64] Lisa Bernstein, *Merchant Law in a Merchant Court: Rethinking the Code's Search for Immanent Business Norms*, 144 U. PA. L. REV. 1765 (1996).

[65] *See supra* text accompanying notes 9–13. In addition, bodies of law that govern relations between an individual and the state – especially tax and welfare policies – may profoundly affect both how households are composed and the internal rules they adopt. For example, if the value of household labor were to be treated as imputed income under the Internal Revenue Code, members would have a greater incentive than they do now to contract out household work. For a useful review of the numerous consequences of American governments' disinclinations to equate household work with paid work, see Katharine Silbaugh, *Turning Labor Into Love: Housework and the Law*, 91 NW. U. L. REV. 1 (1996).

It is a staple of empirical legal scholarship that low-stakes disputes among individuals with continuing relationships tend to be resolved beyond the shadow of the law.[66] While in some contexts this pattern may be partly attributable to lack of confidence in the legal system, in all situations a major reason is the desire to economize on transaction costs. Learning legal rules requires research and perhaps consultation with legal experts. Learning a household's self-generated rules, by contrast, requires little more than being alert at the dinner table. Moreover, legal enforcement is far slower and more costly than more decentralized forms of enforcement. In midgame, household members enjoy ongoing relations (and indeed commonly share enduring ties based on family or friendship). These enduring bonds provide ready future opportunities for the self-help sanctioning of rulebreakers. For a workaday dispute involving small stakes, self-help plainly is far cheaper and faster than seeking relief through the legal system.[67] Resort to law is so expensive that a civil lawsuit between members of a household in midgame is increasingly rare (absent any prospect of collecting from a third party, such as a liability insurance company).[68]

For their part, judges are strongly inclined to let housemates work out their problems on their own. Most notably, courts typically decline to reach the merits of a domestic civil complaint filed by one spouse against the other while the marriage still is in midgame – that is, before the two have either initiated a divorce proceeding or begun to live separately.[69] An ongoing marriage is a highly complex, multi-stranded relationship. Judges understandably are wary

---

[66] *See* sources cited in ELLICKSON, ORDER WITHOUT LAW, *supra* note 35, at 141–47, 256–57.

[67] A pertinent study is Vilhelm Aubert, *Some Social Functions of Legislation*, 10 ACTA SOCIOLOG-ICA 98 (1967), discussed in ELLICKSON, ORDER WITHOUT LAW, *supra* note 35, at 141–42. Aubert found that no lawsuits had been brought under the Norwegian Housemaid Law of 1948 during the first two years it had been in effect because, to curb employer abuse, housemaids continued to rely on their ability to exit from the household.

[68] Although hornbooks note that a co-owner can petition for an accounting while the relationship is ongoing (*see, e.g.,* STOEBUCK & WHITMAN, *supra* note 11, § 5.9, p. 209), few appellate cases involve such actions. *But cf.* Swartzbaugh v. Sampson, 54 P.2d 73 (Cal. Ct. App. 1936) (action by wife against husband and lessee to cancel husband's lease of co-owned real estate). On possibilities of tort litigation between family members, see HOMER H. CLARK, JR., THE LAW OF DOMESTIC RELATIONS IN THE UNITED STATES §§ 10.1–10.2 (2d ed. 1988).

[69] *See, e.g.,* Kilgrow v. Kilgrow, 107 So. 2d 885 (Ala. 1958) (refusing to adjudicate suit between cohabiting spouses over where their seven-year-old child should attend school); McGuire v. McGuire, 59 N.W.2d 336 (Neb. 1953) (rejecting, for reasons of public policy, suit by wife for support payments from husband who lived with her). *But see, e.g.,* Miller v. Miller, 30 N.W.2d 509 (Mich. 1948) (granting wife support payments, on ground of extreme cruelty, against cohabiting husband). *See generally* Marjorie Maguire Shultz, *Contractual Ordering of Marriage: A New Model for State Policy*, 70 CAL. L. REV. 204, 232–37 (1982). *Cf.* Saul Levmore, *Love It or Leave It: Property Rules, Liability Rules, and Exclusivity of Remedies in Partnership and Marriage*, 58 LAW & CONTEMP. PROBS. 221 (1995) (noting that a business partner's exclusive remedy is to terminate the relationship and pursue a "final accounting").

of adjudicating a dispute arising within a single strand, because the losing party is likely to be able to effectively counter the judicial action through self-help responses in other strands of the relationship.[70] For similar reasons, courts also are likely to forbear from involving themselves in disputes arising within ongoing nonmarital households.

The judicial reluctance to intervene in midgame domestic affairs honors basic liberal values. A liberal legal system, after assuring individual rights of exit and bodily integrity, gives household members wide berth to shape their own arrangements. Members should be presumptively free to decide who can join the group and to frame internal policies governing matters such as cuisine, sleeping arrangements, and religious practices.[71] In a liberal polity, candidates for elective office do not propose legislation that would directly regulate how housemates are chosen, bedrooms allocated, and household chores assigned.[72] Indeed, in the United States, government intrusion into these internal household affairs might be held to be an unconstitutional restriction on freedom of association.[73] The Supreme Court has been especially protective of family-based households, particularly when legal authorities have sought to regulate marital and parent-child relations.[74] Households consisting solely of non-kin also have received some, albeit less robust, constitutional protection.[75]

The chief exceptions to this libertarian policy arise out of the considerations that limit freedom of contract in any context: concern for the interests of either helpless insiders or jeopardized outsiders.[76] For example, legal limits

---

[70] Some observers criticize this persistent judicial policy of refusing to intervene in disputes between currently cohabiting spouses. *See, e.g.,* Frances E. Olsen, *The Myth of State Intervention in the Family,* 18 U. MICH. J. L. REFORM 835 (1985); Note, *Litigation Between Husband and Wife,* 79 HARV. L. REV. 1650 (1966).

[71] *Accord* Dagan & Heller, *supra* note 9, at 596 (as long as exit is available and third-party interests are not jeopardized).

[72] *Cf.* the exemptions included in the federal Fair Housing Act, cited *supra* note 12.

[73] *See generally* Kenneth Karst, *The Freedom of Intimate Association,* 89 YALE L. J. 624 (1980).

[74] *See, e.g.,* Troxel v. Granville, 530 U.S. 57 (2000) (holding that application of statute to override mother's control of grandparents' visitation rights violated mother's rights to substantive due process); Moore v. City of East Cleveland, 431 U.S. 494 (1977) (invalidating, as violation of substantive due process, ordinance provision that prevented grandmother from bringing into her household two grandsons who were not brothers).

[75] *Compare* Village of Belle Terre v. Boraas, 416 U.S. 1 (1974) (upholding, against wide-ranging constitutional attack, ordinance that limited composition of a non-family household to a maximum of two adults), *with* City of Santa Barbara v. Adamson, 610 P.2d 436 (Cal. 1980) (striking down, as violation of state constitutional provision, ordinance that limited creation of households of more than four unrelated persons). Arguments in favor of greater legal solicitousness toward family households are arrayed in David D. Haddock & Daniel D. Polsby, *Family As a Rational Classification,* 74 WASH. U. L.Q. 15 (1996).

[76] *See* Ian Ayres & Robert Gertner, *Filling Gaps in Incomplete Contracts: An Economic Theory of Default Rules,* 99 YALE L. J. 87, 88 (1989).

on intrahousehold violence help ensure that individual members indeed are free to exercise their powers of voice and exit.[77] The state similarly may seek to prevent the abuse and neglect of children and to assure their education.[78] Legal systems do not defer to household activities that are nuisances to neighbors.[79]

b. *Ambient Social Norms.* A particular household's practices typically are significantly influenced by informal norms prevalent in larger social circles. In particular, ambient norms governing gender roles are likely to influence allocation of household tasks. Ambient norms are mostly enforced by means of informal social sanctions. The enforcers may be other household members. Or the enforcers may be outsiders, for instance, neighbors who employ gossip to reward good landscaping or to punish lax child supervision. In a liberal society, however, neighbors, like lawmakers, are likely to give a household's members much leeway to structure their own internal rules as long as those rules do not harm the interests of either helpless insiders or affected outsiders.[80]

2. Potential Internal Sources of Household Rules
To complement and (commonly) supplant pertinent laws and ambient social norms, housemates typically generate their own "customs of the household," an analogue to the varying "customs of the manor" that evolved in medieval villages.[81] In so doing, household members encounter a basic issue: how formally to articulate their homespun system of social control. Household rules can emerge inchoately from domestic practice, be negotiated in conversations, or, at the extreme, be put down in writing.

Household members who opt for informality generally prefer unarticulated rules to oral contracts, and are averse to written rules. These informalists also

---

[77] *See generally Developments in the Law: Legal Responses to Domestic Violence*, 106 HARV. L. REV. 1498 (1993). Many legal regimes also have sought to prevent cruelty to household animals (and, where slavery was permitted, to household slaves).

[78] *See generally* Peter David Brandon, *State Intervention in Imperfect Families*, 13 RATIONALITY & SOC'Y 285 (2001). One conception is that the state tries to assure that the rules of a household that contains minor children, incompetent adults, pets, or other helpless members are identical to the rules that would exist if those members were not lacking in capacity. *See* Gary S. Becker & Kevin M. Murphy, *The Family and the State*, 31 J. L. & ECON. 1 (1988).

[79] *See, e.g.*, People v. Wheeler, 106 Cal. Rptr. 260 (Ct. App. 1973) (authorizing correction of unsanitary conditions in commune that posed risk of epidemic).

[80] *See* ALAN WOLFE, ONE NATION, AFTER ALL (1998) (describing broad tolerance of most Americans toward others' modes of living). *But cf.* Richard H. McAdams, *The Origin, Development, and Regulation of Norms*, 96 MICH. L. REV. 338, 412–19 (1997) (on the possibility of "nosy norms").

[81] See 1 WILLIAM BLACKSTONE, COMMENTARIES *74–*75.

are likely to oppose establishment of any sort of formal rulemaking body for their households. Instead, they muddle through their internal disputes case-by-case, thereby establishing unwritten household customs, including customary procedures for domestic decision-making.

Conversely, members may prefer a high degree of formalism – that is, explicit as opposed to unarticulated rules, and written as opposed to oral agreements. Formalists also may warm to the creation of a permanent governing structure, such as a fixed household hierarchy or democratically elected council, responsible for carrying out the household's rulemaking and enforcement functions.

a. *Household-Specific Norms.* There has been scant systematic empirical research on actual household governance practices. I am confident, however, that most readers, drawing on their personal experiences, will agree that informality and muddling through tend to be the order of the day in the domestic sphere. Why do household members gravitate toward informalism? Transaction-cost considerations surely are a large part of the story. Household relations are complex and ever-changing. In all cultures the time-tested strategy for securing a cooperative domestic arrangement has been to live and own with individuals one can trust – that is, with kinfolk or others who share a close and continuing social network.[82] Intimates tend to cluster together in households not only because they value being close to one another for its own sake, but also because a high-trust household environment enables informal internal governance and its associated transaction-cost economies.

A small number of intimates typically can satisfactorily muddle through most household issues by engaging in a long-term process of gift exchange. As discussed above, in a small and trusting social environment, an informal system of give-and-take tends to be cheaper than either explicit contracting or formal governance.[83] In addition, a person may cooperate not only because of possibilities of sanctions by others, but partly or entirely on account of self-sanctioning mechanisms (often the administratively cheapest of all social control systems).[84] Most individuals have internalized norms that support cooperation, especially with intimates. Upon reaching adulthood, a person socialized in this fashion is likely, without external prodding, to help out appropriately around the house, in order either to feel a warm glow or to avoid pangs of guilt. By living exclusively with intimates, members of a household can take advantage of these internalized norms.

---

[82] *See supra* text accompanying notes 21–25. [83] *See supra* text accompanying notes 34–41.
[84] *See* ELLICKSON, ORDER WITHOUT LAW, *supra* note 35, at 243–46.

b. *Explicit Intrahousehold Contracts.* Housemates can anticipate that gift exchange and self-sanctioning may not be sufficient in certain contexts, for example, when participants are likely to disagree on the value of an outcome, face a new challenge of major proportions, or are untrusting (perhaps because they lack intimacy or are nearing endgame).[85] In these sorts of contexts, household members may prefer to contract in advance rather than to relegate the resolution of issues to a subsequent process of give-and-take.[86]

But formal contracting commonly is ill-advised in a domestic setting. For starters, there are the administrative costs of the contracting process itself. In addition, in a relationship as complex and enduring as a domestic one, transaction costs obviate the negotiation of anything approaching a complete contract – that is, one covering all aspects of household affairs. Entering into a contract that governs only a few strands of the multistranded relationship, however, is likely to be a futile exercise. A teenager induced to promise to clean up her room may respond by being more surly at the dinner table. In the end, spontaneous gift exchange usually turns out to be more expeditious than explicit contracting.[87]

If housemates do contract, they are likely to do so orally, not in writing. Particularly at the outset of a relationship, when there are no household-specific customs to build on, household members may converse about how spaces are to be shared, chores performed, and bills paid. Like unarticulated household-specific norms, these oral agreements are mostly enforced both by promisors through self-sanctions and by promisees through self-help sanctions. Resort to the legal system to enforce an oral household contract is virtually inconceivable in midgame (although less so in endgame).[88]

Although rare, written contracts governing household issues are not unknown. Some couples enter into antenuptial agreements. In a residential setting that involves a large number of relative strangers, such as a co-housing community, a written declaration of covenants is to be expected. Even room-mates or co-owners occasionally may put some of their rights and obligations on paper. The main benefit of a written contract, as opposed to an oral one,

---

[85] *See id.* at 246–48.

[86] For insightful exploration of this question in the family setting, see CARL E. SCHNEIDER & MARGARET F. BRINIG, AN INVITATION TO FAMILY LAW 427–75 (2d ed. 2000).

[87] *Cf. supra* text accompanying notes 69–70 (on judges' hesitancy to get involved in an ongoing multistranded domestic relationship).

[88] A variant of the Statute of Frauds may bar judicial enforcement of an oral domestic contract. *See, e.g.*, MINN. STAT. § 513.075 (2002) (court can enforce cohabitation agreement between an unmarried man and woman only if it is in writing and only after termination of the relationship). *But cf.* Morone v. Morone, 413 N.E.2d 1154 (N.Y. 1980) (allowing ex-cohabitant to pursue recovery based on oral contract, but not on implied contract theory).

is that the parties can more readily prove the substance of their agreement to each other in midgame, or to a third party in the event of an endgame dispute.[89] The ritual of signing a document also may have a symbolic significance that increases participants' propensities to enforce it, helping to solidify the arrangement.

Written contracts among housemates, however, have significant, and usually decisive, drawbacks. In a context as complex and long-lived as the household, the transaction costs of negotiating, drafting, and enforcing written provisions covering an adequate number of strands of the relationship typically are forbiddingly high. In addition, a housemate who insists on a written contract – especially with an intimate – signals a lack of trust, a message that itself may poison future interactions.[90] It is notable that legal formbooks (including ones for amateurs) that offer numerous templates for leases, mortgages, sales contracts, and so on, fail to include forms for the governance of platonic relations among either the co-occupants or co-owners of a household.[91]

c. *Formal Governing Structures.* A household with a large number of members unrelated by kinship is particularly likely to founder on a pure system of gift exchange. The members of such a household therefore may not only enter into contracts governing specific substantive domains, but also establish a permanent governing body to issue and enforce rules.[92] This can enable the specialization of labor in internal social control, and also public identification of the agent authorized to represent the group in dealings with outsiders. In some significant historical instances, households have been headed by hierarchs, commonly selected according to rules of inheritance.[93] Examples

---

[89] Particularly in the marriage context, courts are loath to enforce written contracts prior to endgame. *See, e.g.,* Miller v. Miller, 42 N.W. 641 (Iowa 1889), where the court declined to enforce a written interspousal contract in an intact marriage on grounds of public policy, saying in part: "That which should be a sealed book of family history must be opened for public inspection or inquiry. The law, except in cases of necessity, will not justify it." *Id.* at 643. *See also* sources cited *supra* note 69.

[90] *Cf. supra* text accompanying notes 40–41 (on the negative effects of introducing money into household exchanges).

[91] The Nolo Press is a leading purveyor of legal forms to the lay public. Its most relevant publication for household members is *Living Together: A Legal Guide for Unmarried Couples*, a package of legal forms intended for couples possibly headed toward matrimony or children. Otherwise, there appear to be no Nolo Press forms designed to structure relations between either the co-owners or the co-occupants of a household. *See* <http://www.nolo.com> (last visited on July 15, 2000).

[92] *Cf.* ELLICKSON, ORDER WITHOUT LAW, *supra* note 35, at 248–49 (on organizational rules).

[93] Gary Becker's early work on the family assumed that a household is governed by a single "loving head" who altruistically strives to maximize the welfare of all members. *See, e.g.,* Gary

include the ancient extended-family household headed by a *pater familias*,[94] and the English noble household of the Middle Ages.[95] More contemporary examples of these sorts of hierarchical domestic arrangements include dormitories, prisons, and the residential complexes of religious orders. Rule by a hierarch, however, is an anathema for a household committed to equality. In egalitarian settings, a multiperson committee may hold sway – for instance, the designated elders who govern a Hutterite community.[96] Utopian writers commonly envision a fully democratic and participatory system of governance, an ideal reflected in the governance structures of co-housing ventures and some intentional communities.[97]

Members of an ordinary (i.e., small) household, however, rarely establish a formal governing system. The formalization of governance entails process costs and is likely to lead to substantive rigidities. In a liberal society, households with formal governance structures can be expected to survive in the market for household forms only when they are better at augmenting sharable household surplus. Under contemporary conditions, neither formally hierarchical extended-family households nor intentional communities have a good record in competing with small households of informally organized intimates.

B. *The Content of Midgame Rules*

Household rules come in two main types: substantive and procedural.[98] Substantive rules govern members' behavior in using, entering into, and transferring the household premises. These rules are basically designed to prevent

S. Becker, A *Theory of Social Interactions*, 82 J. Pol. Econ. 1063, 1074–83 (1974). As Becker more recently has admitted, this is implausible even for many kinship-based households. *See* Becker & Murphy, *supra* note 78, at 4–5.

[94] On the relatively hierarchical households characteristic of the earliest historical periods, *see* sources cited in Robert C. Ellickson & Charles DiA. Thorland, *Ancient Land Law: Mesopotamia, Egypt, Israel*, 71 Chi.-Kent L. Rev. 321, 355–57 (1995). Aristotle asserts that "every household is monarchically governed by the eldest of kin," an exaggeration even in his day. Aristotle, *supra* note 7, at 9.

[95] See Kate Mertes, The English Noble Household, 1250–1600: Good Governance and Politic Rule (1988).

[96] On governance of Hutterite communities, see Ellickson, *Property in Land*, *supra* note 2, at 1347.

[97] *See* Mark Fenster, *Community by Covenant, Process, and Design: Cohousing and the Contemporary Common Interest Community*, 15 J. Land Use & Envtl. L. 3, 13–14 (1999) (cohousing); Zablocki, *supra* note 62, at 46–47, 250–55 (communes); Ellickson, *Property in Land*, *supra* note 2, at 1348 (kibbutzim).

[98] For a richer taxonomy of rules, see Ellickson, Order Without Law, *supra* note 35, at 132–36. *See also* Elinor Ostrom, Governing the Commons 52–54 (1990) (categorizing rules used by commoners).

excess grabbing and nuisance behavior, and to encourage the supply of inputs that efficiently complement the household economy. Procedural rules govern how the household makes decisions – for example, how it adopts new rules, adjudicates the application of a rule to a given incident, and decides to admit a new member or expel an old one. A household can maximize its sharable surplus by adopting rules that minimize the household's sum of: (1) deadweight losses arising from failures to exploit potential gains from internal trade; and (2) transaction costs. My overarching hypothesis is that housemates, in this close-knit setting, tend to shape their midgame rules in this fashion.[99] In particular, they favor rules that are, to invoke Lisa Bernstein's useful phrase, "relationship preserving."[100]

1. A Household's Substantive Rules

Externalities are a potential problem within a household because of asymmetries in members' information and ability to control actions. To maximize the surplus it can offer members, a household's substantive rules generally should strive to internalize these potential externalities – that is, to make the private product of a member's actions or inactions equal to the product for all household members. This suggests a roughly appropriate general standard of conduct: a member should act as he would act if he were the sole owner-occupant of the premises.[101] Housemates who adhere to this approach thus would impose negative sanctions on an occupant who tracked dirt into the living room and would reward a member who fixed a plumbing leak.

A standard antidote to potential tragedies of a commons is to shift particular spaces or objects from common to individual ownership.[102] This can be lowest-transaction-cost method of internalizing externalities. In addition to developing rules to constrain member conduct in shared spaces, household members therefore may implicitly or explicitly "privatize" certain portions of their domain.[103] By awarding a particular housemate virtually complete control over a particular bedroom, for example, a household can internalize, to

---

[99] This is an application of a broader hypothesis of welfare-maximizing norms that I developed in ELLICKSON, ORDER WITHOUT LAW, *supra* note 35, at 167–83.

[100] See Bernstein, *supra* note 64, at 1796.

[101] *Cf.* RICHARD A. POSNER, ECONOMIC ANALYSIS OF LAW § 3.11, pp. 72–73 (6th ed. 2003) (proposing an analogous rule when ownership is divided between holders of present and future interests).

[102] *See* Harold Demsetz, *Toward a Theory of Property Rights*, 57 AM. ECON. REV. PAPERS & PROC. 347 (1967).

[103] Privatization, of course, is a two-edged sword. While it ameliorates the externality problems that arise out of common property, it also sacrifices the benefits of sharing – among them, risk-spreading, exploitation of scale economies in production and consumption, and the social pleasures of communal interactions. See Ellickson, *Property in Land, supra* note 2, at 1332–62.

that housemate, most of the costs and benefits of the maintenance decisions involving that bedroom.[104] Individual property rights also may be created in portions of the public rooms of a dwelling. By custom or explicit agreement, a member may "have" a particular chair, bookshelf, closet, or parking space.[105] Graduate students who share an apartment commonly treat items of personal property individually brought to it – clothes, sports equipment, books, liquor – as still individually owned and controlled.

2. A Household's Procedural Rules: On the Advantages of Consensus

As previously discussed, the members of a household are highly likely to allocate residual control powers (i.e., ownership) to the suppliers of the household's at-risk capital.[106] Occupants (as opposed to owners), however, are likely to control decisions that affect only the ephemeral quality of the home environment and not the value of residual financial flows. A landlord, for example, doesn't care about the quality of tenants' meals.

How can owners as a group (or occupants as a group) be expected to make decisions? In an intimate household, both groups are apt to use informal procedures. Is debate around a dinner table ever structured according to Roberts' Rules of Order? Would two friends who co-own residential real estate ever prepare a formal agenda to structure their discussions?

In situations where past practices do not provide a clear guide, a household's procedural norms can be expected to call for informal consultations among members of the relevant group. Co-owners' norms thus are likely to require them to consult with one another prior to a capital improvement, a discretionary repair (such as the painting of the dwelling's exterior), or the eviction of an existing occupant. Roommates' norms similarly are likely to require that a dinner invitation to an unusual guest be cleared with other roommates in advance.

When owners or occupants face one of these out-of-the-ordinary decisions, are they more likely to decide by majority vote or by consensus (i.e., implicit unanimity)?[107] Dagan and Heller argue that majority rule usually is

---

[104] In relatively privatized intentional communities, such as Israeli *moshavim* and Amish settlements, households separately own houses and farmsteads. Even in the most collectivized communities, such as Hutterite settlements and *kibbutzim* belonging to the Artzi federation, families have separate bedrooms and at least semi-private sitting rooms. *See id.* at 1346–48 & n.150.

[105] *Cf.* ERVING GOFFMAN, ASYLUMS: ESSAYS ON THE SOCIAL SITUATION OF MENTAL PATIENTS AND OTHER INMATES 244–54 (1961) (on the informal privatization of public spaces in asylums).

[106] *See supra* text accompanying notes 42–62.

[107] These are the main two alternatives considered in Dagan & Heller, *supra* note 9, at 590–96 (discussing commoners' rules of self-governance).

the normatively appropriate procedure for members of a "liberal commons" (a broad category that includes ordinary co-owners).[108] When commoners are intimates, however, Dagan & Heller's position is highly doubtful as both a descriptive and normative proposition. A 1970s survey of 120 intentional communities in the United States, for example, found that these groups (which had 25 members on average) much preferred to proceed by consensus.[109] Members of co-housing developments also prefer this procedure.[110] In contrast to brute majority rule, a process of striving for consensus generates debate that that tends to inform proponents about opponents' concerns. Governance by consensus thus promises to result in both superior decisions (because intensities of preference are better taken into account) and higher levels of satisfaction with the decision-making process itself.

The basic downside of a unanimity rule for decisions, of course, is that it may result in stalemate.[111] For several reasons, however, intimate households (which of course usually include far fewer members than do intentional communities and co-housing developments) are implausible settings for procedural paralysis. First, a housemate is unlikely to hold out solely for strategic reasons in hope of obtaining some sort of side compensation from the frustrated majority. Intimates typically can detect, and punish in future interactions, any one of their number who attempts this ploy. Second, there is little risk that those disadvantaged by a measure will scotch it when they recognize that the measure will help the other housemates by a greater amount. To maximize aggregate household surplus over the long run, intimates who interact repeatedly and along many dimensions have a strong incentive to achieve patterns of compromise in exactly these sorts of situations. In a well-functioning household, a member who relents for the overall good of the group later will be informally compensated when other decisions come before the house. In the long run, a pattern of give-and-take is best for all. And, of course, the fact that a member of a liberal household can exit helps sustain this dynamic of reciprocated compromise.

Rule by consensus may not be feasible when household members are numerous and heterogeneous, or otherwise not closely knit. Under those conditions, one procedural approach is, in the first stage of decision-making, to continue to attempt to establish consensus, and, should that effort fail, to fall back in the second stage to some sort of supermajority voting rule. This two-step procedure

---

[108] They would require unanimity only for decisions that are purely redistributive. *See id.* at 592–93.

[109] *See* ZABLOCKI, *supra* note 62, at 83, 200–01, 250–56 (1980).

[110] *See* Fenster, *supra* note 97, at 13–14.

[111] When too many individuals have veto power, a tragedy of the anticommons may ensue. *See generally* Heller, *supra* note 16.

in fact is sometimes employed in contexts where domestic decision-makers number in the many dozens – for example, in a traditional village commons or a contemporary co-housing development.[112] Unalloyed majority rule among either owners or occupants, if it is ever employed, is to be expected only in the least intimate of households.

IV. CONCLUSION: TOWARD MORE HOMEWORK
ON HOW THE HOME WORKS

This chapter has presented a number of potentially falsifiable propositions about the norms of households, among them that contributors of equity capital to households are empowered to make residual control decisions; that members of households rely more on gift exchange than on explicit bilateral exchange; that written contracts among housemates are rare; that privatization of spaces is common within households; and that the owners (or occupants) of an intimate household prefer to make decisions by consensus, as opposed to majority vote. More systematic empirical work on these issues and others would help reveal fundamental insights about how people cooperate (or fail to cooperate) in managing jointly owned and occupied resources. Heretofore, scholars who have investigated the commons typically have focused on fisheries, pastures, and irrigation networks owned by clusters of households. While this work plainly is valuable, scholars can learn much by lowering their sights to a smaller and more basic human institution – the household itself.

---

[112] See Margaret A. McKean, *Success on the Commons: Comparative Examination of Institutions for Common Property Resource Management*, 4 J. THEORETICAL POL. 247, 260–61 (1992); Fenster, *supra* note 97, at 29–30, 34–35, 43–44 (describing decision-making procedures at three co-housing projects).

5   .commons

Lawrence Lessig

I start with the words of someone famous, and then an account of the deeds of someone not quite so famous, as a way of framing an argument about the commons in cyberspace.

First the words.

In a letter written late in his life, Thomas Jefferson, the first commissioner of the patent office, commenting about the limited scope of patents, had this to say about the very idea of protecting something like an idea:

> If nature has made any one thing less susceptible than all others of exclusive property, it is the action of the thinking power called an idea, which an individual may exclusively possess as long as he keeps it to himself; but the moment it is divulged, it forces itself into the possession of everyone, and the receiver cannot dispossess himself of it. Its peculiar character, too, is that no one possesses the less, because every other possess the whole of it. He who receives an idea from me, receives instruction himself without lessening mine; as he who lites his taper at mine, receives light without darkening me. That ideas should freely spread from one to another over the globe, for the moral and mutual instruction of man, and improvement of his condition, seems to have been peculiarly and benevolently designed by nature, when she made them, like fire, expansible over all space, without lessening their density at any point, and like the air in which we breathe, move, and have our physical being, incapable of confinement, or exclusive appropriation. Inventions then cannot, in nature, be a subject of property.[1]

Patent law could try, Jefferson said, to make property out of inventions; but the idea was against nature. Nature had conspired to make ideas, in the words

---

[1] Letter from Thomas Jefferson to Isaac McPherson (Aug. 13, 1813), *in* 6 THE WRITINGS OF THOMAS JEFFERSON 175, 180 (H.A. Washington ed., 1861).

of the economist, nonrivalous and non-excludable – and nature in the end, he believed, would win.

Those are the words from someone famous. Here's a story less famous.

There's a man whom some of you will have heard of but no doubt most of you will not, who in 1984 began a movement that will, I predict, be understood some day to define the ideals of a generation. This movement is the free software movement; its founder is a MacArthur genius named Richard Stallman. And in 1984, Richard Stallman began a project to build a "free version" of something called the Unix operating system. That free version of Unix was not to be called "Unix"; it was to be called GNU – "Gnu's not Unix." This free version of Unix was to be made available to all to build upon and use as they saw fit.

What's the significance of an operating system?

Computers are boxes of chips and wires; operating systems ("OS") make them run. They make them run not in a physical sense – electricity does that. Rather, they make them run in a logical sense. Operating systems provide the basic platform that enables computers to function; they are a complex of computer software – ordinarily software – that links programs to the machines they run upon. An operating system makes it simple, for example, for a program to display characters on a screen. Without the operating system, every programmer who wanted to display characters on a screen would have to write code to display characters on a screen. Obviously, there are a lot of programmers, and if all programmers had to write that code, that would be a lot of redundant code. So an OS helps eliminate that redundancy by providing a common set of code that others can call upon. Programmers writing code to run on a particular OS platform know about this code; they simply invoke it to achieve the ends they seek. In this sense, an OS is a language for those writing for a particular computer platform; its conventions replace a lot of work that others would have to do.

Unix was the breakthrough OS in the history of computing. Before Unix, an OS was something written for particular machines. IBM built computers; it built an OS that would run on its machines, but this OS would not run on anyone else's machines. If you wrote programs for this OS, then you were writing programs for IBM machines.

Many didn't like this inherent, technological tie linking programs to particular machines. Many wanted to write programs that might run on a number of different machines. And, in particular, companies that didn't want to be linked to a particular computer company wanted the freedom to write programs that would run on more than one machine.

AT&T was such a company. At the time computers were taking off, AT&T was tied up. Regulations forbade it from becoming a computer company. It was a telecommunications company – a state sanctioned monopoly to boot – so regulators were eager to keep its power out of the nascent computer market. So AT&T was forbidden to sell computers or the software to run computers. But it nonetheless needed software to run computers, and it wanted to write the same software to run many computers. So its engineers gave birth to this wonder called Unix – an OS that would cross many computer platforms.

But here was the crucial catch: because Unix couldn't be sold, these engineers were able to convince AT&T that it wouldn't hurt for AT&T to give Unix away. More importantly, these engineers were able to convince AT&T that this OS should be given away *with* its source. That is, not only should people be able to use Unix for free, they should be able to modify and adapt Unix freely. And they should be able to do this by having not just a program called Unix, but also the "source code" that made Unix possible. In other words, they urged AT&T to give away not just an OS, but the code that made the OS run.

If there is list of "most significant decisions" in the history of computing, this decision by a few engineers at AT&T to give the Unix source away is high on that list, for it made real a phenomenon that we may not have otherwise noticed. Very quickly Unix spread to become the foundational operating system for computing in the world: universities adopted it, computer science departments taught it, and millions tinkered with it. A generation of engineers was raised on it. Unix became the language within which computing was understood. And it became all of this because people were free to open, and tinker with, the code. Its source code was given away; people were free to take that source apart; and because they could take that source apart, they could come to understand – they could learn – how it, and computers functioned.

And so here is the last technical idea that is crucial to understanding the argument that I am making: source code. Computers run programs. Programs are code. For code to run, the computer must be able to read the code; for them to be written, humans must be able to read the code. It is in the nature of computers and humans that we can't both read the same thing well. What we can read efficiently is too cumbersome and confused for computers; what computers read efficiently is too complex and arcane for humans to understand. So code gets written first in a language that humans can understand – that's called source code. It is then translated into a language that computers can understand – that's called object code. And then this object code is loaded onto a computer, executed by the machine.

AT&T released not just the object code, it also released the source code. By releasing the source code, more than machines could understand it. By inviting more than machines to understand it, many millions came to understand it, and it became a standard upon which an industry was built.

In 1984, all that changed. In 1984, AT&T was broken up; as a consolation, the computing-related limitations the law had placed on AT&T were removed. AT&T was free to sell computers, and sell software. AT&T thus decided that's exactly what it would do. And so in 1984, AT&T announced that no longer would Unix be free. No longer would its source code be available to any one at all. Any access would have to be licensed; and every license would demand a fee. The enclosure movement came to this fundamental concept in computer science and produced something of a shock. A generation was writing its code for the language of Unix; a company now claimed rights to control the terms of this language.

Richard Stallman was, like many others, angry about this event. He was angry that so much creative energy had been devoted to a platform that now restricted rights to its expression. And so in 1985, Stallman created the Free Software Foundation to espouse a new philosophy in computer science, a philosophy that he believed expressed the implicit beliefs of those who had lived for many years in the land of Unix. This philosophy he expressed in the ideals of the free software movement.[2] Code, Stallman said, should be free; people should be free to share it. Coders should be free to take apart the code built by others, to understand it, to modify it, to improve it.

As I report this idea of "free software," many of you will immediately jump to a reading of these words that is wrong, but usefully wrong. You will hear Stallman saying that software should be gratis; that people should be allowed to take it at no cost; that coders should be permitted to get the resource from others without any compensation to the others. But this is not what Stallman means, even if this mistake may well be squarely intended by his language. For by leading you to this mistaken understanding of his words, Stallman has the chance to correct you. Free, as he says, not in the sense of free beer, but free in the sense of free speech. Software should be free in just the same way that speech is free; even if, as with some speech, to get it you may have to pay a price.

What could such a distinction mean?

If there's no such thing as a free lunch, then there's no such thing as free code. People write code; these people have to eat lunch; so somehow these code writers need money to pay for lunch. Somehow, this code writing has to pay.

---

[2] *See* LAWRENCE LESSIG, THE FUTURE OF IDEAS: THE FATE OF THE COMMONS IN A CONNECTED WORLD 52–54 (2001); PETER WAYNER, FREE FOR ALL: HOW LINUX AND THE FREE SOFTWARE MOVEMENT UNDERCUT THE HIGH-TECH TITANS 9, 34–36, 67, 68 (2000).

Even Stallman gets this, and so there's nothing inconsistent with coders getting paid, and with them selling their code. But what the Free Software Foundation did was support the building of a free version of Unix that could be sold by any distributor; but a version that must carry with it its source code. And by carrying its source code, that meant others were always free to use this software critically. As free speech protects the right to question, others could build upon and, at the same time, question this free Unix; they could modify the source, tinker with the source, that right was always reserved to them. But what they built on this source, or what they did to this source, they were free to sell, and did – so long as they did not bottle up what they originally received for free. For the license that one receives with this free software restricts the rights of the recipient in one important way – however free this software is, one is not free to remove the initial source.

It wasn't Stallman in the end, however, who built this free version of Unix. Like Moses and the promised land, Stallman got just to the edge of completing a free software Unix when a crippling carpal tunnel syndrome made it impossible for him to type. The project, though supported by many, quickly stalled. It took another sort of genius, Linus Torvalds, to supply the missing part to the puzzle – a kernel that plugged into the parts of the operating system Stallman had built. And as ginger to a ginger cake, this tiny part of the overall system then defined the name for the system as a whole. The Linux operating system, as most of you know it – or the GNU/Linux operating system, as those who want to be reminded of the past will call it – now flows freely across the world as a free and open version of Unix. At any moment, from any number of places, one is free to download the source of the Linux OS; but at any moment, from any number of different vendors, one also can buy compiled and functioning code called the Linux operating system. The only rule that governs that code is the rule that governs all free code, and the rule that governed Unix itself before AT&T was free to change the rule – that the source code is delivered as well as the object code, and that the source code must never be locked up. You can change GNU/Linux as you want; you can sell the changes; but you must include the source to the changes you've made.

This is a long introduction to a definition, I realize. But this story establishes all that my definition of a commons will need. For my claim is that the GNU/Linux operating system is a commons in all the ways that a commons is relevant in cyberspace. And my hope is that, with this account vivid in the background, we can see the relevance of these separate elements.

In my view, we should understand a commons as a resource that others may draw upon – as a first cut we could say, without requiring the permission of someone else, or, as I want to refine that idea, without requiring the permission of a *certain kind* of someone else. But let's start with the first cut first.

A commons is a resource that others may draw upon without the permission of someone else. A park, in this sense, is a commons. I am permitted to enter the park, to enjoy its peace, without getting the permission of someone else. An idea in the public domain is a commons in this sense. I need not register with anyone to take and use the theory of relativity. A speech by a member of Congress is a commons in this sense. I don't need a politician's permission to use his speech and ridicule it. The speech is free for anyone to take and do with as he or she wants. A report of the Supreme Court deciding a certain case is a commons in just this sense. One need not ask the permission of a court to cite the holding of a case as authority. It exists out there for anyone to use; it is free of the control of an author or institution. A public road is a commons in just this sense. I can get in my car in San Francisco and drive to my office in Palo Alto without registering with the local authorities, without requesting the permission of any central dispatcher. And finally Unix (before 1984) and GNU/Linux now is a commons in just this sense. I can, if I can, take a version of GNU/Linux and change it; I can take the OS and explore and modify it; I am free to use it to build something different; I am free to use it to criticize it, or ridicule it. I can do this without the permission of anyone else because the essential element that gives me such power – its source – is there for me to use.

I said this definition was a first cut, and so let me now add an important qualification: It may well be, in all these cases, that in fact to use a commons in the sense I would call a commons, I do need the permission of someone else. It may well be that I must ask before I can take. But if that is so, then the resource can still be considered a commons if the reasons for denying access are of a special sort: if they are, as First Amendment lawyers would describe them, *content neutral*. If the reasons are neutral with respect to the particular use, nonetheless they may restrict access for certain reasons. So, for example, a park is still a commons even if it is closed in the evening, or if a nominal admission is charged. Those are restrictions, no doubt; they in a sense require permission. But these restrictions are unrelated to one's ideas, or purpose. I am not rejected if I am a Republican, or if my purpose is to study in the park rather than relax. So too could a toll road still be considered a commons, so long as the toll was neutral, and relatively low. So long as access was not contingent upon holding certain views, or upon membership in the party. And so too could GNU/Linux still be a commons, even if one must agree to a license to get it. The condition is neutral; it restricts, but not to a particular end. It is not picking sides in a debate, or winners in an argument.

In this sense of a commons, my claim is this: that the most important features that of cyberspace so far – the features that more than any other explain its extraordinary growth, and the extraordinary innovation that cyberspace has produced – are the features that most resemble a commons. That without a commons in this sense – without a number of distinct yet overlapping structures that all satisfy the conditions of the definition I have offered – there would have been nothing remotely like the Internet for us to rave about. That all that is unexpected and extraordinary about this space are the parts of this space that are commons.

We can be more specific, however, about the place of the commons within the structure we call the Internet. We can distinguish three "layers" that comprise a communication system. As NYU Professor Yochai Benkler describes it, at the bottom we could describe a physical layer – the wires that connect the phones or the computers or the cable across which television might be broadcast. Above that, the logical layer – the system that controls who gets access to what or what gets to run where. And above that, the content layer – the stuff that gets said or written within any given system of communication.[3]

Each of these layers in principle could be controlled or free. They would be "free" if they were organized in a commons – organized so that anyone could get access on equal terms, whether they had to pay (a fixed and neutral charge) or not. They would be controlled if they were the property of someone else – someone who had a right to exclude, or to grant access or not, based on his or her own subjective reasons.

And the communications system built differs depending on whether these layers are free or are controlled.

Consider four possibilities as we vary whether each of these layers is owned or free.

Speakers' Corner: Orators and loons gather every Sunday in Hyde Park's Speakers' Corner to rage about something or nothing at all. It has become a London tradition. It is a communication system organized in a specific way. The physical layer of this communication system (the park) is a commons; the logical layer (the language used) is also a commons. And the content layer (what these nuts say) is their own creation. It too is unowned. All three layers in this context are free; no one can exercise control over the kinds of communications that might happen here.

Madison Square Garden: Madison Square Garden is another place that people give speeches. But Madison Square Garden is owned. Only those who

---

[3] Yochai Benkler, *From Consumers to Users: Shifting the Deeper Structures of Regulation*, 52 FED. COMM. L.J. 561, 562–63 (2000).

pay get to use the auditorium; and the Garden is not obligated to take all comers. The physical layer is therefore controlled. But like Speakers' Corner, both the logical layer of the language and the content that gets uttered are not controlled in the context of the Garden. They too remain free.

The Telephone System: Before the breakup, the telephone system was a single-unitary system. The physical infrastructure of this system was owned by AT&T; so too was the logical infrastructure – determining how and who you could connect to – controlled by AT&T. But what you said on an AT&T phone (within limits at least) was free: The content of the telephone conversations was not controlled, even if the physical and logical layer underneath were.

Cable TV: Finally, think of cable TV. Here the physical layer is owned – the wires that run the content into your house. The logical layer is owned – only the cable companies get to decide what runs into your house. And the content layer is owned – the shows that get broadcast are copyrighted shows. All three layers are within the control of the cable TV company; no communications layer, in Benkler's sense, remains free.

This range of free and controlled layers constructs very different communication environments. Consider then within this range one more significant communication environment: the Internet.

The Internet is a communication system. It too has three layers. At the bottom, the physical layer, are wires and computers, and wires linking computers. These resources are owned. The owners have complete control over what they do with their wires or computers, or wires linking computers. Property governs this layer.

On top of the physical layer is a logical layer – the protocols that make the net run. These protocols are many, all chucked into a single box called TCP/IP. Their essence is a system for exchanging datagrams, but we miss something important about the system if we focus exclusively on the essence.

For at the core of this logical layer is a principle of network design. At the core of the Internet's design is an ideal called "end-to-end." First articulated by network architects Jerome Saltzer, David Reed, and David Clark, end-to-end or "e2e" says build the network so that intelligence rests in the ends, and the network itself remains simple.[4] Simple networks, smart applications.

The reason for this design was clear. With e2e, innovation on the Internet didn't depend upon the network. New content or new applications could

---

[4] J. H. Saltzer et al., *End-to-End Arguments in System Design* (Apr. 1981), *available at* <http://web.mit.edu/saltzer/www/publications/endtoend/endtoend.pdf>. *See also* David P. Reed et al., *Active Networking in End-to-End Arguments* (May 1998), *available at* <http://<web.mit.edu/saltzer/www/publications/endtoend/ ANe2ecomment.html>.

run regardless of whether the network knew about them. New content or new applications would run because the network simply took packets of data and moved them along. The fundamental feature of this network design was neutrality among packets. The network was simple, or "stupid" in Bell Labs researcher David Isenberg's words,[5] and the consequence of stupidity, at least among computers, is the inability to discriminate. Innovators thus knew that if their ideas were wanted, the network would run it. This network was designed never to allow anyone to decide what would be allowed.

That means that this layer of the network – the feature of the network that distinguished it from all that had been built before – built this network into a commons. One was free to get access to this network, and share its resources. The protocols were designed for sharing, not exclusive use. Discrimination, at the heart of a property system, was not possible at the heart of this system. This system was coded to be free. That was its nature.

This feature is something new in network design. It contrasts, for example, with the design of the original telephone network. The original telephone network was created not to permit uses other than those it allowed; if you had a different use – if you wanted to connect a modem, for example – then you needed the permission of the network owner, AT&T. No doubt sometimes that permission would be granted – when, for example, the technology advanced the business model of AT&T; but equally certain was that permission would be denied when the technology did not advance the model of AT&T. So, for example, when the design of the Internet was first presented to AT&T – not in 1990, or 1984, or 1976, but in 1964 – said AT&T about this technology, "it can't possibly work, but if it did, damned if we are going to allow the creation of a competitor to ourselves."[6]

Allow. This was the essence of the network that predated the Internet: a network owner got to decide how the network would be used. Not allowing anyone the power to say "allowed" is the design of the network that has replaced the telephone network – the Internet. The essence of this design, the essence of how the original architecture was built, was to deny to the network owner this power to "allow."

Thus, on top of a physical layer that is controlled rests a logical layer that is free. And then on top of this free layer is a content layer that is both free and controlled.

The free part is all the content that effectively rests in the public domain. The facts, data, abandoned property, undiscovered theft – this is the content

[5] LESSIG, THE FUTURE OF IDEAS, *supra* note 2, at 38.

[6] JOHN NAUGHTON, A BRIEF HISTORY OF THE FUTURE: THE ORIGINS OF THE INTERNET 107 (1999).

that is open for the taking and that is taken openly. But it also includes a part dedicated to be open: open source or free software, dedicated to be free.

This free resource does more than entertain or build culture; this free resource teaches the world about how this aspect of the net functions, or is free – as in every web page that both displays and carries its source, so that its source can be copied and modified for different displays.

This free content coexists with content that is controlled: software that is sold; digital content – music, movies, greeting cards – that is controlled. You can link to mp3.com and listen to music that is free; you can link to amazon.com and read a book that is controlled. The network doesn't care much about what linking occurs. It is neutral about the linking, and the result of this neutrality is a mix.

This is a picture of the complexity we call the Internet. At the bottom is a physical layer that is controlled; on top of it is a logical layer that is free; and on top of both is a content layer that mixes free and controlled.

This complexity builds an *innovation commons*. And this commons has been the location of some of the most extraordinary creativity that we have seen. Not innovation in just the .com sense, but innovation in the ways humans interact; innovation in the ways that culture is spread; and most importantly, innovation in the ways in which culture gets built. The innovation of the Internet – built into its architecture – is an innovation in the ways in which culture gets created. Let the .com flame; it won't matter to this innovation one bit. The crucial feature of this new space is the low cost of digital creation, and the low cost of delivering what gets created.

We can say more about the commons built at the logical layer. I've pointed to one – to free or open source software – that defined computing before the Internet was really born, and that continues to define all of the major software that now makes the Internet run. Not just the Linux OS, which fuels most of the servers that run on the net, but also open source server software called Apache, or the programs that distribute most of your mail – Sendmail. All this is open source, or free software; all of this is software that gets distributed with its source; all of this source is open for others to change.

But let me point to a few others. Think of the world wide web itself. The world wide web rides on top of a bit of code called html; html is the source that defines how web pages will be displayed. It is a language for building web pages. This language is very recent. It didn't exist before 1991. But in 1991, Tim Berners-Lee and Robert Calloux, working in a research lab in Switzerland, released to the world the specs for this language, and a protocol that would ride on top of the Internet, http; and this protocol and language together make up the world wide web. But that's not what built the world wide web. Instead, what built the world wide web was a single command built into every web browser – a command called "reveal source." Even today, on every major browser, you can go to the edit bar, and invoke this command, reveal source. The source that makes the web page you are looking at tick is then revealed to the user. The user is free to take and copy this code – free in the sense that the technology enables it; no doubt most of this code is copyrighted, so not free in the sense that the law permits it. But free in that people could do it. And they did it. The first generation of the world wide web was built on the stolen copies of other people's web pages; the language of html was learned by this stealing and changing. No one sat down at a book to learn html. People took what was out there, and modified it as they wanted.

The code of the web, too, like free software, in this sense, existed in a commons; anyone anywhere could take this code and use it without the permission of anyone else.

Let me draw together these different kinds of commons that mark the space called the Internet, and suggest what it is about them that makes them so important to the Internet. All of them define resources that anyone can draw upon. That anyone can draw upon without the content based permission of someone else. There is a cost to get access, but the access once granted is not conditioned on content-based, or strategy-based, terms such as, "Does this use compete with our existing business model?" No one in this environment – of open source software, or end-to-end design – is in a position to do anything if a new innovation competes with a dominant design. No response is possible because the space creates no structure sufficient to enforce a response.

This design feature has two important consequences for innovation. First, it flattens the field of potential contributors to the innovation of this space. A broader range of innovators can innovate for the platform; innovation and development are not reserved to a select few. To develop technologies for the Internet, one need only a connection to the Internet; to develop technologies for AT&T's monopoly phone company, one needed to work for, or license to, AT&T. Both requirements impose costs on the innovator – not everyone wants to work for a telephone company; not every good idea is a good idea for a telephone company – and these costs are not present in the Internet. Anyone can play, meaning many more do, meaning many more ideas about how best to develop this space get realized.

Second, this design builds into the design a right to revolt. The network is a platform; the platform is built to be unable to resist revolution. If a new idea comes along, even if this new idea destroys the dominant use of the network, there is no structure, no power, that can resist this new idea. Nothing in this original design gives anyone the power to check one idea over another; nothing in this original design empowers anyone to say "allow."

We can link this design back to the optimism of a revolutionary, Thomas Jefferson. Recall how Jefferson reveled in the conspiracy that nature had launched against the concept of property rights in an idea. How nature had made it impossible for ideas to become property. Ideas would flow freely, this was nature's design; man could do little about this design.

That romanticism about ideas in the Enlightenment is how most now speak about innovation in the Internet. That here, now, the nature of the space is such that innovation can always flourish; that new ideas will always prevail; that old ideas cannot defend themselves. This is the nature of the space, and this nature cannot change.

But it is here, when we put these stories together, that we should see the trouble with this modern Jefferson – and it is with this trouble that I want to end this essay.

For if there is one thing we should know about cyberspace, it is this: nature did not build it. If anything is socially constructed, cyberspace is. How it is constructed is simply a function of its code; its code here, and elsewhere, could be different. If it is built now to enable these two fundamental commons – over platforms, over networks – then it could be built differently to take these commons away. And to the extent you agree with me that these commons contribute to the innovations of the net, how future changes might remove these commons should concern you as well.

Let me end then with three accounts of changes in these commons – actually just one real account, but three indications of where a fuller account could be made. One is from the past (or one wishes it were the past) – Microsoft; one is about the present, and the current struggle over the architecture of broadband Internet access; and one is about the future, about how the future architecture won't be. All three are about changes to the environment of innovation in cyberspace, and all three, I suggest, are examples that, to preserve this environment, we must begin to account.

First the past: Microsoft owned a platform; that platform is the Windows operating system. This operating system has inspired extraordinary innovation upon its platform. By leaving open most of the application program interfaces ("APIs"), by encouraging developers to code to the system, by supporting these projects, and by evangelizing its product, the corporation has done much to assure that the world can build on the platform that Microsoft owns.

But owning the platform means something. In particular, it means the ability to control how the code will evolve. Not perfect control: if Microsoft decided to dump the graphical user interface ("GUI") as the operating system interface on the desktop, and in some radical retro moment, decided to return to the command line, consumers would react; we would flee the platform, but this fleeing and fury would have an effect on the platform. It would reform it, for at the extremes the customers have that power.

Within the extremes, however, within the detail within which a system gets built, customers don't have much power. Within the extremes, the owner of the code gets to decide how the code will evolve. It gets to decide, that is, whether a browser remains a separable product – whether an application or a system service doesn't matter for the moment. It gets to decide whether other products get to run well on the platform. It gets to decide all this because the owner owns the code and the code keeps itself secret. The code is closed, not open. If someone doesn't like how it is developing, what they can do is limited.

This architecture of a closed platform also has an effect on innovation. Or, at least it has an effect on innovation that threatens the underlying platform – that threatens to weaken its power as a dominant force in the network. For if an innovation develops that the platform doesn't like, then a closed code platform can chose to cancel that innovation. It can choose to refuse it, or confuse it, or embrace it and digest it; it can bundle or bind an alternative; it can displace the competitor; it can play many games to make the competing application have to compete more strongly.

This was the argument, at least, of the U.S. government in its recent action against Microsoft. No one could doubt that in a significant way, Microsoft had fueled innovation. But the charges against the company were based on the ability of the company to target innovations it didn't like. Anytime an innovation threatened its control over the platform – over the APIs to which developers wrote – Microsoft, the government claimed, would intervene to kill that innovation. To capture it. To control it. To displace it. To, as a Microsoft executive said to Apple about QuickTime, "knife the baby".[7]

The platform thus chose which innovations were allowed. And it was empowered to choose because the owners control the code. The platform could behave strategically. It had strategic power because it controls its code. To the extent it exercises that strategic power, it undermines the innovation commons built by neutral, common platforms.

Second, the present: I said that the commons that fuels innovation is the commons that exists at the logical layer of the net. This is the commons constituted by the principle of end-to-end; it is the commons that gets built by a set of protocols that don't discriminate. It is the neutral platform upon which innovation happens. And this neutrality is neutrality built into the code.

---

[7] *See* Declan McCullagh, *Knifing the Baby,* Wired News (Nov. 5, 1998), *available at* <http://wired-vig.wired.com/news/politics/0,1283,16082,00.html>.

But this code is not given. The code governing a network is not fixed. The code that governs at one time could be replaced by different code later on. And more importantly, there is nothing that forces people who connect to the net to obey the neutrality of the net. There is no brand called "the Internet" that carries with it a set of assumptions about openness and balance; there is instead a basic set of protocols that anyone is free to supplement by adding other protocols on top.

Anyone is free to change the open commons of the Internet, and some important people are changing it. For example, providers of broadband services.

As the Internet moves from the telephone – from modems and 28.8 or 56k connections – to broadband – to fast, always-on connections, the physical layer across which the Internet travels is different. The dominant technology today for serving this broadband content is cable.

As cable converts itself to make itself open to the Internet, it is modifying the architecture of the Internet in an important way. While the essence of the commons of the Internet is neutrality and simplicity, the essence of what the broadband cable Internet will be is the power to discriminate in content and services. The aim of this form of Internet access will not be openness and neutral platforms; the aim of this form of Internet access will be control over the content that gets played.

For example: Cable companies make a great deal of money streaming video to television sets. That is the core of their legacy monopoly power. Some think it would be useful to stream video to computers. Cable companies are not eager to see this form of competition. So they imposed rules on broadband users – no more than ten minutes of streaming video could be contracted for at any time. When they were smart, they said they were worried about congestion. But when they were honest they said something different. Said Daniel Somers, of AT&T, "we didn't spend 56 billion on a cable system to have the blood sucked from our veins."[8]

Broadband providers will insist that this control is their right – that nothing should interfere with their right to layer onto the free logical layer a system of control. And a budding line of First Amendment doctrine strongly supports this claim.[9]

---

[8] David Lieberman, *Media Giants' Net Change: Major Companies Establish Strong Foothold Online*, USA TODAY, Dec. 14, 1999, at B2.

[9] *See* Robert Corn-Revere, *Broadband Internet Access Debate Heightened by Agencies, Courts, the First Amendment and the Media* (2002), *available at* <http://www.mediainstitute.org/ONLINE/FAM2002/BCTV_B.html>.

These cases are Blade-Runner-esque. Remember one of the million amazing puzzles in that extraordinary film is the slow recognition that the machines are human. Well, here too, with a cable system, it is the increasing recognition that these systems to deliver electricity are in fact First Amendment speakers. Wires plus a certain logic entail the press; and then into the mix comes courts eager to bestow on this press long-standing First Amendment power.

And hence we should expect, as the Internet moves to broadband service, that the rules governing the providers will be different. Unlike the telephone company, these providers will be allowed to discriminate, and discriminate they will. When they do, the open feature of the Internet commons will be removed, with the consequence that innovation will be different.

The two changes that I've described so far are changes at the logical layer of the Internet. The third is a change at the physical layer – or more precisely, a change in how the physical layer gets allocated.

The radio spectrum is a resource. For most of the last century, it was not a resource organized as a commons. Early in the last century, the federal government claimed the right to allocate, through license, the right to use the spectrum. Very quickly, Nobel-quality economists like Ronald Coase noted this was a silly way to allocate a scarce resource, that property rights would better allocate the resource of spectrum.[10]

Both of these models for allocating radio spectrum presume something about the nature of this resource. They both presume that spectrum is the sort of thing that must be allocated. Whether by governments or by the market, the presumption is that radio spectrum is like land; that the only way efficiently to use it is to assure clean and clear rights to use it; and the only issue then is who sets the rights.

Behind this picture is a very crude notion about how radio spectrum works. This notion is that radio waves function like jet-liners, destined to crash and fall to the ground if someone doesn't direct how they should fly.

But this is not at all the nature of radio spectrum. And indeed, as technologists demonstrated more than thirty years ago, there is another way we might allocate spectrum such that it is shared, and any "tragedy" from this sharing would be negotiated by the receivers. Rather than allocating the resource *ex ante*, the resource would be allocated by machines on an "as needed" basis.

The technologies for this are many, and increasingly available; were they deployed, they would enable a fast and efficient use of spectrum. But these technologies would permit a use of radio spectrum that was unallocated, uncontrolled. No property regime would govern who got what, when; no

[10] Ronald H. Coase, *The Federal Communications Commission*, 2 J. L. & ECON. 1 (1959).

rules would limit access based on who had accumulated what set of rights. One's right to broadcast using spectrum would be just as one's right to send email across the Internet; broadcasting and receiving would not require the permission of someone else.

This alternative way of allocating and using radio spectrum is in competition with existing models; it is in conflict with the model of Coase that is increasingly being deployed across the world. Spectrum is being sold, and rights are being created and allocated, with no clear understanding of whether such an allocation system is needed.[11]

The result of this property system will be to remove radio spectrum from a commons; it will require the permission of someone else before one can use the spectrum of this space; and this requirement will thus channel and direct the kinds of uses that can be made. Not controlled by a government, no doubt, but neither free in the sense the Internet initially was. Rather, it is more in line with the structures of access of the world before the Internet, producing the kind of speech that was produced in the world before the Internet.

In all three areas – the past, if true, about Microsoft; the present, if allowed, with cable; the future, if we continue, with wireless – I have described changes in a commons that currently define the environment of the Internet. These changes are occurring because, Jefferson notwithstanding, there is no inherent nature of the net that will preserve the commons of its founding. Yet we are allowing these changes to occur without considering the effect the loss of the commons will have on what is most surprising, and extraordinary, about this space: the reality of an explosion in creativity and innovation that is induced by an environment where property is only imperfectly protected. We will lose this reality if we fail to understand its environment and fail to preserve the commons that is at its core.

---

[11] *See* LESSIG, THE FUTURE OF IDEAS, *supra* note 2, at 225–27, 231–33.

6 How Norms Help Reduce the Tragedy of the Commons: A Multi-Layer Framework for Analyzing Field Experiments

Juan-Camilo Cárdenas and Elinor Ostrom

I. INTRODUCTION

Contemporary economic theory is one of the more successful, empirically verified social science theories to explain human behavior. It does best, however, in the settings for which it was developed – the exchange of private goods and services in an open, competitive market. The theory is based on a theory of goods, a set of rules for social exchange, and a model of human behavior. When the goods involved are easily excludable and rivalrous, and individuals are interacting in a competitive market, theoretical predictions have strong empirical support. When the goods involved are not easy to exclude – such as public goods or common-pool resources (CPRs) – conventional theoretical predictions receive much less empirical support.[1] In a static setting, the conventional predictions are that individuals will not produce public goods and that they will overharvest common-pool resources. The evidence for both predictions is mixed.[2]

---

[1] See SAMUEL BOWLES, MICROECONOMICS: BEHAVIOR, INSTITUTIONS, AND EVOLUTION (2004); COLIN F. CAMERER, BEHAVIORAL GAME THEORY: EXPERIMENTS IN STRATEGIC INTERACTION (2003); Colin F. Camerer, *Bounded Rationality in Individual Decision Making*, 1 EXPERIMENTAL ECON. 163–83 (1998); Colin F. Camerer, *Progress in Behavioral Game Theory*, 11 J. ECON. PERSP. 167 (1997); Herbert Gintis, *Beyond* Homo Economicus: *Evidence from Experimental Economics*, 35 ECOLOGICAL ECON. 311 (2000); John O. Ledyard, *Public Goods: A Survey of Experimental Research, in* HANDBOOK OF EXPERIMENTAL ECONOMICS (John Kagel & Alvin Roth eds., 1995).

[2] See Elinor Ostrom, A *Behavioral Approach to the Rational Choice Theory of Collective Action*, 92 AM. POL. SCI. REV. 1 (1998).

A portion of an earlier version of this chapter has been published as *What Do People Bring into the Game? Experiments in the Field about Cooperation in the Commons*, 82 AGRIS. SYS. 307 (2004). Support received from the National Science Foundation (Grant SBR-9521918) is gratefully acknowledged. Extensive comments by Marten Beckenkamp, Bruno Frey, Mike McGinnis, and James Walker on past versions helped improve this chapter as well as the excellent editing by Patty Lezotte.

In "public goods" experiments, for example, instead of contributing nothing to the provision of a public good, as is predicted by neoclassical theory for individuals pursuing material payoffs, individuals tend to contribute, on average, between 40 to 60 percent of their assets in a one-shot game.[3] In repeated games, the average level of contribution starts at around 50 percent but slowly decays toward the predicted zero level.[4] With nonbinding communication – cheap talk – participants are able to sustain cooperation in public goods experiments for long periods of time.[5] Similarly, participants in common-pool resource experiments approach near-optimal withdrawal levels when they are able to communicate, come to their own agreements, and use agreed-upon punishments if someone deviates from the agreement.[6]

Field studies also find that the theoretical prediction that users are trapped in inexorable tragedies[7] is frequently not confirmed,[8] even though many examples of resources that have been destroyed through overuse have also been documented. Achieving effective, self-organized solutions is, of course, not guaranteed. Attributes of resources and of participants have consistently

[3] *See* DOUGLAS D. DAVIS & CHARLES A. HOLT, EXPERIMENTAL ECONOMICS (1993); R. Mark Isaac & James M. Walker, *Communication and Free-Riding Behavior: The Voluntary Contribution Mechanism*, 26 ECON. INQUIRY 585 (1988); R. Mark Isaac & James M. Walker, *Group Size Effects in Public Goods Provision: The Voluntary Contributions Mechanism*, 103 Q. J. ECON. 179 (1988).

[4] *See* Ledyard, *supra* note 1.

[5] *See* Isaac & Walker, *Communication, supra* note 3; David Sally, *Conservation and Cooperation in Social Dilemmas: A Meta-Analysis of Experiments from 1958–1992*, 7 RATIONALITY & SOC'Y 58 (1995).

[6] *See* ELINOR OSTROM, ROY GARDNER & JAMES WALKER, RULES, GAMES, AND COMMON-POOL RESOURCES (1994). Probably the clearest rejections of theoretical predictions have occurred in ultimatum and dictator experiments where first movers tend to offer second movers a far larger share of the bounty than predicted and where second movers (when given a chance) turn down offers that are not perceived, given the experimental conditions, as being fair. *See* Werner Güth & Reinhard Tietz, *Ultimatum Bargaining Behavior: A Survey and Comparison of Experimental Results*, 11 J. ECON. PSYCHOL. 417 (1990); Alvin E. Roth, *Bargaining Experiments, in* THE HANDBOOK OF EXPERIMENTAL ECONOMICS 253–348 (John H. Kagel and Alvin E. Roth eds., 1995). For a survey of experimental studies in developing countries with similar results in the Dictator, Ultimatum, Trust, Public Good, and Common-Pool Resource games, also see JUAN-CAMILO CÁRDENAS & JEFFREY CARPENTER, EXPERIMENTS AND ECONOMIC DEVELOPMENT: LESSONS FROM FIELD LABS IN THE DEVELOPING WORLD (Universidad de Los Andes, Working Paper, 2005).

[7] *See* Garrett Hardin, *The Tragedy of the Commons*, 162 SCI. 1243 (1968).

[8] *See* DANIEL W. BROMLEY & DAVID FEENY EDS., MAKING THE COMMONS WORK: THEORY, PRACTICE, AND POLICY (1992); NAT'L RESEARCH COUNCIL, COMM. ON THE HUMAN DIMENSIONS OF GLOBAL CHANGE, THE DRAMA OF THE COMMONS (Elinor Ostrom et al. eds., 2002); ELINOR OSTROM, GOVERNING THE COMMONS: THE EVOLUTION OF INSTITUTIONS FOR COLLECTIVE ACTION (1990).

been found to affect initial levels of organization.[9] Political economists face a major challenge to construct a behavioral theory of human choices that includes the classical economic model when applied to the exchange of private goods in full-information market settings, but which assumes a wider range of motivations when individuals face non-private goods and/or interactions outside a market.[10] The theory needs to encompass a full array of goods, a broader model of the individual (including the norms adopted by individuals), the importance of group characteristics, the possibilities for using reputation and reciprocity, and the specific rules used in particular settings. Given the number of variables potentially involved, providing a framework for how they are interlinked is one of the most important next steps toward a new theoretical synthesis. In this chapter, we take a small step in this direction.

In this chapter we explore how norms within groups help reduce temptations of social dilemmas using data from a set of experiments in common-pool resources conducted in the field, as well as information about the individuals and their households, groups, and local context. The framework for the analysis proposes that individuals use different layers of information – from the game payoffs and formal rules to the context where the experiments are conducted – to guide their choices in the experiment and help avoid social dilemmas as much as possible.

In particular, we explore how reciprocity may play an important role in defining the individual strategy followed by players and, thus, the aggregate outcomes that emerge from the use of reciprocity among humans. Further, we show that reciprocity can generate the opposite effect depending on the institutional setting faced by a group involved in a common-pool resource dilemma. Our findings have strong implications for the design and understanding of formal and informal institutions for the management of resources.

In the next section, we present a framework that posits four layers of information that may be used by participants in social dilemma situations that could affect their actions and thus the joint outcomes obtained. The framework, first proposed by Cárdenas,[11] combines inputs from Ostrom's behavioral model of

---

[9] *See* CLARK GIBSON ET AL. EDS., PEOPLE AND FORESTS: COMMUNITIES, INSTITUTIONS, AND GOVERNANCE, (2000); Elinor Ostrom, *Reformulating the Commons, in* PROTECTING THE COMMONS: A FRAMEWORK FOR RESOURCE MANAGEMENT IN THE AMERICAS 17–41 (Joanna Burger et al. eds., 2001).

[10] *See* Albert Hirschman, *Against Parsimony: Three Easy Ways of Complicating Some Categories of Economic Discourse*, 1 ECON. & PHIL. 7 (1985).

[11] Juan-Camilo Cárdenas et al., *Local Environmental Control and Institutional Crowding-out*, 28 WORLD DEV. 1719 (2000).

collective action,[12] Bowles's argument for an endogenous preferences model,[13] and from McCabe and Smith's cognitive model of cooperative behavior.[14]

Conducting economic experiments in the field with nonstudent participants provides a special opportunity to test the hypotheses that can emerge from this framework. Given the specific kinds of information that are available to members from the same rural village who know more about each other than participants brought together in a university experimental laboratory, we then present evidence regarding the impact of these layers of information on decisions made in the experiments reported below.

II. MULTI-LAYER FRAMEWORK FOR THE ANALYSIS OF INFORMATION THAT PEOPLE BRING INTO A GAME

Institutions as "rules of the game" transform key elements involved in the decisions of individuals. Most of these elements enter the decision as information – or lack of it. Individuals, by interacting within institutions, gather information by learning about others and their actions, and about the consequences to them and to others of such interactions, within a specific set of rules and payoffs.

Ostrom earlier argued that studying the context of a game is crucial because institutions affect individuals' decisions to cooperate by performing at least three key tasks.[15] First, institutions reinforce or counteract certain social norms. Second, they allow participants to gather more or less information about the behavior of others. Third, they entitle people to reward and punish certain behaviors with material and nonmaterial incentives. The social sanctioning of norms has been widely studied experimentally[16] and also supported on neurological basis.[17] Individuals are willing to assume material costs in order to maintain social norms and punish violations of them. One might think that this willingness to punish violators, however, will operate within a context

---

[12] Ostrom, *Behavioral Approach, supra* note 2.

[13] Samuel Bowles, *Endogenous Preferences: The Cultural Consequences of Markets and Other Economic Institutions*, 36 J. ECON. LITERATURE 75 (1998).

[14] Kevin A. McCabe & Vernon L. Smith, *Strategic Analysis in Games: What Information Do Players Use?, in* TRUST AND RECIPROCITY: INTERDISCIPLINARY LESSONS FROM EXPERIMENTAL RESEARCH (Elinor Ostrom & James Walker eds., 2003).

[15] Ostrom, *Behavioral Approach, supra* note 2; Elinor Ostrom, *Collective Action and the Evolution of Social Norms*, 14 J. ECON. PERSP. 137 (2000).

[16] Ernst Fehr & Urs Fischbacher, *Third-Party Punishment and Social Norms*, 25 EVOLUTION & HUM. BEHAV. 63 (2004).

[17] Dominique J.-F. de Quervain et al., *The Neural Basis of Altruistic Punishment*, 305 SCI. 1254 (2004).

where potential punishers expect others to respond to social sanctioning, and potential violators expect punishers to invest in sanctioning. Thus, it is not only the rules of the particular game, but also the context in which the players are interacting, that provides the information for voluntary sanctioning against those who break social norms.

As discussed by Crawford and Ostrom,[18] when players share a norm, the payoff structure looks different than the payoff structure for a similar situation in which the players do not share a norm. One can model this preference function by adding or subtracting a delta parameter from the expected material payoff. The payoffs may even reflect a large enough change so that the predicted outcome of the game differs entirely from that predicted by a similar game where players' payoffs do not contain delta parameters. Uncertainty about whether other actors, who have accepted particular certain norms, are present in a situation may be sufficient grounds for changing the behavior of players.

Further, it seems that individuals will *simultaneously* use several sets of information to make their decisions. Prior experimental evidence shows, for instance, that both group identity and the marginal per-capita return (MPCR) in the payoff function increase contributions in public goods games.[19] When an individual faces a game where there is a clear group identity but the MPCR is low, the second effect may overpower the first one, and reduce contributions overall. In this case, the individual is more likely to defect by not contributing to the public good despite the group identity incentive. While the MPCR parameter is information about material payoffs, group identity is information that captures the expected intentions that participants have about each other's likely strategies and the valuation placed on benefits achieved by all of the group as well as by the specific actor. However, they may interact in more complex ways.

The framework we present here is an attempt to organize the kinds of information that individuals may use in making decisions. As a starting point, let us assume that an individual is facing a game with the characteristics of a particular collective-action dilemma. The game has a material payoff structure where the Nash strategy is to defect, but a Pareto-optimal solution is achieved at universal cooperation. And let us also assume that it is very costly to write and enforce contracts among the players to guarantee their universal cooperation.

[18] Sue E. S. Crawford & Elinor Ostrom, *A Grammar of Institutions*, in UNDERSTANDING INSTITUTIONAL DIVERSITY 137–74 (Elinor Ostrom ed., 2005).

[19] *See* Ledyard, *supra* note 1; Jennifer Zelmer, *Linear Public Goods Experiments: A Meta-Analysis*, 6 EXPERIMENTAL ECON. 299 (2003).

Knowing these basic elements and the dilemma involved, what action would a player choose?

Conventional game theory based on the assumption of a self-regarding individual who maximizes her short-run material payoffs will predict a Nash equilibrium, resulting in overexploitation of the commons, or contributions to the public good lower than the social optimum. In fact, most experimental evidence shows that a fraction of the population always follows this prediction. Depending on the specific set of institutions and incentives, however, a significant fraction of individuals do cooperate in these experiments. Arguments explaining this range from the presumed lack of learning and understanding of the game to altruistic preferences of humans.[20] A major factor consistent throughout the literature is the use of reciprocity by participants. When people foresee a repeated game with possibilities of meeting the same players again, the emergence of cooperative behavior is quite frequent. Most of the experimental results with student populations supporting this argument are based on comparing the so-called "strangers" versus "partners" treatments, where groups are formed and shuffled in every round (strangers) versus groups that are maintained across all rounds (partners). When players are certain that they are interacting with the same people over rounds, even though anonymity remains, they take advantage of reciprocity to signal willingness to cooperate by contributing and willingness to punish by not cooperating.

Instead of presuming that all individuals are rational egoists and that they presume everyone else is, we assume that individuals use information to assess the characteristics and types of other players to build a conjecture about the likely actions taken by others. Thus, information enables the player to decide whether to trust the others in the group and cooperate, once they are aware that cooperation can achieve a Pareto-superior outcome. If the information they are able to gather does not provide grounds for assuming a significant fraction of trustworthy partners, then the player is unlikely to cooperate. Or, if a player simply does not see any benefit from cooperating because his utility equals material payoffs, the player will follow the predicted Nash strategy for a finitely repeated game.

We classify the pieces of information that the players gather to construct a framework to explain the way players transform material payoffs of an externally defined game into an internal game. These data can be ordered in four layers of information, namely, the static game, the dynamic game, the group-context, and the identity layer. In summary, players will gather and use information

---

[20] For a meta-analysis of experimental studies on voluntary contributions to public goods, *see* Zelmer, *supra* note 19.

TABLE 6.1. *Layers of information and questions players ask*

Layer	Basic questions
Static game layer	• What material payoffs can I obtain from my actions and those of others in this game? • How much more (temptation payoff) do I obtain from free-riding when others cooperate? • How much do I obtain by cooperating when others do not? (sucker's payoff) • What are the material penalties and rewards involved from my actions?
Dynamic game layer	• What can I learn from previous rounds about others' actions? • What can happen in future rounds of this game because of what happened in previous rounds?
Group-context layer	• Who are the others in the game? • Can they be trusted? Am I trustworthy to them? • Do they usually cooperate in this and similar games? • Do they follow social norms? Are they strong reciprocators or conformists or competitors?
Identity layer	• Do I care if I defect on others? • Do I enjoy cooperating? Or competing? Does my experience in similar games provide hints on how to play this game?

about these layers when facing a collective-action dilemma. Responding to questions such as those shown in Table 6.1, they will guide their decision to cooperate or not.

These layers of information can be expressed in the framework shown as Figure 6.1, which provides examples of specific factors included in each of the layers that transform the game from an external, material payoffs game into an internal game. Players will then transform the payoffs structure into an internal valuation of costs and benefits of actions within a set of individual norms, group-context, and the institutions for the game. The transformation of the internal game is represented in Figure 6.1 as the dotted arrow that crosses all layers of information and then is converted into the decision, in this case, to cooperate or not in a specific moment in time.

The framework implies that, depending on the game structure, individuals try to gather and evaluate as much information as they can about these four layers. For instance, if the game is a one-shot, anonymous game, information about some of the other layers will not provide any benefit to the individual and thus would not be worth the cost. Eventually, an individual moral

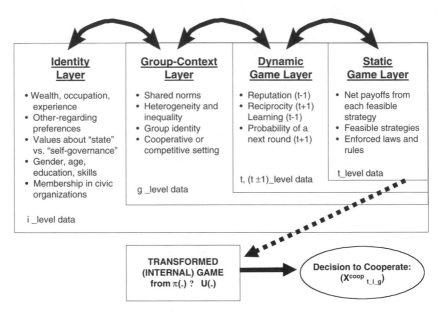

Figure 6.1. A framework of the multiple layers of information players use in the game.

obligation to a certain norm based on the identity layer could play a role, but the layers about the dynamics of the game or the group-context would not be operational. In fact, in competitive markets, less information is usually better, as argued by Smith.[21] Once the game involves repetition, nonanonymity, and externalities among players, net gains may be achieved from gathering additional information, even if costly, to construct a new internal game. The transformed game will then have a different set of payoffs, a different set of preferred strategies, and eventually, in light of the change of behavior over time, a different set of Nash strategies. Depending on the initial distribution of intrinsic preferences and the information revealed, social dilemma games may be transformed into other games, such as an assurance game, with less conflict between individual and collective interest. Also of importance, the new internal game does not have to be a monotonic transformation of the initial material payoffs structure in the static one-shot game nor the same for all players. Let

[21] Vernon L. Smith, *Economics in the Laboratory*, 8 J. Econ. Persp. 113 (1994). This does not preclude market institutions from also allowing for other normative aspects to affect the social efficiency of exchange. The study by Kahneman, Knetsch, and Thaler – showing how fairness norms can affect consumers' perceptions of changes in prices or wages in different directions depending on the source of the shifts – is an example. *Infra* note 35.

us now look in detail at the layers of information proposed in the framework, and some of the relevant literature supporting the importance of this kind of information.

A. *The Static Game Layer*

In the first layer of information, the player observes the structure of material payoffs and feasible strategies for a one-shot game. The set of actions and pay-offs will produce possible Nash equilibria, some of which may be more socially desirable than others. The perception of the game at this layer is affected by the set of formal rules that are effectively enforced. Therefore, the perceived game drawing on this information is in fact the one resulting after applying those formal rules and the material rewards, penalties, or restrictions that are fully enforced.[22] For the particular case of a "common-pool resource" game, the payoffs' structure typically involves a social dilemma where the individual strategy to maximize material payoffs produces, in equilibrium, a socially inefficient outcome, as in any N-prisoner's dilemma game. The particular case of common-pool resources may involve interior solutions, given that the resource may be nonexcludable but subtractable, but still with the properties of a social dilemma.

B. *The Dynamic Game Layer*

In interactions that are repetitive, or at least involve other known participants, the dynamic game layer of information becomes relevant. Most social exchange relations of the collective action type involve more than one round and a nonzero probability of facing the same counterparts in future rounds of the game. Robert Axelrod's argument of cooperation emerging from self-oriented maximizers was based on such grounds.[23] This is particularly true for rural settlements that interact daily in the decisions about using fisheries, forests, or water resources. A robust result in the experimental literature is that when participants are paired or grouped over rounds with the same other players, cooperative behavior is more likely to emerge. The likelihood that the same players meet in future rounds creates several effects in the dynamic game. Since players can learn and have memory, they can both build a reputation

---

[22] Once the enforcement of rules suffers from any kind of transaction costs, the other layers of information enter into play to determine the actual response to a certain formal but partially enforced rule.

[23] ROBERT AXELROD, THE EVOLUTION OF COOPERATION (1984).

and build a history of the reputation built by others. McCabe and Smith, in their cognitive model, suggest a set of modules, one of which involves the process of goodwill accounting.[24] Since the strategy of tit-for-tat produces strong results in the long run against most other strategies, the information that can be gathered about past rounds and the probability of future ones with the same players will create the conditions for cooperation through reciprocity, including retaliation towards noncooperators as a group selection mechanism. It is well-recognized that in experimental public goods environments, even with no possibilities for communication among players, individuals are willing to start contributing at levels above the Nash prediction, but such contribution rates decrease over rounds. However, Isaac, Walker, and Williams report how longer time frames in public goods games produce and sustain higher rates of contributions.[25] These results are important because the canonical analysis of repeated games, by backward induction, predicts that each round be analyzed as a one-shot game given that there are no carry-on effects on payoffs from one round to another. However, repetition in experiments offers other services to cooperation, such as allowing reciprocators to signal their intentions to others, and to build reputations, which are all crucial for the emergence of cooperative equilibria.

Reciprocity has been identified as a social norm that helps individuals reduce the social losses from the tragedy of the commons. When individuals are willing to cooperate if they observe others in their groups cooperating, and when others observe that those same individuals are also willing to punish noncooperative behavior, at a cost, free-riding is discouraged. However, reciprocal behavior can only emerge if the institutional context of the game allows players to signal and to receive the signals, and this can only occur in games where there are repeated rounds, or at least sequential moves, as is the case of the "trust" game.[26] Ostrom posits a set of core relationships – reciprocity, trust, and reputation – that seem to be the key engine of cooperative behavior.[27] Reciprocity needs to be based on trust. Only if I trust others in my group am I willing to engage in cooperative behavior. Otherwise, my personal losses from providing the public good with my cooperation will not be compensated by the gains from my own cooperation. Trust and trustworthiness, to be developed within the individuals in the group, require that players build their own

---

[24] McCabe & Smith, *supra* note 14.

[25] R. Mark Isaac, James Walker & Arlington Williams, *Group Size and the Voluntary Provision of Public Goods: Experimental Evidence Utilizing Large Groups*, 54 J. Pub. Econ. 1 (1994).

[26] Joyce Berg, John Dickhaut & Kevin McCabe, *Trust, Reciprocity, and Social History*, 10 Games & Econ. Behav. 122 (1995).

[27] Ostrom, *supra* note 2.

goodwill accounting of the others. Also, they need to provide the others with the information for their own goodwill accounting.[28] Reputation is the third component of the engine of cooperation as those who build a reputation as a conditional cooperator can expect others to cooperate more frequently with them in the future. Further, reciprocity feeds back on reputation and augments the positive cycle of cooperation. Reciprocators will signal their tit-for-tat strategy to others and will update their beliefs about the possibilities for gains from cooperation but also about the losses from punishment.

There are, however, negative dimensions of reciprocity. Reciprocators can engage in equilibria of mutual punishment with poor efficiency resulting at individual and social levels. Lack of trust and signals of noncooperative behavior in previous rounds will generate a record of noncooperation across individuals that does not promote cooperative actions. If no other institution or sufficiently strong external shock in the game happens for propelling the group out of such equilibrium, no self-governed way exists to emerge from the tragedy. Thus, the same social norm, reciprocity, can drive groups out of the social dilemma or further down into it. This is, in fact, one of the strongest results from the experimental results to be presented below.

C. *The Group-Context Layer*

A third information layer is supported by the notion that a player's decisions are also influenced by learning about additional features of the other players in the interaction. Knowing who the others are is important in the game for several reasons. First, a possibility may exist that the same players will meet in a future round of the game or a similar game. Therefore, reciprocity and retaliation processes will affect future outcomes. Second, an individual's own set of preferences include caring for the well-being of certain others (relatives, friends, neighbors). Third, some natural altruistic preferences toward humans in general might also guide players to cooperate or provide a public good that benefits others.

Evolutionary models where the gains from cooperating or defecting may be affected by the frequency of cooperators and defectors in the group provide grounds for this argument.[29] The information a player has about the composition of the group will determine if there is sufficient trust for choosing to cooperate for mutual gains. Thus, depending on the fraction of trustworthy and opportunistic types observed in a group, the player will have a better estimate

---

[28] McCabe & Smith, *supra* note 14.   [29] *See* Bowles, *supra* note 13.

of the likelihood of cooperation by others and therefore of the gains and costs of cooperating themselves.

Empirical evidence supports this argument. Group identity, group cohesion, and social distance have been shown to affect the likelihood that individuals cooperate. Lawler and Yoon, for instance, show in a series of experiments how the level and equality of power among players increased the frequency of mutual agreements.[30] Kollock provides data from a set of prisoner's dilemma experiments studying how group identity has a direct effect on cooperative behavior.[31] The behavior of college students changed, depending on the information they received about the other players (being from the same fraternity, from any other fraternity, from the same campus, from another campus, from the police department). Significant changes in behavior were found consistent with the existence of strong in-group/out-group effects.[32]

D. *The Identity Layer*

In this fourth layer, the players store and process information about themselves that may affect the feasible strategies or the subjective payoffs from each strategy. Certain values inherent to the player will increase or decrease the subjective payoffs from cooperating or defecting because of the existence

---

[30] Edward Lawler & Jeongkoo Yoon, *Commitment in Exchange Relations: Test of a Theory of Relational Cohesion*, 61 AM. SOC. REV. 89 (1996).

[31] Peter Kollock, *Transforming Social Dilemmas: Group Identity and Co-Operation, in* MODELING RATIONALITY, MORALITY, AND EVOLUTION (Peter A. Danielson ed., 1998).

[32] *See* John M. Orbell et al., *Explaining Discussion-Induced Cooperation*, 54 J. PERSONALITY & SOC. PSYCHOL. 811 (1988). Other nonexperimental evidence might also support how group composition and context may determine cooperation. Alesina and La Ferrara show evidence from U.S. survey data that the participation of individuals in social organizations and activities is higher for more equal and less fragmented localities in terms of race or ethnicity. Alberto Alesina & Eliana La Ferrara, *Participation in Heterogeneous Communities*, 115 Q. J. ECON. 847 (2000). Group heterogeneity and inequality are still presented to be part of the core explanations for collective action since Olson, and more recently with Bergstrom, Blume, and Varian. MANCUR OLSON, THE LOGIC OF COLLECTIVE ACTION: PUBLIC GOODS AND THE THEORY OF GROUPS (1965); Theodore Bergstrom, Lawrence Blume & Hal Varian, *On the Private Provision of Public Goods*, 29 J. PUB. ECON. 25 (1986). Much of the arguments for heterogeneity inducing higher cooperation are based on the asymmetric payoffs structure where the players with higher stakes may be more willing to provide the public good. We would assign such effects to the static game layer in the framework. However, other elements arising from group composition may also enter into play even under a symmetric payoff. One of these cases is the effect that social differences may have in a group, for instance due to wealth. For a more detailed discussion on how wealth differences may have an effect in solving these dilemmas, see Juan-Camilo Cárdenas, Rural Institutions, Poverty and Cooperation: Learning from Experiments and Conjoint Analysis in the Field (unpublished Ph.D. dissertation, University of Massachusetts, 2000).

of other-regarding or process-related preferences. The player's own stock of human capital will affect preferences as well. This information is not necessarily gathered by the player through the institutions of the particular game, but is already stored in her mind and is used depending on the externalities involved in the game.[33]

An example is the pleasure or joy from cooperating or defecting oneself depending on the values or preferences one has about reciprocating, gaining the highest outcome, or observing whether the group does well. We draw on Sen's rejection of egoism and opportunism as the only rationalities possible for humans.[34] Sen's discussion of behaviors based on sympathy – which is still based on egoist rationality – but especially on commitment, which involves other-regarding preferences, can explain why we observe non-negative voluntary contributions in public goods. Also, inherently human traits, such as reciprocal fairness,[35] create reciprocal behavior that goes against the opportunist prediction. Falk, Fehr, and Fischbacher provide a theoretical model that includes in its analysis individual preferences based on reciprocity and fairness, with which it is possible to explain the levels of cooperation in experiments where communication and informal sanctioning are introduced.[36] In their model, an individual's utility increases with his or her own material payoff, but is also affected by the outcomes received by others. This kind of other-regarding preferences model still maintains a utility-maximizing rationality, but one that is based not only on one's own payoffs but also on the outcomes for others.[37] Therefore, the material payoffs game is transformed, but not necessarily in a monotonic fashion, after considering the outcomes of others.

This identity layer is also important when there is imperfect information about the material game (payoffs, strategies, and other players). Past experience in similar games, skills, and education can inform the player about the game. For instance, the framing of the problem can induce the player to bring

---

[33] In the case of transactions under perfectly competitive markets where there are no externalities involved, it is very unlikely that the player will use this layer of information because the perfectly competitive transaction has accounted by definition for all effects on others, and the decision ultimately is based on the price and the demand for it.

[34] Amartya Sen, *Rational Fools: A Critique of Behavioral Foundations of Economic Theory*, 6 PHIL. & PUB. AFF. 317 (1977).

[35] *See* Ernst Fehr & Jean-Robert Tyran, *Institutions and Reciprocal Fairness*, 23 NORDIC J. POL. ECON. 133 (1997); Daniel Kahneman et al., *Fairness as a Constraint on Profit Seeking: Entitlements in the Market*, 76 AM. ECON. REV. 728 (1986).

[36] Armin Falk, Ernst Fehr & Urs Fischbacher, Appropriating the Commons: A Theoretical Explanation (Working Paper No. 55, Inst. for Empirical Research in Econ., Univ. of Zurich, 2000).

[37] *See* James C. Cox, Daniel Friedman & S. Gjerstad, A Tractable Model of Reciprocity and Fairness (Working Paper, Dep't of Econ., Univ. of Ariz., 2004).

elements from prior experiences into the game. Games with exactly the same objective structures produce different behavior depending on the framing.[38] Institutions in field settings can induce different preferences in the way they frame a social exchange situation.[39]

The case for endogenous preferences is also supported by Becker, who proposes a utility function dependent not only on the consumption of the goods, but what he calls *personal capital*, which accounts for "the relevant past consumption and other personal experiences that affect current and future utilities," and *social capital*, which "incorporates the influence of past actions by peers and others in an individual's social network and control system."[40]

A growing, but not yet systematic, area of work is studying whether aspects inherent to the participants participating in an experiment may explain part of their behavior. For instance, gender effects in public goods contributions have been studied for the last decade. The results, as Ledyard reports, are still inconclusive.[41] Accounting for the particular major of the student participating has also been a focus of attention. Early experiments in the 1980s concluded that economics majors showed higher levels of free-riding with modestly strong results.[42] More recently, Cadsby and Maynes reported that nurses showed higher levels of cooperation than economics and business students in a threshold public goods game.[43] These results would also be consistent with the work by Frank, Gilovich, and Regan on the behavior of economics

---

[38] *See* Elizabeth Hoffman et al., *Social Distance and Other-Regarding Behavior in Dictator Games: Reply*, 89 AM. ECON. REV. 340 (1999); Elizabeth Hoffman et al., *Social Distance and Other-Regarding Behavior in Dictator Games*, 86 AM. ECON. REV. 653 (1996).

[39] *See* Bowles, *supra* note 13.

[40] GARY BECKER, ACCOUNTING FOR TASTES 4 (1996).

[41] *Supra* note 1. *See also* Jamie Brown-Kruse & David Hummels, *Gender Effects in Laboratory Public Goods Contribution: Do Individuals Put Their Money Where Their Mouth Is?*, 22 J. ECON. BEHAV. & ORG. 255 (1993). Brown-Kruse and Hummels suggest that contrary to recent propositions that females tend to cooperate more, males contributed at higher rates. Meanwhile, Ortmann and Tichy found that females cooperated more in the first round but that the difference faded by the end of the game because, they argue, of the effect of experience in previous rounds. Andreas Ortmann & Lisa K. Tichy, *Gender Differences in the Laboratory: Evidence from Prisoner's Dilemma Games*, 39 J. ECON. BEHAV. & ORG. 327 (1999). They also report that the gender composition had an impact in behavior, namely, that single sex groups of females showed a higher rate of cooperation than all male groups. This last result would support the arguments about the group-context layer in the framework presented here.

[42] *See* R. Mark Isaac et al., *Public Goods Provision in an Experimental Environment*, 26 J. PUB. ECON. 51 (1985), *reported in* Ledyard, *supra* note 1; Gerald Marwell & Ruth E. Ames, *Economists Free Ride, Does Anyone Else?: Experiments on the Provision of Public Goods*, IV, 15 J. PUB. ECON. 295 (1981).

[43] Charles Bram Cadsby & Elizabeth Maynes, *Choosing between a Socially Efficient and a Free-riding Equilibrium: Nurses Versus Economics and Business Students*, 37 J. ECON. BEHAV. & ORG. 183 (1998).

majors being closer to game-theoretical predictions.[44] In another interesting study, Ockenfels and Weinmann found that East German participants behaved less cooperatively than West German ones in both public goods (ten rounds, 5 person) and solidarity (one-shot, 3 person) games.[45]

E. Cross-Effects between Layers

Notice also in the diagram (Figure 6.1) the two-way arrows above the layers. Any one layer can reinforce or decrease the effect of other layers. Tradeoffs also exist across layers; that is, the relative weight of one layer may increase or decrease because of the information contained in other layers. For instance, if there is such a tradeoff between the additional gains from defection in the one-shot game and the nonmaterial satisfaction of cooperating and allowing the others in the group to benefit, a threshold or a marginal rate of substitution should exist for these. The level of the threshold would depend on the information the player has from the static game layer and the preferences and group layers. The opposite of a tradeoff might be in place also when competitive and egoistic preferences, for instance, reinforce the defection rate with an increase in the temptation payoff, i.e., the difference between the cooperation payoff and the defection one.

Sally has proposed a formal model to introduce the concept of sympathy as a key to determining the willingness to cooperate by a player.[46] He defines sympathy as the "fellow-feeling person i has for person j" and models it as a function of both the physical and psychological distances between i and j. Using our framework, Sally's approach combines the last two layers in the sense that it involves information both about self and about the others when playing the game. In fact, Sally differentiates sympathy from altruism. He uses a reciprocity argument in the former case, since persons will reduce their fellow-feeling for another when they feel they are being manipulated and taken advantage of.

In general, the importance of cross-effects among the factors that determine cooperation has been under studied, particularly in experiments. Ledyard, in fact, mentions the lack of research in this area, on how the marginal effect of one variable depends on the level of another institutional variable.[47] He

---

[44] Robert H. Frank, Thomas Gilovich & Dennis T. Regan, *Does Studying Economics Inhibit Cooperation?*, 7 J. ECON. PERSP. 159 (1993).

[45] Axel Ockenfels & Joachim Weinmann, *Types and Patterns: An Experimental East-West-German Comparison of Cooperation and Solidarity*, 71 J. PUB. ECON. 275 (1999).

[46] David Sally, *On Sympathy and Games*, 44 J. ECON. BEHAV. & ORG. 1 (2001).

[47] Ledyard, *supra* note 1, at 144.

cites the work by Isaac and Walker and Isaac, Walker, and Williams on how the effect of marginal per-capita return (MPCR) on contributions to public goods is affected by group size.[48] In our framework, this suggests that the static game layer – where the MPCR determines the material marginal return from contributions – might interact with the group composition layer.

Another example of cross-effects that can be captured in the lab are provided by Frohlich, Oppenheimer, and Kurki, who conducted an experiment in which a "dictator" game was played among participants who were previously engaged in a two-person production task process that determined the size of the pie to be divided later on.[49] Their main result was that the sharing behavior changed from the conventional dictator game results in the literature. They are able to explain behavior with the choices made previously in the production line and the experimental context of the experimental setting. On the one hand, the generosity of the dictator *increases* with the effort of the other player in the production task. On the other hand, when the design of the experimental protocol opens room for doubt, players tend to move towards more selfish behavior.

F. *Hypotheses about Decision Making Using a Cross-Effects Framework*

We have reviewed experimental evidence on how institutions created in the lab and information brought by the participants affect the decision to cooperate. Further, a cross-cultural comparison using the same experimental design would then be an ideal test of the hypotheses derived from the framework. For example, Henrich[50] and Henrich et al.[51] report on a series of ultimatum, public goods, and dictator games from field experiments with fifteen small-scale societies in twelve countries. The behavior under the same objective game varied with the culture of the group, and differed from the same replication of experiments with university students. We will present more detailed evidence

---

[48] *Id.* (citing R. Mark Isaac & James M. Walker, *Communication and Free-Riding Behavior: The Voluntary Contribution Mechanism*, 26 Econ. Inquiry 585 (1988), and R. Mark Isaac, James Walker & Arlington Williams, *Group Size and the Voluntary Provision of Public Goods: Experimental Evidence Utilizing Large Groups*, 54 J. Pub. Econ. 1 (1994)).

[49] Norman Frohlich, Joe Oppenheimer & Anja Kurki, *Modeling Other-Regarding Preferences and an Experimental Test*, 119 Pub. Choice 91 (2004).

[50] Joseph Henrich, *Does Culture Matter in Economic Behavior? Ultimatum Game Bargaining Among the Machiguenga of the Peruvian Amazon*, 90 Am. Econ. Rev. 973 (2000).

[51] Joseph Henrich et al., *In Search of* Homo Economicus: *Behavioral Experiments in 15 Small-Scale Societies*, 91 Am. Econ. Rev. 73 (2001).

of this later, when we analyze the results of a series of common-pool resources (CPR) experiments where the participants are actual CPR users in three rural villages.

Before we discuss the evidence from field experiments, let us try to make some sense of the elements so far presented about the framework. First of all, we do not argue that all the information in all the layers is used in all exchange situations. Therefore, the question is what information players use and when. The first proposition about the framework is that an individual decides whether or not to gather information from added layers beyond the static game layer depending on the overall structure of the game including the payoffs, the feasible strategies, the others included in the game, and the number of repetitions. Also, bringing this information to the game depends on how available and how costly it is to gather. If players do not know the others in a group involved in a social dilemma transaction, the group-context layer is useless for them, unless it is inexpensive to gather this information. If the player does not assume multiple rounds of the same game with the same players, there is no need to think of the dynamic game layer and its information related to reciprocity.[52]

An extreme case is when a player faces a transaction in a competitive market close to the Walrasian world; that is, where there are many suppliers and buyers, sufficient information about prices of the alternatives, no externalities, and zero transaction costs.[53] In such case, players do not need to use any other layer of information except that generated by the static game. They will compare prices

---

[52] One caveat would be when there is no likelihood of a next round in this game, but the player knows with some certainty that he/she will meet with the same players in an entirely different game. In this case, the one-shot decision to cooperate might be influenced by that. This is developed in much detail in the multilevel and linked games literature. *See, e.g.*, Michael D. McGinnis, *Issue Linkage and the Evolution of International Cooperation*, 30 J. Conflict Resol. 141 (1986); Robert D. Putnam, *Diplomacy and Domestic Politics: The Logic of Two-Level Games*, 42 Int'l Org. 427 (1988).

[53] It is quite striking how well certain predictions based purely on monetary incentives work in experimental settings while predicting poorly human behavior in other types of game structures. In the former, we can mention the case of auction-based market experiments where convergence toward the price-equals-marginal-costs price equilibrium works in a very predictable and robust way. In the latter, we can mention public goods, dictator, and ultimatum experiments. Bowles suggests from the existing experimental work that "the more the experimental situation approximates a competitive (and complete contracts) market with anonymous buyers and sellers, the less other-regarding behavior will be observed." *Supra* note 13, at 89. Notice that the competitive market experiments with no externalities do involve private information by the players. For instance, buyers do not know the marginal cost of sellers. Yet after a few rounds, the system converges towards market-efficient prices. At that equilibrium, as predicted in theory, the maximization of individual material payoffs by each player produces a social optimal solution in the laboratory.

and choose the one that best satisfies their demand for any good or service. In this type of interaction, the transformed (internal) game will probably have the same properties as the material one in terms of Nash equilibria and social efficiency. No real need exists to use other information since there are no coordination failures or externalities in such a market.

A major reason for a player to bring information from the other layers into the game is that a transaction may involve an externality or interdependency not corrected in the static game through enforceable rules and material incentives. A prisoner's dilemma game is the typical case, although not the only one. If possible, every player would like to gather more information to predict the other player's action and then use that knowledge along with their personal norms in choosing whether to cooperate or not.

A second reason for the player to search for information in the other layers is the existence of asymmetric information involved in the transaction. Many social exchange transactions involve some kind of private information that gives players the possibility of deriving extra rents from the transaction. In such situations, it is costly to write and enforce contracts. In common-pool resources, for example, it would be costly for other users or authorities to know the individual withdrawal levels that decrease the availability of resource flows for others. In a firm, workers can invert levels of effort well below what the employer would like, given the difficulty of writing a contract based on effort rather than time at the workplace. Sharecroppers and landlords also find their utility function in conflict because they have different stakes and risks in a game. Polluters would engage in production levels above those that the environmental regulator would like them to, if the monitoring of emissions is imperfect or costly.

In summary, when a game involves externalities and problems of asymmetric information among players, we assume that players will search for additional information from the three other layers and use these to create an internalized vision of the game. Some will be more likely to cooperate because of this information, while others will be more likely to defect. The internal game values will be affected by their preferences (identity layer), the information they gathered about the other players (group-context layer), and the dynamic game conditions. The basic structure of the game in the static game layer alone will not provide a full representation of the game. Players will complement the basic static layer of the game with the other three layers of information they bring.

In the case of dictator, ultimatum, and public goods games, we find the externalities and asymmetric information conditions as reasons to use the other layers of information. Players do affect the payoffs of others in their decisions, and the basic nature of the game impedes enforcing contracts that better align the individual and collective interest. The experimental evidence mentioned above – providing consistent evidence of deviations from the theoretical predictions based only on material payoffs maximization – suggests that other information is brought into the game and can be explained by factors suggested in our framework.

III. EMPIRICAL EVIDENCE FROM THE EXPERIMENTAL LAB

When reviewing the experimental literature, one notices that the third and fourth layers – group-context and identity – are especially related to the kinds of variables that are difficult to control in the lab, as Ledyard argues.[54] Culture, beliefs, group identity, social context, and personal identity are among these. The importance of these factors in forming the context of the game in earlier experiments gives support for the methodological step forward we present in this chapter, that is, to bring the experimental lab to the field and enrich the analysis that Ledyard has identified as important but difficult.

Zelmer has conducted a recent meta-analysis of more than 700 experimental sessions and more than 7,000 rounds of public goods experiments in the lab using the voluntary contribution mechanism.[55] Zelmer finds that, on average, participants contribute about 37 percent of their total endowment even though a zero contribution is the standard theoretical prediction. These results are, however, also accompanied by substantial variance that itself appears to show some consistencies in the meta-analysis. For instance, communication among the players, although not binding, proves quite effective in driving contributions higher. Also, the "partners" treatment where players are matched with the same people over multiple rounds generates much higher contributions than settings where players are matched randomly in every round. Neither communication nor matching protocols should alter the material payoffs of the game for players. Every round is a one-shot N-prisoner's dilemma game for the canonical design of the voluntary contribution mechanism. On the other hand, the structure of the material payoffs game also plays a role, despite the fact that in all cases the zero contribution prediction is the standard prediction. As widely reported in the literature and surveyed by Ledyard and Zelmer,[56] as MPCR increases, so do individual contributions to the public good.

---

[54] *Supra* note 1.
[55] *Supra* note 19.
[56] Ledyard, *supra* note 1; Zelmer, *supra* note 19.

A. *A CPR Experiment in the Field Lab*

Inspired by the common-pool resource (CPR) experimental design of Ostrom, Gardner, and Walker,[57] an economic experiment was conducted in the field during the summer of 1998 for studying the problem of cooperation in local commons dilemmas in rural settings of Colombia. One hundred and twenty *campesinos* participated in a series of repeated-rounds sessions, in groups of eight people, under two different treatments, non-binding face-to-face communication and an external regulation involving an imperfectly monitored and enforced sanction. We also asked each participant to fill out a household survey at the end of each session after all decisions had been made – information that we were able to link to their decisions in the field lab. This link allowed us to test some of the hypotheses discussed in this chapter about the use of layers of information in their decision to cooperate.

The framing of the decision-making environment was that each participant had to decide the time allocated to extracting resources from a forest, between zero and eight months of the year. In every round, each of eight players would write her choice on a slip of paper, in private, and hand it to the monitor who added the extractions of all players and announced only the total extraction level in public. With such information, each player could calculate her own earnings in each round. The incentive structure in these CPR dilemmas was that each participant's earnings increased with her own effort (i.e., time in the forest), but decreased with the group's total effort. The relevant game benchmarks were the social optimal, where every player harvests from the forest only one month yielding Col\$645 (US\$0.50) in each round, and the Nash equilibrium, where everyone would harvest for six months yielding a suboptimal result of Col\$155 (US\$0.12) per round. In the Nash equilibrium, groups would achieve only 24 percent of the social efficiency that could be achieved if every one in the group had pursued the social optimal strategy.

Fifteen groups of eight people participated in a no-communication treatment for about nine rounds, at which point they were told that a new set of rules was to be introduced in the game. The groups were not told in advance when they were in the last round. The monitor stopped further rounds randomly around nine rounds. Five of these groups were told that an *external regulation* (REG) would be introduced to improve the group's earnings by attempting to enforce the social optimum solution. The other ten groups were told that they would have an open and free *face-to-face group discussion* (COM) of about five minutes before each round to comment openly about the game

[57] *Supra* note 6.

developments. In both cases, the groups would interact for another nine rounds or so, but again, the last round would not be announced in advance.

In the case of the external regulation (REG), the participants were explicitly informed that the social optimum would be achieved if every player chose one month in the forest. To achieve such outcome, an inspector (the monitor) would randomly audit one of the players with a probability of 1/16 in each round.[58] If the player had chosen two or more months in the forest, he or she would have a penalty of Col$100 (U.S.$0.08) imposed for each month in excess. These points would be subtracted from the final earnings. This external monitoring and sanctioning was enacted in every round and all players would be eligible for the inspection.

These two institutions, group communication and external regulation, induced significant changes in the behavior of the participants once they were implemented. In the first rounds, they both improved the social efficiency by decreasing the average extraction effort and increasing aggregate earnings. In the case of the external regulation, the expected costs of violation of the rule induced an improvement of social efficiency in the early rounds after the new rule was introduced. Rapidly, however, by the third round of the second stage, the gains were eroded. Selfish behavior, along with an imperfect monitoring, created more overharvesting, even when compared to the rounds *prior* to the introduction of the rule. In other words, the introduction of the external regulation (REG) seemed to have crowded-out the group-oriented preferences that already existed, triggering a strategy of maximization of payoffs based on the low expected cost of the regulation. The hypothesis of the crowding-out of social preference is discussed in more detail in Cárdenas, Stranlund, and Willis.[59] The statistical analysis that follows will demonstrate this phenomenon and the mechanisms that seem to have created such an unexpected outcome.

As for the case of the groups in the face-to-face communication design, we found results consistent with the earlier evidence in the experimental lab at Indiana University. Despite agreements being nonbinding, face-to-face communication (COM) did create and sustain, on average, more cooperation among players, thus substantially increasing social efficiency on average. A wide variation in decisions and outcomes existed, however, when looking at the individual data within groups and across groups. Given that all of the groups faced the exact same payoffs structure and experimental environment, the variation could be attributed to statistical error or unaccounted factors such

[58] This is a relatively high rate of monitoring for most forests where harvesting can occur in widely disparate locations.

[59] Juan-Camilo Cárdenas, John K. Stranlund & Cleve E. Willis, *Local Environmental Control and Institutional Crowding–out*, 28 WORLD DEV. 1719 (2000).

as the characteristics of the participants or the group composition in the field laboratory. The survey that we conducted at the end of the sessions included information about basic demographic variables such as gender; age; education; the participants' economic activities, assets, and occupation; as well as their personal opinions about the role of government and community governance structures. These individual and group data will be used to explore the type of information that could potentially be used by participants to explain variations in strategies adopted within the same experimental treatment.

In order to test for the combined effects of the variables in the layers of the framework, we used a regression analysis model. The model explains the individual level of cooperation in each round as a function of vectors of variables from all of the four layers, given the round-level data from the experiment, the individual-level data we gathered about the participants through the exit survey, and the construction of group-level data for each of the eight player groups. Thus, each observation in the regression corresponds to the decision by one player in a specific round of the game. Individual- and group-level effects were also controlled using a fixed-effects model with dummies for players and groups.

The payoff structure of CPR games, such as the one used here and by Ostrom, Gardner, and Walker,[60] implies a particular feature. These games do not have a dominant strategy for players because of the nonlinearity involved in the harvesting relationship that has an increasing function, but concave shape, and for rather high levels of extraction, a decreasing relationship due to overharvesting that affects the resource. Thus, a medium level of extraction effort would be a Nash strategy for some levels of aggregate of extraction but not for others. To be able to compare choices in different rounds, we construct a proxy for the willingness to cooperate by an individual in a specific round, based on how distant her decision is from the Nash best response and towards the group-oriented strategy.

The dependent variable and our index of cooperation, XDEVIA, is the distance in "months" units from the Nash best response in a specific round.[61] In other words, it measures how much the player was willing to deviate from a purely selfish strategy and toward a group-oriented strategy by reducing their "months in the forest."

---

[60] *Supra* note 6.

[61] XDEVIA allows us to better compare the decisions between the communication treatment and the external regulation that transforms the expected payoffs for players. Notice that the estimation of XDEVIA depended then on the sum of months by the rest of the group, which each player did not know with certainty. We tested the estimations with two options yielding equivalent results, one with the sum of months in the same round, and the other with the sum of months in the previous round.

TABLE 6.2. *Variables that can explain variation in individual choices in the experiment*

Layer	Explanatory variables
Static game layer	Payoffs from each level of individual extraction and for each level of aggregate extraction.
	Penalty for violating the social optimum regulation times the probability of being inspected.
Dynamic game layer	Reduction/increase in the extraction by the others in one's group in previous rounds.
	Number of rounds.
Group-context layer	Previous experience of group members in community projects in the village.
	Wealth heterogeneity associated with private and collective income-generating activities.
	Social distance among group members.
Identity layer	Individual wealth and income dependence on private activities versus production based on CPR resources.
	Individual preferences about external versus self-governing solutions to collective action.
	Personal participation in community organizations.

Our next step was to select a set of variables for the different layers of information from our multilayer framework, which capture the hypothesis that behavior is guided not only by the material payoffs and structure of the game in the first layer, but also by additional information about the individual, the group, and the context where the experiment is conducted. Based on fieldwork, the household survey, and the experimental data, the variables shown in Table 6.2 were considered for the estimation. The particular indices constructed for the estimation of the model are as follows:

DELTAVG7: Change (average reduction) in "months in the forest" by the other seven players in the group, in the previous round. This was calculated as (Σ months by the other 7 players in $t - 1$) − (Σ months by other 7 players in t). This measures the average intentions to cooperate by the rest of the group based on their choices in the previous round. If reciprocity is a factor in the decision, this variable should have a positive sign in the estimation, that is, the player should cooperate − reduce X or increase XDEVIA − after the rest of the group did so, and if the player behaves with the opportunistic logic, a negative sign.

ROUND: Round number. This variable accounts for the learning or adaptation processes in each treatment. Most experiments in common-pool resources and voluntary contributions show a decreasing rate of cooperation over rounds. Opportunistic players should show a decrease in cooperation over time; reciprocators should either increase or maintain cooperation.

AVCOOPLB: Average number of days in nonpaid labor contributed during last year by the group members – a proxy of "cooperative" behavior in community projects. This is based on the anonymous survey filled out at the exit of the session. If participants bring elements from their context to the lab and they have experienced differences in contributions to collective-action projects, this variable should help explain variations in XDEVIA.

HHWEALT2:   Player's household wealth based on land, livestock, and machinery holdings, valued at local prices and adjusted across villages. Based on the individual survey where we collected information about assets in the household.

WLTHDS2A: Wealth distance = Absolute value of the difference between the player's wealth and the average wealth of the other seven players. Based on the individual survey.

WLT_DIS2:   Cross-effect variable = HHWEALT2 * WLTHDS2A. Accounts for differences in the marginal effect of wealth distance for different social (wealth) classes.

BESTATE: A dummy where "1" if individual responded that a "state" organization should manage the local commons from where they extract resources, and "0" otherwise. Based on survey. The coefficient for this variable might show different signs and sizes depending on the institution of the experiment, for instance, the external regulation versus face-to-face communication.

PARTORGS: Number of community organizations the player belongs to or participates in, including parents' associations, cooperatives, water committees, etc. Based on survey. One could predict that those belonging to community organizations might show higher willingness to cooperate with the others in their group.

The sample size is the set of individual decisions made during a set of rounds in a stage – starting at round 2 to allow for the dynamic effects – by each of the eight players and for all the groups under each treatment.[62]

---

[62] Some observations showed missing data on the survey responses, and therefore the slight differences in sample sizes used in the regressions reported on in the table.

Tables 6.3 and 6.4 summarize the results of applying the same model and the same data sets using two different estimators. Table 6.3 uses the simple "ordinary least squares" (OLS) procedure. Table 6.4 shows the results for a "fixed effects" estimator.[63] The results are similar and, as expected, there are some tradeoffs in precision and efficiency between the two estimators. Each table is organized in two major sets of columns for each of the two stages. Stage 1 included data for rounds 1 to 9 where all fifteen groups faced a baseline treatment with no coordination, communication, or regulation allowed.[64] In Stage 2 (rounds 11 to 19), ten groups (COM) faced the possibility of a face-to-face group discussion, while five groups (REG) faced the externally imposed and imperfectly monitored regulation.

The results shed some light on how information from the four layers helps to explain the variation across groups and across players that otherwise is not explained by the material incentives of the game within treatments. Recall that the eight participants in one session or group are members of the same village. Therefore, they share a prior history of experience, reputation, beliefs, and other factors that affect their willingness to cooperate with the other seven people in their group. The overall significance of the model and the significance of many of these variables support our claim that we can explain variation in the willingness to cooperate through the variables chosen.

Let us now turn to some of the most relevant statistical results from these estimations. First of all, most of the relevant conclusions from the OLS estimation remain for the fixed effects model. Also notice how the explanatory power of the model is much higher for the second stage, where each "experimental institution" (communication or regulation) provides a stronger context for the players and induces them to use the information layers in sometimes different ways in their decisions. This is seen not only in the higher Adj.R^2, but also in the significance of several variables, in the second stage.

The absolute value of the intercept deserves a little attention. It is included in the "static" layer of the game under the following rationale. If players were to follow the strategy to maximize their material payoffs through the Nash best response, the mean value for XDEVIA should be zero.[65] Differences across the intercepts can account for changes to the mean value of XDEVIA due to

[63] The fixed effects estimator is a stronger test than the simple OLS because of possible effects created within each group, which would violate the assumption of independence of observations.

[64] In the case of Stage 1, we also pooled the No-COM and No-REG data given that the groups did not know in advance which new rule they would face; therefore, no structural differences should be expected and the data could be pooled.

[65] Note, however, that the predicted value of XDEVIA should be the intercept only when all the independent variables take the value of zero, which would be unfeasible.

TABLE 6.3. *Explaining CPR appropriation as a function of the framework's multiple layers. OLS regression results.*

Models I. (No-COM/No-REG), II. (COM), III. (REG) (Simple OLS estimations)
Independent Variable: XDEVIA = Deviation from the Nash strategy in "months in the forest" units

Label	Variable	Stage 1: Rounds (1 to 9)			Stage 2: Rounds (11 to 19)	
		No-COM	No-REG	Pooled	COM	REG
Static Layer:	INTERCEP	3.6134	3.2035	3.7052	6.9163	11.7069
		8.482	*5.739*	*10.772*	*10.711*	*13.343*
Dynamic Layer:						
Avg. reduction by other 7 players	DELTAVG7	0.3713	0.4239	0.3887	0.2786	0.4381
		3.922	*3.664*	*5.184*	*3.389*	*2.747*
Learning	ROUND	−0.0266	0.0457	−0.0034	−0.0322	−0.4240
		−0.606	*0.701*	*−0.090*	*−0.963*	*−9.020*
Group-Context Layer:						
Avg. labor contributions by group	AVCOOPLB	−0.1095	0.0409	−0.1128	0.0392	0.2121
		−2.917	*0.605*	*−3.525*	*1.116*	*3.527*
Wealth distance	WLTHDS2A	0.3524	−0.7793	0.1554	−1.7917	−4.0839
		1.415	*−1.460*	*0.694*	*−7.932*	*−8.636*
	WLT_DIS2	0.0391	−0.1245	−0.0774	0.5905	1.3955
		0.409	*−0.636*	*−0.894*	*6.936*	*8.171*
Identity Layer:						
Individual's wealth	HHWEALT2	−0.3818	0.6483	0.0198	−1.0475	−1.8788
		−1.848	*1.792*	*0.109*	*−5.549*	*−5.886*
1 if thinks state should solve the problem	BESTATE	0.1540	1.1768	0.3020	−1.0425	1.3334
		0.680	*3.755*	*1.646*	*−5.116*	*4.774*
No. organizations participates in	PARTORGS	0.2231	−0.8796	−0.0466	−0.1132	−0.8657
		2.130	*−4.945*	*−0.513*	*−1.150*	*−5.461*
Sample size	N	583	271	855	676	339
R²-adjusted	ADJR2	4.67%	18.17%	4.58%	14.36%	41.94%

In italics are t-values for rejecting the hypothesis that the estimated coefficient is statistically equal to zero.

TABLE 6.4. *Explaining CPR appropriation as a function of the framework's multiple layers. Fixed effects estimator regression results.*

Models IV. (No-COM/No-REG), V. (COM), VI. (REG) (Fixed Effects Estimator)
Independent Variable: XDEVIA = Deviation from the Nash strategy in "months in the forest" units

Label	Variable	Stage 1: Rounds (1 to 9)			Stage 2: Rounds (11 to 19)	
		No-COM	No-REG	Pooled	COM	REG
Static Layer:	INTERCEP	4.8267	3.5915	−8.5461	7.1965	13.4515
		9.106	*5.714*	*−3.889*	*10.425*	*15.736*
Dynamic Layer:						
Avg. reduction by other 7 players	DELTAVG7	0.3491	0.4434	0.3894	0.2473	0.3700
		3.765	*3.898*	*5.292*	*3.061*	*2.481*
Learning	ROUND	−0.0209	0.0455	0.0015	−0.0549	−0.4231
		−0.486	*0.718*	*0.042*	*−1.638*	*−9.601*
Group-Context Layer:						
Avg. labor contributions by group	AVCOOPLB	−0.0701	−0.2567	1.3915	0.0838	−1.2233
		−1.039	*−2.043*	*5.311*	*1.282*	*−5.858*
Wealth distance	WLTHDS2A	0.1649	−0.1717	0.0902	−1.6522	−1.8301
		0.458	*−0.267*	*0.287*	*−4.959*	*−3.341*
Wealth*Wealth distance	WLT_DIS2	0.1757	−0.2962	0.0006	0.5371	0.5623
		1.452	*−1.256*	*0.006*	*4.876*	*2.838*
Identity Layer:						
Individual's wealth	HHWEALT2	−0.6323	1.0281	−0.0829	−1.0181	−0.5593
		−2.643	*2.462*	*−0.392*	*−4.619*	*−1.575*
1 if believes state should solve the problem	BESTATE	−0.0162	0.8316	0.0620	−1.1979	0.5285
		−0.467	*2.363*	*0.305*	*−5.347*	*1.718*
No. organizations participates in	PARTORGS	0.0822	−0.8098	−0.1494	−0.1646	−0.7149
		0.758	*−4.625*	*−1.608*	*−1.602*	*−4.765*
Fixed Effects (no. dummies)		10 groups	5 groups	15 groups	10 groups	5 groups
Sample size	N	583	276	850	676	344
R² adjusted	ADJR2	10.86%	22.69%	10.67%	18.67%	49.45%

In italics are t-values for rejecting the hypothesis that the estimated coefficient is statistically equal to zero.

the experimental treatment for a specific vector of values for the rest of the independent variables. Notice that the intercept shows a greater value under the REG and COM treatments if compared to the Stage 1 values. However, the greater value of the intercept for REG needs to be interpreted with care. It shows a greater value, but it also involves a much larger negative coefficient for the ROUND variable. As rounds go by, the value of the intercept under the REG institution decreases more rapidly than in the case of COM. This is connected to the dynamics of the reciprocity norm that we now examine in more detail.

B. *Reciprocity as a Social Norm that Affects Collective Action in the Lab*

If a player were to pursue a strategy of self-oriented maximization of payoffs, the effect of a *reduction* in the level of extractions by the rest of the group should be followed by an *increase* in her own extractions as the best response. In fact, greater reductions in the extraction effort should be responded to with a higher level of individual extraction, given the structure of payoffs of a common-pool resource where low levels of aggregate extraction of the resource provide greater incentives for individual extraction given that state of the resource stock. Thus, if anything, the sign of the two coefficients of the variables in the dynamic layer should be negative. In the case of DELTAVG7, its sign should be negative for the reasons just mentioned. In the case of ROUND, repetition could provide the learning environment for the players to approach their Nash strategy, i.e., reduce XDEVIA over time.

We observe, however, that reciprocity, expressed in the positive and significant sign of DELTAVG7, is confirmed for both treatments, COM and REG and during both Stages 1 and 2. A reduction (increase) in extraction by other players is followed by a reduction (increase) in a player's own extraction. The classic tit-for-tat strategy is confirmed for the average player. The larger coefficient in the REG treatment, however, suggests that the negative reciprocity becomes stronger under the external regulation as a result of the crowding-out effect already mentioned for these groups.[66]

Negative reciprocity, caused by the external regulation, appears to crowd out the other-regarding preferences that existed prior to the introduction of the external rule in Stage 1. The larger coefficient for DELTAVG7 in the second stage for REG shows that in this case each player was, on average, increasing her deviation from the Nash best response (in months in the forest) by 0.4381 units for each unit change in the average of the rest of the group. This is almost

---

[66] *See* Cárdenas, Stranlund & Willis, *supra* note 59.

twice the effect of the reciprocity observed in the communication treatment. Nevertheless, in both cases, the effect of reciprocity is present, although paradoxically with opposite effects depending upon the institutional environment. With an undesired effect, and an imperfectly enforceable mechanism, the external regulation triggered the negative reciprocity of players who find no better alternative than to follow their group members, since the experimental design prohibited any communication among players in order to test the effects of a formal rule with imperfect enforcement.

The positive social norm of reciprocity, used in the right direction, is also present in the COM treatment. Group discussions were quite useful to guide the group goals and to reinforce the gains from cooperation and the losses from free-riding behavior.[67] The erosion of cooperation in the REG treatment is also shown by the negative and significant sign of the ROUND variable, compared to the COM groups with different and insignificant results, suggesting that the face-to-face communication institution sustained cooperation over time, other things held constant.

The mechanism of reciprocity is not the only factor that explains variation in the dependent variable. The estimated coefficients for the next layers of information provide some support for the argument that people bring some of the information they have about themselves and others into the game. Regarding the context of the game and the group, we tested two sets of variables. First, we included AVCOOPLB, which measured the average level of actual labor contributions by the group to community projects. By the second stage of the experiment, this variable showed a positive and stronger coefficient in the case of the REG groups. This suggests that players were more likely to follow the external rule, or cooperated more, when they were in groups formed of more collaborative people in settings outside of the lab, and given that all players knew each other and had a known reputation.[68]

Regarding social and economic status, participants with higher levels of actual wealth (HHWEALT2) and wider financial distance to the others in the group (WLTHDS2A) appeared less willing to cooperate.[69] This is consistent with the argument by Sally, who suggests that sympathy – a key factor in

---

[67] For more details on how communication seems to contribute to solve the social dilemma in similar experiments in the field, see Juan-Camilo Cárdenas, T. K. Ahn & Elinor Ostrom, *Communication and Co-operation in a Common-Pool Resource Dilemma: A Field Experiment,* in ADVANCES IN UNDERSTANDING STRATEGIC BEHAVIOUR: GAME THEORY, EXPERIMENTS, AND BOUNDED RATIONALITY: ESSAYS IN HONOUR OF WERNER GÜTH (Steffen Huck ed., 2004).

[68] A variable for the individual contribution to community was tested and showed no explanatory power.

[69] The impact of wealth and the heterogeneity of wealth in a group are discussed extensively in Juan-Camilo Cárdenas, *Real Wealth and Experimental Cooperation: Experiments in the Field Lab,* 70 J. DEV. ECON. 263 (2003).

cooperation – is a direct inverse function of physical and psychological distance between one person and others.[70] In our case, we find that the absolute value of wealth distance between the player and the other seven in her group reduces cooperation. The explanation emerges from a combination of "experience" in similar situations and the context of the group in which each player participates, particularly in terms of social distance. On the other hand, wealth itself can determine cooperative behavior in an individual. Poorer people face similar commons dilemmas more frequently because they own less productive private assets and thus have to access common-pool resources for their subsistence. And, they do so with people of similar levels of wealth or social status. Thus, more homogeneous groups and groups made up of players who depend to a greater extent on similar collective-action situations (because of material poverty), are likely to cooperate at a significantly higher level. The significant and positive sign for the cross-effect variable WLT_DTS2 confirms this theoretical argument.

We also find that individuals have different opinions about the best governance structure to solve these dilemmas. The responses in the exit survey to the question of whether it should be the role of the state or the community to solve the problems of managing natural resources turned out to be significant explanatory variables for the variation in behavior in both treatments. Responses had an opposite effect in the two second-stage treatments. The estimated coefficients for BESTATE suggest that under the external regulation (REG), "state believers" will proportionally comply *more* with the rule, but cooperate *less* under the non-binding, face-to-face communication environment. Those who responded in the survey that a non-state solution was preferred for this type of problem showed higher levels of cooperation in the COM treatment, but lower in the REG treatment. Notice also that for PARTORGS (the number of local community organizations in which the respondent participates), the signs are negative in both cases. The sign is much larger and significant for the REG environment, however, than for the COM treatment. "Natural cooperators" in the field under an experimental "external regulation" environment were less prone to comply with the externally imposed rule.

IV. CONCLUSIONS

By bringing the lab to the field, we enabled participants to use information from multiple levels about the actual context and background of the participants in

---

[70] *On Sympathy, supra* note 46.

these experiments. Bringing the lab to the field can, in fact, enrich the analysis of decision making using experimental methods for various reasons, including gains in relevance and context of the participants. Harrison and List address some of these issues in their survey of field experiments,[71] although they do not extensively cover experiments about collective action and cooperation in settings such as those studied here. Cárdenas and Carpenter[72] survey a now growing number of studies in which researchers have conducted experiments in developing countries and with nonstudent populations. Many of these studies provide strong evidence that pro-social behavior, based on norms of altruism, reciprocity, or fairness, is present in most societies regardless of their level of industrialization. In the experiments reported on here, it is clear that, on average, data from individual choices do not confirm the prediction of universal free-riding. Instead, participants show a willingness to cooperate in diverse dilemma situations.

We have shown econometrically that under the two institutional treatments (self-governance and external regulation), information from the different layers of the framework help explain choices. The variables in these layers may also play different roles depending on the configuration of the other variables present and the institutional environment. Reciprocity is an explanatory factor in both cases for behavior over time. Participants responded with more cooperation when the others showed an average decrease in extraction, and with increased overextraction when the others had increased their extraction. The higher coefficient for the relevant variable DELTAVG7 under the REG treatment suggests a stronger negative reciprocity under this institution, which should explain the strong erosion of cooperation under the REG treatment. In this case, the same social norm can play a beneficial or detrimental role in the solution of the tragedy of the commons.

Regarding these contrasts, preferences of the participants about the actual context of state versus self-governed institutions they face in reality also explain part of the variation in behavior. Those who trust state organizations for managing common resources cooperate more under the regulation treatment, but free-ride more under the communication treatment. Actual wealth and experience with CPR dilemmas also explain variation under the two treatments with equivalent and significant coefficients regarding wealth and variance in wealth in the group. In both cases, wealthier participants – or participants within a group that is more heterogeneous in wealth – were less willing to cooperate, and the coefficients are stronger under the external regulation case.

[71] Glenn W. Harrison & John A. List, *Field Experiments*, 42 J. ECON. LITERATURE 1009 (2004).
[72] *Supra* note 6.

The regression results suggest that people may transform the material payoffs game into their own internal preference function where cooperation may be the best response in some cases when the desired conditions hold with respect to the game, its dynamics, and the individual and group conditions for cooperation to emerge. This argument was also used by Kollock to explain how different contexts and identities of prisoner's dilemma experiments would yield different choices and outcomes for the same payoffs structure.[73] The field experiments we report on here allow us to test the use of such information, and to test some of the arguments developed in the framework of layers of information people use when facing a game for which there is room for strategic behavior, transaction costs, and collective-action dilemmas.

The field experiments reported on in this chapter allowed the participants to use information from their own context, and for researchers to examine the impact of this information on decisions. We found positive support for the arguments derived from our framework. Individuals appear to use diverse layers of information depending on the structure of a game and the context within which they are playing that game. The framework that we have presented provides some initial guidance in organizing the multiple types of variables that appear to affect individual decision making outside a highly competitive market setting. Depending on the context that individuals face, they may dig ever deeper into a set of layers of information that are relevant to their decisions depending on whether the game is ongoing, whether communication is possible, and whether the others and their reputations are known to the players.[74] The approach proposed in this chapter does not invalidate the argument that players are rational. They might not be maximizing the expected *material* payoffs of a one-shot game, but they appear to be optimizing with their strategies in a transformed game where cooperation can yield substantial gains if the required conditions about the choices of others in the group hold. In particular, social norms such as reciprocity and group identity help reduce the tragedy of the commons, particularly within a self-governed institution where players can discuss their strategies, face-to-face, and construct a shared goal as a group.

[73] *Supra* note 31.
[74] *See* Ostrom, *Behavioral Approach, supra* note 2.

PART THREE

JUDICIAL NORMS

7 Judging the Judges: Some Remarks on the Way Judges Think and the Way Judges Act

Lawrence M. Friedman

Judges, as everybody knows, have a very special role in common law legal systems. In common law systems, a good deal of the law is judge-made. An important body of rules, doctrines, and practices developed over time, through case-law, and cannot be tied to any statutory text. Common law decisions created the bulk of the law of contracts and torts, and a good deal of the law of property. The common law mentality extends even to fields of law that do have a text (which, today, most of them do). To a common law lawyer, a statute hardly means anything until it goes through its baptism of fire – getting construed by courts. And some statutes are so vague that they hardly restrict the judges at all; the case-law under such statutes is basically common law. In many areas of law that are, in theory, statutory, significant bodies of doctrine take the form of "interpretations" but are in fact attached to the text (of a statute or regulation) by the thinnest of strings, or no string at all.

In common law countries, legal tradition and education focus heavily on the work of judges. Statutes, laws, regulations, ordinances have multiplied in the last century like rabbits; yet law schools still spend almost all of their time on case-law. The materials that students break their heads over are contained in thick books called "Cases and other materials," but the cases far outnumber and outweigh the "other materials."

In the common law, then, the judge is culturally king. Yet, at the same time, there is a powerful counter-ideology, also within the common law. This is the ideology that rejects the whole idea of "judicial legislation," and insists that judges do not and should not play a creative role. Judges who innovate are thwarting the will of the people, or usurping the role of the legislature, or committing some comparable sin. An older form of this ideology was captured in the saying that judges do not make law; they just find it or declare it. Law is somehow conceived of as pre-existing, as something somehow out there, waiting to be discovered, like the statue immanent in a block of marble. The proper role of the judge is simply to decide according to the law, whatever that might mean. These slogans have significant political meaning. Republicans in particular talk endlessly about the need to fill the bench with "strict constructionists." They never get tired of beating up on "activist" judges. Judges should follow precedent; and rarely, if ever, should they go off on a frolic of their own. In the field of constitutional law, there is a lot of worrying and nagging about "countermajoritarianism," a very long and extremely ugly word.[1] The peoples' elected representatives should make the laws; when judges undo the work of the legislature, or construe some statute to death, they are going against the people; and in a democratic system, this means that they are defying the first principles of government.

The arguments tend to be most passionate on issues of constitutional law, particularly when what is at stake is some high-profile matter like a woman's right to an abortion. Who authorized the judges to be so bold? There are, of course, perfectly good answers to the critics. Constitutional theory, and constitutional cases, use terms like "evolving standards of decency,"[2] or the "living Constitution," or "judicial creativity," or the like, to justify an expansive (and a changing) reading of the Constitution. But my impression is that many scholars who defend the justices actually seem a little hesitant and uneasy. I will not try to summarize the literature on the countermajoritarian controversy, partly because I have never bothered reading most of it. I do recognize, however, the real paradox or dilemma or contradiction of the common law tradition. On the one hand, there is enormous emphasis on the judge, on the personality of the judge, on the brain of the judge, on the philosophy of the judge, on the craftsmanship of the judge, on the skill of the judge in shaping and reshaping legal matter. On the other hand, there is the condemnation of judge-made law and "activism." Yet it was creativity and suppleness which made judges like Brandeis or Cardozo or Holmes or Lemuel Shaw famous. Judges become famous for doing something new and different, for stepping out of the traditional and limited role of a judge. No strict constructionist is ever going to get into the legal equivalent of the Hall of Fame.

In this essay, I want to explore this paradox or contradiction. To a certain extent, I am going to draw on history; but the points I want to make are (I hope) more general.

---

[1] The word, if not the issue, perhaps stems from ALEXANDER M. BICKEL, THE LEAST DANGEROUS BRANCH: THE SUPREME COURT AT THE BAR OF POLITICS 16 (1962).

[2] In *Trop v. Dulles*, 356 U.S. 86 (1958), the Supreme Court held that expatriation as a punishment was "cruel and unusual punishment"; the meaning of the Eighth Amendment, which used the phrase, "must draw its meaning from . . . evolving standards of decency."

I want to begin by drawing attention to three terms that we often hear in discussions of judges and their work – three adjectives, to be precise. Ideally, judges are supposed to be impartial, or independent, or autonomous, or some combination of these. The literature often confuses the three terms. But their meanings are, in my view, quite distinct. A judge can be independent, for example, without being impartial or autonomous. In fact, I am going to argue that this is the normal situation, at least in our own legal system – that is, judges are quite independent, but their autonomy and impartiality are very much less pronounced.

First, a word about the meaning of these three terms. Exact definition isn't possible, and different people might use the terms in different ways; but I sense a certain core distinction between them. Impartial implies neutrality; an impartial judge is not prejudiced, not corrupt, and approaches issues with an open mind. A judge who takes bribes is certainly not an impartial judge; nor is a judge who decides on the basis of prejudice – against blacks or women, for example – though here the terminology is much less clear.

Independent judges are judges who are free from political interference as they go about their work. The government has no right to dictate decisions. Independent judges are the opposite of judges in a dictatorship, who could lose their jobs or their heads if they went against government policy. In the former German Democratic Republic, or East Germany, people spoke of "telephone justice."[3] That is, a judge hearing a sensitive case would get a phone call from higher authorities, suggesting strongly how the case should come out. Even in a more democratic society, a judge is not independent if bad decisions (bad from the standpoint of the administration) can get the judge demoted, or fired, or transferred to the local equivalent of Siberia.

Autonomous seems to have a somewhat similar meaning, but a rather different nuance. It implies some kind of insulation, not from government or authority, though this may also be the case, but rather from pressures in general, political pressures, social pressures, peer pressures, even the vague, unconscious pressures which crowd in on the judge from society in general, and from his or her own values and attitudes. A judge can be autonomous only if the legal system is autonomous. An autonomous legal system is one that marches to its own drummer. It behaves and grows according to its own internal program,

---

[3] *See* Inga Markovits, *Children of a Lesser God: GDR Lawyers in Post-Socialist Germany*, 94 MICH. L. REV. 2270, 2288 (1996).

free (or relatively free) from considerations of politics, economics, and generally from factors in the surrounding society.[4]

Most people, I imagine, when they think of law, justice, or the rule of law, imagine that the ideal judge combines all three of the traits. He or she is impartial, independent, and autonomous. The public seems to have a hard time with the idea that judges play a creative or a law-making role. The judge is supposed to *do* justice, not make it up. To the ordinary person, it is if some giant book is out there somewhere, a book called "the law," and in it are all possible answers to all possible legal questions. To be sure, it is a hard book to read, since it is written in a kind of foreign language. Indeed, reading that language is one of the things judges are trained to do. They are skilled in finding and reading "the law" in this great big book in the sky. Moreover, whatever is not actually in the book, is not part of "the law." Judges must stay away from all these extraneous matters, above all politics and their own opinions about what is good or bad for the country. Everything outside the pages of the book is strictly off limits.

When it looks as if the Supreme Court is eating forbidden fruit, the public – or parts of it, at any rate – reacts in horror and dismay. When the Supreme Court decided *Brown v. Board of Education*, in 1954,[5] many people mounted a particularly vicious attack on famous Footnote 11. The problem of this footnote was that it cited social science sources. James Reston, in the New York Times, complained that the case "read more like an expert paper on sociology," than a legal opinion; and that it relied "more on the social scientists than on legal precedents."[6] There were those who sneered at the Court as "nine sociologists." In my opinion, that was one of the greatest compliments you could have paid the court, but it was certainly not so intended.[7] Of course, the critics of *Brown* were not really objecting to the footnote for some theoretical reason, or because

---

[4] "An autonomous legal system is one that is independent of other sources of power and authority in social life. Legal action ... is ... influenced only by the preestablished rules of the legal system." RICHARD LEMPERT & JOSEPH SANDERS, AN INVITATION TO LAW AND SOCIAL SCIENCE 402 (1986).

[5] 347 U.S. 483 (1954).

[6] N.Y. TIMES, May 18, 1954, at 14.

[7] It also has been said – and should be obvious – that in fact the famous footnote had little or nothing to do with the actual decision. It was make-weight. If someone had told Earl Warren, while he was writing his opinion, that the works cited in the footnote were no good, and proved nothing, he would have simply left them out. It is impossible to imagine that anything else about the decision would have changed. On footnote 11, see RICHARD KLUGER, SIMPLE JUSTICE 705–706 (1976); Lawrence M. Friedman, Brown *in Context, in* RACE, LAW, AND CULTURE: REFLECTIONS ON *Brown v. Board of Education* 49, 61 (Austin Sarat ed., 1997); Michael Heise, Brown v. Board of Education, *Footnote 11, and Multidisciplinarity*, 90 CORNELL L. REV. 279 (2005).

of their views of judicial esthetics. They were upset by what the justices had actually decided. They merely thought the footnote gave them an additional argument – another reason to criticize the Court. The justices had violated their trust. They had eaten a poisoned apple.

There was a similar rumpus over other high-profile cases that seemed to go beyond the traditional role of judges – decisions based (it was thought) on politics or policy. *Roe v. Wade* was one example;[8] and, very definitely, *Bush v. Gore*.[9] Not everybody, to be sure, is skeptical. The Supreme Court can tap a deep reservoir of trust and support. *Bush v. Gore* seemed to split along ideological or political lines; a simple majority handed George W. Bush the presidency on a silver platter. Yet nearly two-thirds of the public, in a poll, thought that the decision was "mostly based on the legal merits of the case."[10] On the other hand, in another poll, most people expressed the view that ideology, and ideas about "what is good for the public" had a definite influence on Supreme Court decisions.[11]

Social scientists of course almost unanimously reject the traditional and formalistic view of judging. They tend to be quite skeptical about judicial independence or autonomy. They certainly reject any notion of timeless, free-floating neutrality; or that judges simply "follow the law." But social scientists do not agree about which factors influence decision-making (other than "the law") and to what extent. There is evidence – which should surprise nobody – that on many issues in federal courts, Democratic judges and Republican judges reach quite different results.[12] Political party, religion, type of education all have a certain influence on decisions; but how much, and for which courts, and which issues, and in which periods – all this remains largely to be explored.

In the light of the evidence, it is a difficult question, whether judges can be truly impartial, at least in one important sense of the term. I will return to this question. Whether they are, can be, or should be autonomous is also a difficult question. In some ways, the question is similar to the question about impartiality. But there is also a key difference. Just about everybody would agree that an ideal judge should be impartial, or at least try to be. Just about everybody would agree that judicial independence is a good idea; it is also pretty much

---

[8] 410 U.S. 113 (1973).   [9] 531 U.S. 98 (2000).

[10] James L. Gibson, Gregory A. Caldeira, & Lester Kenyatta Spence, *The Supreme Court and the U.S. Presidential Election of 2000: Wounds, Self-Inflicted or Otherwise?*, 33 BRIT. J. POL. SCI. 535, 546 (2003).

[11] John M. Scheb II & William Lyons, *The Myth of Legality and Public Evaluation of the Supreme Court*, 81 SOC. SCI. Q. 928 (2000).

[12] Cass R. Sunstein et al., *Ideological Voting on Federal Courts of Appeals: A Preliminary Investigation*, 90 VA. L. REV. 301 (2004).

a going concern in Western countries, including most certainly the United States. But what about autonomy? In my opinion, if we pay attention to the definition of "autonomy," it seems clear to me at least that judges neither can be nor should be "autonomous."

A. *Judicial Independence*

I said in the last paragraph that independence is more or less a going concern, in the developed world. Independence, after all, can be pretty much ensured by giving judges some sort of tenure, or by putting them more or less on a civil service basis. Anything that insulates the judges from the regime in power adds to their independence. On the other hand, John Ferejohn has distinguished between two meanings of independence.[13] A judge, he says, is independent "if she is able to take actions without fear of interference." This is, basically, close to the definition used here. But he also points out that "a person or an institution [is] . . . dependent" if she or it "is unable to do its job without relying on some other institution or group." In this sense, judges are much less "independent." The federal government pays the salaries of federal judges. The state pays state court judges. Moreover, legislature and executive can tinker with jurisdiction of courts, can cut budgets, can hamstring judges by changing procedural rules, and so on. Legislators can also criticize, abuse, and rail at particular judges and particular decisions. They make use of this great privilege from time to time.[14]

In the United States, the elective system would at least seem to be a serious threat to structural independence. In almost every state, judges have to run for office; the citizens can throw them out of office as well as vote them in.[15] This aspect of our system is particularly surprising to foreigners: the fact that yahoos on the street can decide who sits on the California Supreme Court or the New York Court of Appeals. Even more surprising, perhaps, is that every municipal judge, police court judge, traffic court judge, or justice of the peace gets voted in or out, in most parts of the country.

The reality is a little different. Most judges are not particularly worried about these elections. It is not easy to get rid of a judge at the polls. In fact, the rules, in many states, deliberately make it tough to throw judges out of office on election day. This is the thrust of the so-called Missouri plan; it, or variants of

---

[13] John Ferejohn, *Independent Judges, Dependent Judiciary: Explaining Judicial Independence*, 72 S. CAL. L. REV. 353 (1999).

[14] Recently, right-wing political and religious leaders have been particularly active in denouncing "liberal" judges; and in demanding that something be done.

[15] On the rise of the elective principle, see LAWRENCE M. FRIEDMAN, A HISTORY OF AMERICAN LAW 81–82 (3d ed. 2005).

it, were widely adopted in the twentieth century. Under plans of this sort, the governor appoints the judges. He chooses from a list drawn up by a commission of citizens and lawyers. The appointed judge takes office, and serves until the next election. In many states – California is an example – the judges do not run *against* anybody; the public simply votes ja or nein. There is an old saying that you can't fight somebody with nobody. This works most of the time – the overwhelming majority of judges are re-elected[16] – but there are some notable instances in which Mr. Nobody roundly defeated a very palpable somebody. In 1987, California's controversial chief justice, Rose Bird, was tossed out of office. Enough people voted no to cost her her job; and she dragged down two associate justices with her.[17]

It is undoubtedly true, moreover, that the legislature can undo what a court does, simply by passing a law changing the rule or doctrine (constitutional decisions are an important exception). If a court "interprets" a statute, the legislature can either say, that's not what we meant at all; or simply change its collective mind. Even constitutional decisions can be undone, though this is much, much harder; the amendment process is slow and tortuous, at least at the federal level. But this too has happened on occasion: one good example was the income tax amendment (the 16th), which undid a Supreme Court decision of 1895 which struck down a federal income tax law.[18] Upper court judges can slap lower court judges on the wrists, in the course of reversing their decisions. Bad publicity is another control device that can be used against judges. No judge likes to be criticized. No doubt many judges will hesitate before making a decision, or a statement, that is likely to end up in the newspapers and make them look bad. And this certainly happens, from time to time. Judges who make nasty comments from the bench can be flayed in the local press; judges who seem to be coddling criminals, a most unpopular thing to do, can lose their jobs.

All this is true, but even so, as a practical matter, it does not add up to a serious case of nonindependence. Legislatures can and do change the rules; but most of the time they do not, and even when they do, not many people (or judges) seem to consider this a threat to judicial independence, or even to resent it very much. Mostly, it signals nothing more than a disagreement over policy or tactics. In any event, most judicial decisions have such low

---

[16] Not a single sitting judge lost his or her seat in 1998; and only 50 judges out of some 4,500, between 1964 and 1999. Larry Aspin, *Trends in Judicial Retention Elections, 1964–1998*, 83 JUDICATURE 79 (1999).

[17] LAWRENCE M. FRIEDMAN, AMERICAN LAW IN THE TWENTIETH CENTURY 476 (2002).

[18] Pollock v. Farmers' Loan & Trust Co., 158 U.S. 601 (1895). The 21st amendment repealed the Prohibition amendment (the 18th).

visibility that neither the public nor the legislature pay much attention, one way or the other. The legislature may not even take much notice of decisions that "interpret" the work of that very legislature. And only a few judges get in trouble because they say the wrong thing or make a decision that offends some powerful interest.

In other cases, paradoxically, a legislature finds it hard to overturn the work of the judges precisely *because* the subject is so highly charged. When there is a delicate political balance, a court decision can powerfully shift the burden of going forward. Any change has to come through the legislature; but the subject may be too hot to handle or the forces on this and that side may be evenly balanced. "Accomplishing change," says Ronald Gilson, "is more difficult than merely having to protect the status quo." He gives as an example the unpopular Embarcadero Freeway in San Francisco. This stretch of freeway blocked part of downtown from access to the water. A movement to tear the wretched thing down failed to generate enough strength to get results. Then fate stepped in, in the form of 7.1 on the Richter scale. The Loma Prieta earthquake, in 1989, damaged the freeway so badly that it had to be torn down. Now those who were in *favor* of the freeway had to fight to get it up again. The ball was now in their court; and their efforts failed.[19] Many judicial decisions do what the 1989 earthquake did to the Embarcadero Freeway: they disturb a delicate balance, and shift a heavy burden from one side of an issue to the other. Congress and many of the states would not have been willing or able to pass a law outlawing prayers in public schools. The Supreme Court did exactly that.[20] And Congress, though most members (and the public) dislike the decision, has never been able to muster the strength to turn back the clock.

This freeway effect is even more powerful, of course, in constitutional decisions. It would take a constitutional amendment to put prayer back in the public schools; and amending the constitution is an extremely tough mountain to climb. *Roe v. Wade* on the abortion issue, and *Brown v. Board of Education* itself, are other major decisions which show the power of the freeway effect. There is certainly room to argue about the long and even the short term effects of these decisions,[21] but they do illustrate how an independent judiciary can shift the balance of power. As academics, we can testify to the liberating power of lifetime tenure; and so, no doubt, can the justices of the United States Supreme Court.

[19] Ronald Gilson, *Globalizing Corporate Governance: Convergence of Form or Function*, 49 AM. J. COMP. L. 329, 354 (2001).
[20] Engel v. Vitale, 370 U.S. 421 (1962).
[21] GERALD ROSENBERG, THE HOLLOW HOPE: CAN COURTS BRING ABOUT SOCIAL CHANGE? (1991); Michael Heise, *Litigated Learning and the Limits of Law*, 57 Vand. L. Rev. 2417 (2004).

Legislatures – rivals of the courts in some regards – are much less independent than courts under almost any definition of the term. In the 1950s there was absolutely no hope of persuading Congress to get rid of school desegregation. The southern members blocked any movement toward racial equality; indeed, Congress could not even pass a law outlawing lynching. Congress ultimately did pass a strong civil rights bill, in 1964, but only after a long struggle and a civil rights movement and in general a major social process which *Brown v. Board* undoubtedly helped stimulate.

What about judicial elections? Do they impair the independence of judges? Don't elections put judges in the same position as members of the legislature? Theoretically, yes; but practically, not really. They are not, of course, a factor for federal judges. Federal judges are appointed for life. So too in a handful of states – Massachusetts, notably. Elsewhere, despite a few, lurid examples to the contrary, there are elections; but the judges get re-elected with monotonous regularity, as we pointed out. In short, independence seems to be a working reality. It is possible that the situation may change in the future – elections seem to be getting a bit more partisan. But this is conjecture; and about the future to boot.

Actually, independence is much more than a matter of structure. Culture, perhaps, plays an even more important role. Judging is an honorable profession. The judges wear robes; when they enter the courtroom, everyone rises; judges have about them an aura of dignity and fairness. The fact that so many lawyers are willing to take a pay cut for the title "judge" tells us something about the prestige and respect of the judge. Judging has an honorable tradition, on the whole, in the United States; the respect is not entirely undeserved. In many countries, judges are venal and corrupt, and everybody knows it. The record in the United States is much better than this. In particular, the federal judiciary has a terrific record for honesty. Very few federal judges have ever been impeached. The worst scandal involved Judge Martin Manton, a judge on the Second Circuit, in the 1930s. Manton took bribes, was exposed, tried, convicted, and went to prison.[22] This was quite exceptional, however.

Over time, the aura of the high courts has gotten thicker and more mystical.[23] The Supreme Court in particular seems to be protected by a kind of magic barrier of myth and mystery. Franklin D. Roosevelt, as we all know, came

[22] On the Manton scandal, see GERALD GUNTHER, LEARNED HAND: THE MAN AND THE JUDGE 503–13 (1994).

[23] *See generally*, MICHAEL KAMMEN, A MACHINE THAT WOULD GO OF ITSELF: THE CONSTITUTION IN AMERICAN CULTURE (1986).

to grief with his court-packing plan.[24] Even many New Dealers who hated what the Court was doing jumped ship on this issue. FDR was desecrating something holy. The Supreme Court shies away from publicity; it is an almost impenetrable body; it hires no public relations men, gives no press conferences, and stands almost entirely apart from the hoopla of modern government. But all this probably does the Court more good than public relations would; it helps maintain the air of sanctity and independence. The state high courts inspire a lot less awe, but they also have an excellent record, by and large. Scandal and corruption are mostly matters of the lower courts in big cities. Even here, it is a long time since the days of the Tweed ring. Big city machines are not what they used to be; and big city judges are a lot better than they were.

Judges are not free of controversy now; and, despite the aura, have a long history of controversy. In particular, in the early years of the Republic, the impartiality of the judges (or rather the lack of it) was a serious issue. Some federalist judges were wildly partisan, pontificated on the bench, and made their political views quite obvious. Jefferson, when he came to power, was determined to do something about the problem. During his administration, there was a famous attempt – which failed – to impeach Samuel Chase, a justice of the Supreme Court.[25] In a way, the elective principle that developed was a kind of reaction to the problem of the judges. Electing judges was an admission that judges were important people, who made policy and exercised power. To elect them was therefore one way to keep them under control – to make sure they did what the people wanted. It was a way of curbing the independence of the judges.

But the elective principle in this sense was something of a failure. It never quite did the job. And, in time, it fell into a certain amount of disrepute. For various reasons, elites turned against the elective principle. The strength of the elective principle was that it made judges accountable. This was of course also a weakness. What seemed like a great idea in the early part of the nineteenth century seemed quite different in the late nineteenth century, when men like Tweed ran the big cities, when judges were machine politicians, and millions of immigrants seemed willing to trade political loyalty for a Thanksgiving turkey, a dash of patronage, and a modicum of respect. Some judges were indeed corrupt; and the respectable, old-American jurists thought the whole system of

---

[24] There is, of course, a huge literature on this famous episode. *See generally*, WILLIAM LEUCHT-ENBERG, THE SUPREME COURT REBORN (1995).

[25] *See* RICHARD E. ELLIS, THE JEFFERSONIAN CRISIS: COURTS AND POLITICS IN THE YOUNG REPUBLIC 91–107 (1971); Richard B. Lillich, *The Chase Impeachment*, 4 AM. J. LEGAL HIST. 49 (1960).

local politics, including the election of judges, was thoroughly despicable. The Missouri plan, and other such schemes, were in essence schemes to preserve the form of the elective principle, while gutting the substance.

On the whole, I think, it is fair to conclude that judges of the United States are about as independent as anyone has a right to expect. Nobody is perfect; and neither is any institution. We can grant Ferejohn's point; yes, government pays the judges salaries, and can abolish their offices. But in practice neither of these seems to interfere seriously with what we understand to be judicial independence. Judges have done things that frustrate, annoy, and even defy the officials who make out their checks; they are experts at biting the hand that feeds them. I will move on, then, to the other two prongs of my triangle. Are the judges autonomous? Here my answer will be a fairly resounding no. And are they impartial? Here my answer is also no, but in a more qualified and nuanced way.

B. *Judicial Autonomy*

I will begin with the issue of autonomy. Put in crude terms, the question is this: how do judges decide cases? Do they simply follow the law? Is judging simply a matter of craft and training, so that the attitudes and views of particular judges are irrelevant? This is a much vexed and much debated question. We have already referred to a few of the studies that have tried, more or less, to answer the question.

The research tends to focus on difficult and controversial cases. But even on high courts these cases are a minority. For lower courts, they are rare indeed. Most of the time, as far as we can tell, judges of all political stripes, outlooks, backgrounds, and philosophies, tend to come to the same *legal* conclusions in ordinary cases. But social norms, forces, currents, and structures are powerful agents of decision-making, which are refracted prismatically through the minds of the judges. Judge Black and Judge White will come out the same, in most instances, not because the legal system is autonomous, but because the judges are contemporaries, breathe the same air, live in the same country, and share the same social milieu.

There will be other cases, of course, where differences in attitudes and values do make for differences in "legal" results. Before the civil rights era, southern (white) judges and northern (white) judges came out quite differently in race-sensitive cases. Today there are judges of all races; and it is an interesting question whether they differ systematically in their decisions on issues of race. Again, do women judges behave the same as men judges? If in general they do, are there differences in cases of rape or sexual harassment? And, if judges come out quite differently, is it because of social factors, such as race and gender, or is it mostly a matter of *individuals* and their psychological make-up?

Some writers talk about the partial autonomy of law. The question is where the center of gravity lies. Is it in law, or in the social milieu? My own guess is that the center of gravity lies more in the direction of the social milieu. I have to concede a certain amount of autonomy for the legal system; but think it is a small amount, is easy to exaggerate; and that nonautonomy on the whole has the better case. Even deciding "according to the law" does not necessarily make a case for autonomy. After all, "the law" itself is a social product.

Judges tend to describe themselves, on the whole, in formalist terms. They talk about themselves – and probably think of themselves – as part of an autonomous system. The judge must decide according to the law. Making policy? No: that job is for the legislature. Stirling Price Gilbert, a justice of the Supreme Court of Georgia, put it this way, in his autobiography: "No informed judge will dispute the rule that courts are never concerned with what ought to be the law. Their concern is to correctly rule what the law is." Gilbert also quoted from a 1944 resolution of the Texas Bar Association, denouncing the Supreme Court (even before the *Brown* case), and asserting that the Court should remain "free of political, personal, and unworthy motives," and should interpret and declare the law "as it is written, according to tradition and precedent."[26]

What are we to make of statements like this (and there are countless examples)? Henry R. Glick interviewed high court judges in four states, New Jersey, Massachusetts, Louisiana, and Pennsylvania, in a study published in 1971.[27] He asked the judges whether "nonlegal" factors were important to them in deciding cases. The judges in New Jersey said yes; the judges in Louisiana said no. My guess is that most judges would answer more along Louisiana lines than along New Jersey lines.

On the other hand, social scientists and realistic law scholars know that judges *do* make policy; they make policy all the time. This seems both obvious and inevitable. The policy-making function is particularly true for high profile cases; and most cases before the United States Supreme Court are high-profile cases. It would be almost insulting to give examples; there are far too many of them. It is also obvious that outcomes vary with the values and attitudes of particular judges. Otherwise, why would anybody care who gets on the Supreme

---

[26] Stirling Price Gilbert, A Georgia Lawyer: His Observations and Public Service 147, 149 (1946).
[27] Henry R. Glick, Supreme Courts in State Politics: an Investigation of the Judicial Role (1971).

Court? And why would Roosevelt have wanted to pack the Court? But every-body knows that Scalia and Thomas are not the same as Ginsburg or Stevens.

As we have already seen, there is an interesting and fairly substantial body of research that has tried to find out what impact certain variables – political party membership, for example – have on decisions, in both high and low courts, on church and state, environmental protection, and a broad range of issues. Some of the studies *do* find significant variation in results, correlated with the variables they tested; there is dispute, however, about exactly how much the variables explain – is it a lot, or something more modest.[28] But what about the way the judges describe themselves; what about their vigorous denials that they pay attention to anything but "law." Are they simply fooling themselves? Or are they fooling us – hiding behind a screen, like the Wizard of Oz? Are they naive? Or disingenuous? All of these are possible. Are they mouthing sentiments about autonomy because they feel they are supposed to? Possibly. But maybe, if you recite pious platitudes long enough, you may come to believe them. These are, after all, the safest sentiments to have. If you have been nominated for a federal judgeship, and are about to be grilled by hostile Senators, you had better espouse the most naive positions imaginable – that is, if you want to be confirmed.

Is it possible, too, that the judges are simply wrong about what they do and how they do it? Yes. It must seem like colossal gall for a professor, who has never been a judge, and never will be, to claim to read the minds of judge, or to tell these men and women that they are mistaken about themselves and their work. Yet we are all capable of blindness about ourselves. Specifically, we tend to assume much more autonomy, in our ordinary lives, than we actually have. We constantly make decisions that, in our view, are totally our own, when in reality they are nothing of the sort. It is like buying clothes off the rack. We are sure this shirt or this dress is entirely our own choice. Nobody forced us to buy; it's our taste, our decision entirely. And in a sense it is. But we have no control over *what* shirts or dresses are for sale. And our ideas of what is nice or fashionable is affected by forces we do not understand, and are hardly even aware of. Thousands of families name their children Justin or Dustin or Tracy or Casey, something they decide for themselves, without compulsion. But why do these names sound appealing? There are so many aspects of our lives that we take for granted. Perhaps only a brilliant anthropologist, looking in on us from outside, studying our tribe for years and years, can come to know how

---

[28] For a discussion, see Gregory C. Sisk & Michael Heise, *Judges and Ideology: Public and Academic Debates about Statistical Measures*, 99 Nw. U. L. Rev. 743 (2005). *See also* Cass Sunstein et al., *supra* note 12.

indeterminate our determinate decisions really are; and how determinate the seemingly indeterminate.

Decision-making, I think, is a two-stage process for judges, whether they know it or not. First comes the decision whether to be "formalist" or not. That is, most of the time, judges do in fact decide to look for the better "legal" argument; or find that argument persuasive. Yet this decision itself is socially determined. What makes a case seem cutting edge, rather than cut and dried? What makes a judge think one case will be socially significant, and another of no consequence except to the litigants? These too are socially determined. Factors outside "the law" make a judge feel (consciously or unconsciously) that a case calls for something other than merely following "the rules," or sticking to "precedent."

To most of us, it seems really obvious that cases are significant if they're about abortion rights, or whether the Constitution allows us to execute a 17-year old. It would also seem obvious which cases are totally routine. But these are, of course, social judgments. Doctrines, arguments, judgments are all products of their times. Culture, history, politics determine which ones seem reasonable or persuasive, and which ones do not. The arguments in *Plessy v. Ferguson*,[29] which justified segregation of the races, strike us today as both wrong and pernicious. But eight Supreme Court justices at the time felt otherwise.

I don't mean to suggest that a judge *literally* says or thinks: this is really significant; I had better cast a wider net. But judges are not deaf and dumb; they are not newborn babies. They read the newspapers, they know what is and what is not controversial, and they know or think they know which cases might create an uproar; and which simple tort or contract cases might affect nobody except the immediate parties. These feelings surely affect the process of deciding; or deciding how to decide. The more sophisticated judges know this. Over a century ago, Stephen Field, who later served on the United States Supreme Court, put it this way: "[W]e cannot shut our eyes to matters of public notoriety. When we take our seats on the bench we are not struck with blindness, and forbidden to know as judges what we see as men."[30]

In any event, so long as there are some decisions where the judge, consciously or not, brings in "nonlegal" considerations, then *all* decisions in a sense have this quality. That is, the decision to be formalist or "legal" is not dictated by the law itself; but by other factors. That a judge can choose to be legalistic, or

---

[29] 163 U.S. 537 (1896).
[30] Ho Ah Kow v. Nunan, 12 F. Cas. 252, 255 (1879). The case concerned the "Queue Ordinance," which required cutting off the queue of prisoners in San Francisco. The ordinance was supposed to be a health measure; but Field called that a "mere pretense"; the true purpose was to inflict extra punishment on the Chinese.

not, and to what degree, means, paradoxically, that in a real sense no decision is formalist or mechanical, even when the judge thinks it is, and when it reads that way.

The most powerful decisionmaker then is the framework of norms and values and ideas floating about in society. Of course, this is not an easy proposition to prove. "Social norms" are not clear-cut, simple, and universal entities. There are perhaps some ideas, values, and attitudes that just about everybody in society shares, more or less. But there are also, in any given culture, quite a range of norms, values, ideas, attitudes, and feelings. We have conservative judges and liberal judges and all sorts of gradations in between. We have judges who are conservative on this issue and liberal on that issue and vice versa. The judges can be arranged along various dimensions, so as to form a nice, ordinary bell-shaped curve. This would be true in any generation; but what is important is that the bell curve itself travels and shifts and moves through space and time.

Thus, the most conservative Supreme Court justice today is far more liberal on issues of race than the most liberal justice of the nineteenth century. Compare the majority and minority opinions in *Plessy v. Ferguson* with any recent Supreme Court decision on race – even if the modern decision is one which (for example) rejects affirmative action. In *Plessy*, there was one dissenter, John Marshall Harlan. But Harlan, who seemed so far ahead of his time, uses language when he talks about race that would be considered racist today. Ironically, conservative justices today pay homage to Harlan. They like to use (misuse, I think) Harlan's phrase about a color-blind constitution; in fact they trot out this phrase as an excuse for getting rid of preferences for minorities. But they are conservative only about these preferences, about arrangements which (they think) give minorities *more* rights than white people; none of them would be willing to go back to segregation – to a situation, almost universal a century ago, where racial minorities had *less* rights than white people.

Similarly, with regard to issue after issue: take censorship and pornography. The most conservative justice or judge today would allow things to be printed, spoken, or shown, that could never get by the most liberal judge of a century ago. We know it when we see it, but what we know and see today is not what we knew or saw in, say, 1850; or even 1930. Legal arguments that were persuasive in the past seem ridiculous today; arguments made today are taken seriously that would have been laughed off the boards in the past, or rejected in shock.[31] Would anybody today argue seriously to the Supreme Court or a state high court that the 14th Amendment outlaws a minimum wage law? Nobody a century ago would have argued for gay rights, or even *mentioned* such an

[31] On this point, see Lawrence M. Friedman, *Taking Law and Society Seriously*, 74 CHI.-KENT L. REV. 529 (1999).

idea as a constitutional right of privacy, which includes the right to condoms, abortions, and consensual same-sex relations.

We know, too, that "conservative" and "liberal," to take these two crude labels, refer exclusively to *contemporary* conservatives and liberals. Chief Justice Rehnquist, as a young clerk to Justice Robert Jackson in 1952–53, wrote a memo of "random thoughts" in which he stated, quite baldly, that he thought *Plessy v. Ferguson* "was right and should be re-affirmed."[32] Later, in 1971, when Rehnquist had been nominated to the Supreme Court, he claimed that the memo was not really what *he* thought, it just reflected Jackson's "tentative views"; he told the Senate "I fully support the legal reasoning and the rightness . . . of the *Brown* decision."[33] I doubt that he was being completely candid. But in any event, he recanted whatever views he once had on the subject of school segregation and the *Plessy* case. The world marches on. People change. The obvious becomes dubious, the dubious obvious. Conservatives fell all over themselves praising Clarence Thomas, a right wing black man nominated to the Supreme Court in 1991. Thomas was married to a white woman. Two or three decades earlier, Clarence Thomas would have been excoriated for this behavior, and could even have gone to prison in some states; miscegenation was against the law.[34] For generations, interracial marriage was totally taboo. Avoiding the dangers of "mongrelization" was one of the strongest arguments the South could advance against anything that smacked of racial equality.

All of this suggests, quite strongly, a point that should be obvious to everybody except some lawyers and judges; judges are not and cannot be truly autonomous. Their apparent autonomy is either a legend or an illusion. If it is a legend, it is, of course, a legend that many judges firmly believe in. Or perhaps judges take it as an ideal: something difficult to get to, but worth striving for. But Dorothy is never going to reach this Emerald City.

I do not want to overdo the point. Autonomy and non-autonomy are not either-or propositions. There may be degrees and gradations. Some judges may be more inclined to look for a "legal" answer than others; and, as I have suggested, all judges often do so, simply as a matter of indifference or indecision. In some periods, there may be more autonomy than in other periods. Certainly, different fields of law, in any given society, may evoke different responses from judges. Moreover, there are undoubtedly real differences between high courts

---

[32] For the text of this memo, see N.Y. TIMES, Dec. 9, 1971, at 26.
[33] *Id.*
[34] The Supreme Court swept the last of these laws aside in *Loving v. Virginia*, 388 U.S. 1 (1967); and the decision was unanimous. Loving, who was white, had married a black woman; the laws of Virginia made such marriages a crime.

and lower courts. Lower courts may have less leeway than the courts that sit in judgment on top of them.

But even this is far from obvious. Lower courts do not publish their decisions. Most cases never get appealed. In practice, then, trial court judges have a good deal more freedom in practice than they enjoy in theory. Trial courts may be able to get away with matters that a high court would find more troublesome – just as the jury, which deliberates in secret and gives no reasons for its decisions, has a kind of freedom, a suppleness, that judges, who have to justify what they do, may lack.

Do these remarks hold mainly for the common law countries and their judges? Are civil law courts more bound by laws and legal traditions than common law courts? This is a common understanding (or misunderstanding).[35] In those countries, there is a strong prevailing myth: judges do not, cannot, and should not make law. They are nothing more than mouthpieces of the (statutory) law. The *theory* in civil law countries assigns judges to a much more subordinate role than the *theory* in common law countries. The practice is another question. It is difficult to measure the performance of civil law judges (or any judges) in a rigorous way. Their lack of autonomy is probably just as illusory as the analogous belief in the common law system. One thing seems clear, even in the civil law world: the times are changing, and with it, theories of judicial role and behavior. Judicial review, for example, has been sweeping the civil law world. A court, like the German constitutional court, which has the power to invalidate acts of the German parliament, is not a bashful court; it does not behave the way civil law courts traditionally behaved. It has more power, and it exercises it. The activist *lower* court judge has also made a startling appearance, in recent years, in Italy and Spain, to take two prominent examples. In both countries, judges have been raising a tremendous stir. It is enough to refer to the *mani pulite* (clean hands) campaign by the judges in Italy;[36] and the Pinochet affair coming out of Spain.[37]

C. *Impartiality*

I turn now to our third term, impartiality. Here again our approach has to be somewhat careful; the word can be used in a number of senses. "Impartial," in one simple but important sense, means nothing more than *honest*. A judge

---

[35] John Henry Merryman, The Civil Law Tradition 34–38 (2d ed. 1985).

[36] David Nelken, *The Judges and Political Corruption in Italy*, 23 J. L. & Soc'y 95 (1996).

[37] *See* David Sugarman, *The Pinochet Precedent and the 'Garzón Effect': On Catalysts, Contestation and Loose Ends*, Amicus Curiae, July–Aug. 2002, at 10.

like Judge Manton, who took bribes, was certainly not impartial. In this regard, American judges do very well on the scale of impartiality. Most of them try to deal fairly with the litigants; they will recuse themselves if they see some sort of conflict of interest.

But judges most certainly have prejudices, presuppositions, attitudes, points of view, and so on; and the question is, to what extent do these affect the outcome of cases? Here impartiality tends to merge in meaning with autonomy. The line between "bias" and "responsiveness to social norms" is extremely slippery and hard to draw. A judge who always decides in favor of rich against poor, or poor against rich, or black against white, or white against black, is not "impartial." But what about a judge who thinks economic efficiency is really important; so that he or she always tries to reach the more efficient result? Or the judge who thinks it is right to give the benefit of the doubt, in borderline cases, to the underdogs? Is such a judge impartial? One fairly crude way to draw the line might be this: a *conscious* tilt makes a judge less impartial; an *unconscious* tilt makes the judge less autonomous.

We have already referred to the literature on judicial decision-making. Scholars have tried to find out whether such factors as age, race, sex, background, education, or political party make a difference in decision-making. This is not easy research; in part it is often hard to say whether some result is liberal or conservative, or pro- or anti-labor, for example. Also, judges, like most human beings, are complicated and at least partly unpredictable. In addition, it is impossible to tell, in most cases, whether what is measured is judicial impartiality or judicial autonomy. That is, we may be able to find some sort of tilt or tendency; but it is much harder to tell whether the tilt is conscious or not, or what brings it about.

Either way, whether attitudes are conscious or not, we *know* that they matter, at least for some kinds of decisions. Otherwise, we would be unable to distinguish William Rehnquist from William Brennan. After all, we *can* predict, pretty well, how Scalia and company will vote on certain issues. The judges sometimes like to fool us, but we are right much more often than we are wrong. It makes a difference who gets to sit on the Supreme Court, and on the federal courts (and state courts) in general. And everybody knows this.

D. *The Time Dimension*

Judging is obviously a somewhat different enterprise in different societies. It is also an enterprise that changes over time. In the United States, Karl Llewellyn thought he detected a master historical narrative: judging moved from what he called the Grand Style to the Formal Style and back again (he hoped) to the Grand Style. The Grand Style judges were sensitive to policy, and boldly innovative. They brushed aside technicality, cited few "authorities," and worried about the social consequences of their decisions. The Grand Style flourished in the first half of the nineteenth century. John Marshall, Lemuel Shaw, and James Kent were among the great Grand Style judges. The Formal Style judges were wooden, literal, and conceptual; they hid their personalities behind strings of citations. They were deliberately formalist. These judges, according to Llewellyn, flourished in the last half of the nineteenth century.[38]

Another account, which centers a good deal on the Warren court, comes in a right wing and a left wing version. The left wing version is that activist conservative courts did a lot of mischief in the late nineteenth century, and in the first few decades of the twentieth century. The Supreme Court was one of the worst offenders; it handed down reactionary decisions in cases like *Lochner v. New York*[39] and *Hammer v. Dagenhart*.[40] The justices hated organized labor and consistently thwarted the will of the people. These justices also made trouble for Roosevelt and the New Deal; and they scuttled a good deal of his program.[41] But then came activist liberal courts, starting from the dates of the late New Deal. These courts tried to make our national ideals a reality. They struck down race discrimination and sex discrimination; they expanded the rights of criminal defendants. When liberals talk about this period, on the whole they leave out a discussion of the will of the people. The whole point was to protect the unpopular and the suffering. During the *Lochner* era, the "people" were workers, and the underclass. Now we begin to hear about the tyranny of the majority. The liberal heroes are the judges of the Warren court; the Burger and Rehnquist courts meet with far less approval.

The right wing version of the story praises the old courts as sound and sensible. They did their best to protect property rights and help a stable economy. They upheld the Constitution, and honored traditional values. Then came

---

[38] Karl N. Llewellyn, *Remarks on the Theory of Appellate Decision and the Rules or Canons About How Statutes Are to Be Construed*, 3 Vand. L. Rev. 395 (1950).

[39] 198 U.S. 45 (1905). In this case, the Supreme Court voided a New York statute regulating the hours of work of bakers.

[40] 247 U.S. 251 (1918). Congress had enacted a law which tried to keep goods which were the product of child labor out of the stream of interstate commerce. The Court struck this statute down, by a 5 to 4 vote.

[41] For example, in *Schechter Poultry Corp. v. United States*, 295 U.S. 495 (1935), the Court declared the National Industrial Recovery Act unconstitutional.

the fire-eating liberals, and Earl Warren, and upset the apple-cart. The liberals did some good things (nobody dares criticize the *result* in *Brown v. Board of Education*),[42] but they did a lot of bad things too. They decided cases in the criminal justice field – like the *Miranda* case[43] – which tied the hands of the police and favored thugs over citizens. They invented "affirmative action" and allowed discrimination on the basis of race – though this time the discrimination worked against white people. They discovered a mysterious right of "privacy" and did Satan's work on abortion and gay rights. Now it is time, conservatives say, to rein in the judges and restore some sort of balance. The right also claims, as we have seen, that the way to do this is to appoint judges who are "strict constructionists," men and women who will mind their own business and follow the law. But this is probably not really what they mean. What they really want is activism on the conservative side.

Another story, more subtle and complex, but clearly related, is the story told by Max Weber, though of course he was not writing about the United States. Here the progression among legal systems, the grand sweep of history, with regard to law-making and law-finding, evolves or develops from irrationality to formal rationality, which is (roughly speaking) legal autonomy, and the use of strict legal logic.[44] The high point was a legal order that was highly "systematized," a stage in legal development which Weber associated with the great Continental codes of the nineteenth century. But Weber also detected a certain amount of decay in the system. Formal rationality (strict and systematic legal logic) was under pressure from substantive rationality; this meant that judges were taking into account political, social, economic, ethical, and cultural factors.[45] Weber has been dead quite a while; but if he were alive, he would find, I am sure, that the process he described was accelerating.

If Weber is right, then judges were once strongly autonomous, but are evolving away from autonomy. But his account rests on a very flimsy empirical basis. There is really no way to tell whether the formal rationality of the Continental judges was anything more than a facade, or a style of writing opinions. There is no way to go beyond the style. Not even a CAT scan can read minds. Consider

---

[42] There are, however, quite a few who criticize the way the opinion was reasoned or written, or both.

[43] Miranda v. Arizona, 384 U.S. 436 (1966), which laid down rules the police were supposed to follow whenever they arrested someone and sought to interrogate him.

[44] "Irrational" methods are those that "cannot be controlled by the intellect." A prime example would be decisions by oracle, or through the use of trial by battle. MAX WEBER ON LAW IN ECONOMY AND SOCIETY 63 (Max Rheinstein ed., 1954).

[45] *See id.* at 318–21.

the case of Judge Manton, the corrupt judge, mentioned earlier. Take a flock of Manton opinions, some that were bought and paid for, some that were not. Give the opinions to a group of skilled lawyers and law professors. Ask them to find the fakes – the corrupt decisions, the ones that were bought and paid for. It would be next to impossible. But of course, as any lawyer could gladly tell you, a good advocate can always argue either side of a tough contested issue. Any judge with talent can write an opinion on either side of the issue as well – perhaps it would be more accurate to say that any judge can do this if he has the benefit of well-written briefs on both sides. A judge can write an opinion justifying any possible outcome in any case which makes it to the appellate level. This means that we cannot tell if formalist judges were really formalists, or whether this was just their way of playing the game. The high point of formalism was a period in which the work of the judges was controversial; formalism was a safe disguise. This seems true for the judges in Llewellyn's second period; and it was perhaps true as well for the Weber's German jurists of the nineteenth century.

In sum, judges are neither autonomous nor impartial (in the strong sense of this term). Of course, this does not tell us very much about what they actually do, and how and why they do it. What are the social forces that mold their behavior? If we see a kind of liability explosion in the field of torts, as we do, how do we explain it? It happened all over the United States in the twentieth century. It followed more or less the same path in Kansas or Vermont as in California and New York. Was it because of insurance, or the New Deal, or sunspots, or the invention of air conditioning? What lies behind no-fault divorce and rights for people in wheelchairs, and the discovery rules in the code of civil procedure, and the erosion of the at-will doctrine in employment law? All of these, and hundreds more, are questions about legal culture, and about the social, economic, and political forces that bear on the law. None of the questions has an obvious answer. But clearly none of them can be answered in terms of the unfolding of strict legal logic.

On the independence of judges: the question is not whether our judges are independent – on the whole they are. The real question is: what difference does this make? We insulate them from partisan politics, at least to a degree. We do not, cannot, and should not insulate them from the vast glacial and volcanic movements of society. Yet the *structure* of the judiciary does have an influence. Judges behave differently from legislatures. How different, and in what regards? These are, as we suggested, difficult but in principle answerable questions – answerable empirically, of course. Scholars have given us at least some tentative answers. A lot more research needs to be done. Legal scholars, alas, are not very good at answering empirical questions. They are intoxicated by the heady liquor of what they consider big ideas. They tend too to look down on "mere empiricism"; it is slow, time-consuming, and you might, God forbid, have to know something about statistics. Moreover, in the world of the law schools, the way to get ahead, to get a name for yourself, is to float some vast normative balloon. It is likely, then, that only social scientists can come to the rescue. Some already have.

8 Judicial Independence in a Democracy: Institutionalizing Judicial Restraint

John Ferejohn and Larry D. Kramer

The Constitution establishes the judiciary as a co-equal department of the federal government and protects its members from political interference by granting them life tenure and prohibiting Congress from reducing their salaries. Yet Congress is free to decide whether to create lower federal courts at all, to define their jurisdiction narrowly or widely, to establish rules of procedure, and to determine the size of the judiciary's budget. Moreover, federal courts are not only staffed by presidential nominees, they must also rely on the executive branch to enforce their judgments. From this perspective it is hard not to agree with Alexander Hamilton who noted in Federalist 78 that the judiciary, having neither purse nor sword, is the "least dangerous branch." Hamilton, it must be said, offered this as assurance to those who feared the new constitution might establish independent and unaccountable judges as threats to liberty. But he surely worried that the complex ways in which federal judges were embedded in the political structure and their dependence on the political branches might undermine their capacity to withstand political pressures.

A contemporary observer might be forgiven for thinking, after two centuries of practice, that these concerns about the independence of the federal courts were overblown. Starting with its clever and cautious stance in *Marbury v. Madison*, the Supreme Court has proved more than capable of protecting its institutional powers relative to the other branches and, even more, relative to the state governments. Indeed, from a practical standpoint, the Court has gone well beyond mere independence to assert a position of "supremacy" over the Constitution that was not even imaginable to Alexander Hamilton or John

This chapter is a substantially revised version of *Independent Judges, Dependent Judiciary: Institutionalizing Judicial Restraint*, 77 N.Y.U L. REV. 962 (2002).

Marshall. The domain of law has, of course, grown immeasurably since the Founding. And the judiciary has grown with it – expanding immensely in size and importance. There are nearly a thousand federal judges and twenty times that many at the state level, and these judicial legions have not shied from involving themselves in every aspect of public and private life. Partly as a result, the whole court system has become more organizationally complex and more capable of creating general rules in the context of particular disputes. Neither the Founders nor their opponents could have envisioned something like today's three tier federal judiciary, which is formally structured to enable the Supreme Court to eschew worrying about the need to correct errors in individual cases in order to focus on shaping legal and constitutional policy generally and regulating the sprawling judicial leviathan.

As the Anti-Federalist Brutus saw, the question of judicial independence is inseparable from the question of the power of the judiciary relative to the other parts of government, and relative to the people themselves. To create independent judges is to risk creating a government of judges rather than law, a system that fits poorly in a democracy. There are ways in which judges need to be responsive to democratic forces. Certainly they ought to apply legitimately-enacted statutes and they ought not to claim unauthorized jurisdiction or ignore congressional impeachments. Independence must be balanced with accountability: a ticklish sort of problem.

We try to develop a theory of judicial independence that accounts for the restraints that federal judges actually face. But while this is ultimately a surprisingly complex task, the necessary first steps seem clear. To begin, we need a workable definition of judicial independence and an accurate description of the institutional arrangements through which it may be accomplished. With a better understanding of how our system of judicial independence actually works, we can begin to explore what, if anything, makes these arrangements stable and to address normative questions about whether judges have too much or too little independence.

In Parts I and II, we consider what independence is meant to accomplish. We argue that independence and accountability are not ends in themselves. Each is a *means* toward a more fundamental goal: the construction of a well-functioning judiciary within the constitutional order. That either or both must be sacrificed to a degree simply is not a problem if done in the service of this objective. Of course, this dual concern for both independence and accountability necessitates a complex institutional design. The constitutional scheme, therefore, mixes various structural arrangements – some protecting the independence of judges, others making them accountable – in an effort to create a properly balanced judicial system.

Parts III and IV examine how the balance between independence and accountability in the federal system is maintained by a system that protects individual judges from direct outside interference while making the institution in which they work vulnerable to control by the political branches of government. This institutional dependence requires that the judiciary is a self-regulator: it has created a system of self-imposed institutional and doctrinal constraints that keep judges within the bounds required by institutional vulnerability. The resulting equilibrium usually works well enough that the political branches seldom need to exercise their power or even to threaten doing so. We will demonstrate that the specific mechanisms operating to control or regulate federal judges include a variety of judicially-created doctrines not usually thought of in connection with judicial independence.

I. INDEPENDENCE AND ACCOUNTABILITY: PROTECTING THE ADJUDICATORY PROCESS

What *do* we mean when we talk about the need for judicial independence? Everyone agrees that we need "decisional independence," meaning the judges' ability to adjudicate facts and interpret law in particular cases "free from any outside pressure: personal, economic, or political, including fear of reprisal,"[1] at least as long as judges are likely to decide cases according to acceptable legal standards. Everyone also agrees that certain forms of popular or legislative contribution are not only permissible, but indispensable. If the legislature changes the applicable law, for example, judicial decisions obviously ought to reflect this fact. But what about "branch independence"? Is the judiciary free "to operate according to procedural rules and administrative machinery that it fashions for itself through its own governance structure"?[2] Or may the other branches play a role in determining rules and procedures? And how about other forms of political influence such as judicial elections? Most of the states have decided that judges can be made to run for election or retention and even be subject to recall. Is this an interference with judicial independence that undermines the judiciary's capacity to render justice? Or is it a recognition that our judiciaries operate in a democratic setting and that well-crafted regulations do not threaten independence in an important way?

---

[1] Archibald Cox, *The Independence of the Judiciary: History and Purposes*, 21 U. DAYTON L. REV. 566, 566 (1996).

[2] Gordon Bermant & Russell R. Wheeler, *Federal Judges and the Judicial Branch: Their Independence and Accountability*, 46 MERCER L. REV. 835, 845 (1995).

A shortcoming of conventional notions of judicial independence is that they conflate various threats to the adjudicatory process. In particular, they fail to distinguish between corruption of the political process – failures of political agency that lead politicians or other powerful actors to interfere in adjudication for their own private purposes – and endemic properties of popular government that may undermine judicial independence. Recall that James Madison's most profound insight was that the greatest threat to justice in a republican system comes from the most democratic parts of the government:

> Wherever the real power in a Government lies, there is the danger of oppression. In our Governments, the real power lies in the majority of the Community, and the invasion of private rights is *chiefly* to be apprehended, not from acts of Government contrary to the sense of its constituents, but from acts in which the Government is the mere instrument of the major numbers of the constituents.[3]

As Madison saw, majoritarian pressures are especially threatening to judicial independence in a republic,[4] and because (as Tocqueville noted later) these pressures may be "total" in pervading civil society (through the media, for example, or "public opinion") as well as being expressed in ordinary political processes.[5] The principle underlying judicial independence calls for hindering undue political pressures of *every* kind, and especially majoritarian pressures, if they would interfere with a well-functioning judiciary by distorting its decision-making process.

At the same time, the majority is entitled to influence adjudication in certain ways. Judicial independence in a democracy requires proper accountability as well as strict protections for adjudication. Making judges independent of politicians and other lawmakers frees them from certain foreseeable pressures to ignore the "law" in rendering a judgment but it also frees them from acceptable pressures to follow properly enacted laws and, in this way, liberates them to make law in ways that may itself be problematic. If no one is empowered to judge the judges, what do we do about lawless courts and irresponsible judging?

---

[3] Letter from James Madison to Thomas Jefferson (Oct. 17, 1788), *in* 11 THE PAPERS OF JAMES MADISON 295, 298 (Robert A. Rutland et al. eds., 1978). "This is a truth of great importance," Madison continued, "but not yet sufficiently attended to. . . . " *Id.* Madison was, in fact, baffled and frustrated by the failure of his fellow Framers and Founders to grasp this axiomatic point. *See* Larry D. Kramer, *Madison's Audience*, 112 HARV. L. REV. 611, 678 (1999).

[4] Majorities are the most serious problem for judges not because they are more likely to interfere than corrupt officials, but because they are incorrigible within a democratic system, whereas official corruption can be discovered and corrected.

[5] *See Symposium on Judicial Independence*, 25 HOFSTRA L. REV. 703–815 (1997), which explores the problem of media criticism of judges and their decisions.

The question of judicial accountability can be broken down into two further problems. The first is simply the danger that judges will act for improper reasons. Judges have friends and financial interests and ideologies; they have loves and hates and passions and prejudices just like the rest of us. How do we prevent judges from ignoring or misapplying the law for their own inappropriate reasons? The second issue springs from realist-inspired insights concerning law's indeterminacy. No one really believes that law is wholly indeterminate, but virtually everyone recognizes that modern jurisprudential tools create a range of legitimate choices in almost any given case. And even those who believe in objectively "right answers" appreciate that the process by which these answers are generated hinges on arguments and judgments of a kind about which reasonable people can (and will) subjectively disagree.[6] Even two judges of superhuman intelligence, each of whom is completely free of cognitive biases, will predictably produce systematically different outcomes in litigated cases. Yet we have no purely *legal* grounds for preferring one set of results to another, no consensus within the legal community on "the" one true jurisprudence. In this way, a judge's choice of methodologies and his or her exercise of discretion are imbued with an inescapably political dimension, which justifies a claim that the majority ought to have a say over what courts do.[7]

Questions about whether the Constitution demands "branch" or "decisional" independence are thus revealed as instrumental and pragmatic, rather than matters of principle pertaining to some free-standing concept of judicial independence. To secure a well-functioning judiciary within a democratic constitutional scheme, we can choose among a varied assortment of institutional alternatives to achieve multiple overlapping goals. One catches a glimpse of just how broad the range of strategic possibilities is from surveying the different approaches taken in our federal Constitution and in the fifty states.[8] These utilize everything from judicial elections to civil-service protections to life tenure, from impeachment to judicial self-discipline to removal for

---

[6] The classic argument here would be RONALD DWORKIN, TAKING RIGHTS SERIOUSLY 126–30 (1977).

[7] This problem is most acute when it comes to constitutional interpretation, because it is so much more difficult to overturn the courts' decisions, but insofar as legislative overruling is not transaction-costs free, the same concern exists in the domain of statutory interpretation and common-law adjudication.

[8] For surveys, see ANTHONY CHAMPAGNE & JUDITH HAYDEL, JUDICIAL REFORM IN THE STATES (1993); HARRY P. STUMPF & JOHN H. CULVER, THE POLITICS OF STATE COURTS 14–35 (1992); Paul D. Carrington, *Judicial Independence and Democratic Accountability in Highest State Courts*, 61 LAW & CONTEMP. PROBS. 79, 113–25 (1998).

cause, from independent judicial budgetary control and rulemaking authority to administration through the executive branch and legislatively prescribed rules of procedure, from deferential review of decisions rendered by independent executive agencies to *de novo* appellate review to jurisdiction stripping. The number of possible arrangements is endless, though differences in actual systems are surely generated by historical accident and indigenous cultural traits as often as through deliberate constitutional engineering. Accordingly, our task in the remainder of this paper is to explain how the balance between independence and accountability is maintained within the United States federal judiciary.

II. THE FEDERAL SYSTEM: ACCOUNTABLE INSTITUTIONS, PROTECTED JUDGES

We argue that the federal system's basic strategy for balancing independence and accountability is to protect individual judges while making the court system democratically accountable in various ways. Life tenure and salary protection – together with potent cultural norms stemming from colonial history and the Framers' outspoken determination to make national judges secure[9] – give individual federal judges generous protection from essentially all forms of direct coercion. These independent agents are, at the same time, situated within an institution that is exposed and vulnerable to a wide array of controls by the political branches. The ability of Congress to control such things as the judiciary's budget and jurisdiction creates opportunities for a trenchant political response to objectionable judicial behavior. As a result, individual judges are subjected only to *indirect* pressure through threats to deprive the courts of resources or to curtail their jurisdiction. The tools available to Congress are

---

[9] State constitutions adopted after 1776 generally gave judges more independence than they had under British rule, particularly by providing for them to hold office during good behavior. *See* WILLI PAUL ADAMS, THE FIRST AMERICAN CONSTITUTIONS 266–71 (Rita Kimber & Robert Kimber trans., Univ. of N.C. Press 1980); MARC W. KRUMAN, BETWEEN AUTHORITY AND LIBERTY: STATE CONSTITUTION MAKING IN REVOLUTIONARY AMERICA 122–23 (1997). Experience during the Confederation period and an emerging new conception of the courts' role in separation of powers led to greater appreciation of the need for a strong and independent judiciary, and the Framers of the Constitution made federal judges especially secure. GORDON S. WOOD, THE CREATION OF THE AMERICAN REPUBLIC 1776–1787, at 453–56 (1998); Charles Gardner Geyh & Emily Field Van Tassel, *The Independence of the Judicial Branch in the New Republic*, 74 CHI.-KENT L. REV. 31, 35–48 (1998). According to Gerhard Casper, "by comparison with all the state constitutions, Article III represents the extreme solution: an appointed judiciary serving at a guaranteed salary for life, subject only to impeachment. Not a single state constitution had gone that far." GERHARD CASPER, *The Judiciary Act of 1789 and Judicial Independence*, in SEPARATING POWER 132, 137–38 (1997).

cumbersome and blunt, and federal lawmakers can seldom make pinpoint attacks directed at specific judges or particular decisions. Instead, political pressure from Congress or the executive (or the public, for that matter) tends be exerted on a wholesale basis – a reaction to accumulated grievances or general trends – rather than aimed at overturning particular judgments.[10]

The pressure can nevertheless become quite intense, its mere threat a cause for anxiety. Judges are, generally speaking, a cautious lot, which is hardly surprising for officials whose decisions deal with controversial public matters but who lack access to most normal channels for acquiring political capital. The judiciary's capital is intellectual and reputational, limited to what it can acquire through effective job performance, and the sort of thing that quickly wears thin in the face of persistent criticism.[11] Consequently, the mere threat of political retribution from Congress has, we argue, turned the judiciary into an effective self-regulator – a point we will attempt to substantiate in Part III. Federal judges have concocted an impressive body of doctrinal limitations, creating a buffer zone that minimizes their chances of stepping heedlessly into political thickets. Obviously the federal judiciary sometimes finds itself at the center of controversy, but less often than one might expect given the degree of individual autonomy offered its members. Indeed, if federal courts have sometimes managed to be effective in controlling politics, this may be attributable partly to the fact that their interventions are so rare: the product of a politically astute, institutional self-abnegation.[12]

III. MECHANISMS OF POLITICAL CONTROL

As noted above, individual judges are generally well guarded from direct political punishment or pressure. The only means by which Congress can penalize

---

[10] There are obvious exceptions. Truly high profile cases in the Supreme Court – the occasional *Roe v. Wade* or *Brown v. Board of Education* – may have immediate and specific political repercussions. But the structure of judicial protection in the federal system makes this a rare event. More typical is political resistance to a course of decisions rendered over a period of years, as happened, for example, with the criminal procedure decisions of the Warren Court or the substantive due process cases of the *Lochner* era.

[11] All the more inasmuch as judges cannot ethically take to the airwaves to respond publicly to criticism of their decisions. *See* MODEL CODE OF JUDICIAL CONDUCT CANON § 3(b)(9) (1998); Stephen J. Fortunato, Jr., *On a Judge's Duty to Speak Extrajudicially: Rethinking the Strategy of Silence*, 12 GEO. J. LEGAL ETHICS 679, 685–90 (1999).

[12] This basic idea is familiar from ALEXANDER BICKEL, THE LEAST DANGEROUS BRANCH: THE SUPREME COURT AT THE BAR OF POLITICS (1962), though Bickel's analysis was confined to the Supreme Court and consisted more of exhortation than any kind of institutional explanation of an observable phenomenon.

a particular judge's errant behavior is through impeachment,[13] a largely tooth-less threat used in practice to remove judges only when extreme misconduct can be proved.[14] There is another means by which politicians can influence individual judges, though it consists of a carrot rather than a stick and is con-trolled by the President rather than Congress. We mean, of course, the promise of promotion to a higher court. Presidents can – and today most often do – select Supreme Court Justices and circuit court judges from the ranks of sit-ting circuit and district judges,[15] giving rise to concern that potential nomi-nees may change their behavior on the bench to please the President or his advisors.[16]

Another check on the judiciary is in the hands of the executive. The judi-ciary can accomplish nothing unless the executive branch enforces its orders, a point that "has not been lost on the federal executive or on the states and their executives."[17] In practice, Presidents have usually backed even controver-sial rulings from the Court, though state governors have been more willing to stare the Court down.[18] Andrew Jackson apparently ignored judicial mandates in two cases involving the Cherokee Indians (leading to an apocryphal story that has Jackson grumbling about how John Marshall should enforce his own

[13] *See Hearings of the National Commission on Judicial Discipline and Removal* app. B at 20–21 (1993) (concluding that any statutory provision for removing Article III judges by means other than impeachment, or for diminishing the salary even of criminally convicted Article III judges, would be unconstitutional).

[14] Whether impeachment was originally meant to be quite this inconsequential is uncertain. Some of the Framers spoke against including any power to impeach in the Constitution for fear that such power could be exploited for political purposes. *See* THE FEDERALIST NO. 65 (Alexander Hamilton) at 439–45; JACK N. RAKOVE, ORIGINAL MEANINGS 260–61, 264–65 (1996). Once the decision to include impeachment had been made, however, the Founding generation's history and experience probably led them to anticipate more frequent resort to the device than has been true in practice. *See* PETER CHARLES HOFFER & N. E. H. HULL, IMPEACHMENT IN AMERICA, 1635–1805, at 1–95 (1984).

[15] *See* DEBORAH J. BARROW ET AL., THE FEDERAL JUDICIARY AND INSTITUTIONAL CHANGE 22–23, 89–90, 94–96 (1996); Daniel Klerman, *Nonpromotion and Judicial Independence*, 72 S. CAL. L. REV. 455, 460–61, fig. 1 (1999).

[16] There is some evidence, mostly anecdotal, to justify this fear. *See* Mark A. Cohen, *Explaining Judicial Behavior or What's "Unconstitutional" about the Sentencing Commission?*, 7 J. L. ECON. & ORG. 183, 188–89 (1991); Mark A. Cohen, *The Motives of Judges: Empirical Evidence from Antitrust Sentencing*, 12 INT'L REV. L. & ECON. 13, 27 (1992).

[17] Stephen B. Burbank, *The Architecture of Judicial Independence*, 72 S. CAL. L. REV. 315, 323 (1999).

[18] *See* DWIGHT WILEY JESSUP, REACTION AND ACCOMMODATION: THE UNITED STATES SUPREME COURT AND POLITICAL CONFLICT, 1809–1835 (1987); Leslie Friedman Goldstein, *State Resis-tance to Authority in Federal Unions: The Early United States (1790–1860) and the European Community (1958–94)*, 11 STUD. AM. POL. DEV. 149 (1997).

decisions).[19] But, as Barry Friedman has pointed out, Jackson's travails with the Court took place when the struggle over judicial review was still young, and Jackson stood behind the Court when more controversial questions threatening the Union were at stake.[20] With the notable exception of the Lincoln Administration, moreover, subsequent Presidents have shied away from following Jackson's example. Lincoln ignored an order by Chief Justice Taney to release a prisoner in *Ex parte Merryman*,[21] and his cabinet (under Andrew Johnson) gave equally scant respect to the Supreme Court's command in *Ex parte Milligan* that military trials cease.[22]

While Presidents may rarely ignore orders of the Supreme Court, executive enforcement of politically unpopular decisions is often willfully lackluster – even in the face of widespread disregard for the Court's mandate. The failure of the desegregation cases to accomplish anything until political winds changed and a new President and Congress made civil rights enforcement a priority is well known.[23] The Court's school prayer decisions are still ignored in many parts of the country,[24] and continued resistance to *Roe v. Wade* has left abortion unavailable as a practical matter in many places.[25] Additional instances can easily be documented and multiplied, particularly if we look to the treatment of lower court decisions. The federal bench is quite sensitive to the danger of half-hearted executive support – as indicated, for example, by the Supreme Court's savvy handling of the remedial issue in

[19] *See* Worcester v. Georgia, 31 U.S. (6 Pet.) 515 (1832); Cherokee Nation v. Georgia, 30 U.S. (5 Pet.) 1 (1831). Barry Friedman draws even this example into question, observing sensibly that "there is some question, first, whether there was anything in either case for the Executive to enforce and second, whether Jackson felt he had the practical ability to enforce the mandate." Barry Friedman, *The History of the Countermajoritarian Difficulty, Part One: The Road to Judicial Supremacy*, 73 N.Y.U.L. Rev. 333, 400 (1998). On whether Jackson made his famous remark to John Marshall, see Richard P. Longaker, *Andrew Jackson and the Judiciary*, 71 Pol. Sci. Q. 341, 349 (1956).

[20] Friedman, *supra* note 19, at 394–404.

[21] 17 F. Cas. 144 (D. Md. 1861) (No. 9487). *See* Carl Brent Swisher, Roger B. Taney 550–56 (1935).

[22] *Ex parte* Milligan, 71 U.S. (4 Wall.) 2 (1866); Mark E. Neely, Jr., The Fate of Liberty 176 (1991) ("[T]he *Milligan* decision had little practical effect. It was written in thunderously quotable language . . . [but d]espite unmistakeable condemnation, trials by military commission continued.").

[23] *See* Gerald N. Rosenberg, The Hollow Hope 42–82 (1991).

[24] *See* Robert S. Alley, Without a Prayer 21–24 (1996); Frank S. Ravitch, School Prayer and Discrimination 3, 73 (1999).

[25] *See* Janet Hadley, Abortion: Between Freedom and Necessity 1–17 (1996); Mira Weinstein, *Who Still Has a Choice?*, Nat'l NOW Times (Nat'l Org. for Women, Washington, D.C., 1998), <www.now.org/nnt/01-98/roe.html>.

Brown II[26] – and judges are conscious that they should not take executive backing for granted. Moreover, the mere threat of executive nonenforcement can be a powerful deterrent. The precariousness of the judges' standing in this political equilibrium is underscored each time a high executive official attacks the federal bench for acting politically or, as Attorney General Edwin Meese did in the mid-1980s,[27] publicly muses about resurrecting Lincoln's position on the limits of judicial authority.

If relatively few devices are available that can target judges or their decisions, a great many more can be directed at the institution of the judiciary as a whole. These include the appointment power, which affords the political branches of government – and especially the President, in whose hands this power chiefly lies – considerable leverage to shape (or reshape) the bench.[28] Court-packing in the dramatic fashion of FDR's notorious gambit may be off the table for now, but more subtle forms of court-packing – such as adding judgeships to the lower courts or making ideologically driven appointments – have long and distinguished pedigrees in American politics.[29] The beauty of using appointments to control the bench is that it fosters democratic accountability without

[26] Brown v. Bd. of Educ., 349 U.S. 294 (1955). *See* Robert B. McKay, *"With All Deliberate Speed":* *A Study of School Desegregation*, 31 N.Y.U.L. Rev. 991, 999–1000 (1956).

[27] Edwin Meese III, *The Law of the Constitution*, 61 Tul. L. Rev. 979, 984–85 (1987).

[28] *See* Barry Friedman, *"Things Forgotten" in the Debate over Judicial Independence*, 12 Ga. St. U. L. Rev. 737, 763 (1998). In recent years, Congress has tried to limit the President's control over appointments by refusing to approve his nominees, hoping thus to force a compromise on who is nominated. The big losers in this game, apart from the nominees (who may be put through the ringer for several years), are the other federal judges, who find themselves deprived of much-needed assistance in coping with an expanding caseload. Such are the costs of divided government.

[29] *See* Barrow et al., *supra* note 15, at chs. 2–5. Court packing got off to an early and rocky start in the Judiciary Act of 1801, which (among other things) created numerous new positions to be filled by the already defeated Federalist President John Adams. Richard E. Ellis, The Jeffersonian Crisis 15–16 (1971). Jefferson later complained bitterly about Adams's willingness to make these appointments, saying that it was "personally unkind" of Adams to appoint some of Jefferson's "most ardent political enemies" in this fashion, and that "[i]t seemed but common justice to leave a successor free to act by instruments of his own choice." Letter from Thomas Jefferson to Abigail Adams (June 13, 1804), *in* 8 The Writings of Thomas Jefferson 306, 307 (Paul Leicester Ford ed., G. P. Putnam's Sons 1897). The Republican response to the Federalist scheme – which included not only the impeachment of Samuel Chase, but also a controversial law firing the newly appointed judges by abolishing their court – probably constituted the most serious assault on judicial independence in American history. *See* Ellis, *supra*, at 3–52, 76–82; Geyh & Van Tassel, *supra* note 9, at 77–85. Interestingly, court packing survived the controversy and has thrived, while the Jeffersonian remedy of abolition soon faded into disrepute. *Cf., e.g.,* William S. Carpenter, Judicial Tenure in the United States 78–100 (1918) (discussing Congress's rejection of the option to fire judges when their court is abolished in dealing with the short-lived Commerce Court).

in any way threatening judicial independence: the political branches have a regular means to keep the bench in line with prevailing attitudes, but individual judges are immune from further pressure or obligation once they have been appointed.[30] The weakness of the appointment power in this regard is that turnover rates for federal judges are often low – approximately three percent per year in the 1990s[31] – which makes this an undependable method for fine-tuning the judiciary's political complexion. Past practice indicates that increasing the size of the judiciary can be used to enhance the effectiveness of using appointments to change or control the federal bench, especially during periods when one of the two major parties controls both Congress and the Presidency.[32]

When we turn to Congress, moreover, we find a richer array of tools available with which to rein in a rambunctious judiciary.[33] Surely the most important of these is Congress's control over the budget – no less effectual in subduing the third than the second branch.[34] The gravity of this power in respect to the

---

[30] Bear in mind that gratitude and the sense of obligation most of us naturally feel toward our patrons can be a motivating force. Judge Kozinski, for example, has candidly acknowledged his continuing sense of duty to those who appointed him:

It doesn't happen every time I write an opinion, but every so often I come to a close case and I ask myself the question: "Would Ed Meese approve?" . . . The question, for me, isn't what the actual Ed Meese thinks. The question is: Am I living up to be the kind of judge the people who appointed me thought they were appointing? Am I the kind of judge I represented myself to be?

Alex Kozinski, *The Many Faces of Judicial Independence*, 14 Ga. St. U. L. Rev. 861, 865 (1998). Writers of legal mythology like to focus on renegades like Justices Brennan or Blackmun (though whether and to what extent either of these Justices really were renegades is a complicated issue), but the kind of thinking divulged here by Judge Kozinski is surely far more common.

[31] *See* Richard A. Posner, The Federal Courts 31 (1996); Harry P. Stumpf, American Judicial Politics 208–10 (2d ed. 1998); Emily Field Van Tassel, Why Judges Resign: Influences on Federal Judicial Service, 1789–1992, at 9 (1993).

[32] Barrow et al., *supra* note 15, at 90–96. The appointments process as a device for controlling the judiciary has also been enhanced at times by politically astute judges, who timed their retirements to ensure that they were replaced by someone who was ideologically compatible. *Id.* at 94.

[33] *See* David P. Currie, *Separating Judicial Power*, 61 Law & Contemp. Probs. 7, 11–12 (1998). *Cf.* Friedman, *supra* note 28, at 758 ("[t]he list [of devices tried to control courts] is long").

[34] *See* Bermant & Wheeler, *supra* note 2, at 848–50. Although the judicial budget makes its way to Congress via the executive Office of Management and Budget (OMB), the President is obliged by statute to forward the judiciary's request without change, and by long tradition executive branch officials do not even comment on the judicial proposal. 28 U.S.C. § 605 (2002); 31 U.S.C. § 1105(b) (2002); John M. Slack, *Commentary, Funding the Federal Judiciary*, 82 W. Va. L. Rev. 1, 8 (1979). Indeed, the OMB provoked a firestorm of protest from the judiciary in 1993 when it packaged the judiciary's submission to Congress along with its own budget and budget-cutting proposals, which included an 18 percent cut in the judicial budget. Bermant & Wheeler, *supra* note 2, at 849.

judiciary has grown over time, as the federal bench changed from a modest operation into today's massive bureaucracy, which oversees extensive facilities across the country and boasts a nonjudicial staff in excess of 30,000.[35] Judges must worry about funds to keep this machine running, and especially to hire capable staff and supply them with adequate resources (which include computer and research support, courthouse security, storage facilities, press offices, and much more). With these additional needs has come increased sensitivity to how the judiciary's budget is dealt with in Congress.[36] Judicial administrators are acutely conscious of competing for resources with other agencies and departments of government,[37] and the judiciary has already witnessed how budget cuts can wreak havoc on its ability to manage the caseload.[38] Even putting aside the power of Congress to inflict de facto pay cuts on judges by declining to adjust their salaries for the cost of living,[39] an underfunded court is a distinctly unpleasant place to work.

Of almost equal importance to the budget is Congress's power to define the subject-matter jurisdiction of the federal courts. Scholars continue to debate the extent to which federal legislators can withhold jurisdiction conferred in Article III,[40] but there is no need to rehearse their excruciatingly technical arguments, because even the most aggressive readings of Article III recognize that Congress has wide latitude to regulate the business of the federal courts.[41] That allowed, most discussions of congressional regulation dwell on laws that deprive federal judges of power to hear a particular case or class of cases because of its controversial nature, or what has come to be known as "jurisdiction stripping."

---

[35] Judith Resnik, *Judicial Independence and Article III: Too Little and Too Much,* 72 S. CAL. L. REV. 657, 663, 668 (1999).

[36] *See* JUDICIAL CONFERENCE OF THE U.S., LONG RANGE PLAN FOR THE FEDERAL COURTS 85–96 (1995) [hereinafter LONG RANGE PLAN]; Bermant & Wheeler, *supra* note 2, at 847; Deanell Reece Tacha, *Independence of the Judiciary for the Third Century,* 46 MERCER L. REV. 645, 648 (1995).

[37] *See* Richard S. Arnold, *Money, or the Relations of the Judicial Branch with the Other Two Branches, Legislative and Executive,* 40 ST. LOUIS U. L. J. 19, 22–26 (1996) (former chairman of the Judicial Conference's budget committee describing various problems in protecting the judicial budget from executive and congressional cost-cutting plans).

[38] *See* Tacha, *supra* note 36, at 650 ("[D]epending on the difficulties of any particular budgetary year, courts have had to suspend civil trials and civil juries, cease to pay appointed defense attorneys, and engage in a host of temporary budget-shifting mechanisms.").

[39] *See* Am. Bar Ass'n, *An Independent Judiciary: Report of the ABA Commission on Separation of Powers and Judicial Independence* pt. 2, 1997 A.B.A. SEC. REP. 28–29, <http://www.abanet.org/govaffairs/judiciary/report.html> [hereinafter ABA Report].

[40] For a discussion of the range of views on this question, see RICHARD H. FALLON, JR. ET AL., HART & WECHSLER'S THE FEDERAL COURTS AND THE FEDERAL SYSTEM 358–87 (4th ed. 1996).

[41] *Id.*

Congress's record in this domain is perplexing from a political perspective and uncertain from a legal one. Several efforts were made to curtail Supreme Court review of state court judgments during the Marshall era, but none was enacted.[42] Early in Reconstruction, a more aggressive Congress successfully divested the Supreme Court of appellate jurisdiction in habeas corpus cases, acting specifically to prevent the Court from deciding the then-pending case of *Ex Parte McCardle*.[43] But while the Court appeared to submit to this flagrant battery by dismissing McCardle's petition and agreeing that Congress could regulate its appellate jurisdiction, the Justices snuck in a technical loophole that left the case's meaning equivocal.[44] Subsequent events have done little to clarify matters, mainly because further examples of similar legislation are hard to find. There is the Norris-LaGuardia Act, which called a halt to federal judicial interference in labor organizing by narrowly restricting the courts' authority to award injunctive relief in cases "involving or growing out of a labor dispute."[45] But every other effort to enact legislation depriving federal judges of jurisdiction for the purpose of undoing a controversial ruling has failed. According to one group of influential commentators, "[a]t least since the 1930s, no jurisdiction-stripping bill has become law."[46] Failed bills represent a virtual (albeit incomplete) honor roll of controversial twentieth century rulings and include proposals to deprive federal judges of power to review everything from the admissibility of confessions in state criminal cases,[47] to the use of busing as a remedy in school desegregation cases,[48] the apportionment of state legislatures,[49] laws regulating or restricting subversive activities,[50] laws regulating abortion,[51] and laws permitting school prayer.[52]

The chronic failure of these efforts to divest federal courts of jurisdiction could easily mislead one into believing that Congress cannot, as a practical

---

[42] *See* Gerald Gunther, *Congressional Power to Curtail Federal Court Jurisdiction: An Opinionated Guide to the Ongoing Debate*, 36 STAN. L. REV. 895, 896–97 (1984).

[43] *Ex parte* McCardle, 74 U.S. (7 Wall.) 506 (1868). *See* 6 CHARLES FAIRMAN, THE OLIVER WENDELL HOLMES DEVISE: HISTORY OF THE SUPREME COURT OF THE UNITED STATES 459–66 (1971).

[44] While dismissing the pending appeal because Congress had repealed the provisions of the Habeas Corpus Act of 1868 under which the appeal had been brought, the Court suggested that it could still review habeas cases brought before the Court under section 14 of the Judiciary Act of 1789 (74 U.S. at 515) – a suggestion upon which it soon acted in *Ex parte Yerger*, 75 U.S. (8 Wall.) 85 (1868).

[45] 29 U.S.C. §§ 101–105 (2002).   [46] FALLON ET AL., *supra* note 40, at 351.

[47] *See* S. 917, 90th Cong. (1968).

[48] *See* S. 3388, 92d Cong. (1972); H.R. 13916, 92d Cong. (1972); H.R. 13915, 92d Cong. (1972).

[49] *See* H.R. 11926, 88th Cong. (1964).   [50] *See* S. 2646, 85th Cong. (1957).

[51] *See* H.R. 867, 97th Cong. (1981).

[52] H.R. 326, 97th Cong. (1981); H.R. 865, 97th Cong. (1981).

matter, effectively control federal judges by regulating their jurisdiction. But this takes too narrow a view of jurisdiction stripping by confining it to retaliatory measures crudely aimed at specific rulings. Looked at more broadly, we see that Congress routinely dispossesses federal courts of authority to hear cases or award remedies because of concern for how the judges might rule or in order to circumscribe their ability to interfere with congressional objectives. The discussion below, which canvasses a number of examples without by any means offering an exhaustive inventory, should suffice to convey the breadth and significance of congressional involvement in policing federal jurisdiction – and its potential importance for a branch of government that hardly relishes having its authority curtailed.[53]

Perhaps the most striking congressional actions are those which limit the authority of courts by taking them away from federal courts altogether. To this end, federal lawmakers have constituted a variety of non-Article III tribunals – so-called legislative or Article I courts – to adjudicate federal claims and interpret and apply federal law. Congress has never pursued a systematic strategy of using these courts, but it has over the years employed them in a variety of important contexts.[54] Familiar examples from the past include the old territorial courts, which heard claims in the federal territories prior to statehood, and the Court of Customs Appeals, which had a monopoly over disputes involving tariffs and trade duties.[55] More recent and still functioning examples of non-Article III courts include the Tax Court, the Claims Court, the Court of International Trade, the courts of the District of Columbia, and bankruptcy judges.[56] Taken together, this is hardly an insignificant portion of federal business.[57]

---

[53] This entirely natural posture is evident from the vociferous but predictable opposition of federal judges to any measure that threatens their stature. Indeed, the whole elaborate planning process within the Judicial Conference is mainly an effort to preserve the dignity and prominence of the federal courts from potential diminution by Congress. *See* LONG RANGE PLAN, *supra* note 36.

[54] For an excellent discussion of these and other specialized courts (some of which are Article III courts), see Rochelle Cooper Dreyfuss, *Specialized Adjudication*, 1990 BYU L. REV. 377 (1990).

[55] *Id.* at 383 n.14, 389–91.   [56] *Id.* at 383 nn.13–14, 384–88, 402–05.

[57] Creating an Article I court does not enable Congress to escape independent judicial scrutiny altogether. The Constitution requires that rulings of legislative courts be subject to at least minimal appellate review in an Article III tribunal (though the law respecting how much review has become Dickensian in its intricacy). Having begun with the very reasonable, and reasonably coherent, decision in *Crowell v. Benson*, 285 U.S. 22 (1932), the Court has in recent years handed down a series of complicated and confusing opinions that are a delight for teachers of federal courts but a nightmare for everyone else. *See* Granfinanciera, S.A. v. Nordberg, 492 U.S. 33 (1989); Commodity Futures Trading Comm'n v. Schor, 478 U.S. 833 (1986); Thomas v. Union Carbide Agric. Prods. Co., 473 U.S. 568 (1985); Northen Pipeline Constr. Co. v. Marathon Pipe Line Co., 458 U.S. 50 (1982).

But the largest evasion of judicial processes occurs though congressional delegations of authority to executive agencies to interpret law and adjudicate disputes. There is, in truth, little or no difference between a legislative court and an executive agency with respect to the power to implement and apply law, unless it is that agencies often have even greater authority than Article I courts. In addition to conducting formal adjudication, many agencies have substantial rulemaking and prosecutorial responsibilities. We take no position on the validity or desirability of this practice. We merely note that, as a result, an immense proportion of federal law can be interpreted and applied by polit-ical bodies, subject only to the most limited sort of appellate review in an Article III tribunal.[58] We find it noteworthy as well that, while these delega-tions may once have been defended on grounds of scientific or bureaucratic expertise, contemporary theory frankly acknowledges the political nature of the practice.[59]

Finally, Congress has undertaken direct management of the federal judiciary by regulating court rules and procedures. That federal lawmakers have this power has never been in issue. Five days after passing the First Judiciary Act, Congress followed up by directing federal courts in each state to apply the same procedures in actions at law "as are now used or allowed in the supreme courts of the same [state]."[60] Two-and-a-half years later, Congress opted for a different solution in equity: because some states had not yet developed any substantial equity practice, Congress instructed federal judges to follow settled "rules and usages" of equity courts – subject, however, to "such regulations as the Supreme Court...shall think proper from time to time by rule to prescribe."[61] With minor variations, this system remained in force for more than a century. In 1912 the courts began to claim the right to produce its own regulations. In that year the American Bar Association, with vigorous support from Chief Justice Taft, launched a determined campaign to extend the Supreme Court's rulemaking authority to actions at law.[62] Political opposition from a variety of directions

---

[58] In some instances, such as prison reform litigation and immigration law, Congress has even found ways substantially to impede or even to deny reviewability. *See* Illegal Immi-gration Reform and Immigrant Responsibility Act of 1996, Pub. L. No. 104–208, 110 Stat. 3009–3546 (codified as amended in scattered sections of 8 U.S.C.); 18 U.S.C. § 3626(e)(2) (2002) (imposing special procedural requirements on injunctions regarding prison conditions).

[59] *See, e.g.*, Richard B. Saphire & Michael E. Solimine, *Shoring Up Article III: Legislative Court Doctrine in the Post* CFTC v. Schor *Era*, 68 B.U. L. REV. 85, 91 (1988).

[60] Act of Sept. 29, 1789, ch. 21, § 2, 1 Stat. 93.   [61] Act of May 8, 1792, ch. 36, § 2, 1 Stat. 275.

[62] *See* Edson R. Sunderland, *The Grant of Rule-Making Power to the Supreme Court of the United States*, 32 MICH. L. REV. 1116, 1116–17, 1123–24 (1934). ABA interest had first been stirred five years earlier by Roscoe Pound's famous speech on "The Causes of Uncertainty and Delay in the Administration of Justice." This prompted the formation of a committee to make appropriate

confounded these efforts until 1934, when the Rules Enabling Act was finally adopted.[63] The Supreme Court approved its first set of rules (including one that merged law and equity) four years later, and for the next half-century the federal judiciary was responsible for making and revising its own procedures with little congressional interference or involvement.[64]

All that changed in the early 1980s, when Congress "unexpectedly began to flex its legislative muscle in the procedural rulemaking arena."[65] Impatient with how certain problems were being handled by courts and by the Judicial Conference, Congress stepped in to impose its own solutions. Two developments in particular merit brief discussion. First, congressional dissatisfaction with criminal sentencing led to administratively-formulated guidelines under the Sentencing Reform Act of 1984,[66] together with a number of separately-enacted, mandatory minimum sentences for particular offenses.[67] The judicial reaction to these laws has been predictable: judges almost uniformly abhorred the guidelines, which the Supreme Court recently declared unconstitutional,[68] and they detest mandatory minimum sentences – viewing both as ill-conceived meddling by legislative interlopers.[69]

recommendations for procedural reform. *See* Edgar Bronson Tolman, *Historical Beginnings of Procedural Reform Movement in This Country – Principles to Be Observed in Making Rules*, 22 A.B.A. J. 783, 784 (1936).

[63] Rules Enabling Act, Pub. L. No. 73–415, 48 Stat. 1064 (1934). On opposition to the Act, see CHARLES E. CLARK ET AL., HANDBOOK OF THE LAW OF CODE PLEADING § 9, at 35 (2d ed. 1947). For a detailed recounting of the entire legislative history, see Stephen B. Burbank, *The Rules Enabling Act of 1934*, 130 U. PA. L. REV. 1015 (1982).

[64] The Federal Rules of Evidence are an important exception, as political divisions within the bench and bar, together with certain other unusual circumstances, drew Congress in – though the federal legislature ultimately made few changes of significance to the original draft approved by the Supreme Court. *See* 21 CHARLES ALAN WRIGHT & KENNETH W. GRAHAM JR., FEDERAL PRACTICE AND PROCEDURE § 5006 (1977).

[65] Linda S. Mullenix, *Judicial Power and the Rules Enabling Act*, 46 MERCER L. REV. 733, 735 (1995) [hereinafter Mullenix, *Judicial Power*]. *See also* Linda S. Mullenix, *Hope Over Experience: Mandatory Informal Discovery and the Politics of Rulemaking*, 69 N.C. L. REV. 795, 798–800 (1991).

[66] Pub. L. No. 98–473, 98 Stat. 1987 (codified as amended at 28 U.S.C. §§ 991–998 (2002)).

[67] *See, e.g.*, Anti-Drug Abuse Act of 1986, Pub. L. No. 99–570, 100 Stat. 3207; *Federal Prison Population: Present and Future Trends, Hearings Before the Subcomm. on Intellectual Prop. & Judicial Admin. of the House Comm. on the Judiciary*, 103d Cong. 15 (1993).

[68] *See* United States v. Booker, 125 S. Ct. 738 (2005); Blakely v. Washington, 542 U.S. 296 (2004).

[69] *See* FEDERAL JUDICIAL CENTER, PLANNING FOR THE FUTURE: RESULTS OF A 1992 FEDERAL JUDICIAL CENTER SURVEY OF UNITED STATES JUDGES 15, 37 (1994). According to Judge José Cabranes, that the sentencing guidelines leave trial courts with some discretion only makes matters worse: "produc[ing] a game of tug of war between the bureaucracy and the bench, as the Sentencing Commission struggles to incorporate or repudiate the exceptions articulated by individual judges or appellate courts." Judge José Cabranes, Address at the University of Puerto Rico Law School (Oct. 1993), *in Cabranes Rips Sentencing Rules*, LEGAL TIMES, Apr. 11, 1994, at 17.

A second example of congressional interference in judicial procedure is the Civil Justice Reform Act of 1990 (CJRA),[70] enacted by Congress to address "mounting public and professional concern with the federal courts' congestion, delay, expense, and expansion."[71] This controversial law – in the words of one critic, the "most sweeping procedural rule reform since promulgation of the federal rules in 1938"[72] – takes authority away from the Judicial Conference's Civil Rules Advisory Committee and places it instead in the hands of ninety-four district-level committees acting pursuant to a statutorily-prescribed case-management policy. On a superficial level, this looks like just one more instance of policymaking devolution, consistent with a more general political trend that began around 1980.[73] Against the background of twentieth-century developments in procedure, however, the Act also represents a significant "redistribution of the procedural rulemaking power from the federal judicial branch to the legislative branch."[74] The Judicial Conference, in its Long Range Plan for the Federal Courts, spoke forthrightly in its opposition to this sort of congressional activity – noting that it is "troubling . . . that bills are introduced in the Congress to amend federal rules directly by statute, bypassing the orderly and objective process established by the Rules Enabling Act." The judges beseeched Congress "at the conclusion of the period of experimentation and evaluation" prescribed by CJRA to allow the judiciary to resume "promoting nationally uniform rules of practice and procedure" through its own familiar processes.[75] Bowing to pressure from Congress, the Judicial Conference said it was willing to "enhance outside participation" in the process, but clearly the Conference regards its rulemaking authority as an important facet of judicial independence.[76] Articulating a sentiment widely shared among judges, Linda Mullenix explains:

> A judiciary that cannot create its own procedural rules is not an independent judiciary. Moreover, a judiciary that constitutionally and statutorily is entitled to create its own procedural rules, but must perform that function

---

[70] Civil Justice Reform Act of 1990, Pub. L. No. 101–650, 104 Stat. 5089.

[71] LARRY D. KRAMER, REPORT OF THE FEDERAL COURTS STUDY COMMITTEE 3 (1990). The Civil Justice Reform Act grew directly out of the report issued by the Federal Courts Study Committee (FCSC), created by Congress in 1989 to investigate these problems and recommend reforms. *See id.* at 31.

[72] Mullenix, *Judicial Power, supra* note 65, at 737.

[73] *See* Keith E. Whittington, *Dismantling the Modern State?: The Changing Structural Foundations of Federalism*, 25 HASTINGS CONST. L. Q. 483, 505 (1998).

[74] Linda S. Mullenix, *The Counter-Reformation in Procedural Justice*, 77 MINN. L. REV. 375, 379 (1992).

[75] LONG RANGE PLAN, *supra* note 36, at 58, 59.

[76] *Id.* at 59. *See also* ABA Report, *supra* note 39, at 52–54.

under a constant cloud of congressional meddling and supercession, is truly a subservient, non-independent branch.[77]

IV. JUDICIAL SELF-RESTRAINT

In principle, the various devices available to the political branches to obstruct the courts afford ample means to cow or even cripple the federal judiciary. Life tenure and salary protection would count for little on a bench whose mandates were ignored, whose budgets were reduced to the point where daily administration was impossible, or whose jurisdiction or procedures left judges with little authority or flexibility. Presidents *can* ignore the courts' orders, but they seldom do so. Congress *can* manipulate the budget, the jurisdiction, and the procedures of the federal courts and, as recounted above, federal legislators have occasionally done so. But legislative oversight remains sporadic, its range modest, and it would be fatuous to maintain that Congress has significantly degraded or repressed the federal judiciary. The most one can say is that the political branches have formidable means by which to humble the courts and *could* significantly debase the institution of the judiciary, not that they have done so. Still, to say that Congress and the executive *can* stifle the federal courts is, in our view, to say quite a lot, particularly since the courts boast no comparable power to hit back.[78] If Congress and the executive have seldom exercised their power to impair the judiciary, however, this may be because the judiciary has acted in such a way that Congress and the executive have seldom felt the need to do so. That is, given the judiciary's political weakness relative to the other branches, we should expect it generally to conduct its business in such a way as to minimize the number and severity of any showdowns.

---

[77] Mullenix, *Judicial Power, supra* note 65, at 734.
[78] On this point, we think Alexander Hamilton had it exactly right in *The Federalist* No. 78 when he observed that the Court would be "the least dangerous to the political branches" because it would be "least in a capacity to annoy or injure them." To quote his familiar language:

The Executive not only dispenses the honors, but holds the sword of the community. The legislature not only commands the purse, but prescribes the rules by which the duties and rights of every citizen are to be regulated. The judiciary, on the contrary, has no influence over either the sword or the purse; no direction either of the strength or of the wealth of the society; and can take no active resolution whatever. It may truly be said to have neither Force nor Will, but merely judgment; and must ultimately depend upon the aid of the executive arm even for the efficacy of its judgments.

THE FEDERALIST No. 78, at 522–23 (Alexander Hamilton) (Jacob E. Cooke ed., 1961). If the Court seems more powerful than Hamilton here prophesies, this may be, as we suggest below, because of its careful husbanding of political capital and its attentiveness to signals from the political branches.

This pattern of judicial deference can be illustrated by a sequence of events early in our history. There was considerable uncertainty about the proper role of federal judges during the early years of the Republic, and an overly-politicized Federalist bench provoked a major crisis by 1800.[79] Lawyers have tended to fix their attention on *Marbury v. Madison*,[80] celebrating it as some sort of triumph for judicial supremacy, when in fact *Marbury* was a rearguard action by a Court in full flight after a ruthless political offensive. Much more important at the time were the impeachments of Pickering and Chase and the Judiciary Act of 1802 – in which Congress made clear its determination to put the federal bench in its place by abolishing a number of newly-created judgeships and firing the judges, by delaying a Supreme Court sitting for over a year, and by restoring the despised ordeal of circuit-riding.[81] The actual resolution of the crisis was reflected not in *Marbury*, which passed by with little fanfare,[82] but rather in the Court's meek submission to this congressional mugging in *Stuart v. Laird*[83] and in the cessation of open politicking by Federalist judges.[84] The resulting settlement, which left the Supreme Court much more deferential to Congress (though not to the states), endured for many decades. And, while interbranch relations have obviously evolved since then, they have on the whole been relatively stable, subject as predicted to periodic, brief crises (of which 1856 and 1937 are the most famous, with another one possibly brewing right now).

Our general thesis is, then, that the judiciary will conduct its business in ways designed to stave off political confrontations. What is especially interesting in this regard is the manner in which it is accomplished. A judiciary staffed by hundreds of judges, each with life tenure and an irreducible salary, cannot trust its individual members always to act discreetly – cannot, that is, count on them all to avoid trouble by exercising Alexander Bickel's famous "passive virtues."[85] Safety requires institutional and doctrinal barriers that reduce the need for judges to attend to such matters in each case. We divide the judiciary's

---

[79] *See* ELLIS, *supra* note 29, at 1–35; DUMAS MALONE, JEFFERSON THE PRESIDENT: FIRST TERM, 1801–1805, at 110–56 (1970).

[80] 5 U.S. (1 Cranch) 137 (1803).

[81] ELLIS, *supra* note 29, at 36–52; 2 GEORGE LEE HASKINS & HERBERT A. JOHNSON, THE OLIVER WENDELL HOLMES DEVISE: HISTORY OF THE SUPREME COURT OF THE UNITED STATES 151–63 (Paul A. Freund ed., 1981).

[82] ELLIS, *supra* note 29, at 65–67.

[83] 5 U.S. (1 Cranch) 299 (1803). *See* ELLIS, *supra* note 29, at 53–68; Dean Alfange, Jr., Marbury v. Madison *and Original Understandings of Judicial Review: In Defense of Traditional Wisdom*, 1993 SUP. CT. REV. 329, 362–365 (1993).

[84] *See* ELLIS, *supra* note 29, at 69–75; KEITH E. WHITTINGTON, CONSTITUTIONAL CONSTRUCTION: DIVIDED POWERS AND CONSTITUTIONAL MEANING 20–65 (1999).

[85] BICKEL, *supra* note 12, at 111–98.

self-policing devices into two main categories. On the one hand are mechanisms of internal discipline that operate to correct individual judges when they ignore or misapply established rules and practices. On the other are principles of jurisdiction or justiciability that operate to remove whole categories of cases from federal judicial cognizance. Rather than merely ensuring that law is properly applied, these principles withdraw potentially controversial issues from direction by the federal courts, leaving them to be addressed in other fora.

A. *Internal Discipline*

Two principal devices serve this purpose for the federal judiciary. First and foremost, of course, is the process of appellate review. Appeals reduce the risk posed by wayward judges by ensuring that multiple judicial voices are heard before any particular judgment becomes final. As Barry Friedman notes, the federal system provides an appeal as of right to the Court of Appeals, thus ensuring that at least four judges will consider any objectionable decision.[86] But that is not all, he adds, for:

> there are en banc hearings in divisive or difficult cases, and, for truly important cases, the Supreme Court is always available. The fact of the matter is that many, many judges might review a case. The more controversial the decision, the likelier it is that a great amount of judicial review will follow. This collective judgment is very valuable. It may be divided at times, and those times may cause controversy, but by the time the appellate process is complete, many judges will have spoken.[87]

The effectiveness of appellate review is not simply a matter of giving more than one judge an opportunity to rule, though this is undoubtedly important. As Lewis Kornhauser and Lawrence Sager have convincingly argued, the development of an appellate hierarchy with collegial courts at the higher levels and stringent rules of vertical stare decisis operates structurally to ensure that no individual judge can, by his or her actions alone, inflict too much damage on the judiciary by making aberrant or overly ambitious decisions.[88] Beyond even this, horizontal stare decisis among the district and circuit courts is relatively weak, while the Supreme Court seldom hears an issue that has not had time to percolate in the lower courts and is generally reluctant to ignore what a strong majority of those courts has decided. As a result, even within this hierarchical

---

[86] Friedman, *supra* note 28, at 763.   [87] *Id.*

[88] Lewis A. Kornhauser & Lawrence G. Sager, *Unpacking the Court*, 96 YALE L. J. 82, 115–17 (1986).

structure, the process of establishing settled precedents remains decentralized –
enhancing the amount and quality of collective deliberation underlying the
judiciary's interpretations of law.[89]

In addition to appellate review, the federal judiciary exercises control over
its members through internal disciplinary procedures. Prior to mid-century,
circuit judges informally exercised loose disciplinary control over the district
courts.[90] Congress sought to regularize their authority in 1939, enacting a
statute that established each court of appeals as a judicial council with a mandate to ensure that "the work of the district judges shall be effectively and
expeditiously transacted."[91] This statute accomplished little, however, partly
because of continuing reservations about its constitutionality.[92] By the mid-
1970s, mounting evidence of problems in the judiciary, together with support
from the Judicial Conference that helped overcome lingering constitutional
doubts, led Congress to consider revising and strengthening the disciplinary
process. It took six years to hammer out a compromise, but in 1980, with the
Judicial Conference's backing, Congress finally passed the Judicial Councils
Reform and Judicial Conduct and Disability Act.[93]

---

[89] The allocation of authority between judge and jury and between trial and appellate courts
also has obvious implications for our ability to police deviant outcomes. Whenever judges give
deference to juries, or appellate courts give deference to trial courts, we increase the risk that
controversial rulings will be left standing. At the same time, numerous other considerations
must be taken into account in determining who should decide what: considerations of efficiency
and economy, of relative expertise, of political commitments to a role for lay deliberation, and
of making the trial the main focus of adjudication. Such questions present modern versions of
the monumental battles fought between Hamiltonians and Jeffersonians in the early nineteenth
century, and between Democrats and Whigs a few decades later, over such matters as whether to
permit lay judges, whether to preserve the jury's role in finding law, when to allow judges to direct
a verdict, and whether even to permit the publication of written judicial opinions. *See* John Reid,
Controlling the Law: Jeremiah Smith, William Plumer, and the Politics of Law in the Early
Republic: New Hampshire, 1791–1816 (Nov. 2001) (unpublished manuscript, on file with Dean
Larry Kramer). These struggles between trained lawyers striving to professionalize the legal
process and democratic leaders who fear surrendering control of law to trained professionals
obviously affect the question of independence. We nevertheless defer consideration of this
interesting subject for the present, because its details are unimportant for our present purpose –
which is simply to identify and underscore the place of appellate review in the analysis. Insofar
as other decisions about how to structure litigation also bear on the relative independence or
accountability of judges, these too should be kept in mind.

[90] Bermant & Wheeler, *supra* note 2, at 841.

[91] An Act to Provide for the Administration of the United States Courts, and for Other Purposes,
ch. 501, § 306, 53 Stat. 1223, 1224 (1939).

[92] *See, e.g.,* Sam Ervin, *Separation of Powers: Judicial Independence*, 35 LAW & CONTEMP. PROBS.
108, 121–27 (1970).

[93] Pub. L. No. 96–458, 94 Stat. 2035 (1980) (codified as amended in scattered sections of 28
U.S.C.). A useful account of the background and history of this legislation is found in Stephen

The Act expands and formalizes the judiciary's disciplinary process. It autho-
rizes anyone who believes that any federal judge "has engaged in conduct prej-
udicial to the effective and expeditious administration of the business of the
courts" or "is unable to discharge all the duties of office by reason of mental or
physical disability" to complain in writing through the office of the clerk of the
court of appeals for the circuit in which that judge sits.[94] The Act specifies how
the chief judge and circuit judicial council should respond to complaints, and
it empowers the council to impose remedies.[95] These include certifying the
judge as disabled, formally requesting his or her retirement, imposing a freeze
on the assignment of new cases, and delivering a private or public reprimand;
the council may not order the removal of a sitting district or circuit court
judge.[96]

Both the success and the constitutionality of the Judicial Conduct and Disability Act remain debatable. Perceptions in Congress that the courts were not
taking their responsibilities under the Act seriously simmered throughout the
1980s, kept warm by the judiciary's tardiness in enacting rules to implement
it.[97] Goaded by pressure from Congress, the Judicial Conference eventually
proposed rules, and courts began making more active use of their disciplinary
authority.[98] Congress nevertheless appointed a Commission in 1990 to investigate whether the Act was working and to recommend changes if needed.[99]
The Report of the National Commission on Judicial Discipline and Removal,
issued in 1993, included numerous recommendations, but it reaffirmed the
basic structure for judicial discipline and strongly supported its constitutionality.[100] "[T]he existing federal system," said the Commission, "is working reasonably well and is capable of improvement."[101] Although ninety-five percent
of complaints made under the Act had been dismissed,[102] the Commission

B. Burbank, *Procedural Rulemaking under the Judicial Councils Reform and Judicial Conduct and Disability Act of 1980*, 131 U. PA. L. REV. 283, 291–308 (1982).

[94] 28 U.S.C. § 372(c)(1) (2002) *repealed by* Pub. L. 107–273, 116 Stat. 1855 (2002). The authorization is now part of the 21st Century Department of Justice Appropriations Authorization Act. 28 U.S.C. § 351 et seq. (2002).

[95] 28 U.S.C. §§ 352–361. For a brief description, see Stephen B. Burbank, *Politics and Progress in Implementing the Federal Judicial Discipline Act*, 71 JUDICATURE 13, 15 (1987).

[96] *See id.*   [97] *See* Burbank, *supra* note 95, at 13–14.

[98] *See id.* at 13–23.

[99] *See* National Commission on Judicial Discipline and Removal Act, Pub. L. No. 101–650, §§ 409–410, 104 Stat. 5124, 5124–25 (1990).

[100] NATIONAL COMMISSION ON JUDICIAL DISCIPLINE AND REMOVAL REPORT 14–17, 147–55 (1993).

[101] *Id.* at 124.

[102] A study done by for the Commission by Jeffrey Barr and Thomas Willging found that of 2,405 complaints filed between 1980 and 1991, corrective action was taken in only 73, including only 5 formal reprimands. *See* Jeffrey N. Barr & Thomas E. Willging, *Decentralized Self-Regulation*,

found that "nearly all" of these dismissals were "justified and appropriate," and also that many complaints "were resolved by corrective action taken on the part of the judge complained against."[103] Indeed, "the very existence of the Act has facilitated informal resolutions of misconduct or disability problems by chief judges and circuit councils, without need for a formal complaint under the Act."[104] The Supreme Court has yet to rule on the constitutional question, but several lower courts have already upheld the legislation.[105]

A number of other devices that are available to the federal judiciary in disciplining its members should be mentioned, if only briefly. Appellate courts sometimes use their opinions not only to correct legal errors, but also to reprimand lower court judges for controversial actions or comments.[106] They may also reassign cases to a different judge on remand.[107] Extraordinary writs like mandamus and prohibition can be used to correct particularly flagrant misbehavior by lower court judges.[108] Finally, the chief judge in a circuit or district has authority to control the assignment of cases, though Norma Johnson's recent difficulties in the District of Columbia may put a damper on further use of this power.[109]

B. *Doctrinal Limitations*

As important as these "administrative" tools may be, the federal judiciary has devised a far more important assortment of doctrinal principles that limit the possibility of politically controversial judicial entanglements. Of course, no one ever sat down to plan how or where to introduce doctrines of self-restraint, and these rules have emerged haphazardly over time. For similar reasons, the

---

Accountability, and Judicial Independence Under the Federal Judicial Conduct and Disability Act of 1980, 142 U. PA. L. REV. 25, 52, tbl.9 (1993).

[103] EXECUTIVE SUMMARY TO THE REPORT OF THE NATIONAL COMMISSION ON JUDICIAL DISCIPLINE AND REMOVAL 9 (1993).

[104] *Id.*

[105] *See In re* Certain Complaints, 783 F.2d 1488, 1502–15 (11th Cir. 1986); Hastings v. Judicial Conference of the United States, 593 F. Supp. 1371, 1378–85 (D.D.C. 1984), *aff'd in part and vacated in part*, 770 F.2d 1093 (D.C. Cir. 1985); McBryde v. Comm. to Review Circuit Council Conduct & Disability Orders, 83 F. Supp.2d 135, 151–56 (D.D.C. 1999), *aff'd in part and vacated in part*, 264 F.3d 52 (D.C. Cir. 2001).

[106] *See* Bermant & Wheeler, *supra* note 2, at 844 & n.40 (citing cases).

[107] Liljeberg v. Health Servs. Acquisition Corp., 486 U.S. 847, 862–70 (1988); Dyas v. Lockhart, 705 F.2d 993, 997–98 (8th Cir. 1983); United States v. Robin, 553 F.2d 8, 9–10 (2d Cir. 1977).

[108] ROBERT L. STERN ET AL., SUPREME COURT PRACTICE 493–501 (7th ed. 1993).

[109] *See Judges Scrap Rule Used in Hubbell, Trie Cases*, COM. APPEAL (Memphis), Feb. 3, 2000, at A4, 2000 WL 4438380; *Inquiry Clears Chief D.C.Judge of Steering Cases of Clinton Friends*, COM. APPEAL (Memphis), Feb. 27, 2001, at A6, 2001 WL 9428019.

doctrines do not all take the same form: some exclude whole cases, while others merely limit the timing or scope of judicial involvement. What they share in common is the aim and effect of curbing judicial responsibility in potentially sensitive areas of law and policy. Taken as a whole, the extent of this judicial abstinence turns out to be impressive indeed.

For ease of exposition, we have divided the relevant principles into three categories: (1) principles of justiciability, (2) principles of federalism, and (3) rules of constitutional interpretation. We do not purport to offer an exhaustive inventory; that would require a short treatise at the very least. We have instead sought simply to chart the major lines of institutionalized judicial self-restraint, which should suffice to make our point. Thus prompted, most lawyers will already be familiar with the additional details of the particular doctrines.

1. Principles of Justiciability

In 1798, the Federalist-controlled Congress set out to annihilate the Republican opposition by, among other things, enacting the Alien and Sedition Acts.[110] Republicans denounced these laws as unconstitutional in resolutions promulgated through the Virginia and Kentucky legislatures, which they controlled.[111] Their efforts were, in turn, promptly denounced by Federalist-dominated assemblies in ten other states.[112] State legislatures "are not the proper tribunals to determine the constitutionality of the laws of the general government," these legislatures replied, insisting that this duty "is properly and exclusively confided to the judicial department."[113] Not so, protested the Virginians, in a famous report authored by James Madison: We cannot depend on the judiciary because, for one reason, "there may be instances of usurped power, which the forms of the constitution would never draw within the controul of the judicial department."[114] The scope of judicial powers were then tightly constrained by the procedural rules that made many lawsuits hard to bring. Between the need to fit one's case into one of the forms of action, limitations on joinder of

---

[110] See Manning J. Dauer, The Adams Federalists 198–205 (1953); Stephen G. Kurtz, The Presidency of John Adams 308–13 (1957).

[111] See Adrienne Koch, Jefferson and Madison: The Great Collaboration 184–87 (1950).

[112] See Stanley Elkins & Erik McKitrick, The Age of Federalism 726 (1993).

[113] The quotes in text are from the reply approved by the state of New Hampshire on June 14, 1799. 4 Jonathon Elliot, The Debates in the Several State Conventions, on the Adoption of the Federal Constitution 538–39 (photo. reprint 1987) (Ayer Company Publishers, Inc., 2d ed. 1836). For the replies of six other states, see *id.* at 532–39.

[114] Report on the Alien and Sedition Acts (Jan. 7, 1800), *in* James Madison 608, 613 (Jack N. Rakove ed., 1999) [hereinafter Madison Report]. This was consistent with Madison's position at the Philadelphia Convention. *See* Notes of James Madison (Aug. 27, 1787), *in* James Madison, Notes of Debates in the Federal Convention of 1787, at 535, 538 (indexed ed. 1984).

parties and claims, the division of law and equity, restrictive rules of personal jurisdiction, and a variety of other obstacles, there were indeed many disputes that never assumed a form suitable for litigation.[115] Over time, of course, this changed. The forms of action were replaced by code and then notice pleading; many new causes of action were recognized; law and equity were merged and the rules of joinder were liberalized (including the expansion of class actions); the requirements for personal jurisdiction and service of process were eased; and so forth.[116] As a result, a much larger portion of real world behavior could be fashioned into a viable lawsuit. Over the same period, the development of the regulatory state vastly expanded the amount of activity that is either an object or a subject of government regulation, again augmenting potential sources of litigation.

The federal judiciary has responded to these changed circumstances by inventing a whole series of doctrinal constraints that significantly reduce the scope of its potential authority. Taken together, these require that cases assume a certain form and achieve a level of particularity and focus before they can become proper subjects for adjudication. Certainly the range of justiciable claims is larger than it was in Madison's time. But as a result of these doctrines, it is also smaller than it might otherwise be. From a technical standpoint, the Supreme Court has grounded its doctrinal innovations in the language of Article III, specifically in the words "cases" and "controversies" in the provisions conferring federal jurisdiction.[117] Hence, these limitations on justiciability are sometimes referred to as the "case or controversy requirement." But no one seriously believes that the Framers chose these words with anything like the Supreme Court's doctrinal framework in mind or that the Court's justiciability rulings are anything other than a judicially-invented gloss on the Constitution.

The Court found it necessary to impose justiciability restrictions from its earliest days. Take the prohibition on advisory opinions, which one leading commentator calls "the oldest and most consistent thread in the federal law of justiciability."[118] In July 1793, Secretary of State Thomas Jefferson wrote to the Justices of the Supreme Court on behalf of President Washington, requesting advice on a number of matters pertaining to America's obligations under the treaty of alliance with France and to her legal options were she to remain

---

[115] *See* FLEMING JAMES, JR. ET AL., CIVIL PROCEDURE 12–23 (5th ed. 2001); STEPHEN C. YEAZELL, FROM MEDIEVAL GROUP LITIGATION TO THE MODERN CLASS ACTION 267–91 (1987).

[116] *See id.*; JACK H. FRIEDENTHAL ET AL., CIVIL PROCEDURE 244–29 (3d ed. 1999).

[117] *See infra* notes 137–144 and accompanying text.

[118] CHARLES ALAN WRIGHT, LAW OF FEDERAL COURTS 65 (5th ed. 1994).

neutral in the war between France and England.[119] Famously, the Court refused to answer, explaining in a letter that separation of powers, together with text that seemed to authorize the President to call for opinions from the heads of executive departments only, "are considerations which afford strong arguments against the propriety of our extrajudicially deciding the questions alluded to."[120]

Against the background of politics at that time, the Court's self-limitation has to be seen as an attempt to sidestep political controversy. The matter of neutrality was fraught with meaning. It symbolized how the United States would respond to the French Revolution. As Lance Banning once remarked, the bitterness of the split aroused by the revolution in France "has been exceeded only once in American history, and that resulted in civil war."[121] Even George Washington's seemingly impregnable reputation could not withstand such passions, and the President's decision to steer America on a neutral course provoked the first open attacks on his previously untouchable character and judgment.[122] John Jay and his brethren had no desire to be drawn into this fray. The mere announcement that their opinion had been sought touched off negative commentary in Republican newspapers, which added to the furor already generated by the willingness of a federal circuit court to try Gideon Henfield for privateering actions on behalf of France (not to mention the still-recent ruling in *Chisolm v. Georgia* that private citizens could sue states in federal court).[123] Recognizing, as John Jay wrote to Rufus King in December 1793, that "[t]he foederal Courts have Enemies in all who fear their Influence on State objects,"[124] the Justices were not about to squander political capital

---

[119] Letter from Thomas Jefferson to the Justices of the Supreme Court (July 18, 1793), *in* 26 THE PAPERS OF THOMAS JEFFERSON, 11 MAY to 31 AUGUST 1793, at 520 (John Catanzariti ed., 1995). The actual questions, twenty-nine in all, were sent to the Court separately the day after Jefferson's letter. 33 THE WRITINGS OF GEORGE WASHINGTON, JULY 1, 1793–OCTOBER 9, 1794, at 15–19 (John C. Fitzpatrick ed., 1940).

[120] Letter from John Jay and the Associate Justices of the Supreme Court (James Wilson, John Blair, James Iredell & William Paterson) to George Washington (Aug. 8, 1793), *in* 15 THE PAPERS OF ALEXANDER HAMILTON: JUNE 1793–JANUARY 1794, at 110, 110 n.1 (Harold C. Syrett ed., 1969). The sixth Justice, William Cushing, was not present in Philadelphia due to illness.

[121] LANCE BANNING, THE JEFFERSONIAN PERSUASION 209 (1978).

[122] *See* JAMES ROGER SHARP, AMERICAN POLITICS IN THE EARLY REPUBLIC 81–82 (1993).

[123] STEWART JAY, MOST HUMBLE SERVANTS: THE ADVISORY ROLE OF EARLY JUDGES 160 (1997). Henfield was acquitted by a jury, which scarcely relieved the intense anxiety of Republicans concerned by the willingness of federal judges to make common law crimes a basis for federal prosecutions. *See* HARRY AMMON, THE GENET MISSION 70–71 (1973). *Chisholm v. Georgia*, 2 U.S. (2 Dall.) 419 (1793), had been decided the previous February, provoking censure and criticisms that were still reverberating in July. JAY, *supra*, at 162–63.

[124] Letter from John Jay to Rufus King (Dec. 22, 1793), *in* 2 THE DOCUMENTARY HISTORY OF THE SUPREME COURT OF THE UNITED STATES, 1789–1800: THE JUSTICES ON CIRCUIT 1790–1794, at 434 (Maeva Marcus ed. 1988).

unnecessarily. So they refused to answer. There were of course sound constitutional justification for this refusal, but there is also little doubt that the charged political atmosphere had much to do with the decision of the Court to steer clear of this particular controversy.

Over time, the Court has refined and extended the rule against advisory opinions in ways the Justices deemed necessary to preserve its essence. In the early years of the Republic, and even after the Jay Court had declared against advisory opinions, federal judges happily entertained lawsuits that had been contrived by the parties.[125] But this attitude changed, as the Supreme Court became increasingly uncomfortable with actions that were feigned for the sole purpose of obtaining a judicial opinion.[126] In *United States v. Johnson*,[127] the Court ruled explicitly that a suit brought by the plaintiff at the request of a defendant (who had also financed and directed the litigation) must be dismissed: an "honest and actual antagonistic assertion of rights," the Court held, is "a safeguard essential to the integrity of the judicial process."[128] Some uncertainty remains as to the precise line between an illegitimate contrived case and a legitimate test one, but it is generally accepted today that feigned litigation is nonjusticiable.[129] Similarly, the Court has held that litigants must have genuinely adverse interests and that a judgment of the court one way or the other must have some effect on the parties.

The requirement that a ruling of the court have some actual effect on the parties has manifested itself in a variety of settings. Judicial rulings must be final, at least as respects the controversy before the court, and thus not subject either to further review or to being disregarded by executive officials.[130] Congress may revise the law, but it may not reverse a particular judgment rendered.[131] Most

---

[125] *See, e.g.*, Fletcher v. Peck, 10 U.S. (6 Cranch) 87 (1810); Hylton v. United States, 3 U.S. (3 Dall.) 171 (1796); 1 CHARLES WARREN, THE SUPREME COURT IN UNITED STATES HISTORY: 1789–1835, at 146–47, 392–95 (rev. ed. 1926); Susan Low Bloch, *The Early Role of the Attorney General in Our Constitutional Scheme: In the Beginning There Was Pragmatism*, 1989 DUKE L. J. 561, 612 (1989).

[126] *See, e.g.*, Chicago & Grant Trunk Ry. Co. v. Wellman, 143 U.S. 339, 345 (1892) ("It never was the thought that, by means of a friendly suit, a party beaten in the legislature could transfer to the courts an inquiry as to the constitutionality of the legislative act."); Lord v. Veazie, 49 U.S. (8 How.) 251, 255 (1850) (dismissing an action docketed by consent to get before the Supreme Court as "in contempt of the court and highly reprehensible").

[127] 319 U.S. 302 (1943).   [128] *Id.* at 303–05.

[129] *See* ERWIN CHEMERINSKY, FEDERAL JURISDICTION 50 (3d ed. 1999). *Cf.* Evers v. Dwyer, 358 U.S. 202 (1958) (allowing suit to challenge segregation on buses although plaintiff rode bus on one occasion only for the purpose of instituting the litigation).

[130] *See* Chicago & S. Air Lines v. Waterman S. S. Corp., 333 U.S. 103, 111–13 (1948); Hayburn's Case, 2 U.S. (2 Dall.) 409, 410 (1792).

[131] *See* Plaut v. Spendthrift Farm, Inc., 514 U.S. 211 (1995).

important for present purposes, a controversy between adverse parties must continue to exist at every stage of the proceedings. If events subsequent to the filing of a case or an appeal resolve the dispute, the action must be dismissed as moot.[132] Despite exceptions for special situations,[133] mootness doctrine operates as a significant restraint on what courts do, particularly in today's world, where settlements are common at every stage in litigation.

We need to understand "standing" doctrines in much the same way. The advent of the regulatory state brought legislation creating countless new interests that had not been protected at common law. At the same time, the Supreme Court recognized a myriad of new constitutional rights that did not resemble traditional forms of liberty or property. These changes forced courts to address, in the words of one leading group of commentators, "who, if anyone, should be able to sue to ensure governmental compliance with statutory and constitutional provisions intended to protect broadly shared interests of large numbers of people."[134] Issues arising from governmental regulation might have opened the doors of the courthouse to practically anyone unhappy with almost anything the government did. Instead, the Supreme Court circumscribed access to the judiciary by fabricating the doctrines of standing and ripeness.

There was no doctrine of standing prior to the middle of the twentieth century. The word "standing" made scattered appearances, but it was unattached to any analytical framework because no such framework was needed.[135] Litigants invariably based their claims on legal interests of a type long recognized at common law. Even in suits raising constitutional challenges, plaintiffs typically complained about official action that caused them some form of traditional physical or economic harm – a trespass or a conversion or something like that.[136] While the Supreme Court tried, initially, to import this traditional private-law model in its early encounters with the new administrative state, this private-law model proved too unforgiving, and excluded too many of the government's new activities. And, after a brief detour that momentarily promised

[132] *See* DeFunis v. Odegaard, 416 U.S. 312 (1974); Liner v. Jafco, Inc., 375 U.S. 301 (1964); Henry P. Monaghan, *Constitutional Adjudication: The Who and When*, 82 YALE L. J. 1363, 1383–86 (1973). For discussion of whether the mootness doctrine is a matter of the courts' power under Article III or merely a question of policy, see the exchange between Chief Justice Rehnquist and Justice Scalia in *Honig v. Doe*, 484 U.S. 305, 329–42 (1988) (Rehnquist, C. J., concurring) (Scalia, J., dissenting). Although the Chief Justice resisted the idea of mootness as a constitutional limitation, the Court has clearly held otherwise.
[133] These are surveyed in CHEMERINSKY, *supra* note 129, at 129–143.
[134] FALLON ET AL., *supra* note 40, at 137.
[135] *See* JOSEPH VINING, LEGAL IDENTITY: THE COMING OF AGE OF PUBLIC LAW 55–56 (1978).
[136] *Id.* at 20–33.

an extravagantly expansive doctrine,[137] the Court settled on a framework that imposes substantial limits on the reach of the federal courts.[138]

Describing this doctrine concisely is difficult, because the cases are such a jumbled mess. In its present guise, however, the law of standing consists of three main requirements, ostensibly grounded in Article III, together with a handful of subconstitutional "prudential" limitations that are sometimes hard to disentangle from the constitutional ones. In terms of Article III, a party must have suffered an "injury in fact" that consists of something more than ideological opposition to what government is doing: there must be some material harm that is "distinct and palpable,"[139] rather than "conjectural" or "hypothetical,"[140] and that is suffered personally.[141] The plaintiff's harm must also be "fairly traceable" to the challenged action and it must be "likely to be redressed by the requested relief."[142] A plaintiff who satisfies these constitutional requirements may still be excluded from federal court, however, if he or she runs afoul of a judicially developed prudential limitation, such as presenting a claim that is too "generalized,"[143] or seeking relief when the plaintiff is not "arguably within the zone of interests to be protected or regulated" by the substantive law at issue.[144]

---

[137] *See* Association of Data Processing Serv. Orgs. v. Camp, 397 U.S. 150 (1970) (allowing competitors to challenge Comptroller decision allowing banks to provide data processing services because competitors were "arguably within the zone of interests" protected by relevant federal statute); Flast v. Cohen, 392 U.S. 83 (1968) (allowing taxpayer to challenge statute under Establishment Clause). As is discussed below, *Data Processing*'s "zone-of-interests" test has been converted over the years from an extension of standing into a limitation. *See infra* note 144.

[138] *See* WRIGHT, *supra* note 118, at 67–83; Cass R. Sunstein, *Standing and the Privatization of Public Law*, 88 COLUM. L. REV. 1432, 1434–51 (1988).

[139] Warth v. Seldin, 422 U.S. 490, 501 (1975).   [140] City of L.A. v. Lyons, 461 U.S. 95, 102 (1983).

[141] *See* Lujan v. Defenders of Wildlife, 504 U.S. 555, 563 (1992); United States v. Students Challenging Regulatory Agency Procedures, 412 U.S. 669, 687 (1973); Sierra Club v. Morton, 405 U.S. 727, 734–45 (1972).

[142] *See* Allen v. Wright, 468 U.S. 737, 751 (1984).

[143] *See* Schlesinger v. Reservists Comm. to Stop the War, 418 U.S. 208, 217 (1974) (dismissing action to enjoin members of Congress from serving in military reserves on the ground that this violated constitutional prohibition against legislators holding other civil offices); United States v. Richardson, 418 U.S. 166, 179–180 (1974) (dismissing complaint arguing that a statute authorizing CIA to keep its budget secret violated Constitution's requirement of regular accounting of expenditures).

[144] When this condition was first articulated in 1970, it was with the purpose of liberalizing the law of standing. The Court offered the zone-of-interests test in lieu of the then still-prevailing private-law model, explaining that the requirement of standing was distinct from the traditional "legal interest" test and could be more easily satisfied. *See* Association of Data Processing Serv. Orgs. v. Camp, 397 U.S. 150, 153 (1970). When the Court subsequently erected the tripartite Article III test described above, it preserved the zone-of-interests requirement while transforming it into an additional condition that needs to be satisfied in cases challenging agency action under the Administrative Procedures Act. In *Air Courier Conference v. American Postal Workers Union*,

Ripeness, like standing, is a creature of the administrative state, though also like standing it is now applied in many situations not involving agency action.[145] Where standing addresses the propriety of allowing a particular party to litigate, ripeness asks whether the subject matter is ready for adjudication; it deals with *when* review is appropriate. Ripeness doctrine seeks to separate actions that are premature from those that are fit to be litigated. It is the obverse of mootness, defining when it is too soon rather than too late for federal court action. Courts use the ripeness doctrine to avoid ruling if an alleged injury is speculative or may never occur, thus sidestepping unnecessary judicial involvement.[146] Ripeness issues often intersect with overbreadth or void-for-vagueness challenges in the First Amendment context,[147] and they have been important in limiting the scope and timing of review in Takings Clause cases.[148] Among the most significant uses of ripeness has been to avoid requests for equitable relief in cases challenging certain kinds of practices by the government, especially in the area of law enforcement.[149]

---

498 U.S. 517 (1991), for example, the Supreme Court held that the postal workers' union could not challenge the United States Postal Service's decision to suspend its monopoly over certain routes, because the union was not within the zone of interests protected by the Postal Express statutes. *Id.* at 524–25.

[145] *See, e.g.*, cases cited *infra* note 149.

[146] *See* Abbott Labs. v. Gardner, 387 U.S. 136, 148–49 (1967). *See also* Toilet Goods Ass'n v. Gardner, 387 U.S. 158 (1967) (holding that cosmetics manufacturer could not yet challenge FDA regulation because only punishment at this stage was suspension of sales certificates).

[147] *See* Times Film Corp. v. City of Chicago, 365 U.S. 43, 44–46 (1961); Adler v. Bd. of Educ., 342 U.S. 485, 504 (1952) (Frankfurter, J., dissenting).

[148] *See* Pennell v. City of San Jose, 485 U.S. 1 (1988); Williamson County Reg'l Planning Comm'n v. Hamilton Bank, 473 U.S. 172, 186 (1985); Gene R. Nichol, *Ripeness and the Constitution*, 54 U. CHI. L. REV. 153, 166–67 (1987).

[149] The plaintiffs in *O'Shea v. Littleton*, 414 U.S. 488 (1974), for example, sought an injunction to combat what they claimed was a longstanding and continuing pattern of discriminatory law enforcement against blacks. The Court dismissed their claim. That some of the plaintiffs had allegedly been victims of these discriminatory practices in the past was not enough to convince the Court that their complaint presented a live case or controversy within the meaning of Article III. While "past wrongs are evidence bearing on whether there is a real and immediate threat of repeated injury," the requested relief still depended on finding that similar violations would occur in the future. *Id.* at 496. "But it seems to us," the Court said, "that attempting to anticipate whether and when these respondents will be charged with crime and will be made to appear before either petitioner takes us into the area of speculation and conjecture." *Id.* at 497. The Court has employed this reasoning to turn back a variety of analogous challenges over the years, using justiciability to avoid becoming enmeshed in continuously monitoring another branch of the government. *See, e.g.*, City of L.A. v. Lyons, 461 U.S. 95 (1983) (challenge to use of chokeholds by Los Angeles police); Rizzo v. Goode, 423 U.S. 362 (1976) (addressing action to enjoin a variety of practices by Philadelphia police); Laird v. Tatum, 408 U.S. 1 (1972) (concerning action to enjoin Army surveillance of civilian political activity).

Finally, we may consider the political question doctrine which represents a perfect illustration of the self-restraint thesis. Unlike standing or ripeness, which limit only when or by whom a challenge can be brought, the political question doctrine removes whole categories of constitutional law from judicial consideration altogether because the subject matter is deemed inappropriate for resolution by judges. It is a very old doctrine, as old as *Marbury v. Madison*, where Chief Justice Marshall said:

> By the Constitution of the United States, the President is invested with certain important political powers, in the exercise of which he is to use his own discretion, and is accountable only to his country in his political character, and to his own conscience.... Questions, in their nature political, or which are by the constitution and laws, submitted to the executive, can never be made in this court.[150]

It is also confusing or perhaps merely confused; or perhaps it is not a "doctrine" at all. Commentators have puzzled about how this aspect of *Marbury* fits with Marshall's *other*, more famous declaration that it is "the province and the duty of the judicial department to say what the law is."[151] They have wondered what the Court means by questions "in their nature political," since judges deal with political questions all the time.[152] They have insisted that, properly understood, the political question doctrine is not a matter of justiciability, but is merely a question of giving appropriate deference to the judgments of coordinate departments.[153] The Court, in the meantime, has made things worse by steering an erratic and inconsistent course in how it has used and explained the political question doctrine over time. Given our dynamic conception of judicial independence, it is not surprising that the Court deals with some political questions but not others. Nor does it matter whether the doctrine is formally a question of jurisdiction or simply a matter of deference to coordinate branches. What matters is that, over time, the Supreme Court has declared that federal courts could not, and so should not, deal with certain questions because they are too dangerous institutionally. These are not necessarily the most controversial questions, though they are plenty controversial (or would be if the Court

---

[150] 5 U.S. (1 Cranch) 137, 165–70 (1803). That the substantive question at issue in *Marbury* was of this nature still did not stop Marshall from lecturing Jefferson about what he should have done, and it was this, rather than the exercise of judicial review, that provoked what hostility the Court's decision received. *See* ELLIS, *supra* note 29, at 66.

[151] *See* Martin H. Redish, *Judicial Review and the "Political Question,"* 79 Nw. U. L. Rev. 1031 (1984).

[152] *See* CHEMERINSKY, *supra* note 129, at 144–45.

[153] *See* HERBERT WECHSLER, PRINCIPLES, POLITICS, AND FUNDAMENTAL LAW 11–14 (1961); Louis Henkin, *Is There a "Political Question" Doctrine?*, 85 YALE L. J. 597, 622–23 (1976).

tried to resolve them). They are, rather, potentially controversial questions in areas where courts are more at sea than usual. As Alexander Bickel elegantly explained nearly three decades ago, the core of the political question doctrine combines:

> the Court's sense of lack of capacity, compounded in unequal parts of (a) the strangeness of the issue and its intractability to principled resolution; (b) the sheer momentousness of it, which tends to unbalance judicial judgment; (c) the anxiety, not so much that the judicial judgment will be ignored, as that perhaps it should but will not be; (d) finally ("in a mature democracy"), the inner vulnerability, the self-doubt of an institution which is electorally irresponsible and has no earth to draw strength from.[154]

So, the Court declared that it had no role to play in enforcing the Guaranty Clause when asked to judge the winner of a small scale civil war in Rhode Island.[155] And it has made very clear that its competence is limited when it comes to foreign policy, renouncing any authority to decide when a war has begun or ended,[156] when a foreign government can be or has been recognized,[157] whether a treaty survives the fall of a foreign government,[158] and how the President may use his war powers.[159] Likewise, the Court has shied away from certain questions involving the structure of politics, including some important aspects of political parties.[160] And, of course, the Court had found that challenges to the impeachment process are nonjusticiable.[161] This is but a sampling of cases invoking the political question doctrine, but enough, we think, to convey its essential flavor – which is the erratic and inconsistent

---

[154] BICKEL, *supra* note 12, at 184.

[155] Luther v. Borden, 48 U.S. (7 How.) 1, 46–47 (1849). The Court has reaffirmed this holding in other contexts. *See, e.g.*, Pacific States Tel. & Tel. Co. v. Oregon, 223 U.S. 118 (1912) (declining to review state's use of ballot initiatives); Taylor & Marshall v. Beckham, 178 U.S. 548 (1900) (declining to review state's resolution of disputed gubernatorial race).

[156] Commercial Trust Co. v. Miller, 262 U.S. 51, 57 (1923).

[157] United States v. Belmont, 301 U.S. 324, 328 (1937); Oetjen v. Central Leather Co., 246 U.S. 297, 302 (1918). The Court has also held that recognition of Indian tribes is a political matter. United States v. Sandoval, 231 U.S. 28, 45–47 (1913).

[158] Terlinden v. Ames, 184 U.S. 270, 288 (1902). *Cf.* Goldwater v. Carter, 444 U.S. 996, 1002–04 (1979) (plurality holding that rescission of treaties is a political matter).

[159] *See* CHEMERINSKY, *supra* note 129, at 157–58 (discussing lower court cases refusing to review challenges to United States military policy in Vietnam, El Salvador, and Persian Gulf).

[160] *See* O'Brien v. Brown, 409 U.S. 1 (1972) (refusing to decide challenge to the seating of delegates at 1972 Democratic Convention).

[161] Nixon v. United States, 506 U.S. 224 (1993) (not *that* Nixon: challenge by District Court Judge Walter Nixon to Senate procedures in trying his impeachment).

renunciation of jurisdiction in cases where the Court feels it has little to offer and something to lose.

2. Principles of Federalism

Federalism is the principal source of political friction among American governmental institutions, and the federal courts have been as vulnerable to federalist objections as rest of the national government. The debate over Article III in Philadelphia and during Ratification was dominated by fears that a powerful federal bench would swamp the state courts, fears that drove judicial politics in the early Republic and have persisted ever since.[162] The federal courts have been subjected to pressures to curtail their authority vis-à-vis state courts, and this pressure has produced a number of major controversies over time. A consequence of these historic struggles has been to make federal judges particularly sensitive to jurisdictional conflicts with state courts. This sensitivity is certainly justified. The statutes that confer federal jurisdiction are extremely broad. Diversity jurisdiction, for example, which has existed since the first Judiciary Act, is conferred over all civil actions that meet a $75,000 amount-in-controversy requirement and are "between citizens of different states."[163] Federal question jurisdiction is bestowed in equally generous terms and extends (with no minimal amount in controversy) to all civil actions "arising under the Constitution, laws, or treaties of the United States."[164]

But, in order to manage these expansive statutes, the Supreme Court has, in both cases, interpreted the statutory language narrowly to exclude a huge portion of the cases that are potentially within its reach. Take diversity jurisdiction. The Constitution requires no more than what has come to be known as "minimal diversity": there must be *a* plaintiff who is from a different state than *a* defendant.[165] Nothing in the language of the statute requires more than this, which was true also of the first statute to confer diversity jurisdiction in 1789.[166] Yet in one of its earliest decisions interpreting the reach of federal jurisdiction, the Supreme Court held that the statute requires "complete diversity" – meaning that *every* plaintiff must be from a different state than *every* defendant.[167] The requirement of complete diversity keeps an enormous number of

---

[162] See ELLIS, *supra* note 29, at 10–16.   [163] 28 U.S.C. § 1332(a)(1) (2002).
[164] *Id.* § 1331.
[165] See State Farm Fire & Cas. Co. v. Tashire, 386 U.S. 523, 530–31 (1967).
[166] Judiciary Act of 1789, ch. 20, § 11, 1 Stat. 73, 78 (allowing federal jurisdiction where "the suit is between a citizen of the State where the suit is brought, and a citizen of another State"). The requirement that one of the parties be from the state where the suit was brought was eliminated in the Act of March 3, 1875, ch. 137, § 1, 18 Stat. 470.
[167] See Strawbridge v. Curtiss, 7 U.S. (3 Cranch) 267 (1806).

multiparty cases out of federal court, an effect that is exacerbated by parties who manage to avoid unwanted federal litigation by artfully selecting their opponents.[168]

Federal courts have been even more active, and considerably more creative, in finding ways to limit federal question jurisdiction. As Chief Justice Marshall opined in *Osborn v. Bank of the United States*,[169] the Constitution permits Congress to confer jurisdiction over any case in which a federal interest might be denied or impaired even *indirectly* by a state law ruling; there could be federal jurisdiction whether or not the federal "ingredient" had to be pleaded as part of the plaintiff's claim and even if it were not actually contested in the lawsuit.[170] But, while recognizing that Congress has broad power to confer federal jurisdiction, the Supreme Court has never read legislation concerning federal questions anywhere near this broadly, but has instead limited it in a variety of ways over the years. The most prominent judicially-crafted limitation on federal question jurisdiction is the "well-pleaded complaint rule." This holds that, for statutory purposes, "a suit arises under the Constitution and laws of the United States only when the plaintiff's statement of his own cause of action shows that it is based upon those laws or that Constitution."[171] Federal question jurisdiction exists, in other words, only if one of the essential elements of the plaintiff's claim is federal or raises a federal question – something to be determined "upon the face of the complaint unaided by the answer...."[172] This is crucial because, since 1887, defendants have been allowed to remove a case to federal court only if the plaintiff could have filed it there in the first

---

[168] While parties may artfully plead themselves out of federal court, there is a statute that precludes them from similarly scheming their way in. *See* 28 U.S.C. § 1359 (depriving district court of jurisdiction over actions "in which any party, by assignment or otherwise, has been improperly or collusively made or joined to invoke the jurisdiction of such court").

[169] 22 U.S. (9 Wheat.) 738 (1824).

[170] *Osborn* itself was an easy case for federal jurisdiction: the Bank of the United States (BUS) was suing for an injunction to prevent state officials from seizing its assets pursuant to a state tax that the BUS claimed was unconstitutional under *McCulloch v. Maryland*, 17 U.S. (4 Wheat.) 316 (1819). More difficult was *Osborn*'s companion case, *Bank of the United States v. Planters' Bank of Georgia*, 22 U.S. (9 Wheat.) 904 (1824), in which the BUS sued a state bank for refusing to honor bonds. The only conceivable federal questions were the capacity of the BUS to sue and to make a contract to purchase bonds – potential defenses that were not being raised by the defendant. Having noted in *Osborn* that ordinary contract cases of this sort were the hardest in which to justify federal jurisdiction, the Court in *Planters' Bank* nevertheless upheld the federal court's power to hear the case, referring readers back to *Osborn* which, Chief Justice Marshall said, "fully considered" and disposed of the matter. *Id.* at 905. The Court obviously feared that, given state hostility to the BUS, a state court might deny its claim by misapplying state law, effectively destroying the federal bank without having to say a word about federal law.

[171] *Louisville & Nashville R.R. Co. v. Mottley*, 211 U.S. 149, 152 (1908).

[172] *Gully v. First Nat'l Bank*, 299 U.S. 109, 113 (1936).

place.[173] The result is a substantial diminution in federal question jurisdiction through the elimination of cases in which the federal issue comes up as a defense or a reply to a defense.

Federal courts have further circumscribed federal question jurisdiction with a variety of abstention doctrines under which they renounce or refuse to exercise authority otherwise conferred by Congress for the specific purpose of avoiding undue frictions with the states. Because these doctrines have been crafted by federal judges on a case-by-case basis over the past sixty years, their contours – including even the number of separate abstention doctrines – remain only partly defined.[174] As a technical matter, abstention can be justified on statutory interpretation grounds: the federal courts ought to interpret broad grants of jurisdiction narrowly to take account of circumstances in which exercising jurisdiction appears troublesome; Congress is then implicitly invited to overrule or modify the courts' decisions if Congress decides that they are wrong. In the case of abstention, the Supreme Court has also invoked the discretion traditionally available to judges asked to award equitable relief, and it is unclear whether abstention is ever permitted in a damages action.[175] Be that as it may, what matters for present purposes is that the various abstention doctrines all share a common concern for avoiding "needless federal conflict with the states"[176] in order to advance "harmonious federal-state relations."[177] Whether postponing jurisdiction to avoid unsettled state law, as in *Pullman* abstention,[178]

---

[173] *See* 28 U.S.C. § 1441(a)–(b) (2002).

[174] The Supreme Court refers sometimes to two and sometimes to three abstention doctrines, while a leading treatise refers to four forms of abstention plus the related doctrine of "Our Federalism." *Compare* Ohio Bureau of Employment Servs. v. Hodory, 431 U.S. 471, 477 (1977) (listing two abstention doctrines), *with* Colorado River Water Conservation Dist. v. United States, 424 U.S. 800, 814–16 (1976) (listing three abstention doctrines), *and with* 17A CHARLES ALAN WRIGHT ET AL., FEDERAL PRACTICE AND PROCEDURE § 4241, at 28–29 (1988) (listing four abstention doctrines plus "Our Federalism").

[175] *See* Quackenbush v. Allstate Ins. Co., 517 U.S. 706, 730–31 (1996) (limiting *Burford* abstention to cases involving equitable relief, but noting that federal court might properly postpone exercising jurisdiction in some damages actions); *id.* at 733 (Kennedy, J., concurring) (noting that abstention might be proper in damages claims in other contexts); *id.* at 731–32 (Scalia, J., concurring) (joining Court's opinion only because he understands that it does rule out abstention in any case involving only damages).

[176] Burford v. Sun Oil Co., 319 U.S. 315, 327 (1943).

[177] Louisiana Power & Light Co. v. City of Thibodaux, 360 U.S. 25, 29 (1959).

[178] Railroad Comm'n v. Pullman Co., 312 U.S. 496 (1940). *Pullman* abstention comes into play whenever the resolution of a federal constitutional issue turns on an unsettled question of state law: the federal court is required to abstain from exercising its admitted jurisdiction so that the parties can refile in state court and have the state law issue settled there. In *Pullman* itself, for example, the Supreme Court ruled that the lower federal courts should have refrained from deciding a challenge to an assertedly unconstitutional order of the Texas Railroad Commission

or renouncing jurisdiction to avoid interfering with a state regulatory scheme, as in *Burford* abstention,[179] or ongoing state judicial proceedings, as in *Younger* abstention,[180] the basic premise is the same: to avoid entangling federal courts in controversies likely to generate friction with state governments.

Two final doctrines warrant brief discussion while we are on the subject of abstention. Although neither is formally classified as "an abstention doctrine," both resemble these doctrines closely enough to be included at this point. First is the so-called Rooker-Feldman doctrine, named after two Supreme Court cases holding that plaintiffs may not use 42 U.S.C. § 1983 to challenge state court judgments.[181] Although there appears to be federal jurisdiction under both sections 1331 and 1343(3) to argue that a state court decision deprived the plaintiff of a federal right, federal scrutiny of state court judgments is ordinarily confined to appellate review in the Supreme Court. The Rooker-Feldman

so that state courts could decide whether the Commission lacked authority to issue the order under state law. *Id.* at 500. In theory, federal proceedings are merely postponed pending resolution of the state law issue in state court; the plaintiff may reserve the right to return to federal court, if still necessary, for a decision on the federal issue once the state proceedings have concluded. *See* England v. La. State Bd. of Med. Exam'rs, 375 U.S. 411, 421–22 (1964). In practice, problems of delay and the expense of litigating twice renders this right more illusory than real.

[179] *Burford*, 319 U.S. at 332. *Burford* abstention calls for federal judges to decline jurisdiction where this would disrupt or interfere with a complex state administrative program. *See id.*; Alabama Pub. Serv. Comm'n v. S. Ry. Co., 341 U.S. 341, 345 (1951). It differs from *Pullman* in two respects. First, because abstention is justified to permit state courts to administer regulatory schemes that require harmony and consistency, it applies without regard for the presence of a federal question (i.e., even if jurisdiction is based on diversity). Second, the federal court dismisses the action rather than merely postponing the exercise of its jurisdiction. *Burford* is closely related to *Thibodaux* abstention, which calls upon federal courts to defer to state courts on questions like eminent domain, which involve matters "close to the political interests of the state" that are "intimately involved in the sovereign prerogative." *Thibodaux*, 360 U.S. at 28–29. *See* Kaiser Steel Corp. v. W. S. Ranch Co., 391 U.S. 593 (1968) (per curiam). Like *Burford*, *Thibodaux* applies even in the absence of a federal question, but only if state law is unclear. *See* County of Allegheny v. Frank Mashuda Co., 360 U.S. 185 (1959).

[180] Younger v. Harris, 401 U.S. 37 (1971). *Younger* stands for the proposition that federal courts will not assert jurisdiction when doing so interferes with certain categories of pending state judicial proceedings. By far the most complicated of the abstention doctrines, the main problem has been how broadly or narrowly to define the class of proceedings requiring abstention. In its most recent encounter with the problem, *New Orleans Public Service, Inc. v. Council of the City of New Orleans (NOPSI)*, 491 U.S. 350, 373 (1989), the Court emphasized that the mere availability or pendency of state judicial proceedings was not enough to exclude federal jurisdiction. *Id.* at 373. Reaffirming the applicability of *Younger* to any criminal and civil enforcement proceedings, the Court limited its use in private civil litigation to "orders that are uniquely in furtherance of the state courts' ability to perform their judicial functions." *Id.* at 367–68. No one is yet sure just what this means.

[181] *See* District of Columbia Court of Appeals v. Feldman, 460 U.S. 462, 482 (1983); Rooker v. Fiduciary Trust Co., 263 U.S. 413 (1923).

doctrine thus bars a party losing in state court "from seeking what in substance would be appellate review of the state judgment in a United States district court, based on the losing party's claim that the state judgment itself violates the loser's federal rights."[182] Second is the venerable "domestic relations" exception to diversity jurisdiction, which excludes "the whole subject of the domestic relations of husband and wife, parent and child," together with probate matters, from federal jurisdiction.[183] The exception does not preclude every action between family members, but it does deprive federal judges of power to probate wills, administer estates, or hear cases "involving the issuance of a divorce, alimony, or child custody decree."[184] Often criticized by commentators, federal judges have steadfastly adhered to this self-imposed qualification on their authority.

Judicial regulation of unlawful detention has been a central constitutional concern throughout history, centering around the writ of habeas corpus in England and the United States, where it has often been a federalism issue. Federal judges had no authority to grant the Great Writ to state prisoners until after the Civil War, when Congress gave them the power as part of its effort to reconstruct the South.[185] The same Congress also slapped the Supreme Court down when it threatened to use this power in a way that interfered with congressional plans,[186] but the Justices avoided further controversy by limiting habeas corpus relief to cases in which a state sentencing court lacked jurisdiction over the prisoner.[187] As time passed, the Court relaxed its austerity a bit, expanding the writ by allowing prisoners to challenge their sentences for a handful of additional reasons.[188] But it was not until the Warren Court got hold of it that habeas corpus jurisdiction took off. Beginning in 1953, with the decision in *Brown v. Allen*,[189] followed a decade later by the dramatic trilogy

---

[182] Johnson v. De Grandy, 512 U.S. 997, 1005–06 (1994).

[183] *Ex parte* Burrus, 136 U.S. 586, 593–94 (1890); CHEMERINSKY, *supra* note 129, at 300–01.

[184] Ankenbrandt v. Richards, 504 U.S. 689, 704 (1992).

[185] *See* Act of Feb. 5, 1867, ch. 28, 14 Stat. 385.   [186] *See supra* note 43 and accompanying text.

[187] *See* CHARLES H. WHITEBREAD & CHRISTOPHER SLOBOGIN, CRIMINAL PROCEDURE 972 (3d ed. 1993); Paul M. Bator, *Finality in Criminal Law and Federal Habeas Corpus for State Prisoners*, 76 HARV. L. REV. 441 474–83 (1963).

[188] *See, e.g.*, Waley v. Johnston, 316 U.S. 101 (1942) (coerced guilty plea); Johnson v. Zerbst, 304 U.S. 458 (1938) (ineffective assistance of counsel); Moore v. Dempsey, 261 U.S. 86 (1923) (mob-dominated trial); *Ex parte* Siebold, 100 U.S. 371 (1879) (defendant convicted under unconstitutional statute); *Ex parte* Lange, 85 U.S. (18 Wall.) 163 (1873) (double jeopardy). The Court made these extensions by analogizing the denial of the right in question to a flaw so fatal as, in effect, to deprive the trial court of jurisdiction. According to Bator, it was only in *Waley* that the Court finally abandoned this fiction. Bator, *supra* note 187, at 495.

[189] 344 U.S. 443, 463–64 (1953) (holding that federal district court may relitigate constitutional claims previously decided in state court). Eric Freedman argues that *Brown v. Allen* produced

of *Fay v. Noia*,[190] *Sanders v. United States*,[191] and *Townsend v. Sain*,[192] the Supreme Court liberated federal trial courts to rehear virtually any federal claim de novo while removing various other procedural obstacles that had formerly limited the use of the writ. Not surprisingly, the use of habeas corpus soared, particularly after the 1963 trilogy. Only 560 petitions were filed by state prisoners in 1950, a number that had crept up to 660 by 1955, two years after *Brown v. Allen*, and 871 by 1960; in 1965, nearly 5,000 such petitions were filed, and this grew to more than 9,000 by 1970.[193] Even adjusting for changes in the prison population, there was a more than ten-fold increase in the number of habeas corpus petitions filed between 1962 and 1970.[194]

By around 1970 the Court's activities had provoked substantial opposition in the states and from the public at large. Richard Nixon ran for office on a law-and-order platform, vowing to undo the Warren Court's criminal-coddling (a goal in which he was aided by the opportunity to make four appointments during his first term in office). Responding to the pressure, and with its new members, the Supreme Court soon reversed courses. As quickly as it had begun, the federal judiciary's foray into state criminal justice ended, as the Burger and Rehnquist Courts handed down an uninterrupted stream of decisions erasing everything its predecessor had done to make habeas corpus more broadly available. To list just a few examples (in no particular order), the Court toughened the exhaustion requirement,[195] limited the filing of successive petitions,[196] circumscribed the cognizable issues,[197] required greater deference to state fact-finding,[198] weakened the test for harmless error,[199] barred review

no momentous changes and that later decisions revolutionized the writ. Eric M. Freedman, *Milestones in Habeas Corpus: Part III*: Brown v. Allen: *The Habeas Corpus Revolution that Wasn't*, 51 ALA. L. REV. 1541 (2000).

[190] 372 U.S. 391, 438 (1963) (procedural default in state court will not bar habeas claim unless petitioner "deliberately bypassed" opportunity to present the claim below).

[191] 373 U.S. 1 (1963) (establishing liberal rules allowing successive petitions).

[192] 372 U.S. 293 (1963) (defining circumstances when federal court should defer to findings of fact made by state court).

[193] *See* FALLON ET AL., *supra* note 40, at 1363 (reporting statistics).

[194] *See* Charles D. Weisselberg, *Evidentiary Hearings in Habeas Corpus Cases*, 1990 BYU L. REV. 131, 162–63 (noting that fewer than 0.5 petitions filed per 100 prisoners in 1962 grew to 5.05 in 1970).

[195] *See* Rose v. Lundy, 455 U.S. 509 (1982); Larry W. Yackle, *The Exhaustion Doctrine in Federal Habeas Corpus: An Argument for a Return to First Principles*, 44 OHIO ST. L. J. 393, 424–31 (1983).

[196] *See* McCleskey v. Zant, 499 U.S. 467 (1991).

[197] *See* Stone v. Powell, 428 U.S. 465 (1976) (holding that Fourth Amendment exclusionary rule claims are not cognizable in habeas corpus proceedings).

[198] *See* Keeney v. Tamayo-Reyes, 504 U.S. 1 (1992); Sumner v. Mata, 455 U.S. 591 (1982).

[199] See Brecht v. Abrahamson, 507 U.S. 619 (1993).

of claims that had been procedurally defaulted in state court,[200] and forbade petitioners from raising arguments based on anything other than wholly settled legal principles.[201] Indeed, so little remains of the writ today that teachers of federal courts (including one of us) have begun either to drop the subject from their classes altogether or to treat it as a matter of mostly historical interest.

We consider two final issues of longstanding historical import in debates about the federal judiciary: its powers with respect to common law, and the doctrine of state sovereign immunity. Few issues were more controversial in the early Republic than the relationship between the federal courts and the common law. Thomas Jefferson wrote, for example, that

> Of all the doctrines which have ever been broached by the federal government, the novel one, of the common law being in force & cognizable as an existing law in their courts, is to me the most formidable. All their other assumptions of un-given powers have been in the detail. The bank law, the treaty doctrine, the sedition act, alien act, the undertaking to change the state laws of evidence in the state courts by certain parts of the stamp act, &c., &c., have been solitary, unconsequential, timid things, in comparison with the audacious, barefaced and sweeping pretension to a system of law for the U.S., without the adoption of their legislature, and so infinitely beyond their power to adopt. If this assumption be yielded to, the state courts may be shut up, as there will then be nothing to hinder citizens of the same state suing each other in the federal courts in every case, as on a bond for instance, because the common law obliges payment of it, & the common law they say is their law.[202]

To understand why Jefferson and his supporters found this business so menacing, we need to recapture the peculiar station of the common law in the eighteenth century. The common law was then seen not as a method of reasoning but as a distinct substantive *field* of law, one that covered most of the ordinary affairs of life in a world where legislative statutes were still somewhat exceptional.[203] The content of the common law was a set of principles produced (or legislated) in judicial opinions, ultimately derived in principle from "maxims and customs . . . of higher antiquity than memory or history can

[200] *See* Coleman v. Thompson, 501 U.S. 722 (1991) (overruling Fay v. Noia, 372 U.S. 391 (1963)); Wainwright v. Sykes, 433 U.S. 72 (1977).
[201] *See* Penry v. Lynaugh, 492 U.S. 302 (1989); Teague v. Lane, 489 U.S. 288 (1989).
[202] Letter from Thomas Jefferson to Edmund Randolph (Aug. 18, 1799), *in* 7 THE WRITINGS OF THOMAS JEFFERSON 383–84 (Paul Leicester Ford ed., 1896).
[203] *See* Larry D. Kramer, *The Lawmaking Power of the Federal Courts*, 12 PACE L. REV. 263, 281–83 (1992).

reach."[204] Two political implications followed for the Americans. First, a government could choose to "receive" the common law's body of principles for itself, but doing so required an express positive political act in its constitution or by way of legislation.[205] Second, once a government had adopted the common law, its judges were authorized to interpret that law in all the cases to which it applied, employing the uniquely legal form of "artificial reasoning" by which judges molded the principles of the common law to fit the exigencies of the day.

Given this understanding, the Republicans' panic over the Federalist position is easily grasped. Common law offenses could be committed against the federal government only if that government had received the common law. Yet, if it had, suits based on common law would automatically present federal questions that could be litigated in federal court as cases "arising under the Laws of the United States"[206] – an extension of federal jurisdiction that made a mockery of Article III's carefully prescribed limits. Moreover, federal "reception" had it actually occurred would have obliterated Article I's enumeration of legislative powers. Such an expansion of federal authority was, to Republicans, not just unthinkable, but obscene. And so they fervently, passionately, denied that federal reception had taken place and therefore that federal courts could exercise jurisdiction to hear common-law crimes[207] – a position the Supreme Court officially endorsed in 1812, in the wake of Republican political ascendancy.

Of equal longevity is the doctrine of state sovereign immunity, so much in the news of late. For our purposes, the story begins in 1793, when the Supreme Court provoked an outcry by ruling in *Chisolm v. Georgia*[208] that citizens of South Carolina could bring suit in federal court against the state of Georgia on a contract claim. This led a short two years later to the adoption of the Eleventh Amendment. By its terms, the Eleventh Amendment did no more than literally

---

[204] 1 WILLIAM BLACKSTONE, COMMENTARIES ON THE LAWS OF ENGLAND 67 (Univ. of Chi. ed., Univ. of Chi. Press 1979) (1765).

[205] Thus, upon declaring their independence, eleven of the original thirteen colonies immediately adopted "receiving statutes" expressly incorporating the common law as state law. *See* ELIZA-BETH GASPAR BROWN, BRITISH STATUTES IN AMERICAN LAW 1776–1836, at 24–26 (1964); Ford W. Hall, *The Common Law: An Account of Its Reception in the United States*, 4 VAND. L. REV. 791, 798–800 (1951).

[206] U.S. CONST. art. III, § 2, cl. 1.

[207] In addition to Jefferson's letter to Randolph, *supra* text accompanying note 202, see Madison's lengthy and scholarly (though no less impassioned) repudiation of the Federalists' argument in his Report of 1800 defending the Virginia Resolves, Madison Report, *supra* note 114, at 632–44.

[208] 2 U.S. (2 Dall.) 419 (1793).

overturn the holding in *Chisolm*.[209] And based on its language, together with
certain assumptions about Federalist aims, many commentators have argued
that state sovereign immunity should be limited to cases like *Chisolm* – diversity
cases based on state law – and not extend to claims arising under federal
law.[210] While this could be a plausible position, the Supreme Court itself
has never espoused it. According to the Court, the Eleventh Amendment
reaffirms a general principle of state sovereign immunity that never should have
been questioned in the first place.[211] Whether rightly or wrongly, moreover,
the Court has stuck to this position with remarkable consistency throughout
American history. It has, when necessary, modified or reshaped aspects of the
broader doctrine to account for changing circumstances. So, for example, in
Ex parte Young,[212] changes in the nature of governmental activity led the Court
to enlarge the personal cause of action that had been traditionally available
against individual officials.[213] And in a line of cases beginning with *Edelman*

---

[209] See U.S. CONST. amend. XI ("The Judicial power of the United States shall not be construed to
extend to any suit in law or equity, commenced or prosecuted against one of the United States
by Citizens of another State, or by Citizens or Subjects of any Foreign State.").

[210] See CLYDE E. JACOBS, THE ELEVENTH AMENDMENT AND SOVEREIGN IMMUNITY 90–105 (1972);
William A. Fletcher, A *Historical Interpretation of the Eleventh Amendment: A Narrow Construction of an Affirmative Grant of Jurisdiction Rather than a Prohibition Against Jurisdiction*,
35 STAN. L. REV. 1033 (1983); John J. Gibbons, *The Eleventh Amendment and State Sovereign
Immunity: A Reinterpretation*, 83 COLUM. L. REV. 1889 (1983); James E. Pfander, *History and
State Suability: An "Explanatory" Account of the Eleventh Amendment*, 83 CORNELL L. REV.
1269 (1998). These commentators have been supported in recent years by a persistent minority
on the Supreme Court.

[211] Hans v. Louisiana, 134 U.S. 1, 11–12 (1890). As the Court recently explained, the states' immunity thus "derives not from the Eleventh Amendment but from the structure of the original
Constitution itself." Alden v. Maine, 527 U.S. 706, 728 (1999).

[212] 209 U.S. 123 (1908).

[213] The impact of sovereign immunity was, from the first, softened by the opportunity to sue personally the government official allegedly responsible for a wrong. The plaintiff would bring an
action based on an ordinary common law theory, such as trespass or conversion; the defendant-
official would answer that his conduct was authorized by law; and the plaintiff would reply that
this law was illegal or unconstitutional, an argument that, if successful, stripped the official
of any protection. See David P. Currie, *Sovereign Immunity and Suits Against Government
Officers*, 1984 SUP. CT. REV. 149, 154–56 (1984). Because most governmental activities in the
late-eighteenth and early-nineteenth centuries required officials to enter land or seize property
or do something that fell within one of the common-law forms of action, this "official action"
meant that a remedy was available as a practical matter for most aggrieved plaintiffs. There were,
to be sure, some instances in which sovereign immunity effectively barred all relief because no
action was possible against the official personally, but these were rarer than one might otherwise
suppose. See *id.* at 151.
    By the late-nineteenth century, government was doing new sorts of things that did not require
an official to do anything encompassed by a traditional common-law cause of action. (*Ex parte*

v. Jordan,[214] the Court limited the forms of relief available in such actions to reflect new sorts of claims being brought.[215] But with very few exceptions (since overturned),[216] the Supreme Court has adhered closely to the idea that states

> *Young*, for example, involved allegedly confiscatory rate regulation that was enforced through ordinary criminal proceedings at a time before any action for malicious prosecution was available.) This new development threatened to upset the traditional balance between immunity and liability, leaving many more plaintiffs without any remedy at all. The Court solved the problem by enlarging the official action: holding that government officials could be sued personally for acting with apparent authority in violation of federal law, essentially the same theory as underlies § 1983. In so doing, the Court closed a potential gap in the availability of relief, restoring the traditional balance without having to repudiate or alter state sovereign immunity itself.
>
> This explains, by the way, why the modern Court's repeated insistence that actions under *Ex parte Young* are some sort of latecomer that involve a legal fiction is mistaken. *See, e.g.,* Pennhurst State Sch. & Hosp. v. Halderman, 465 U.S. 89, 105, 111–14 , n.25 (1984). The "fiction" that officials could be sued personally for illegal action taken in their official capacity has been built into sovereign immunity from the start. All *Ex parte Young* did was to enlarge this cause of action in a thoroughly conventional manner to reflect new activities not already covered by common law.

[214] 415 U.S. 651 (1974). *See* Idaho v. Couer d'Alene Tribe, 521 U.S. 261 (1997); Green v. Mansour, 474 U.S. 64 (1985); Quern v. Jordan, 440 U.S. 332 (1979); Hutto v. Finney, 437 U.S. 678, 689–70 (1978); Milliken v. Bradley, 433 U.S. 267, 288–91 (1977).

[215] Under *Ex parte Young*, plaintiffs could obtain injunctive relief to compel an official to cease illegal or unconstitutional official activity. This worked well for many decades, but the expansion of class actions and the development of new causes of actions in the 1960s and 1970s began to put pressure on the doctrine. In *Edelman*, for example, the plaintiff class sought declaratory and injunctive relief against Illinois state officials for withholding welfare payments, asking both that future payments be made and that past payments be adjusted. The Court concluded that an injunction awarding past payments was formally and functionally so indistinct from a damages action against the state that it could not be permitted. The cases since *Edelman*, cited *supra* note 214, all reflect the Court's ongoing effort to regulate the remedy in such a way as to preserve the state's immunity without at the same time rendering the official action meaningless.

[216] *See* Pennsylvania v. Union Gas Co., 491 U.S. 1 (1989); Parden v. Terminal Ry., 377 U.S. 184 (1964). *Parden* held (1) that just by engaging in regulated activity the state constructively waived its immunity; and (2) that federal statutes should be construed liberally to find that Congress has abrogated a state's immunity. *Parden*, 377 U.S. at 190, 196. The second holding was overturned in *Welch v. Texas Department of Highways and Public Transportation*, 483 U.S. 468, 475–77 (1987), followed a few years later by the reversal of the first holding in *Florida Prepaid Postsecondary Education Expense Board v. College Savings Bank*, 527 U.S. 627, 635 (1999). *Union Gas* held – in what must stand as one of the Court's all-time most tortured and poorly reasoned opinions – that Congress could constitutionally abrogate a state's sovereign immunity by exercising its power under the Commerce Clause. *Union Gas*, 491 U.S. at 23. It was overturned a short seven years later in *Seminole Tribe v. Florida*, 517 U.S. 44, 72 (1996).

The only other important decision that even arguably reflects a different, less stringent, understanding of state sovereign immunity is *Fitzpatrick v. Bitzer*, 427 U.S. 445 (1976), which ruled that Congress could abrogate state sovereign immunity by exercising its powers under Section 5 of the Fourteenth Amendment, which was specifically designed to empower Congress to reform state government.

cannot be sued in federal courts – thus avoiding a broad category of potentially troublesome political controversies.

3. Rules of Constitutional Interpretation

While only a microscopic fraction of cases present questions of constitutional law, the stakes in the debate about judicial independence are perceived to revolve mainly around the Constitution. This is partly because the charter's national character means that everyone is interested in it and pays attention, especially to Supreme Court decisions. And it is partly because the handful of cases every year, or every few years, that present genuinely important issues of constitutional law go far toward defining our national legal identity. For many, then, the question of judicial review and the question of judicial independence are one and the same – which makes it all the more striking (and important) to realize just how little the federal courts actually do, even in this domain. In saying that federal courts do little in the domain of constitutional law, we mean, of course, relative to what the text and best understanding of the Constitution suggest that they might otherwise do. The point is similar to one that our colleague Lawrence Sager first made some two decades ago, that the Constitution is to a striking degree "underenforced."[217] "Our constitutional jurisprudence," Sager observed, "singles out comparatively few encounters between the state and its citizens as matters of serious judicial concern":

> After threats to speech, religion, and the narrow band of activities that fall under the rubric of privacy, after the disfavor of persons because of their race or gender (or possibly, because of their nationality or the marital status of their parents), and after lapses from fairness in criminal process, the attention of the constitutional judiciary rapidly falls off. By default, everything else falls in the miasma of [judicially unenforced] economic rights.[218]

If Sager's reckoning of what courts do seems anything but modest, consider the much larger domain of things that are within the judicial reach but that the judiciary has chosen not to grasp. Start with the clauses granting affirmative powers to Congress and the Executive, virtually all of which have historically been left to the essentially unlimited discretion of the political branches.[219]

---

[217] Lawrence Gene Sager, *Fair Measure: The Legal Status of Underenforced Constitutional Norms*, 91 HARV. L. REV. 1212 (1978); Lawrence G. Sager, *Justice in Plain Clothes: Reflections on the Thinness of Constitutional Law*, 88 NW. U. L. REV. 410 (1993) [hereinafter Sager, *Justice in Plain Clothes*].

[218] Sager, *Justice in Plain Clothes*, *supra* note 217, at 410–11.

[219] *See* Larry D. Kramer, *Putting the Politics Back into the Political Safeguards of Federalism*, 100 COLUM. L. REV. 215, 227–33 (2000).

These include some rather important powers, too, such as the war power,[220] the treaty power (and foreign affairs generally),[221] and the powers to tax and spend.[222] The Court has recently begun to exercise aggressive judicial scrutiny under the Commerce Clause and Section 5 of the Fourteenth Amendment,[223] and its rhetoric in these cases suggests the possibility of an even more dramatic expansion of judicial interference.[224] If so, both history and our model would predict trouble. In the meantime, and for the moment at least, the Court's actual intrusions remain modest. Separation of powers is another arena in which the degree of judicial deference is remarkable. Here the Court has occasionally intervened – when it has viewed the text or some settled practice as unmistakably clear,[225] or when Congress has sought to aggrandize its own position in the separation of powers scheme[226] – but apart from these relatively narrow circumstances, the Court has for the most part left the political branches free to experiment. Hence the independent agencies, and legislative courts, and broad delegations of authority, and executive agreements, and much, much more. We are not saying that the Court plays no role in separation of powers; that would be a gross exaggeration. But in thinking about judicial independence, one needs to focus on the eighty or ninety percent of the glass that is empty as well as the ten or twenty percent that is full.

Even when we turn to the domain of individual rights, where the Court has been its most active, we mostly find restraint. Start with the Equal Protection Clause, which is theoretically applicable to everything government does, because all laws draw lines and create legal categories. Yet rather than use the clause ambitiously, the Court created tiers of scrutiny – strict, intermediate,

---

[220] There is no single case dealing with the war powers, which have evolved even more than most as a matter of practice and experience over time. But the courts have never interfered here. For a general discussion, see 1 LAURENCE H. TRIBE, AMERICAN CONSTITUTIONAL LAW 657–70 (3d ed. 2000).

[221] *See* Perez v. Brownell, 356 U.S. 44 (1958); United States v. Curtiss-Wright Export Corp., 299 U.S. 304 (1936); Missouri v. Holland, 252 U.S. 416 (1920).

[222] *See* South Dakota v. Dole, 483 U.S. 203 (1987); Helvering v. Davis, 301 U.S. 619 (1937); Steward Machine Co. v. Davis, 301 U.S. 548 (1937).

[223] *See* Board of Trustees v. Garrett, 531 U.S. 356 (2001) United States v. Morrison, 529 U.S. 598 (2000); Kimel v. Florida Bd. of Regents, 528 U.S. 62 (2000); United States v. Lopez, 514 U.S. 549 (1995).

[224] *See* Larry D. Kramer, *The Supreme Court, 2000 Term: Foreword: We the Court*, 115 HARV. L. REV. 4, 130–58 (2001).

[225] *See* Clinton v. City of N.Y., 524 U.S. 417 (1998) (striking down line-item veto); Immigration & Naturalization Serv. v. Chadha, 462 U.S. 919, 951–59 (1983) (finding legislative veto unconstitutional).

[226] *Compare* Humphrey's Ex'r v. United States, 295 U.S. 602 (1935) (holding that Congress can limit President's removal power), *with* Myers v. United States, 272 U.S. 52 (1926) (ruling that Congress cannot give itself removal power), *and* Bowsher v. Synar, 478 U.S. 714 (1986) (same).

and rational basis. Carefully confining the first two categories to a small subset of laws, the Justices allocated the vast majority of what government does into the third category, which means leaving it undisturbed.

Indeed, the use of rational basis scrutiny is ubiquitous in constitutional law, liberating most of what government does from serious judicial oversight whether it be under the Due Process Clause, the Takings Clause, the Contract Clause, or the Necessary and Proper Clause. The Court has effectively read the Fourteenth Amendment's Privileges and Immunities Clause out of the Constitution, while completely ignoring important parts of the Bill of Rights, including the Second and Ninth Amendments. To be sure, a few recent decisions suggest that clauses everyone thought were completely dead – like the Takings Clause or the Privileges and Immunities Clause – may have a bit of life in them after all.[227] But barely breathing is a long way from being a significant restriction on politics, and dire or hopeful predictions about a renaissance in the protection of economic liberties seem farfetched in reality.

The Court has been more aggressive with some provisions of the Constitution. There is the law of privacy, and, as Sager suggests, the Court's equal protection jurisprudence has been quite aggressive in the areas of race and gender. First Amendment doctrine is similarly robust, both as to matters of speech and religion. But the Court's once equally robust criminal procedure jurisprudence has fallen on hard times, and most of the rights recognized in the halcyon days of the 1960s have long since been undone. In much the same way, while adhering to its practice of policing the political system on matters of race, the Court has retreated from more daunting problems like political gerrymandering.[228] On the whole, then, if one considers how easily the Justices could make their presence felt over a much broader range of governmental activity, it is hard not to agree with Sager that the domain the Court has put beyond the reach of constitutional case law is "considerable."[229]

C. *Evaluating Equilibrium*

The federal judiciary has surrounded itself with an elaborate system of institutional and doctrinal devices of self-restraint. The principal reason for doing so is to protect itself against likely interventions from the political branches or from the people themselves. Indeed, from our point of view, the remarkable

---

[227] *See* Saenz v. Roe, 526 U.S. 489, 502–04 (1999) (interpreting Privileges and Immunities Clause); Nollan v. California Coastal Comm'n, 483 U.S. 825 (1987) (applying Takings Clause).
[228] *See* Davis v. Bandemer, 478 U.S. 109 (1986).
[229] Sager, *Justice in Plain Clothes*, *supra* note 217, at 410.

fact is how reluctant the federal judiciary has historically been to take an expansive view of its jurisdiction or its authority. Even when the political branches encourage courts to take a more active role in guiding social change, judges have established doctrinal barriers permitting them either to decline the invitation or to respond in a circumscribed and cautious manner. There have undeniably been periods when the federal courts were more aggressive – the *Lochner* Court is the most famous example, though the Rehnquist Court gave it a run for its money and the Roberts Court seems likely to continue on the same path – but such periods are rare, and their accomplishments often prove fragile and evanescent. Not surprisingly, the Supreme Court has generally been at the center of this institutional conservatism. This is so because the Court is uniquely in a position to take the perspective of the whole federal judiciary into account and to seek the public good of imposing judicial restraint. So, while some judges or some lower courts might, at times, undertake a venturesome jurisprudence, the Supreme Court will usually limit or stop these experiments if they threaten to provoke a political retaliation that would affect the federal court system generally.

It is, of course, possible to see in this picture, a judicial system that is *too* vulnerable to external political pressures, one that anticipates retaliation at every turn and imposes self-denying ordinances in response to foolishly imagined as well as real political threats. Does this accurately describe our federal courts? Should we say that the Marshall Court was cowardly in *Marbury* and *Stuart v. Laird* for failing to throw down the gauntlet to the Republicans? Or was it farsighted in finding a way to salvage some tactical advantage out of what might have been a disastrous period for the courts? In *Marbury*, Chief Justice Marshall successfully preserved the Court's just budding authority to review statutes and to interpret the Constitution, institutional prerogatives that have grown in authority and importance over time. Marshall was not permitted the luxury of assuming that these prerogatives were securely embedded in the constitutional fabric, though we take them for granted today. Faced with an imminent and dangerous threat to the authority of the judiciary, he found a way to craft *Marbury* that recognized and took account of political reality without abandoning his understanding of fundamental principles, at least not entirely.

The idea of a constitutional democracy rests on two ideas, democracy and the rule of law, reflecting two separate conceptions of legitimacy: democratic legitimacy, which flows from the responsiveness of policy to the people's will; and legal legitimacy, which arises from the fact that judicial decisions can be understood to fit within an accepted, ongoing legal system. Because we as a people insist on both values, we are particularly vulnerable to the moments when they tug in opposite directions. We ask our leaders to pull us back from these dangerous moments, and doing so occasionally requires some fancy footwork. This chapter has emphasized the role played by judicial leaders, those sitting on the Supreme Court, but we could in another setting speak of political leaders like Dwight Eisenhower, who accepted unpopular judicial decisions in order to avert a constitutional crisis. For the reality of judicial independence ultimately depends on the interactions among these leaders, acting within a malleable institutional framework that encourages them to behave responsibly while still protecting the interests of their institutions.

9   Black Judges and Ascriptive Group Identification

Kathryn Abrams

The literature on judicial independence has begun to be enriched by what might be described as its complement: a focus on judicial interdependence – that is, judicial connection or affiliation with identifiable groups in the larger population, members of whom will predictably appear before the courts. Judges are, as a normative matter, assumed or exhorted to be independent; yet they may also have, as a descriptive matter, connections to or affinities for different groups within their jurisdictions. Works arguing that these affinities shape the process or outcomes of adjudication date back to the legal realists; and they have recently served to challenge the norm of independence.[1] But these works have tended to elide a set of more difficult questions: How precisely does judicial interdependence affect the operation of the judicial role? Is judicial connection with particular groups simply in tension with impartiality, or might a more interdependent judicial stance be in some ways consistent with impartiality, or help to refine our understanding of what impartiality for situated decisionmakers might mean? In order to confront these questions more directly, I propose to examine judicial interdependence in the context of one kind of affinity: ascriptive group membership, or membership in certain socially-salient groups or categories, which tends to be assigned through a series of complex social processes, on the basis of visible, largely immutable characteristics such as gender or race.

This chapter begins by considering several related literatures that highlight judicial interdependence or connection with particular groups. Particularly prominent within this examination are literatures that focus on judges' identifications with those who share their group membership. For while judges' *group*

---

[1] The form of "independence" that is most frequently at issue in this particular debate is independence from the perspectives of the parties before the court, or from any specific vantage point on a controversy. This quality is also described as objectivity or impartiality.

membership, in and of itself, may communicate certain messages to the public, even more important is the question of judges' *affinities or identifications* with members of their group(s), and the way that these judicially-perceived connections shape judges' performance of their roles. Works within these literatures are often premised on a tension between judicial action reflecting affinity and judicial objectivity or impartiality; and they focus primarily on justifying the departure from impartiality that interdependence seems to entail. This emphasis on largely theoretical justification has obviated, or even replaced, a more concrete examination of how ascriptive group affinities, or identifications, actually operate in the context of judicial decisionmaking. In this essay I undertake such an examination, looking at the characteristic of race. I focus first on empirical data concerning the way in which decisionmaking does or does not vary with the race of the judge. My primary emphasis, however, is on a kind of analysis that tends to be lost in highly conceptual arguments about the effects of ascriptive group membership on judging: a phenomenological account of judging – that is, an analysis of the ways that individual judges experience their affinities with their ascriptive groups as operating in the context of their judicial role, and draw on these identifications as they implement their judicial roles. In particular I discuss a series of more than a dozen extended narratives by African-American judges about how race shapes their approach to adjudication and other tasks connected with their lives as judges. I conclude that these narratives provide concrete and sometimes unexpected ways of understanding the operation of racial group identification in judging, that serve more often to reinforce or reinterpret than they do to undermine the norm of judicial independence or objectivity.

I. APPROACHING INTERDEPENDENCE

The question of judicial interdependence with, or connection to, groups within the larger population has been approached from several perspectives. The issue is raised in a particularly blunt way by the election of some state judiciaries. Judges who must campaign for their positions, seek re-election, or face the prospect of recall cannot be wholly insulated from the views of their constituents, in the manner assumed by theorists of judicial independence. On the contrary, they develop an acute awareness of both the issues facing their districts and the substantive preferences of those who elect them: an awareness that some judges have described as influencing their decisions. The elected judge's role as a "representative" – responsive or accountable to, if not more directly influenced by, constituents – has also been highlighted in cases holding judicial districts to be subject to the minority vote dilution protections of the Voting Rights Act.[2] Finally, the necessity of judicial campaign finance has sharpened the question of constituent influence, as judges have developed not only diffuse electoral reliance on constituents who may have identifiable views, but more focused financial reliance on constituents who may have identifiable litigation-related interests.[3] Despite the provocative facts surrounding this instance of judicial interdependence, the debate over the role of elected state court judges has generated more heat than light. Perhaps because the link that tethers judges to their constituents is so menacingly frank – and the potential for departure from the norms of independence, understood not simply as impartiality but the practical freedom of a judge to decide for herself, is so great – normative arguments are rarely made about the virtues of this form of connection between judges and their constituents.[4] Moreover, with the exception of a few unseated judges who have been momentarily candid about the constraining effects of constituent opinion,[5] judges themselves have not been forthcoming enough about the effects of electoral influence either to elaborate on the effects of such connections on their work, or to commend such interdependence as the source of new judicial norms.

The remaining literatures in which the question of judicial interdependence has been raised are distinct, in that they *do* embody strong normative claims about the virtues of judicial connection with particular groups. In some of these literatures, moreover, the interdependence they explore arises not from electoral relations but from judges' membership in ascriptive groups. Perhaps the most familiar, in this regard, is feminist literature from the late 1980s and early 1990s that argued that adjudication could be improved by an approach that sought to foster more imaginative connection with the lives of litigants and more appreciation of the effects of adjudication on those lives. Scholars such as Judith Resnik,[6] Martha Minow, and Elizabeth V. Spelman[7] argued that the

---

[2] *See* Chisom v. Roemer, 501 U.S. 380 (1991); Chisom v. Edwards, 839 F.2d 1056 (5th Cir. 1988).

[3] *See* Kathryn Abrams, *Some Realism about Electoralism: Rethinking Judicial Campaign Finance*, 72 S. Cal. L. Rev. 505 (1999).

[4] These arguments were of course made in the nineteenth and early twentieth centuries, when the election of judges was first being implemented. In the contemporary period, however, analysts more frequently characterize elected state judiciaries as an inevitable feature of the institutional landscape, and direct their energies toward mitigating the most problematic effects of this feature.

[5] *See* Joseph Grodin, *Developing a Consensus of Constraint: A Judge's Perspective on Judicial Retention Elections*, 61 S. Cal. L. Rev. 1969, 1980 (1988) (acknowledging that electoral pressures may have affected his decisionmaking in one or more critical cases); Philip Hager, *Kaus Urges Reelection of Embattled Court Justices*, L.A. Times, Sept. 28, 1986, at A23 (similar acknowledgment by late California Supreme Court Judge Otto Kaus).

[6] Judith Resnik, *On the Bias: Feminist Reconsideration of the Aspirations for Our Judges*, 61 S. Cal. L. Rev. 1877 (1988).

[7] Martha Minow & Elizabeth V. Spelman, *Passion for Justice*, 10 Cardozo L. Rev. 37 (1988).

venerated norm of objectivity, when understood as entailing abstraction or emotional distance from the life circumstances of litigants, could produce blindness to the effects of legal decisionmaking and judicial failure to take responsibility for the concrete, human consequences of decisions. A process of imaginative or empathic connection with the parties and their dilemmas – which seemed to undermine objectivity by encouraging too intimate an emotional or even cognitive engagement with the circumstances of the parties – could actually be understood to promote sound and responsible decisionmaking.

This literature was not straightforwardly about ascriptive group membership: the process of imaginative connection was recommended to all judges, in connection with all groups of litigants. However, in another sense, membership in the group "women" was implicated in this normative position. The posture of imaginative or empathic connection corresponds to the modes of cognition or decisionmaking some theorists have associated with women,[8] or with epistemological claims (i.e., for experiential forms of knowledge and concrete, situated reasoning) advanced by feminists[9] and associated with women. Some of this scholarship even sought to derive this approach from the work of women judges.[10] Perhaps more importantly, while some judges discussed in this literature – Justices Brennan and Blackmun primary among them – could engage in strong empathic connection with claimants whose lives were completely unfamiliar to them, this posture is easier to assume for claimants whose lives most strongly resemble one's own, a situation approaching the effects of ascriptive group membership. As it emerged during this period, this scholarship on imaginative connection sought primarily to problematize a particular account of objectivity – objectivity as a posture of stringent and intentional distance from the lives of litigants – and to introduce, in broad terms, a possible alternative. It did less to elaborate what the stance of empathic engagement meant for judges in their decisionmaking: Was such thinking particularly applicable to sanctions or remedies (the phase of adjudication in which lives were actually disrupted), or did it also play into decisions about liability? Was empathic identification an intuitive response that had simply been derailed by the conventional injunction to maintain distance from the parties, or did it have to be exercised like a muscle? Did such identification emerge more readily toward some parties than toward others, and, if so, how did a judge respond to such disparities? Because

---

[8] *See, e.g.,* Carol Gilligan, In a Different Voice: Psychological Theory and Women's Development (1982).

[9] *See* Kate Bartlett, *Feminist Legal Methods,* 103 Harv. L. Rev. 829 (1990), *and* Susan Williams, *Religion, Politics, and Feminist Epistemology: A Comment on the Uses and Abuses of Morality in Public Discourse,* 77 Ind. L. J. 267 (2002).

[10] *See* Resnik, *On the Bias, supra* note 6, at 1928–29 (discussing work of Shirley Abrahamson).

of these failures of elaboration, this literature does not make clear whether this new mode of decisionmaking simply disrupts or potentially refines prevalent notions of objectivity. What we see is more a juxtaposition of prototypes than a fully fleshed-out account of interdependent decisionmaking.

The final body of scholarship to address questions of interdependence and ascriptive group membership is a small but growing literature on the normative contributions of a racially diverse bench – that is, a judiciary that includes increasing numbers of judges of color. Scholars seeking to advocate the racial diversification of the bench have asked whether diversity can be defended in terms that are substantive as well as symbolic. The effort to mount a substantive defense of the contributions of judges of color has entailed an interesting tension: the more these judges are thought to embody or bring to adjudication an identifiable perspective, the more this account of their approach to adjudication seems to conflict with the longstanding mandate of judicial objectivity or impartiality. The most common way of resolving this tension has been to look at the judiciary as a group and employ the metaphor of cross-sectionality. This conceptualization comes, of course, from work on the jury, and has been brought to the discussion of the bench by scholars such as Sherrilyn Ifill[11] and Martha Minow.[12] If one considers the judiciary, as a whole, as analogies to the jury, it becomes structurally impartial – or broadly reflective of the range of views that could arise in adjudication – only if it embodies many different, as opposed to one dominant, perspective. Racial diversity understood as contributing a set of substantively distinct perspectives could therefore be understood not only as salutary but as necessary for the achievement of structural impartiality.[13]

This analogy might be challenged for begging a number of critical questions: Do we actually expect the same characteristics of decisionmaking from judges as from a jury? And how can we talk about cross-sectionality in the judiciary, in the aggregate, when most judges decide alone, rather than in collegial groups? My reservation about the analogy, for purposes of this paper, is different. The cross-sectional account fails to address the dynamics produced by ascriptive group membership decisionmaking by *individual* judges. In its move to the aggregate, it assumes a kind of direct, representational relation between individual judges of color and members of their ascriptive group – a relation that is not only potentially reductive of a more complex connection,

---

[11] Sherrilyn Ifill, *Judging the Judges: Racial Diversity, Impartiality and Representation on State Trial Courts*, 39 B. C. L. REV. 95 (1997).

[12] Martha Minow, *Stripped Down Like a Runner or Enriched by Experience*, 33 WM. & MARY L. REV. 1201 (1992).

[13] *See* Ifill, *Judging the Judges, supra* note 11 (arguing that structural impartiality of this sort can be viewed as constitutionally required).

but posits an apparently inevitable tension between ascriptive group member-ship and impartiality. We need an account of the effects of ascriptive group membership – in this case, racial group membership – that tries to answer these questions about individual decisionmaking, rather than assuming them for the purposes of talking about judges in the aggregate.

One scholar, Sherrilyn Ifill, recognized this problem and asked what racial-group representation that has substantive, as well as symbolic, dimensions means for the decisionmaking and the impartiality of individual judges.[14] Her answer is that one can identify, across broad population groups, differences in perspective between blacks and whites on many issues that come before the courts, particularly at the state level. But individual judges do not straight-forwardly act on these differences; they more often simply bring them to the table – in both collegial deliberations and in the ongoing choice among inter-pretive possibilities that constitutes decisionmaking for the individual judge. This reconciliation permits judges to reflect particularized group perspectives and to reflect the impartiality that academics and the public have traditionally demanded from judges.

Ifill's work reflects a deft theoretical reconciliation – and more awareness of the pitfalls of neglecting individual adjudication than many others who write in this area. However, it leaves important issues unresolved. What exactly does it mean to "bring [a group-based perspective] to the table"? And how do judges who are as thoroughly socialized to these perspectives as Ifill appears to assume satisfy themselves by simply offering these perspectives in the course of deliberation? Is it difficult to abstract from, or make choices against, the explanatory "narratives" conferred by group-based experience[15] if, as this anal-ysis suggests, these narratives shape so many, almost subconscious, quotidien responses? If earlier accounts posit too much distance between group-based per-spectives and the conventional demands of impartiality, Ifill's account seems to tie them too neatly together. It might be easier to imagine this act of com-promise or transcendence if Ifill had supplied more concrete details about how judges move from a particular group-based response to the decision about how it should bear on a particular instance of adjudication. In other words, it would be useful to know more about judges' group-based *identifications*: not simply judges' group membership and its presumed effects, but their own *understandings of their relationship to their group*, and their implications for judges' approach to their roles.

---

[14] Sherrilyn Ifill, *Racial Diversity on the Bench: Beyond Role Models and Public Confidence*, 57 WASH. & LEE L. REV. 405 (2000).
[15] *See id.* at 439–49 (describing race-based "narratives").

These difficulties suggest, once again, that we need a better picture of how group-based perspectives operate, in order to answer the question of exactly how such perspectives shape our understanding of judicial objectivity. In the remainder of this paper, I will begin to develop a more detailed account, by drawing on two distinct bodies of work. First, I will begin by surveying a more traditional, empirical literature on the effects of race, gender, and other similar characteristics on judicial decisionmaking. This literature does not distinguish between group membership and group identifications; moreover, it does not find significant variation in most indices of judicial decisionmaking, when it compares black judges with white judges, often of similar tenure and political vantage point. This literature supports my intuition that we may need to go beyond accounts of group membership to more nuanced examinations of group affinities or identifications, to understand more fully the roles that race plays for members of the judiciary. Second, I embark on this latter task by examining a group of first-person narratives by African-American judges. These narratives illuminate a variety of ways that race-derived perceptions and experiences have affected judges' understanding of their relationship to their ascriptive group, their approaches to judging, and their objectivity.

II. GROUP MEMBERSHIP AND DECISIONAL EFFECTS

One classical way of assessing the impact of ascriptive group membership on judicial roles has been to consider decisional effects. A series of empirical studies, spanning the period from 1979 to 2001, have sought to assess the effects of race on judicial decision making.[16] These studies have had different foci and surveyed different groups of judges. One study, for example, analyzed the decisions of judges who were Carter appointees, comparing white judges to

---

[16] *See* Orley Ashenfelter, Theodore Eisenberg & Stewart J. Schwab, *Politics and the Judiciary: The Influence of Judicial Background on Case Outcomes*, 24 J. LEGAL STUD. 257 (1995); Jon Gottschall, *Carter's Judicial Appointments: The Influence of Affirmative Action and Merit Selection on Voting on the U.S. Courts of Appeals*, 67 JUDICATURE 165 (1983); Gregory C. Sisk et al., *Charting the Influences on the Judicial Mind: An Empirical Study of Judicial Reasoning*, 73 N.Y.U. L. REV. 1377 (1998); Cassia Spohn, *The Sentencing Decisions of Black and White Judges: Expected and Unexpected Similarities*, 24 LAW & SOC'Y REV. 1197 (1990); Daniel Steffensmeier & Chester L. Britt, *Judges' Race and Judicial Decision Making: Do Black Judges Sentence Differently?*, 82 SOC. SCI. Q. 749 (2001); Thomas M. Uhlman, *Black Elite Decision Making: The Case of Trial Judges*, 22 AM. J. POL. SCI. 884 (1978); Thomas G. Walker & Deborah J. Barrow, *The Diversification of the Federal Bench: Policy and Process Ramifications*, 47 J. POL. 596 (1985); Susan Welch et al., *Do Black Judges Make a Difference?*, 32 AM. J. POL. SCI. 126 (1988).

black judges among Carter appointees[17]; another looked at the decisions of federal district court judges on the constitutionality of the Federal Sentencing Guidelines, during the period before the Supreme Court first ruled on this question.[18] Still others looked at the decisions of larger groups of federal or state judges, across a wider docket of cases, and sought to isolate the effects of race within those groups.

The most noteworthy feature of these studies is that they find no consistent, and only a few salient, differences in decisionmaking that correlate with the race of the judge. These studies do not find significant differences in decisionmaking among black and white judges in areas including economic regulation, sex discrimination, and – surprisingly, to some observers – civil rights. The only area in which a few studies found race-related differences in decisionmaking was criminal law; moreover, these differences were subtle, rather than categorical, and variable from study to study. In Gottschall's 1983 study of Carter appointees to the courts of appeals, the author found that in a comparison of decisions by white male and black male judges, black judges found in favor of claims of the accused/prisoners at a rate of 79 percent, whereas white judges found in favor of claims of the accused /prisoners at a rate of 53 percent.[19] A study by Welch et al., which looked at sentencing decisions by state court judges in an unidentified urban metropolitan area, found that in the initial decision to incarcerate, black judges tended to be more even-handed toward black and white defendants, whereas white judges tended to be more severe with black defendants.[20] As to the length of sentences, however, black judges tended to give lighter sentences when all sentences were aggregated, but tended to be more severe than white judges when defendants were white, and more lenient than white judges when defendants were black. However, a recent study by Steffensmeier and Britt found that black judges sent convicted defendants, both black and white, to prison more frequently, though they concluded that the race-of-judge effect were small, and the reasoning employed by the different groups of judges in sentencing was substantially similar.

The most frequent conclusion of these studies however, was that the race of the judge was not a strong or predictable determinant of decisional outcomes. Thomas Walker and Deborah Barrow's study concludes that "black and white [federal district] judges displayed markedly similar decision-making records" in multiple legal fields, including criminal law and procedure.[21] Gottschall's

---

[17] Gottschall, *Carter's Judicial Appointments, supra* note 16.
[18] Sisk et al., *Charting the Influences, supra* note 16.
[19] Welch et al., *supra* note 16, at 131–35.   [20] *Id.*
[21] *See* Walker & Barrow, *supra* note 16, at 613–15.

study of Carter appointees finds comparability in all but the criminal field. Sisk
et al., surveying the field in their study of decisions on the Federal Sentencing
Guidelines, conclude that "studies of trial judges in the very context of criminal cases and criminal sentencing have uncovered very little variation in the
behavior of judges based upon race."[22] And Cassia Spohn's study of the sentencing decisions of black and white judges notes "remarkable" similarities in
sentencing decisions of black and white judges, and finds race-of-judge effects
very limited.[23]

These findings seem to be consistent with my earlier intuition that a cross-
sectional notion – that judges from different racial backgrounds bring to collective decisionmaking distinctive decisional inclinations derived from their
group-based experience – may be an insufficiently nuanced tool for explaining
how racial group membership and affinity affects the judge's role. Black judges,
for example, might be expected to have a range of perceptions about civil rights
or economic regulation that are distinct from those of white judges; but these
differences in perception or assumptions do not seem consistently or even per-
ceptibly to translate into different decisional outcomes. This suggests that there
may be a more complicated story about the way that experiences, assumptions,
and racially-grounded explanatory "narratives" operate for judges as they perform their official role. Thus, first-person accounts that explore precisely these
questions may help us to articulate that more complicated picture.

III. INTERROGATING INTERDEPENDENCE

To begin this task, I analyzed a series of first-person narratives by judges who
have precisely the kind of ascriptive group membership I have discussed above:
African-American jurists. The literature that elicits or examines such perspectives is surprisingly scant, a product perhaps of the relatively recent racial

---

[22] Sisk et al., *supra* note 16. As to race, the study finds that: 1) while minority judges invalidated the
   guidelines by a larger percentage (71 percent v. 60 percent) than white judges, this difference
   was not statistically significant; 2) the race-of-judge variable didn't approach significance in any
   of the multiple phases of analysis with one exception – of judges striking down the guidelines
   as unconstitutional, minority judges were significantly more likely than white judges to strike
   down the guidelines on the grounds that due process guaranteed defendants a right to individual sentencing by a judge operating with full discretion. (Only 42/192 judges invalidated the
   guidelines on this ground, so it was a nonmainstream position.). Fifty-eight percent of whites
   who addressed the due process claim invalidated the guidelines on this ground; ninety percent
   of the minority judges who addressed the due process claim invalidated the guidelines on this
   ground.
[23] Spohn, *supra* note 16, at 1211–14.

integration of the bench, as well as a reluctance on the part of academics,[24] and judges themselves, to perturb longstanding assumptions about judicial impartiality or objectivity. One volume that proved a useful point of departure in this effort was Linn Washington's collection, *Black Judges on Justice*,[25] in which fourteen African-American state and federal judges reflect on the ways that race bears on their decisionmaking, as well as on other aspects of their judicial role and on the possibilities for justice in the legal system more generally. All of these judges consider themselves to be African-American, but beyond that, they are a fairly heterogeneous group. Two have biracial heritage; three are women. They span a range of ages, geographical areas, educational backgrounds, prior professional experience and years on the bench. Most are Democrats, although three or four (depending on one's definition) are Republicans. They are fairly equally divided between the federal and state benches.

I should stress that in analyzing the interviews in this volume, and supplementing them with the few available others,[26] I do not intend to offer *conclusions* about the racial identifications of black judges as a group. Although the number of African-American jurists nationwide is still frustratingly small,[27] one cannot hope to say anything about the proclivities of this group by examining a "sample" of fourteen.[28] What these narratives provide is rich and potentially

---

[24] As I note above, this reluctance extends both to traditionalists and to their critical counterparts. *See supra* Part II. While traditionalists assume that judges, in pursuit of objectivist aspirations for their role, can and do abstract from the perceptual or normative effects of group-based identity or affiliation, many critical scholars assume that these effects operate in a straightforward or unitary way. My suggestion is that we unsettle both of these assumptions by investigating, in a more differentiated and nuanced fashion, the way that these effects operate in the many different tasks associated with the judicial role.

[25] *See* LINN WASHINGTON ED., BLACK JUDGES ON JUSTICE (1994).

[26] *See, e.g.,* BRUCE WRIGHT, BLACK ROBES, WHITE JUSTICE (1987).

[27] *See, e.g.,* Ifill, *supra* note 11.

[28] Questions of the representativeness, as well as the size, of this group would also inevitably arise. As I observe later, *infra* text accompanying note 30, those judges who would agree to participate in a volume that, as a matter of conceptual orientation, focused on the significance of racial identification for black judges, most likely have a sense of affiliation or identification with their racial group – however it plays out in practice – which might not be shared by all members of that group.

There are also unavoidable difficulties with the "self-reporting" that forms the basis of my analysis here, particularly among a group of professionals who are widely expected to enact or embody certain norms, including the very norms at issue in this analysis: objectivity or impartiality. Judges may feel, consciously or subconsciously, that they would compromise themselves, or compromise members of their racial group, by describing the effects of race on their judicial functioning in a way that deviated too sharply from these norms. Thus we might expect to see subtle, or not so subtle, efforts by judges to describe their group-based affinities in terms that are more or less consistent with broader judicial norms. This is a possibility that

valuable material that may help legal analysts to take the first steps beyond cross-sectional analyses that assume certain consequences of judicial group member-ship, toward more subtle or differentiated accounts of the ways in which group identification might bear on a judge's understanding of her role. They may help us to formulate hypotheses that could subsequently be investigated in the larger population of African-American judges, or judges of color more broadly, yielding useful information about the consciousness of important segments of the judiciary, and enabling scholars to rethink, in more empirically-grounded fashion, notions of judicial impartiality or objectivity.

How do the African-American judges whose statements are analyzed here express, or act on, or experience their connections with their communities, in the context of their judicial roles? It may be useful to ask, first, whether there are judges in this group who do not articulate a specific connection with members of their group. The answer is there are few if any; this should be placed in context, however, because judges who had no sense of themselves as members of their racial group would be unlikely to want to be interviewed for a book like *Black Judges on Justice* or to write a book like Bruce Wright's, *Black Robes, White Justice*, or, for that matter, to see their lives as district court judges, for example, as worthy of book-length focus.[29] There are, however, judges whose connection with their ascriptive communities appears to be minimal, or who regard the consequences of their group membership as primarily symbolic. There is one judge who talks primarily about the responsibility to be an "exemplar of Black excellence,"[30] a role that entails some awareness of group-based history and tradition, but that depends primarily on integrity, relentless work, and analytic skill. One or two other judges talk about the effects of their role as making things "fairer," or making the legal system more legitimate in the eyes of racial minority groups.[31] This latter goal reflects a general concern about the system affect of people of color, but neither of these last views seems to indicate a connection predictably potent enough to bear on decisional outcomes, or challenge the norm of objectivity.

must be borne in mind, although, as we will see, some of the judges whose accounts I will analyze reveal a willingness to depart from or reinterpret those norms that is surprising and bracing.

[29] In his empirical study of black judges, *Race Versus Robe*, Michael David Smith notes that some judges to whom he sent a written survey instrument responded angrily that they did not think of themselves as black judges and did not wish to participate in a study that hypothesized for them that kind of identity. See MICHAEL D. SMITH, RACE VERSUS ROBE: THE DILEMMA OF BLACK JUDGES (1983).

[30] See WASHINGTON, BLACK JUDGES ON JUSTICE, *supra* note 25, at 226 *et seq.* (interview with Judge Timothy Lewis).

[31] See id.

Most judges in this group, however, combine these more symbolic understandings with actions, decisions, or analytic postures that more substantively reflect their racial group membership. Many of the judges interviewed for *Black Judges on Justice* describe black judges as having a race-related obligation to effect certain goals or undertake certain actions that are not incumbent on white judges.[32] Not all of these mandates have specific decisional consequences. They vary from speaking up against the subtle effects of racism,[33] to "acting like a 'real' black and trying to solve the problems of the community"[34] to "be[ing] part of the leadership that is saying things that people don't want to hear."[35] But they are indicative of a range of potential ways in which the judicial role of these African-American judges might look different from that of their white counterparts. Let us now examine how these perceived obligations have played out in practice.

Many judges reflected a commitment to their ascriptive group that is expressed through judicial actions outside the adjudicative process, or even through actions that are not distinctively judicial. Members of this group who were state court judges, in particular, committed themselves to a variety of activities in their local communities, many of which addressed members of their ascriptive group (defined either as African-Americans or as people of color) in particular, or addressed substantive issues of particular interest to this group. Several mentioned making presentations to school children, particularly at schools with substantial poor or minority populations, or hosting school children during their visits to the courthouse.[36] These visits were described by some of these judges in explicitly group-based terms, as "giving hope" to children of color, or contributing to their view of the justice system as one that insured equality for all.[37] One or two also volunteered in their communities at activities like tutoring, or working with youth of color, usually from poorer areas.[38] Of the judges who chose to become involved in their communities in ways that exceeded their formal judicial duties, most showed a particular interest in addressing problems of crime, an issue they described as bearing in particular on young African-American men.[39] Some of these judges expressed a feeling of

---

[32] Ten of the fourteen judges interviewed for the book articulated some sense of obligation that I would characterize in this way.

[33] *See generally* Washington, Black Judges on Justice, *supra* note 25, at 72 (Theodore A. McKee).

[34] *See id.* at 46 *et seq.* (Joseph Brown).   [35] *Id.* at 45 (Veronica S. McBeth).

[36] *See* Washington, Black Judges on Justice, *supra* note 25.

[37] *See id.* at 38, 174 (Veronica S. McBeth, Henry Bramwell).

[38] *See id.* at 46 *et seq.*, 91 *et seq.*, 211 *et seq.* (Joseph Brown, Reggie Walton, Abigail Rogers).

[39] *See id.* at 46 *et seq.* (Joseph Brown).

responsibility for bringing local leaders together to address problems of crime and criminal justice; one state court judge described himself as a playing the role of a "village chieftain."[40] Others highlighted their responsibility, exercised through speeches and commission work, for helping policymakers to see the larger social problems that bear on the incidence of crime in urban areas, or condition the responses of the criminal justice system.[41]

Both federal and state judges in this group demonstrated a strong commitment to increasing the numbers of judges of color on the bench. Although some focused specifically on African-Americans, a substantial number spoke of racial minorities more generally and some also spoke about women.[42] This commitment seemed to be an important means of expressing a connection with other members of their ascriptive group, which judges acted on in a number of different ways. Most (including a Republican appointed by President Bush)[43] vocally criticized public officials for their failure to appoint African-American or other minority judges.[44] Several worked in their local or state legal communities to promote African-American candidates for the bench, including one state court judge who conducted lectures for minority lawyers on strategies for enhancing their attractiveness as potential judicial candidates.[45] Several more served on state bar commissions on racial equity, examining both judicial appointments and the treatment of minority clients, lawyers, and court personnel in state legal systems.[46]

If the above are the nondecisional (and even nonjudicial) means by which black judges act on their connection with members of their racial group, these connections also seem to be vindicated through forms of substantive decision-making. Perhaps the most conspicuous is the interest reflected among these judges in experimentation with innovative criminal sanctions. Several judges working at the state court level spoke of work they had done developing nontraditional solutions to the problem of crime.[47] These ranged from the sanctioning of "reverse theft" – the victim was authorized to enter the home of the convicted defendant and take a specified number of items of his choice – to the requirement that convicted pimps establish scholarship funds for prostitutes,

---

[40] *Id.* at 46 (Joseph Brown).

[41] *See* WASHINGTON, BLACK JUDGES ON JUSTICE, *supra* note 25 (some judges opt for a more professional/organizational approach rather than a community-based approach to these issues).

[42] *See id.*   [43] *See id.* at 230 (Timothy Lewis).

[44] *See generally* WASHINGTON, BLACK JUDGES ON JUSTICE, *supra* note 25.

[45] *See id.* at 191 (Charles Smith).

[46] *See id.* at 27 *et seq.*, 145 *et seq.*, 186 *et seq.* (Veronica McBeth, George Crockett, Jr., Charles Z. Smith).

[47] *See id.* at 27 *et seq.* (Veronica McBeth), 46 *et seq.* (Joseph Brown), 65 *et seq.* (Theodore McKee), 186 *et seq.* (Charles Z. Smith).

to the requirement that convicted felons pursue literacy programs, Graduate Equivalency Degrees, or read the works of black theorists such as W. E. B. DuBois or Malcolm X. The judges who experimented with these alternative sanctions – along with several of their more traditional African-American colleagues – decried the high numbers of young black men in prison and the use of mandatory sentencing guidelines.[48] They expressed doubt that such "containment" strategies reflected promise in combating urban crime. Some of them also stressed the power that the sentencing judge has over the conduct of a convicted criminal, and advocated that that power be used to improve the lives of both victims and perpetrators of crime, rather than simply to remove convicted criminals from the streets.

Others expressed views about the operation of the criminal justice system that one could imagine bearing on decisions in the area of criminal law, particularly those relating to sentencing. Many of these views tend to place the criminal responsibility of African-American offenders in the context of larger social problems and governmental decisions. Some judges were fairly explicit about the likely effects of these understandings on their adjudicative decisionmaking. One state court judge said specifically that his perspective as an African-American had led him to consider lack of education and job security in criminal dispositions.[49] A federal judge volunteered that he had come to have a different view of which convicted criminals were most subject to rehabilitative efforts than that evinced by most white judges. He said that an African-American perpetrator who had spent his youth in circumstances of poverty and pervasive crime and had resisted their influence until nearly the age of maturity showed far more potential for future self-discipline than a white youth who had been given every advantage of economic comfort and skin privilege and had nonetheless succumbed to the temptations of crime.[50]

Other judges offered accounts of complex social responsibility for crime that might or might not bear on matters such as sentencing decisions. Almost half the judges interviewed, including those working at both federal and state levels, said that the crime problems of urban areas required systematic government approaches to poverty and unemployment that were not currently being undertaken.[51] Two federal judges stated, in connection with the drug problems prevalent in many urban areas, that black males were being targeted in enforcement efforts, but were neither the original source of the problem nor the largest

---

[48] *See id.* at 69–71, 108 (critiques of mandatory sentencing by Theodore McKee and Reggie Walton).
[49] *See* WASHINGTON, BLACK JUDGES ON JUSTICE, *supra* note 25, at 188 (Charles Z. Smith).
[50] *See id.* at 73 (Theodore McKee).
[51] *See* WASHINGTON, BLACK JUDGES ON JUSTICE, *supra* note 25.

financial beneficiaries of the drug traffic.[52] Several judges also stated that the intense veneration of wealth and diminished respect for life that characterized many criminal defendants reflected values that poor African-American shared with, and often learned from, highly privileged whites.[53] While many of these contextualizing responses pointed the finger at powerful persons or institutions apart from the black community, some placed responsibility with members of that community itself – but the effect of such beliefs on actual decisionmaking seems even less clear than with the previous assumptions. Three judges cited the breakdown of the family as a source of the increase in crime, with two judges citing the negative influence of single mothers in raising young black men.[54] One federal judge talked about the need for "containment" and the imperative for black leaders to "get tough" on members of the black community engaged in crime.[55]

In another group-based commitment with potential decisional implications, many judges stressed that they felt an obligation, as people of color in a position of relative power, to speak out when they saw instances of racial injustice. Four judges expressed this as an obligation to highlight subtle effects of racism that might go unappreciated by many whites.[56] While this obligation could, for some, be vindicated by public statements, others saw it as extending to actions on the bench. One judge detailed numerous contexts in which he had spoken out about racism among members of the bench and bar.[57] Two spoke of times they had intervened to highlight and stop racist statements by witnesses, attorneys, or court personnel in their own courtroom.[58] Some were, finally, specific about the way that this mandate had affected their decisionmaking in specific cases. One state criminal judge gave examples of contexts in which he had rejected prosecutorial requests to deny bail to large groups of suspects, when he believed that the requests reflected a strategy of containment against accused parties who were African-American.[59] Two other federal judges described cases in which they had denied motions for their recusal which they saw as predicated on the unjust and unjustified assumption that race (or gender) eroded the objectivity of minority and

---

[52] *See id.* at 61,106 (Joseph Brown, Reggie Walton).
[53] *See id.* at 46 *et seq.*, 68–69 (Joseph Brown, Theodore McKee).
[54] *See id.* at 66 (Joseph Brown, Reggie Walton).   [55] *See id.* at 171 *et seq.* (Henry Bramwell).
[56] *See* WASHINGTON, BLACK JUDGES ON JUSTICE, *supra* note 25.
[57] *See id.* at 247 *et seq.* (Bruce Wright). *See also* WRIGHT, BLACK ROBES, WHITE JUSTICE, *supra* note 26.
[58] *See* WASHINGTON, BLACK JUDGES ON JUSTICE, *supra* note 25.
[59] *See id.* at 165–70 (George Crockett, Jr.).

female decisionmakers in a way that it did not in the case of white male jurists.[60]

Finally, a majority of these judges stated that their experience as persons of color had helped create in them a different posture toward the parties before them, and a critical vantage point on some of the arguments that were made in their courts. Many stated that their experience had helped to remove some of the barriers that frequently existed between courts and certain parties, particularly criminal defendants.[61] It was a recurrent theme in these narratives that there is a universe of difference between the narrow, highly privileged background that many white judges come from and the extremely harsh lives of many criminal defendants. These judges believed that many white judges simply knew nothing of the circumstances or lives of those whose cases they adjudicated. This made it more likely that they would resort to stereotypes in thinking about those before them. As one federal judge, who had had previous experience as a state criminal judge said, "when you see a young black guy charged with a crime, there's a prejudice about what's going on in urban communities." He added that, while some of this was based in fact, "this particular kid may not be a part of it."[62] Many of these judges argued that their own experience growing up in poorer neighborhoods, or being closely acquainted with people who had grown up in such neighborhoods, gave them a perspective on the experience of those before them that made it difficult simply to resort to stereotypes. As one state judge said, "I'm from South Central Los Angeles; I know what it's like to get jacked up on a wall by the police."[63] One state judge said that her group-based experience made it possible for her to see blacks who were accused even of the most serious crimes in human terms.[64] Two others stated that their familiarity with the circumstances of black offenders meant that they were able to "speak their language." Interestingly, this experiential proximity did not always translate into a posture of greater empathy or leniency. Two judges remarked, for example, that this familiarity made it easier for them to see when they were being given what one of them referred to as a "lame line" by a black defendant.[65]

Several judges noted that their own experiences of being discriminated against in public accommodations, educational institutions, or courtrooms made it easier for them to see subtle discrimination in action. These were

---

[60] *See id.* at 3 *et seq.* (Leon Higginbotham), 127 *et seq.* (Constance Baker Motley).

[61] *See* WASHINGTON, BLACK JUDGES ON JUSTICE, *supra* note 25.

[62] *Id.* at 68 (Theodore McKee). [63] *Id.* at 49 (Joseph Brown).

[64] *See id.* at 44–45 (Veronica McBeth). [65] *Id.* at 50 (Joseph Brown).

among the most poignant sections of these narratives, when judges related being shown to a portion of a restaurant where other black families "just happened to be" seated, or having a conference hotel call the police because management believed that a bar association party of black lawyers and judges was becoming "unruly."[66] The judges noted that these experiences gave them a critical eye, and helped them to see how perspective shapes decisionmaking and, in particular, how it can produce blindness and insensitivity on certain kinds of issues. Although this critical frame of reference was frequently brought to bear on actions taken by white people, it was also capable of inspiring self-scrutiny. One judge remarked that once she saw this problem in other people, it became easier to see it in herself as well.[67] Finally, several judges stated that their experiences of victims of prejudice had given them a deep commitment to the articulated goals of equal justice under law. As one state judge said, "persons of color understand the importance of being fair to other persons because we don't want other persons to have the negative experiences we've had." His experience as a person of color, this judge concluded, "makes me more sensitive, more aware of the need for treating all persons as decent human beings."[68]

IV. DYNAMICS OF IDENTIFICATION

Even among so small a group, the complexity of response revealed by these narratives quickly undermines the notion that there is a predictable set of decisional leanings associated with group membership, or that such membership produces in judges a straightforward affinity with the ascriptive community that is in tension with the demands of objectivity or impartiality. On the contrary, these qualitative accounts of the (self-) perceptions of African-American jurists help to explain phenomena such as the lack of decisional divergence among the black and white Carter appointees discussed earlier. These variant accounts reflect certain broad patterns, which could be used to organize and inform future investigations; I focus here on two. Yet even these unifying perceptions are experienced and implemented in very different ways by the judges surveyed. In the following exposition, I will identify both the recurring themes and the highly diverse ways that they are given meaning by different judges.

The first, and perhaps the most salient, is the sense of *responsibility* to their ascriptive community that is articulated by these African-American

---

[66] WASHINGTON, BLACK JUDGES ON JUSTICE, *supra* note 25, at 121 (Damon Keith).
[67] *See id.* at 32–33 (Veronica McBeth).   [68] *Id.* at 188 (Charles Smith).

judges. Interestingly, that community is not always defined simply as African-American. Often the judges' responsibility to their community seems to flow from "outsider" characteristics that African-Americans share with other people of color, or even with white women; in other contexts, judges articulate responsibilities to particular subgroups such as poor African-Americans, or African-American men. There is a consistent sense that the office of the judge provides valuable opportunities to facilitate inclusion of these marginalized groups, and to foster awareness of the present circumstances that contribute to their disadvantage.

One of the most interesting revelations of these narratives is that many of these opportunities occur outside the traditional, decisional role that has been the focus of scholarly analysis. The state judges interviewed, in particular, seemed to feel that their positions both empowered them, and made it incumbent upon them, to take a role in their communities on questions of criminal justice or educational or economic opportunity that bore with particular weight on African-Americans. Many judges on both federal and state benches were aware of the symbolic value of their roles in signaling the potential of African-Americans to attain positions of leadership in the legal system, and the potential of the legal system to respond to claimants from a variety of different racial, ethnic, and economic groups. They felt a responsibility to make themselves visible, whether in giving school children tours of their courthouses, or in addressing meetings of the bench and bar. The federal judges, in general, held themselves at a greater remove from their communities and from activities that might be regarded as "political." But they joined with their state counterparts in serving on race equity commissions and acting to recruit more people of color to the bench. The view that there should be greater racial diversity on the bench was shared by every judge in the group, including registered Republicans, judges professedly "tough on crime," and judges who considered Justice Clarence Thomas among their professional heroes.

A large number of these judges voiced a sense of obligation to make visible – particularly to those who did not suffer them – the subtle social and institutional dynamics that perpetuate the disadvantage of African-Americans, or people of color. This sometimes meant describing a problem regarded as individual or characterological in its complex and constitutive social context; it sometimes meant revealing seemingly unremarkable or neutral beliefs to be actually discriminatory or potentially disadvantaging. While some of these beliefs remained background elements of judicial consciousness, others were implemented in judicial decisionmaking. For state judges, these efforts to highlight broader social dynamics sometimes led to the imposition of novel remedies or the consideration of additional factors in the process of sentencing.

For both federal and state judges, the task of highlighting the dynamics of subordination often meant identifying and curtailing instances of subtle or unrecognized racial discrimination by witnesses, advocates, and court personnel. This pattern is connected with a broader sense of obligation to speak difficult – often racially-related – truths that might not be observed or articulated by others. Some judges remarked on the self-awareness that these habits tended to foster: the ability to glimpse the blind spots produced by unreflective perceptivity could be applied to oneself as well as others. But the most obvious, and most frequently intended, beneficiaries of these practices were members of the group(s) impeded by unrecognized prejudice. This wide range of strategies enact a prevalent, shared sense among these jurists that ameliorating the disadvantage of the members of one's group – though not simply or even predictably through decisional outcomes – is part of one's moral and professional responsibility *as a judge*.

A second shared feature of these narratives is a sense of deep and nuanced familiarity with the (varied) circumstances and life patterns of members of the African-American community. This familiarity or knowledge need not determine outcomes, but it often shapes the terms in which cases are conceived or parties are characterized. This knowledge impedes the resort to stereotypes by putting what might otherwise be viewed as group-based or characterological traits in a broader social context. While the local knowledge of these judges may reflect categories or understandings that are shared by some members of the majority (white) population – the breakdown of the family as a source of the increase in crime, for example – it is also alert to exceptions (while some prejudice about urban communities was based in fact, "this particular kid may not be a part of it"), and moves persistently toward more contextual or power-aware explanations (e.g., black teens' veneration of expensive consumer goods is part of a pattern originated and reinforced by the more privileged).

A second stance that comes out of this contextual familiarity is a greater distrust than one might expect to see in judges, of emotional and experiential distance in adjudication. Many of these judges decried the cluelessness of white jurists about the life circumstances of poor, black defendants. While their greater familiarity did not always lead to more leniency in dealing with these defendants (for some judges, their knowledge permitted them to understand what it was like to be "jacked up on a wall by the police"[69]; for others it enabled them to recognize when the defendant was feeding them "a lame line"[70]); it reflected a richer understanding of circumstances, which produced more careful and accurate adjudication. Some judges expressed the view that

[69] *See supra* note 63.   [70] *See supra* note 65.

such knowledge not only helped them to assess credibility, but also facilitated communication in criminal cases when they "spoke [the defendants'] language." Others observed that it helped them to see some of the most ostensibly unsympathetic parties before them "in human terms"[71] – a goal that was frequently characterized as desirable for all judges, in dealing with all parties.

One interesting aspect of these patterns of judicial perception is that they can be understood not as moving judges in the direction of greater partiality toward members of their group, but as eliminating the barriers – whether they be stereotyped understandings, blind spots of which one was unaware, or communication-scrambling distance – that have prevented some judges from addressing these group members fairly when they come before the court. Something similar is true about the stated commitment of some of these judges to treating all parties more fairly, specifically because of their experience with discrimination: it could be described as tending less in the direction of partisanship, and more in the direction of impartiality. An increase in objectivity – where objectivity is defined quite traditionally as an ability to look without prejudice or preconceived notions at the parties before the court – might be described as a consequence of group-based membership for many of these judges. These judges also suggest the need to expand conventional notions of objectivity to include a definition familiar to feminists and other critical legal theorists: awareness of the inevitable partiality of all perspectives and willingness to test a range of affinities and commitments for their blind spots and limitations.

V. AGENDAS FOR RESEARCH

As interesting and provocative as these patterns may be for our understanding of racial and group-based identifications, and the possible meanings of judicial objectivity, they remain only suggestions or hypotheses until they can be investigated more systematically. A starting point would obviously be to put a series of questions about the meaning and implications of one's racial identification for the many tasks associated with the judge's role to a significantly larger group of judges. While the elaboration of a full agenda for empirical research is beyond the scope of this article, it may be useful to identify some of the other promising avenues for future inquiry.

One such issue concerns possible differences between federal and state judges. Many of the strongest suggestions that black judges' sense of

[71] *See supra* note 64.

responsibility to their group can (and perhaps should) be vindicated outside their courtrooms, in the larger venues of their communities, came from state court judges. This might not be surprising, given the norms of insulation surrounding the federal judiciary, and the closer relations between many state judges and their immediate geographic communities, which are sometimes constituted or reinforced by an electoral mode of judicial selection. It would be useful to investigate whether the extent to which, or the vehicles through which, state judges vindicated their senses of responsibility to their ascriptive groups varied with their mode of selection. It would also be valuable to probe whether understandings of "appropriate" judicial detachment animated a different response among federal judges, or whether judges altered their extrajudicial efforts on behalf of their group – to more neutral activities such as working for greater diversity among the federal judiciary – when they were appointed to the federal bench.

It would also seem important, at both state and federal levels, to investigate how perceptions of group identification manifested themselves in the context of adjudication. This inquiry might be particularly fruitful in the context of doctrinal areas that are premised on a more rigorously individualized notion of the legal subject. How might a judge with a more complex view of the social context and contribution of criminal conduct adjudicate cases within a conceptual structure of criminal justice that is grounded in stringent notions of individual responsibility? How might judges who have come to recognize innumerable subtle dynamics of discrimination adjudicate cases involving equal protection claims that must be resolved within a narrower framework of "discriminatory intent"? How judges of color accommodate, or strive to transform, frameworks that may not reflect some of their experientially-informed perceptions would be a valuable question for empirical investigation.

There is a risk, however, that the understandings of judicial objectivity, or group-based identification, that emerged from such research might be conceived as anomalous, or even operate to marginalize "outsider" jurists, if scholars did not also investigate the identifications of white jurists. White judges, after all, have a racial-group membership just as minority judges do. To neglect this would be to partake of the same error that led parties to seek the recusal of Judges Leon Higginbotham and Constance Baker Motley, on the ground that their race, but not the race of white judges, would make it impossible for them to view a race discrimination claim objectively.[72] Yet it would also be naive to assume that racial-group membership functions in the same ways for white

---

[72] For a thoughtful discussion of these and other recusal cases involving black judges, see Sherrilyn Ifill, *Judging the Judges, supra* note 11.

judges as it does for judges of color. To begin with, group-based affinity with a numerically predominant and socially privileged group might well produce a different kind of effect than interdependence with a systematically disadvantaged group. Second, and relatedly, for most white people, and many white judges, their race is "transparent"[73]: they scarcely notice that they have one, let alone reflect on what their construction by that race means for their approach to legal decisionmaking. It may be useful to investigate the consciousness of white judges who have been repeatedly and systematically involved in kinds of cases – criminal cases, school desegregation, voting rights, or affirmative action cases – that would tend to make them more aware of race, and make their own race, and any affinities they experienced to their own racial group, less transparent to them. Or it may be useful to probe the identifications of white judges with some smaller group – a group identified not only by race but by class or ethnic origin,[74] for example – to whom they may be better able to perceive their connection.

These initial suggestions about group-based identifications, and the broader research agendas toward which they point, make clear that the great promise of a more diverse bench accrues not just to the groups whose members gain access to judicial roles or to the parties whose cases are illuminated by a broader range of experiences and sensibilities. The richer range of perceptions and understandings that inclusion makes available – encompassing forms of independence and forms of interdependence – may assist legal analysts in articulating more comprehensive notions of judicial objectivity, and more nuanced understandings of the judicial role.

---

[73] *See* Barbara Flagg, *"Was Blind But Now I See": White Race Consciousness and the Requirement of Discriminatory Intent*, 91 MICH. L. REV. 953 (1993).

[74] The affirmative action opinions of Justice Antonin Scalia, for example, sometimes appear to reflect an identification with working class, ethnic whites whom he views as likely to suffer, in particularly acute ways, from race-conscious remedies. *See* Adarand Constructors, Inc. v. Pena, 515 U.S. 200 (1995) (Scalia, J., concurring in part and concurring in judgment); City of Richmond v. J. A. Croson Co., 488 U.S. 469 (1989) (Scalia, J., concurring).

10 Judicial Norms: A Judge's Perspective

Harry T. Edwards

In reflecting on "judicial norms," I will offer some views on judicial restraint, independence, impartiality, autonomy, and interdependence. I will also stress the importance of collegiality in judicial decisionmaking and highlight what I see to be the advantages of a diverse judiciary.

In amplifying my views, I will comment on three essays: John Ferejohn and Larry Kramer, *Judicial Independence in a Democracy: Institutionalizing Judicial Restraint*; Lawrence Friedman, *Judging the Judges: Some Remarks on the Way Judges Think and the Way Judges Act*; and Kathryn Abrams, *Black Judges and Ascriptive Group Identification*. This will allow me to lend a judge's perspective to the analyses offered by these preeminent legal scholars.

I. SOME COMMENTS ON PROFESSOR FEREJOHN'S AND DEAN KRAMER'S *JUDICIAL INDEPENDENCE IN A DEMOCRACY: INSTITUTIONALIZING JUDICIAL RESTRAINT*

The chapter authored by Professor Ferejohn and Dean Kramer is a long and scholarly piece which attempts to rationalize institutional doctrines of judicial restraint employed by the federal courts in the United States. I want to begin by saying that, in my view, Professor Ferejohn and Dean Kramer have got it basically right in their essay. The Constitution makes judges dependent on the political branches in a variety of ways. Individual judges are not terribly vulnerable to control from the political branches, but the judiciary as a whole is somewhat vulnerable. As a result of this arrangement, the judiciary has developed a set of self-imposed institutional doctrines of restraint. By regulating itself, the judiciary protects its ability to have its judgments effectuated. At the same time, a judge's ability to make decisions independently is largely preserved.

Professor Ferejohn and Dean Kramer offer a wealth of authority to explain the institutional doctrines of restraint. Their analysis of the case law is comprehensive and thoughtful. At places in their chapter, the authors seem to suggest that federal judges sometimes have gone too far in applying doctrines of restraint. I may disagree with them on certain aspects of this argument, but this is a minor issue. Overall, I found their legal analysis to be sterling.

There is one major piece of the thesis in *Judicial Independence*, however, with which I disagree. The paper identifies three principal types of mechanisms that the political branches arguably might use to obstruct the courts. One type of obstruction is *enforcement-related*: the political branches could ignore judges' mandates. A second type of obstruction pertains to *judicial administration*: our budgets could be cut, and our daily affairs regulated to the point that it would be hard for us to do our jobs. And a third type of obstruction relates to the *scope of judicial power*: federal judges' jurisdiction could be limited or stripped.

In my view, only one of these threats looms large to judges in a way that actually encourages us to engage in self-restraint, and that is the possibility that our mandates might not be carried out by the executive or legislative branches. This ever-present possibility gives my judicial colleagues and me a compelling reason to restrain ourselves from rendering decisions that deviate from the rule of law or that overreach the boundaries of our authority. In other words, in my view, concern over the enforcement of judicial mandates, more than any other factor, underlies much of the doctrine associated with judicial restraint.

A. *Self-Restraint and Judicial Mandates*

In the fall of 1997, I traveled to the People's Republic of China as part of a Ford Foundation program to conduct a series of lectures on the federal courts in the United States. My audiences were composed of judges and legal scholars who were principally situated in or near Beijing and Shanghai. I was naturally interested in learning what aspects of our judicial system seemed to them especially striking or unusual. It turned out that, more than anything else, the Chinese judges and legal scholars wanted to understand how judges in the United States were able to make their judicial pronouncements enforceable. Their interest in this issue is unsurprising when you realize that, because of the historical politicization of the judiciary, judicial decisions often are not enforced by other governmental authorities in China.

"Judicial independence" was an oxymoron to the Chinese judges. This came as no surprise. A judiciary that cannot expect its judgments to be executed as a matter of course cannot be described as independent. Judges who need to

convince or cajole other government actors to do what is expected of them
have no choice but to make all of their decisions with an eye on whether those
decisions will be enforced. Indeed, a number of judges and legal scholars with
whom I spoke frankly acknowledged that some important judicial decisions in
China are simply mandated, from "behind the scenes," by political officials.

So what did I tell the Chinese judges who wanted to know the secret of
judicial independence in the United States? I told them, in no uncertain
terms, that *self-restraint* has been a crucial key to the success of the judiciary in
the United States in establishing the enforceability of its decisions. I described
the comparatively weak position of the U.S. judiciary should the executive or
legislative branches choose to ignore our judgments. And I explained that our
courts have been careful to adhere to the limits placed on their authority by
the Constitution and have developed policies of restraint and deference that
minimize conflicts with the other branches.

One important feature of this account of judicial independence and self-
restraint is that it is *dynamic*. For enforceability to emerge, judges over time
must collectively develop the habit of self-restraint. And the executive and
legislative branches need to develop, over time, the habit of obeying judicial
judgments. The other branches will only develop the habit of obedience if they
accept the constitutional legitimacy of judicial action. Self-restraint helps build
up the courts' constitutional legitimacy over time, along with other elements
of judicial decisionmaking, like following the rule of law and adhering to
binding precedent. Over time, self-restraint by judges contributes to a practice
of enforcing judicial judgments. As this practice becomes entrenched, the
judiciary achieves real independence. Once judicial independence comes into
being, however, it needs to be guarded and protected. Judicial self-restraint
therefore helps both to generate and to preserve judicial independence.

The point I want to emphasize is that the awareness that we can do little to
compel enforcement of our judgments is a real, recurring element in judicial
thinking. As a result, our decisional independence relies significantly on the
habit of enforcement. It is therefore hardly surprising that judges' determination to make sure that their judgments are enforced is the overwhelming
concern that drives judicial self-restraint.

B. *Administrative Obstruction: Annoyance without Threat*

The second threat to judicial independence that Professor Ferejohn and Dean
Kramer identify is administrative obstruction. Make no mistake: administrative
obstruction is real and dangerous, for it may substantially impair the ability
of the courts to do their job as efficiently and professionally as possible. My

almost seven years as Chief Judge of the D.C. Circuit gave me a real taste of administrative obstruction, so I understand its potentially pernicious effects.

Before I offer some examples of what I mean, let me first make it clear that, in my view, administrative obstructions do not impede the *decisional* independence of the judiciary. The reason is simple. In my experience, most judges do not believe there is any real connection between congressional cooperation or interference and the content of the decisions we reach as judges. Indeed, I have not seen evidence that Congress decides to make judges' lives difficult administratively because it either likes or dislikes the kinds of decisions we are making. Instead, I have found these sorts of actions to be based on a variety of political considerations that are really quite independent of any particular judicial decisions. Thus, no matter how we decide particular cases, Congress' actions in the administrative realm depend on its own complicated political incentives and motivations. And, more importantly, these actions do not have any appreciable influence on the *decisional* independence of the judiciary.

Administrative obstruction can, however, be terribly burdensome to the judiciary. Let me give you an example, one that I know well. Congress must fund all courthouse construction, and so courthouse construction becomes a line item in the federal budget. This legislative appropriations function is not in itself a threat to an effective judiciary. But in the process of deciding to allocate funds, Congress and the President can sometimes turn courthouse funding into political football.

Just before I took over as Chief Judge of the D.C. Circuit, several independent studies confirmed that an annex to the federal courthouse in Washington, D.C. should be built to solve serious problems of safety, security, and space in the existing building, and Congress approved funding for a building design. The courts, architect, and various government agencies then engaged in nearly seven years of work, thousands of man-hours of effort, and the expenditure of over $6 million in appropriated funds to design a new annex. We faced unanticipated political problems, however, once the design work was done.

In the spring of 2000, the Office of Management and Budget ("OMB") suddenly, without consulting with any officials in the judicial branch, announced that it would not support any courthouse building project unless the building was premised on a design that contemplated "courtroom sharing" by trial judges. In the case of the D.C. Circuit, OMB claimed that its new courtroom-sharing requirement would save $5 million on a $109 million construction project. That assessment was short-sighted for we were able to demonstrate that, if the D.C. Circuit was forced to redesign the annex, the building project would be delayed by over two years and the net cost of a building with four fewer courtrooms would be nearly $6 *million more* than the building that had been designed with the four disputed courtrooms included. We finally secured funding for construction, but only after I and my staff spent countless hours preparing testimony and appearing before a number of congressional committees to plead our case.

The worst part of the process was that OMB officials really did not seem to care about the truth of the matters in dispute. They appeared to be on a mission to force "courtroom sharing" on the federal courts, no matter what the cost. Unsurprisingly, the judiciary as a whole has been far from pleased with OMB's unilateral attempt to force trial judges to "share" courtrooms pursuant to a formula developed solely by officials in the executive branch with no input from the judicial branch.

It is clear that political gamesmanship of this sort affects the ability of judges to do their jobs efficiently. And it puts judges in an uncomfortable situation, because we have no natural constituency to lobby for us and we do not feel at ease ourselves in doing battle in the political arena. Yet, there is nothing about the way Congress or the President acts on our funding requests that would lead judges to think that these political actors are trying to influence us in deciding cases. And given the many diverse personalities and strong characters among federal judges – all of whom are equally affected by sub-par facilities – I think it is fanciful to suppose that day-to-day political decisions over matters such as courthouse funding cause members of the judiciary to develop institutional doctrines of restraint. It simply does not happen. Furthermore, the kind of politics that affects funding for things such as courthouse projects is not typically issue-specific. Thus, when the political branches tie up or slow down judicial activity through their politicking, they may affect the efficiency of the judicial process, but not its content.

There is another way in which Congress can engage in costly administrative obstruction, and that is by isolating the judiciary from the currents of intellectual life in the law. Many federal judges teach, lecture, judge moot courts, or serve on bar association committees. These all are valuable mechanisms for making certain that we know what is going on in the legal world and the life of the mind outside our courtrooms. Many judges, myself included, find this sort of contact to be profoundly valuable. It enhances the quality of our judicial work by extending the range and depth of our thinking. Yet, there have been some moves in Congress to limit or obstruct the way judges interact with the rest of the legal world.

Let me offer a couple of examples. A few years ago, when I was Chief Judge of my circuit, a subcommittee of the Senate Judiciary Committee sent questionnaires to Chief Judges inquiring in extraordinary detail about the work practices and habits of the members of their courts. One question even asked about my secretary's work assignments and patterns! Many of the purported inquiries were more like statements than questions. One strand of the questionnaire appeared aimed at suggesting that judges on my court should spend less time interacting with the legal academy. In responding to the questionnaire, I explained that interactions with the outside world serve to enhance our minds, helping to make us better judges. I explained that when I teach, I am more learned; and when I am more learned, I am better able to grasp the cases that come before me on the court. Beyond this straightforward syllogism, though, it should be obvious that more ethically permissible intellectual engagement means better judges. Answering the questionnaire was a demeaning and pointless exercise, but the Chief Judges had no choice, because the judiciary's operating funds come from Congress.

The proposed Judicial Education Reform Act of 2000, known as the "Kerry-Feingold Bill," is another example of possible administrative obstruction. Under the bill, the Board of the Federal Judicial Center ("FJC") would have been given the power to determine whether a federal judge would be allowed to participate in seminars and conferences sponsored by law schools, bar associations, and other such institutions. In other words, judges' lawful extrajudicial activities would have been subject to censorship by the FJC. This threat to our academic and intellectual independence was great enough to elicit a strong protest, both from the Judicial Conference of the United States and from Chief Justice Rehnquist in his 2000 Year-End Report on the Federal Judiciary.

The Kerry-Feingold Bill and other such proposals that seek to regulate judges' lawful activities outside of the courtroom are odious forms of censorship. Such proposals are also shortsighted. Most federal judges are not wealthy. Our salaries, which are less than those that some of our law clerks receive as young associates at some big-city firms, certainly do not make us rich. That means that, if we are going to attend conferences, lectures, and symposia such as the conference that led to this book, we need to do so as the guests of the academic or other institutions that fund them. To the extent that Congress chooses to constrain our ability to travel and engage intellectually, Congress will be getting worse judges, judges less engaged with legal colleagues outside the narrow judicial world.

But if Congress does choose to obstruct judges' intellectual development by limiting teaching or lecturing or attending symposia, there is no reason to think that our *decisional* independence will be limited. Judges will still be able to decide cases as they see fit pursuant to the rule of law. It is just that we would be doing our jobs less well, because we would not have the benefit of the educational development produced during our interactions with thoughtful colleagues outside the courthouse.

My point, then, is that administrative obstruction is serious business, much more serious than most people realize. There is no doubt that Congress can act in a way that will adversely affect the quality of the judicial work product. This matters profoundly to individual judges, to the judiciary generally, and to the country. But I do not accept the view that administrative obstruction threatens decisional independence. Administrative obstruction is not a precise enough weapon to be targeted only at certain judges or certain outcomes. It is therefore largely unconnected to the outcomes of the cases that judges try and decide.

C. *Limitations on Jurisdiction*

The third type of obstruction that Professor Ferejohn and Dean Kramer identify pertains to limitations on the jurisdiction of the federal courts. Here I also disagree with the authors, but for a different kind of reason. I agree that administrative obstruction is dangerous, but I think that at its worst it threatens only decisional quality, not decisional independence. With regard to limitations on jurisdiction, however, I would contend that a proposal in Congress to strip or alter the jurisdiction of a federal court is not really a threat to the judiciary at all.

Federal courts are courts of limited jurisdiction, not general jurisdiction. Normally, that means that it is up to Congress to provide the definition of the scope of our jobs. My goal as a judge is not to wield the maximum power that I can get in the most independent way possible. It is, rather, to decide the cases that are properly before me by exercising my independent judgment under the law. When and if Congress decides to take away jurisdiction over a given category of cases, those cases no longer fall within my job description.

I do not mean to suggest that jurisdiction-altering acts never affect the judicial function, or that judges care little about such matters. Judges' strong opposition to legislation such as the federal Sentencing Guidelines proves otherwise. But, I can see no meaningful connection between judges' reactions to such acts and the development of institutional doctrines of restraint.

In thinking about this issue, I recalled a story that I once heard about an exchange between Judge Learned Hand and Justice Oliver Wendell Holmes, Jr. One day, following lunch together, as the two men parted on the steps of the Supreme Court, Hand is supposed to have said to Holmes, "Do justice." And Justice Holmes is supposed to have answered, "Justice? We don't do justice here. We just follow the rules of the game."

I do not embrace the view that judicial work has nothing to do with justice. And, to be fair, Justice Holmes probably never really thought so either. In all likelihood, the point he was making is that a judge's job is to apply the laws as they exist. The judicial function is not to reach out to the maximum number of cases, or to guard zealously the broadest possible jurisdiction. Most judges, I think, see the job as I do: as a serious undertaking in which we do the best we can to apply the law fairly and to decide cases in the manner that seems correct to us under the law. Judicial independence is absolutely essential to performing this task. But the threat of limiting jurisdiction has no appreciable impact on our capacity to decide cases independently pursuant to established law.

D. *Collegiality and Independence*

It is appropriate, I think, to conclude this part of my essay by mentioning an aspect of judicial practice that has seemed increasingly important to me over the last decade: the practice of collegiality.[1] By collegiality I mean an attitude among judges that says, we may disagree on some substantive issues, but we all have a common interest and goal in getting the law right. What is more, because in the federal judiciary we all have life tenure, we as judges are in this together. We are, in a word, one another's colleagues.

A culture of collegiality means, in practice, that we respect one another's views, listen to one another, and, where possible, aim to identify areas of agreement. It does not mean that we horse trade with the law, nor does it mean that we decline to express our views about the law in the strongest terms. Collegiality does mean, however, that even when I disagree with another judge, I recognize that we are part of a common endeavor, and that each of us is, almost always, acting in good faith according to his or her own view of what the law requires.

The reason I am raising the issue of collegiality in the context of the *Judicial Independence* essay is that I view collegiality as relevant to the development of the institutional practices of self-restraint that Professor Ferejohn and Dean Kramer see as key to establishing and maintaining judicial independence. The reason for self-restraint by judges in the way we conceive the judicial role has a lot to do with how judges see themselves in collective terms. That is where collegiality becomes relevant to judicial self-restraint.

Because I see myself as engaged in a common endeavor with my judicial colleagues, it follows that I have the interests of the judiciary as a whole at heart. I would still feel bound by my oath to the Constitution if I did not feel a collegial bond with my colleagues, but beyond that I would be a freelancer. When there is little or no judicial collegiality, there is less incentive for judges

---

[1] My views on this subject are explained fully in Harry T. Edwards, *The Effects of Collegiality on Judicial Decision Making*, 151 U. PA. L. REV. 1639 (2003).

to exercise self-restraint. Absent collegiality, we would see, far more than we do, judicial cowboys, outliers who abuse their decisional independence and thereby subvert the rule of law.

In other words, collegiality is important not only for working together effectively, but also at a deeper structural level. An attitude of judicial collegiality helps reinforce judges' incentives to behave in a principled and responsible fashion. I think that any discussion of judicial independence, either at the level of institutions or individuals, should take this practice of collegiality into account.

II. SOME COMMENTS ON PROFESSOR FRIEDMAN'S *JUDGING THE JUDGES*

In his essay *Judging the Judges*, Professor Friedman reflects on a "real paradox or dilemma or contradiction in the common law tradition."[2] On the one hand, he says, this tradition puts so much emphasis on the personality, brain, philosophy, craftsmanship, and skill of the judge "in shaping and reshaping legal matter"; and, yet, on the other hand, the tradition condemns judicial activism, the kinds of "creativity and suppleness which made judges like Brandeis or Cardozo or Holmes or Lemuel Shaw famous."[3] He explores notions of judicial "impartiality" (neutrality, open mindedness), "independence" (freedom from political interference), and "autonomy" (independence from social norms, "from the not-legal"). He concludes that judges are neither impartial nor autonomous. His conclusions, so far as I can tell, are based primarily on his sense of history and his intuitions about how judges judge.

Professor Friedman's critique of judges is quite harsh. He says that judges believe themselves to be insulated from society and therefore autonomous. But in truth, according to Professor Friedman, judges are heavily influenced by social, nonlegal pressures in their decisionmaking. He is wrong on both counts.

> Very few judges nowadays think of themselves as monks, cloistered in the judicial realm, largely oblivious to the world around them. We interact socially in many ways and with many people and, in my view, this improves the quality of our decisionmaking. This does not mean, however, that a judge's social interactions invariably destroy the capacity for independent, honest, and impartial decisionmaking. My view on these matters is that an appellate

[2] Lawrence M. Friedman, *Judging the Judges: Some Remarks on the Way Judges Think and the Way Judges Act*, this volume *supra* pp. 139–40.
[3] *Id.* at 140.

judge has not only the right, but the duty to involve himself in the world. If he is to continue developing as a person after he comes on the bench – and if he is to decide cases as well as he is able – he should maintain a diverse group of friends, travel widely, give speeches (that do not engage political disputes or improperly pertain to matters before the court), and seek out opportunities for exchanges of ideas. I believe that these things can be done easily without a judge infringing his responsibility to insure honest, fair and thorough treatment of the cases before the court, and also without any "appearances of impropriety."

While a judge typically will not need to resort to personal beliefs in deciding cases, some consideration of these beliefs may be unavoidable in the occasional "very hard" case where the legal arguments are indeterminate. In such a case, a judge's informed and critical development of his beliefs is a prerequisite to intelligent resolution of the dispute. Further, in all cases, the nature of one's personal beliefs should be consciously, rather than subconsciously, recognized. The likelihood of such recognition occurring will be heightened when a judge remains intellectually active and aware of the world around him. In other words, a judge who openly seeks legitimate exchanges of ideas, and thereby continues to cultivate personal beliefs, is in a good position to evaluate and minimize the influence of such beliefs in most cases. The real threat that a judge's personal ideologies may affect his decisions in an inappropriate case arises when the judge is not even consciously aware of the potential threat.[4]

Professor Friedman sees judges as mostly incapable of avoiding personal biases, ideological preferences, and political leanings in deciding the cases before them. In other words, he seems to believe that judging is largely an unprincipled function. I do not accept Professor Friedman's premises.

I maintain that "federal appellate judging, although not 'infallible' or 'unaffected by ideological influences,' is 'significantly constrained.'"[5] For the most part, judges are governed by and apply discernible legal principles. The legal system is therefore largely coherent and predictable. I have written extensively on this subject, so I will not repeat myself here.[6] Rather, I would prefer to

---

[4] Harry T. Edwards, *The Role of a Judge in Modern Society: Some Reflections on Current Practice in Federal Appellate Adjudication*, 32 CLEV. ST. L. REV. 385, 409–10 (1983–84).

[5] Brian C. Murchison, *Law, Belief and Bildung: The Education of Harry Edwards*, 29 HOFSTRA L. REV. 127, 162 (2000) (quoting Edwards, *The Role of a Judge in Modern Society, supra* note 4, at 403).

[6] *See, e.g.*, Harry T. Edwards, *Collegiality and Decision Making on the D.C. Circuit*, 84 VA. L. REV. 1335 (1998); Harry T. Edwards, *The Effects of Collegiality on Judicial Decision Making, supra* note 1; Harry T. Edwards, *The Judicial Function and the Elusive Goal of Principled Decisionmaking*, 1991 WIS. L. REV. 837 (1991); Harry T. Edwards, *Judicial Review of Deregulation*, 11 N. KY. L. REV. 229 (1984); Harry T. Edwards, *The Growing Disjunction Between Legal Education*

highlight a telling section of Professor Friedman's paper to show why his critique of the judicial function is suspect.

Near the conclusion of his essay, just before he pronounces that judges are neither impartial nor autonomous, Professor Friedman offers the following argument:

> Consider the case of Judge Manton, the corrupt judge, mentioned above. Take a flock of Manton opinions, some that were bought and paid for, some that were not. Give the opinions to a group of skilled lawyers and law professors. Ask them to find the fakes – the corrupt decisions, the ones that were bought and paid for. It would be next to impossible. But of course, as any lawyer could gladly tell you, a good advocate can always argue either side of a tough contested issue. Any judge with talent can write an opinion on either side of the issue as well – perhaps it would be more accurate to say that any judge can do this if he has the benefit of well-written briefs on both sides. A judge can write an opinion justifying any possible outcome in any case which makes it to the appellate level.[7]

This argument mirrors the naysayer view of judging,[8] but it fails from the weight of its own fallacious reasoning.

First, Professor Friedman's example of the corrupt Judge Manton offers no useful support for his thesis. Lawyers and law professors might not be able to pick out the "fake" opinions, because the judgments in those cases might be correct. In other words, it is true that we do not tolerate judges whose opinions are "bought and paid for"; but the fact that an opinion is corrupt does not mean that the judgment reached was wrong. An honest judge might have reached the same result.

Second, Professor Friedman says that "a good advocate can always argue either side of a tough issue." However, this tells you absolutely nothing about judicial impartiality or autonomy. Of course most good lawyers can marshal arguments on both sides of an issue, but that does not mean that both sides are equally meritorious under the law. The more telling point is that great lawyers can argue both sides of a case and then predict the correct outcome on the merits. Great lawyers, like great judges, assess the merits of their cases pursuant to applicable legal principles. Indeed, the reason that so many cases are not

---

and the Legal Profession, 91 MICH. L. REV. 34 (1992); Harry T. Edwards, *Public Misperceptions Concerning the "Politics" of Judging: Dispelling Some Myths About the D.C. Circuit*, 56 U. COLO. L. REV. 619 (1985); Edwards, *The Role of a Judge in Modern Society, supra* note 4, at 409–10; Harry T. Edwards, *To Err Is Human, But Not Always Harmless: When Should Legal Error Be Tolerated?*, 70 N.Y.U. L. REV. 1167 (1995).

[7] Lawrence M. Friedman, *Judging the Judges: Some Remarks on the Way Judges Think and the Way Judges Act, supra* pp. 158–59.

[8] *See* Edwards, *The Judicial Function, supra* note 6, at 852–54.

litigated is because lawyers explain to their clients that the likelihood of their prevailing on the merits is not good.

Finally, Professor Friedman asserts that "any judge with talent can write an opinion on either side of the issue. . . . A judge can write an opinion justifying any possible outcome." This is a specious contention, because not every opinion reflects the *correct* judgment. Principled decisionmaking – which entails decisions that are based on the applicable rules of law – demands judgments that are faithful to the law. And it is the role of a judge to adhere to the law in deciding cases. When we are disdainful of this mission, we are transparently corrupt; and smart lawyers and judges know when a judicial decision is lawless. There are some "very hard" cases in which there are no *right* answers, so appellate judges sometimes "make law."[9] These cases are relatively few, however. In most cases, judges are significantly constrained in applying the law.

I sometimes hear it said by naysaying lawyers that they can predict the outcome of a case in my court as soon as the panel of judges is announced. This invariably calls to my mind the story of the New England eccentric who claims that by clapping his hands he can keep away the alligators. When his crusty Cape Cod neighbors ask him how he knows this technique works, he slyly responds: "Seen any alligators around here lately?" Smart lawyers appearing before my court can predict the outcome of cases because they know how to assess the merits of the claims – lawyers know that weak appeals will be rejected and strong appeals will be sustained. Outcome is rarely affected by the particular judges assigned to hear a case, as evidenced by the fact that most judgments from my court are unanimous.

Professor Friedman's *questions* regarding the independence, impartiality, and autonomy of federal judges are important. We must continue to assure ourselves that judges are faithful to the mission of principled decisionmaking, so my concern with his paper is not with the questions raised. Rather, I am troubled by some of his *assertions* – based largely on his own intuitions – that find little real credence in the judicial function that I know and practice. And I remain of the view that

> our judicial system will be unable to tolerate public misperceptions beyond a certain point of distortion. Our tolerance level has not yet been surpassed, but I think that we are on a fast track heading in the wrong direction. And if we continue on this course, we will destroy our grand vision of a judicial function premised on principled decisionmaking.[10]

[9] Edwards, *The Role of a Judge in Modern Society, supra* note 4, at 388.
[10] Edwards, *The Judicial Function, supra* note 6, at 853.

III. SOME COMMENTS ON PROFESSOR ABRAMS' *BLACK JUDGES AND ASCRIPTIVE GROUP IDENTIFICATION*

The chapter *Black Judges and Ascriptive Group Identification* takes a very different look at questions relating to judicial independence and impartiality. In her essay, Professor Abrams examines judicial interdependence in the context of ascriptive group membership. In particular, Professor Abrams seeks to determine whether African-American judges bring a different perspective to the judicial function and, if so, whether that perspective has any decisional or other effects.

Professor Abrams's principal finding is unsurprising: the judges who were the focus of her study manifested few perspectives explicitly traceable to race that had the potential to bear on substantive decisionmaking. To the extent that these African-American judges were found to respond to perceived needs of their ascriptive communities, they did so mostly in situations external to the formal judicial role. And the consequence of group-based membership for many of the judges in the sample was "an ability to look without prejudice or preconceived notions at the parties before the court,"[11] but without affording those parties any special decisional advantage because of racial affinity.

In light of my comments on the chapter by Professor Friedman, I surely can find no fault with Professor Abrams's thesis. My race does not determine my judgments. If I sometimes bring unique perspectives to the judicial conference room, perspectives that help to sort out some of the issues that come before the court, that is a good thing. But there is no "race card" to be played in judicial deliberations. And minority judges have no monopoly on "an ability to look without prejudice or preconceived notions at the parties before the court." In my experience, open-minded judges come in all shades.

Professor Abrams's findings are, as she concedes, based on a very limited sample. Thus, her conclusions can claim no empirical purity. And much of the evidence upon which she relies comes from the sample judges' "self-reporting" narratives, that is, from "a group of professionals who are widely expected to enact or embody certain norms, including the very norms at issue in [the] analysis, objectivity or impartiality."[12] Her study data are thus somewhat suspect. But Professor Abrams understands the limits of her study, offers no bold claims, and promises further studies. The importance of Professor Abrams's piece is to show both that there is no good evidence to support the fears of those who might believe that African-American judges are driven by

[11] Kathryn Abrams, *Black Judges and Ascriptive Group Identification*, this volume, *supra* p. 227.
[12] *Id.* at 217, n. 28.

ascriptive group membership in their decisionmaking, and that there is decent anecdotal, and some empirical, evidence to suggest otherwise.[13]

After reading the Abrams essay, an agent provocateur might ask: if ascriptive group membership is largely irrelevant in the judicial process, then why worry about racial or sexual diversity on the federal bench? Professor Abrams offers one answer – a more diverse judiciary helps all judges to remain mindful of "the inevitable partiality of all perspectives."[14] With this understanding, judges are less likely to fall prey to the temptations that trouble Professor Friedman.

Diversity also enhances the benefits of collegiality among judges, which in turn enhances decisionmaking. A court composed of judges with a diversity of professional experiences and personal perspectives makes for better-informed deliberations.[15] It provides for constant input from judges who have seen different kinds of problems in their pre-judicial careers and, indeed, have sometimes seen the same problems from different angles.[16] We all gain from this diversity, by listening to and taking seriously the views of our colleagues.

IV. CONCLUSION

I reject the view that judges are largely lawless in their decisionmaking, influenced more by personal ideology than legal principles. I believe that principled decisionmaking is not a foolish idea. In my view, it is the worst indictment for judges to be labeled political partisans and to be seen as result-oriented in their decisionmaking.[17] Judicial independence helps to ensure impartiality and autonomy in the judiciary. Judicial self-restraint, in turn, helps to preserve judicial independence, because it promotes public confidence in the work that judges do. Collegiality among judges invariably enhances their performance, because it allows judges to trade ideas without acrimony, which in turn advances principled decisionmaking.

> [W]hat I mean is that judges have a common interest, as members of the judiciary, in getting the law right, and that, as a result, we are willing to listen,

[13] *See* Harry T. Edwards, *Race and the Judiciary*, 20 YALE L. & POL'Y REV. 325 (2002) (contending that that the race of a judge should not, and normally does not, determine his or her judgments).

[14] Kathryn Abrams, *Black Judges and Ascriptive Group Identification, supra* p. 227. I make the same point in Harry T. Edwards, *Race and the Judiciary, supra* note 13, at 329–30.

[15] *See* Edwards, *The Effects of Collegiality on Judicial Decision Making, supra* note 1, at 1668; Edwards, *Collegiality and Decision Making on the D.C. Circuit, supra* note 6, at 1360–62.

[16] *See* Ruth Bader Ginsburg, *Reflections on Way Paving: Jewish Justices and Jewish Women*, 14 TOURO L. REV. 283, 284 (1998).

[17] Harry T. Edwards, *Reflections (On Law Review, Legal Education, Law Practice, and My Alma Mater)*, 100 MICH. L. REV. 1999, 2007 (2002).

persuade, and be persuaded, all in an atmosphere of civility and respect. Collegiality is a *process* that helps to create the conditions for *principled* agreement, by allowing all points of view to be aired and considered. Specifically, it is my contention that collegiality plays an important part in *mitigating* the role of partisan politics and personal ideology by allowing judges of differing perspectives and philosophies to communicate with, listen to, and ultimately influence one another in constructive and law-abiding ways.[18]

And the collegiality that I mean to describe embodies an ideal of diversity and envisions judges drawing on their differences in the process of working together to get the law right.[19] Judicial performance is not flawless, but our system of an independent judiciary mostly works.

---

[18] *See* Edwards, *The Effects of Collegiality on Judicial Decision Making, supra* note 1, at 1645 (internal footnote omitted).
[19] *Id.* at 1666.

PART FOUR

THE INFLUENCE
OF LAW ON NORMS

11 Normative Evaluation and Legal Analogues

Amartya Sen

Custom, that unwritten law
By which the people keep even kings in awe.

So wrote Charles Davenant, in *Circe*, about three hundred years ago. There are not many kings left in the world, but custom, in various forms, does still link closely with law. Indeed, norms and laws are intimately connected and influence each other. The influences work in both directions.

Norms have an impact on the actual rules of operation in a society in at least two distinct ways. First, the conduct and behavior of people are influenced, to varying extents, by the established norms in a society. Norms can impose obligations and constraints which work like law, and this is perhaps the most direct manifestation of norms as "unwritten law" to which Charles Davenant referred. At the very least, norms can supplement legal rules (the "written law," as it were) that are in force.

To consider an often discussed example, the enforcement of economic contracts can be made much easier if the power of legal force is supplemented by appropriately conformist behavior. Voluntary compliance can, in this sense, play an auxiliary but important part in the enforcement of contracts, for which policing may be the last resort. This recognition, incidentally, is not in conflict with Douglass North's critical argument, which I find entirely persuasive, that "neither self-enforcement by parties nor trust can be completely successful," and that "a coercive third party is essential" for the enforcement of contracts.[1] But as North himself points out, to accept the stubborn necessity of institutional enforcement does not require us to believe that "ideology or norms do not matter; they do."[2] Norms and their operation cannot altogether supplant

[1] DOUGLASS C. NORTH, INSTITUTIONS, INSTITUTIONAL CHANGE AND ECONOMIC PERFORMANCE 35 (1990).
[2] *Id.*

legal rules and their enforcement, but they can certainly supplement the latter effectively, which is the point at issue here.

Second, norms can motivate law and have a substantial influence on what gets codified as law. This can work either directly through legislation, which may be influenced by demands linked to norms and established values and priorities, or through judicial interpretation of what the legal codes actually say or mean, which too can respond to prevailing values and general "moral sentiments" (to use Smith's terminology). Even if we do not want to go as far as Cicero in claiming that "the good of the people *is* the chief law,"[3] it is hard to deny the role of established norms in influencing legislation and judicial interpretations.

A. *Legal and Normative Thinking*

I have begun by discussing the influence of norms on the law, but that is not what is going to be the principal focus of this essay. Rather, I am mainly concerned with influences that work in the converse direction, in particular the way frameworks of law and legal thinking influence the discussion and formulation of norms. Since these connections from law to norms have received less attention than the connections that work in the opposite direction – from norms to law – they need, I believe, more explicit examination. In discussing the relationship between norms and the law, we must pay attention to influences that work in both directions, and this is why I have begun by acknowledging the importance of the influence of norms on law. But the main concern in this essay is with the influence of law and legal thinking on norms and normative thinking.

I should, however, also warn that my task is not confined to praising the virtues of legal or quasi-legal thinking in moral affairs. I argue that the influence of legal analogy and legal thinking has sometimes been quite counterproductive in ethics and political philosophy. I am particularly concerned with the arbitrary narrowing of the range and reach of moral and political analyses resulting from the tendency to concentrate too exclusively on some very specific – and rather confined – legal frameworks. My task, therefore, is *both* (as it were) to bury Caesar and to praise him. My hope is that a more explicit consideration of the role of legal thinking in moral and political analysis can serve a constructive as well as critical purpose.

---

[3] CICERO, DE LEGIBUS bk. III, iii, 8.

B. *Poverty and Norms*

Let me illustrate some of my points by considering a practical concern of great importance, namely, poverty. That the need to remove poverty must be crucial for the ethical adequacy of any system of social norms has been well discussed for a long time – most effectively, in recent decades, by John Rawls.[4]

One of the clearest articulations of this priority can be found in Adam Smith. "No society," he argued, "can surely be flourishing and happy, of which the far greater part of the members are poor and miserable."[5] Indeed, it is not adequately recognized (given the championing that Smith gets from the hard-nosed political commentators from the right) that even Smith's severe criticism of state intervention in many fields of economic activities drew, to a significant extent, on his fear that state intervention would typically be in favor of the rich and the powerful (including capitalist employers – "the masters," as he called them), rather than the workers and the poor. Indeed, Smith's distinction between helpful intervention and harmful interference turned substantially on the way the workers are treated compared with their "masters." He wrote in *The Wealth of Nations*:

> Whenever the legislature attempts to regulate the differences between masters and their workmen, its counsellors are always the masters. When the regulation, therefore, is in favour of the workmen, it is always just and equitable, but it is sometimes otherwise when in favour of the masters.[6]

Whether or not we agree with Smith's political radicalism and his extreme suspicion of the rich (on which he wrote very extensively both in *The Wealth of Nations* and in *The Theory of Moral Sentiments*), his arguments on the centrality of poverty and disadvantage in the acceptability of social norms are powerful pointers to the need for focus in examining the relationship between norms and the law.

There is, however, an important question regarding the nature and characteristics of poverty. Even though poverty is often defined simply as lowness of income, it is more adequately seen as the lack of the capability to have a minimally acceptable quality of life. Poverty, seen in this broader perspective, is not just the characteristic of having an income level below a prespecified

---

[4] JOHN RAWLS, A THEORY OF JUSTICE (1971).

[5] ADAM SMITH, AN INQUIRY INTO THE NATURE AND CAUSES OF THE WEALTH OF NATIONS 91–101 (Clarendon Press 1976) (1776).

[6] *Id.* at 157–58. On the interpretation of Smith as a political economist, see EMMA ROTHSCHILD, ECONOMIC SENTIMENTS: ADAM SMITH, CONDORCET, AND THE ENLIGHTENMENT (2001).

minimum, but more fundamentally a deprivation of basic capabilities. Thus characterized, the analysis of poverty has to be concerned with various ways in which a person may fail to have these minimal capabilities.[7] In terms of causal determinants, the domain of poverty analysis has to include not merely a lack of economic means, but also the deprivation of political freedoms, civil rights, educational and other social opportunities, health facilities, and other enabling conditions. Inadequacies in any of these fields can impoverish the ability of women and men to have minimally acceptable lives. Furthermore, deprivations in these diverse fields can reinforce each other.[8] To illustrate, lack of political freedom can contribute to economic insecurity; economic and social deprivation can lead to bad health and premature mortality; the denial of basic health care and education can sustain economic poverty.[9] The recent literature on human rights, on which I shall have something to say presently, has been particularly concerned with deprivation and poverty in a wide variety of fields.

C. *Normative Reasoning and Human Rights*

I turn now to the influence of the law and legal thinking on ethical norms and political assessment. This influence can work in a great many different ways. I shall concentrate here on two particular examples of the extensive impact of legal analogy on moral and political reasoning: (1) skepticism about the idea of normative rights (including the legitimacy and scope of human rights), and (2) the idea of a hypothetical contract (such as Rawls's "original position") as a foundational device for substantive ethics and political philosophy.

I begin with the first. Legal rights and duties can serve as analogues in analyzing normative claims regarding rights and duties. When a proposal is made to extend the domain or scope of moral thinking or to alter its substantive demands, the understanding and assessment of what is being proposed can

---

[7] I have discussed this perspective in INEQUALITY REEXAMINED (1992) and DEVELOPMENT AS FREEDOM (1999).

[8] *Development as Freedom* is, to a great extent, occupied in exploring the interconnections between freedoms in different spheres.

[9] For example, the diversity of influences that can contribute to health failures (going well beyond problems with health care delivery) can be of great significance in assessing health policy, including the demands of health equity. The reach and relevance of these interconnections are discussed in the splendid Harvard thesis of Jennifer Prah Ruger, Aristotelian Justice and Health Policy: Capability and Incompletely Theorized Agreements (1998) (Ph.D. dissertation, Harvard University).

be made easier by looking for its legal analogue. Legal concepts can thus help to clarify what is to be morally sought as well as to communicate the results of ethical deliberations. Indeed, concepts of rights and duties have such strong legal associations that it is quite natural to invoke legal comparisons in conducting normative scrutiny. It can, for example, be very tempting to ask how a proposed extension or curtailment or revision of some claims regarding moral rights and duties would be legislated, even if there is no real intention for one reason or other to undertake any such legislation. Law can speak loud and clear, and moral reasoning may have use for that legal voice.

This articulation has not, however, been invariably helpful in understanding extra-legal concepts, such as human rights. Human rights differ from legal rights that a citizen of a country enjoys in two different ways. First, the idea of human rights extends beyond what the system of law in a country recognizes as rights. They are normative claims, regarding what is important and what needs consideration and support. They differ, therefore, from rights that are specifically legislated or otherwise incorporated within the limits of justiciable law (this may or may not hold for human rights, even to those human rights that are widely accepted). The government of a country can, of course, dispute a person's *legal right*, say, not to be tortured (there may be no such legislated right), but that will not amount to disputing what is seen as the person's *human right* not to be tortured.

Second, the normative status of the human right of a person does not arise from his or her citizenship, or nationality, or membership in a legally relevant collectivity. The notion of human rights builds on our shared humanity. They differ, therefore, from constitutionally created rights guaranteed for specified people (such as American citizens or Frenchmen). Human rights go not only beyond the established law anywhere, but also beyond claims arising from any particular denominational category (such as citizenship), in contrast with the common identity of all human beings.

The idea of human rights has been both strongly championed and severely resisted in recent years. It has become a veritable battleground not merely because the notion of human rights is resisted by people who lack sympathy for the assertion of these alleged rights (such as the spokesmen or other officials of authoritarian governments), but also because many analysts who are not out of sympathy with the politics or ethics that go with the championing of human rights nevertheless find the idea of human rights to be conceptually muddled, particularly in the form in which these rights are asserted. This is where, I would argue, the use of simple analogies with legal rights has played a rather counterproductive role.

D. *Legal Analogy and Normative Status*

This is, in fact, not quite a new debate, and in some ways represents a return to intellectual disputes that occurred more than two hundred years ago. The idea that "natural rights" may exist irrespective of legal rights is, of course, quite ancient. It was often used to justify privilege and to reject the claims of human well-being, particularly of the underdogs of society, and it was sharply attacked, especially in that form, by Jeremy Bentham.[10] By taking a no-nonsense view of rights as claims that *result from* legislation, rather than what *motivates* legislation, Bentham found it easy enough to describe "natural rights" as "nonsense," and the concept of "natural and imprescriptible rights" as "nonsense on stilts."[11] (I take this to be a special species of nonsense that is artificially elevated by props.) Bentham did, of course, take a great interest in rights, not as moral or political priors to legislation, but as institutional implications of legislation. In discussing the typology of rights (Bentham was a true pioneer in this exercise, along with Austin), and in linking the idea of appropriate legislation with the social goal of utility maximization, Bentham made substantial contributions to the literature of legal rights. But by insisting on a fairly literal interpretation of all rights as legislated rights, he managed to dispense with one of the major tools of moral and political reasoning.

That tool had been used earlier (Bentham was right to think) in defense of privilege and vested interests. But as a general device of thought that can accommodate morally and politically reasoned claims and correlated duties, the concept of rights had other possible uses. Indeed, Bentham's own attack on natural rights as "nonsense" was aired primarily at the French declaration of the "rights of man" in 1789, linked to the French Revolution. These claims of what we would now call "human rights" vastly extended the scope and reach of rights-based reasoning in a radically egalitarian direction. However, Bentham, the legalist, was severely critical of this use of the idea of rights (well reflected in his pamphlet, *Anarchical Fallacies*). The plausibility and advantage of thinking in terms of rights in demanding more equity and more humanity was extensively brought out, during Bentham's time, by Tom Paine and Mary Wollstonecraft, who were contemporaries of Bentham. Indeed, Paine's *Rights of Man* and Wollstonecraft's *The Vindication of the Rights of Women*, which were published in the same year, 1792, broadened the political and moral horizon exactly in the opposite direction to the one that Bentham had advocated.

---

[10] Jeremy Bentham, An Introduction to the Principles of Morals and Legislation (1789).

[11] *Id.*

E. *The Domain of Human Rights*

Contemporary disputations of the idea of human rights sometimes follow the Benthamite line (though there is another – conceptually independent – line of criticism which I must also examine presently). In this view, the notion of human rights must be nonsense (if not quite elevated nonsense – "on stilts"), since rights are post-legislative phenomena and cannot precede legislation. This argument need not take the form of disputing that we may have good reason to demand fresh legislation to incorporate what are taken to be human rights, and may have excellent grounds for agitating in that direction. Indeed, Bentham himself had done a good deal of just that (even though the normative motivation, in his case, came from utility rather than any prelegal concept of right). There would, however, in this view, be no right until the appropriate legislation, or a suitable judicial reinterpretation, had occurred.

This position, I would argue, seriously limits and constrains the richness of moral and political ideas that can invoke the notion of rights for articulation, analysis, and communication. To claim that a person has a certain right and others have corresponding duties can be a powerful moral or political statement. A nonlegislated claim that is seen as a human right differs, for that reason, from a nonlegislated claim that is *not* seen as a human right. The language of normative rights reflects two distinct but interrelated concerns: (1) it aims at the *freedom* of the right-holder to do certain things or achieve some conditions, and (2) it demands some correlate *obligations* on the part of others (which can take the form of noninterference *or* of positive assistance) to help in the realization of this freedom by the right-holder. To illustrate, person A's right not to be assaulted concerns both (1) freedom of A to avoid being assaulted, and (2) the obligation of others to help A to have that freedom by not assaulting A, and even perhaps by assisting him to avoid being assaulted by others (more on the latter presently).

In terms of broadly consequential reasoning, which both Paine and Wollstonecraft implicitly invoked, and which I have tried to investigate elsewhere,[12] the comprehensive outcome can be judged to have been worsened on each of these – distinct but interrelated – grounds. If person B were to assault A, this would be a violation of A's right and a breach of B's duty not to assault anyone. Both can figure in a broadly consequential accounting, and the moral and political force of such rights and duties can be extremely important even if they have not emanated from legislation. This line of reasoning can, of course,

---

[12] I have discussed that issue in *Rights and Agency*, 11 PHIL. & PUB. AFF. 3 (1982), and *Consequential Evaluation and Practical Reason*, 97 J. PHIL. 477 (2000).

be questioned and scrutinized on substantive moral or political grounds, but it can hardly be summarily dismissed as "nonsense" simply on the basis of an exclusionary analogy with legal rights.

It is also important to note in the context of recognizing the far-reaching distinction between legal rights and normative rights (such as a normatively valued but nonlegislated human right) that it is not in general cogent even to presume that if a normative right is important, then it must necessarily be appropriate to try to legislate and institutionalize it as a legal right. The recognition of a human right may have its own importance and work in its own sphere of influence (as social norms generally do, through influencing behavior). For example, in a male-dominated traditionalist society (where significant family decisions are typically taken by the husband on his own), the social recognition of a wife's "human right" to be consulted in family decisions may be a very important move. But it does not follow that a human right of this kind should be put into the rule books through legislation – perhaps with the husband's being arrested, locked up, or otherwise punished by the state if he were to fail to consult his wife. Similarly, the human right to social respect or dignity involves different spheres of activity, some of which can be included in the domain of formal legislation (such as outlawing the practice of untouchability), while others are mainly matters of attitudinal change (such as altering the lack of regard for the "low-born") on which legislation would be difficult and most likely quite ineffective. Many human rights can serve as important constituents of social norms, and have their influence and effectiveness through personal reflection and public discussion, without their being necessarily diagnosed as pregnant with potential legislation. Human rights have their own domain of relevance and, while there may be substantial intersections between this domain and that of appropriate proposals for legislation, the two domains need not be congruent.

F. *Human Rights and Corresponding Obligations*

There is another line of criticism of human rights, to which I referred earlier, and which too is strongly influenced, if only implicitly, by an analogy with legal rights. This takes the form of arguing that any right must be coupled with an exactly specified correlate duty which imposes particular duties on specific persons or agencies. This is certainly true of many legal rights. For example, if a person enters into a legally binding contract to deliver some goods at some price, then the right of the recipient to have those goods at that price is exactly matched by the duty of the provider to supply those goods at that price. Even when the coverage of legal obligations is not focused on only one person or agency, there can be an exact correspondence. For example, a property right takes the form of combining the entitlement to private property with an exact obligation on the part of everyone else to respect that entitlement, rather than violating it through, say, theft or robbery. We know exactly who is being asked to do what. Since this kind of an exact correspondence often does not hold for what are claimed to be human rights, they should be at best seen (so the argument runs) as loose expressions of goodwill – perhaps even of a lump in the throat – rather than as rigorous formulations of anything that can be seen as rights.

The affirmation of human rights sometimes involves such an exact correspondence, but not always. For example, the human right not to be arbitrarily arrested (no matter whether the laws of the land prohibit arbitrary arrest or not) is quite exactly characterized (the state, in particular, must do no such thing). In contrast, the idea that people have a right to health care or to escape starvation demands, generally though imprecisely, that all those who are in a position to help must consider what they can do to prevent these deprivations from occurring. Human rights can take either form, *with or without* pinpointing specific duties for fully specified obligation-bearers.

The distinction has a close connection with Immanuel Kant's contrast between "perfect" and "imperfect" obligations.[13] Kant spent a good deal of effort in exploring both kinds of obligations. However, in modern explorations of the Kantian tradition, it is the role of "perfect" obligations that has tended to receive overwhelming priority (so much so that the fact that Kant did extensively discuss imperfect obligations is sometimes entirely overlooked). The inclination to concentrate exclusively on perfect obligations is more in conformity with the legal concept of rights, and the invoking of imperfect obligations related to human rights is sometimes seen with suspicion because of the disanalogy involved with legal frameworks.

In contrast, when human rights are embedded in a broad system of consequential evaluation of a kind that Paine or Wollstonecraft or Condorcet (a great theorist of the French Revolution), or for that matter Adam Smith, implicitly but firmly invoked, the accommodation of imperfect obligations as correlates of normative entitlements or human rights becomes much easier to grasp. I have discussed this issue elsewhere,[14] and can draw on that analysis here. Violations of obligations – perfect and imperfect – associated with human rights that are taken to be important can be seen as making the states of affairs worse, in a

---

[13] Immanuel Kant, Critique of Practical Reason (L. W. Beck trans., Bobbs-Merrill 1956) (1788).

[14] *See* Amartya Sen, *Consequential Evaluation and Practical Reason, supra* note 12.

broad consequential system. Even when someone is not directly involved in the violation of a perfectly specified obligation (for example, person A's being assaulted by person B), he or she may have a general duty to help (in this case, to try to prevent B's assault on A). This duty, through a consequential link, may be rather loosely specified (telling us neither who must particularly take the initiative, nor how far he or she should go in doing this general duty), but this broadly formulated imperfect obligation to help may nevertheless be a significant – indeed momentous – moral demand (for reasons that Kant discussed).

In fact, neglect or disregard of obligations – imperfect as well as perfect – can be incorporated into consequential analysis and can be taken into account in the normative evaluation of states of affairs. For example, if a person were severely assaulted in full view of others and her cries for help were completely ignored, it could be argued, in terms of plausible norms, that three bad things had occurred: (1) the victim's freedom was violated and so was her right not to be assaulted, (2) the assaulter transgressed the immunity that others should have from intrusion (in this case, a violent intrusion) and violated his duty not to assault others, and (3) the others who did nothing to help the victim also transgressed their imperfect obligation to help others in the way they could be expected to provide. They are interrelated failings, but distinct from each other.[15]

In contrast with this inclusive accounting, any system of rights that ignores all claims other than those associated with perfect obligations (in analogy with legal obligations) will miss something of potential significance in the field of social norms. This is a serious loss, and the corresponding conceptual impoverishment has had the effect of taking the notion of human rights to be conceptually muddled and problematic in a way it need not be.

There is, in fact, no inescapable conflict with legal thinking in all this (since legal theorizing can be contingently adapted), but there is some tension with the way the analogy with legal rights has contributed to premature suspicion of the important idea of human rights. The belief, often articulated, that human rights are well-meaning but unrigorous nonsense draws on an odd view of rigor.

G. *Contracts and Fairness*

I turn now to the second example, identified earlier, for examining the effects of particular legal analogies on social norms and normative thinking. The analogy is with a legal contract, which has been extensively used in contemporary moral

---

[15] I have discussed these interrelated but distinct concepts in *Consequential Evaluation and Practical Reason, supra* note 12.

and social philosophy. The approach is to a great extent inspired by Kantian practical reasoning,[16] but it has had a remarkable revival over the last half a century. It is well illustrated by the preeminent departure in ethics and political philosophy of our time, to wit, John Rawls's theory of justice as fairness, which draws substantially on an analogy with the legal device of a binding contract.[17] The contractarian approach has also been extensively used by other analysts, for example, by John Harsanyi, to develop a modern approach to utilitarianism,[18] and by James Buchanan, in laying the foundations of a new political economy based on ideas of contracts and consent.[19] I concentrate here on John Rawls's analysis, though some of the issues raised also apply to the other examples of the contractarian approach.[20]

The contract that is invoked by Rawls (and in fact by the other contractarian authors as well) is an imagined one that is settled in a hypothetical state of primordial equality – what Rawls calls the "original position" – where people do not yet know who precisely they are going to be in the actual society. Since no one knows who exactly he or she is going to be in real life, there is a quality of impersonality here that is meant to eradicate special pleading based on vested interests. This is seen as meeting the demand of "fairness." The rules for the basic structure of the society that are put into the hypothetical contract in the original position are taken to be "just" precisely because they emanate from a fair process yielding an impartially derived contract. The analogy with a negotiated contract, to which compliance is expected in actual social behavior, is central to the foundations of this approach of "justice as fairness."

Questions can be raised about the way Rawls reads the likely contents of the contract that would emerge in the original position and about the rules of justice for the basic structure of the society that he argues would be incorporated in the social contract. Indeed, I have questioned the plausibility of the Rawlsian formulae in earlier writings, and have even proposed some alternatives, focusing particularly on the need to take more direct note of people's actual freedoms (or "capabilities") rather than their holdings of resources and

---

[16] KANT, CRITIQUE OF PRACTICAL REASON, *supra* note 13.

[17] *See* JOHN RAWLS, POLITICAL LIBERALISM (1993); A THEORY OF JUSTICE (1971); *Justice as Fairness*, 67 PHIL. REV. 164 (1958).

[18] JOHN HARSANYI, ESSAYS IN ETHICS, SOCIAL BEHAVIOUR AND SCIENTIFIC EXPLANATION (1976).

[19] JAMES M. BUCHANAN & GORDON TULLOCK, THE CALCULUS OF CONSENT: LOGICAL FOUNDATIONS OF CONSTITUTIONAL DEMOCRACY (1962); JAMES M. BUCHANAN, THE LIMITS OF LIBERTY: BETWEEN ANARCHY AND LEVIATHAN (1975); *Individual Choice in Voting and the Market*, 62 J. POL. ECON. 334 (1954); *Social Choice, Democracy and Free Markets*, 62 J. POL. ECON. 114 (1954).

[20] I have attempted a more extensive critical review of the contractarian approach in my Wessons Lectures at Stanford University, "Democracy and Social Justice" (Jan. 2001).

primary goods on which Rawls concentrates.[21] With those specific issues I am not directly concerned here, and I do not further pursue those arguments here. My focus, rather, is on the use of the analogy with a legal contract and the contractarian approach in general.

One point to note straightaway is that any contractarian approach is deeply dependent on the identification of a fixed group of persons who are involved in the process of contracting. The contract is between a specified group of individuals including some persons but not others. As Rawls puts it:

> Justice as fairness recasts the doctrine of the social contract . . . the fair terms of social cooperation are conceived as agreed to by those engaged in it, that is, by free and equal citizens who are born into that society in which they lead their lives.[22]

Even when the policies of one country affect the lives of others elsewhere, their interests or concerns cannot be directly accommodated through the process of contractarian participation. At least some additional device would have to be added to the structure of country-based contracts to give them some hearing. I shall come back to that issue presently, since it is quite central to the adequacy of political and moral thinking about global inequality and poverty, but before that I want to consider some structural aspects of the contractarian approach.

The Rawlsian framework works through the congruence of three groups of people, and this is part of the discipline of relying exclusively on the device of a contract:

(1) "the negotiating group": those who can be seen as negotiating an "as if" legal contract with each other, in the original position, about the basic structure of the society within which they will each live,

(2) "the affected group": those whose interests are directly involved, and

(3) "the evaluating group": those whose fair and impartial judgments must count in judgments of justice involving all the people whose interests and lives are directly or indirectly affected.

The contracting group of people in the original position is simultaneously "the negotiating group," "the affected groups," and "the evaluative group." The insistence on congruence of this kind is difficult to avoid given the logic of contractarian reasoning, especially in the Rawlsian form, in which the original

---

[21] I have presented various lines of questioning in Collective Choice and Social Welfare (1970); Development as Freedom (1999); Inequality Reexamined (1992); *Equality of What?*, *in* Tanner Lectures on Human Values (S. McMurrin ed., 1980); *Justice: Means versus Freedoms*, 19 Phil. & Pub. Aff. 111 (1990).

[22] Rawls, Political Liberalism, *supra* note 17, at 23.

position would lead to elaborate and fixed rules about the basic structure of the society which are then put into institutional practice. Such institutional rules and legal requirements are not easy to arrange across the borders between different countries, and this is indeed one reason for not being able to include in the contractarian approach people who are not "born into that society in which they lead their lives," even if their interests are strongly affected, and even if their own judgments are of great moral and political interest. The rigidity of contractual reasoning imposes some serious loss here.

H. *International versus Global Justice*

It is, of course, possible to supplement this nation-by-nation fragmented analysis of justice by the demands of international justice. In fact, in this supplementary exercise, we can even think of an international get-together – again hypothetical – for arriving at a negotiated understanding of guiding principles for national policies towards other nations. This would be something like an international "original position," in which the representatives of the nations contract together and work out what they might reasonably owe to each other – one "people" to another. The working of such interpolity interaction and the demands of international justice have been recently investigated by John Rawls himself in the form of exploring what he calls "the law of peoples."[23] The "peoples" – as collectivities – in distinct political formations consider their concern for each other and the imperatives that follow from such linkages. The principles of justice as fairness can be used to illuminate the relation between these political communities.

Would such a framework be adequate for an understanding of "global justice?" I would argue that while it provides some insights into the nature of "international justice" (especially in the skilled and sensitive hands of Rawls, even though he refrains from making specific claims regarding global justice in his own conclusions), it nevertheless falls short of providing an adequate understanding of justice or fairness in the global arena. In this particularist conception of nation-by-nation justice, the demands of global justice – in so far as they emerge – operate through *interpolity* relations rather than through *person-to-person* relations, which are central to an appropriate discernment of the nature and content of global justice.

Global justice is not merely an international or intersocietal issue, but primarily one of justice among persons spread across the world. The questions that

---

[23] *See* JOHN RAWLS, THE LAW OF PEOPLES (1999).

remain outside the domain of international justice as formulated through the idea of the "laws of peoples" are quite plentiful. How should note be taken of the role of direct relations between different people across borders whose identities include, inter alia, solidarities based on classifications *other than* those of nationality or political unit, such as class, gender, social or political convictions, or professional obligations? People in different parts of the world interact with each other in many different ways – through commerce, through literature, through political agitations, through global NGOs, through the news media, through the internet, and so on. Their relations are not all mediated through governments or representatives of nations.[24]

Indeed, interpersonal relations in the world may go far beyond international interactions. To illustrate, a feminist activist in America who wants to do something to remedy particular features of women's disadvantage in Africa or Asia, draws on a sense of identity that does not work primarily through the sympathies of one nation for the predicament of another.[25] Her identity as a fellow woman may be more important in this particular context than her citizenship. Even the identity of being a "human being" – perhaps our most basic identity – may have the effect, when adequately appreciated, of broadening our viewpoint, and the imperatives that we may associate with our shared humanity may not be mediated by our membership of collectivities such as "nations" or "peoples."

Global justice cannot but embrace identities that go well beyond citizenship. These issues have become especially prominent in recent years, partly as a result of protesting demonstrations – from Seattle and Washington to London and Prague. One of the first features to note about the recent demonstrations against globalization is the extent to which these protests are themselves globalized events. They draw on people from very many different countries and distinct regions in the world. And many of their concerns relate to global issues of poverty and inequality, broadly defined. This is not the occasion for me to try to present an analysis of needed institutional response to deal with issues of global justice and equity (this I have tried to do elsewhere).[26] The concerns of the

---

[24] This relates to the general issues of plural identity as well as reasoned choice of identity, which I have discussed in my 1998 Romanes Lecture at Oxford, REASON BEFORE IDENTITY (1999), and in IDENTITY AND VIOLENCE: THE ILLUSION OF DESTINY (2006).

[25] There is a related issue of the tyranny that is imposed by the privileging of an alleged "cultural" or "racial" identity over other identities and over nonidentity based concerns. *See* K. ANTHONY APPIAH & AMY GUTMAN, COLOR CONSCIOUSNESS: THE POLITICAL MORALITY OF RACE (1996); SUSAN MOLLER OKIN ET AL., IS MULTICULTURALISM BAD FOR WOMEN? (1999). I also discuss this issue in my REASON BEFORE IDENTITY (1998), and *Other People*, NEW REPUBLIC, Dec. 12, 2000, at 23–30.

[26] *See* AMARTYA SEN, DEVELOPMENT AS FREEDOM (1999). See also the text of my Commencement Address at Harvard University, *Global Doubts*, HARV. MAG., Sept.–Oct. 2000, at 68, and my book IDENTITY AND VIOLENCE: THE ILLUSION OF DESTINY (2006).

demonstrators are often reflected in roughly structured demands and crudely devised slogans, and the *themes* of these protests have been consistently more important than their *theses*. In the present context, it is, however, particularly important to recognize that the sense of identity which finds expression in these movements – and also in many other expressions of global concern – goes well beyond national identities and international relations. The world is not just a collection of nations, but also of persons, and international justice cannot exhaust the claims of global justice. The nation-by-nation approach of justice as fairness loses out to something substantial in moral and political analysis, particularly in relation to issues of global inequality as well as the importance of human rights – economic, social, political, cultural, medical – across the world.

I. *Population Variation and Contractarian Impasse*

The contractarian approach is also in particular difficulty in dealing with any policy decision that may influence the size or composition of the population, since that would vitiate the fixity of the contracting group. This would certainly make it impossible to consider population policies through this device. The rub would lie in the undecidability as to *who* are to be included in the hypothetical deliberations in the original position that can, directly or indirectly, change the size or composition of the population. People who would not be born under some social arrangement cannot be seen to be evaluating that arrangement – a "nonbeing" cannot assess a society from the position of never having existed (even though there would have been such a person had a different policy been chosen). On the other hand, to leave out all those who may be potentially born under one policy or another but who are not invariably there would be to disenfranchise them systematically in the original position.

An as-if contract between exactly *all* the affected parties (under different policies) is, thus, not possible, and there will always be the possibility of underinclusion or overinclusion (either "Type 1" or "Type 2" error). Indeed, the size and composition of the population are bound to be affected by any substantial variation of general economic and social policy (not just population policy), through changes in marriages, mating, cohabitation and other parameters of reproduction, which are invariably influenced by social changes.[27] Thus, the problematic disenfranchisement is not confined only to the special question of what can be thought of as dedicated population policies. Any policy change would tend to change the group that would be born and whose interests would have to be taken into account, and this makes it impossible

---

[27] *See* DEREK PARFIT, REASONS AND PERSONS (1984).

to achieve a consistent congruence of the affected group and the negotiating group. The contractarian approach, drawing on the analogy of a legal contract between a fixed set of parties, is full of internal tension, even if we abstract, for the moment, from the presence of different countries and distinct societies in the world.

J. *The Impartial Spectator and the Model of Arbitration*

Is there any alternative to the contractarian approach, used by Immanuel Kant, and by recent theorists such as Rawls, Harsanyi, Buchanan, and others, without losing the quality of impartiality that can be rightly seen to be central to fairness and justice? I would argue that there is. Indeed, a particularly interesting approach to impartiality was proposed by Immanuel Kant's contemporary, Adam Smith, who had quite a different formulation of the problem of fairness, invoking an "impartial spectator," rather than contracting parties.[28] The basic idea is pithily put by Smith in *The Theory of Moral Sentiments*, in the context of judging one's own conduct, as the requirement to "examine it as we imagine an impartial spectator would examine it," or as he elaborated in a later edition of the same book: "to examine our own conduct as we imagine any other fair and impartial spectator would examine it."[29]

In fact, Smith's analysis of "the impartial spectator" has some claim to being the pioneering idea in this general enterprise of formulating fairness that so engaged the world of European enlightenment. Smith's ideas were not only influential among such enlightened theorists as Condorcet (who was also a pioneering social choice theorist),[30] but Immanuel Kant too knew *The Theory of Moral Sentiments* (originally published in 1759), and commented on it in a letter to Markus Herz in 1771 – though he referred to him as "the Englishman Smith."[31]

---

[28] ADAM SMITH, THE THEORY OF MORAL SENTIMENTS (D. D. Raphael & A. L. Macfie eds., Clarendon Press 1976) (1790).

[29] *Id.* at bk. III, 1, 2. The extended version occurs in the sixth edition. On the points of emphasis, see the discussion in D. D. Raphael, *The Impartial Spectator, in* ESSAYS ON ADAM SMITH 88–90 (Andrew S. Skinner & Thomas Wilson eds., 1975).

[30] See KENNETH ARROW, INDIVIDUAL VALUES AND SOCIAL CHOICE (extended ed. 1963) (1951), on the importance of Condorcet's role. I discuss the role of Condorcet and his influence on modern social choice theory initiated by Arrow, in my Nobel lecture, *The Possibility of Social Choice*, 89 AM. ECON. REV. 349 (1999). There are, in fact, major indirect influences of Adam Smith on contemporary social choice theory, but I shall not try to explore these connections here.

[31] *See* D. D. Raphael & A. L. Macfie, *Introduction* to ADAM SMITH, THE THEORY OF MORAL SENTIMENTS 31 (1976).

However, the impartial spectator as a judgmental device has some important differences from the framework that emerges from the analogy with a legal contract. While the contractarian approach attempts to eliminate the influence of vested interests by imagining a contract – in the original position – in which people are unaware of their own exact identities and thus of their own special interests, the Smithian approach of the impartial spectator tries to do this through examining how things would look to a "fair and impartial spectator." In doing this, there is, of course, a need to place oneself in the position of others, but this exercise is not restricted by the need to stick to a fixed group of negotiators, whose interests have special status over those of all others.

While the imagined impartial spectator in the Smithian moral exercise has to be impartial between the parties (or would-be parties) whose interests or priorities may clash, this is not a person who is involved "internally" in the negotiations. Indeed, at the risk of some oversimplification, it can be said that Adam Smith's use of the impartial spectator relates to Immanuel Kant's use of a social contract in a somewhat similar way in which models of fair *arbitration* relate to those of fair *negotiation*. The judgment imagined can be invoked from outside the perspectives of the negotiating protagonists – indeed can come from "any other fair and impartial spectator" (as Smith put it) – and the linkage between the negotiating parties (bound by the contract) and the fair evaluators (doing impartial evaluation) is, thus, firmly broken.

There is no need in the Smithian approach to have a fixed group of negotiating parties who are the ones who are affected and who also do the evaluation. This avoids a serious difficulty faced by the contractarian approach. In particular, there is no analogous demand here of the congruence of the negotiating group, the affected group, and the evaluating group. Indeed, there is no negotiating group here at all (since the analogy with a legal contract is dropped), and the evaluation need not be done from the confined perspective of a fixed subset of the set of all who may be, one way or another, affected.

So the impasse related to population variability does not arise here. Furthermore, there is no necessity to confine the domain of the analysis to the members of a given nation, who are closely tied to each other through the elaborate institutional framework of a given society ("who are born into that society in which they lead their lives," as Rawls put it). The universalism of Smith's concept of fairness is, in this sense, much less restrictive.

I am not arguing here that the Smithian approach is in every way superior to the Kantian or Rawlsian procedure based on a strong analogy with a legal contract. There are many other issues that would have to be considered in making an overall comparative judgment. No unique and canonical device may be needed anyway to investigate the demands of justice, since moral and political analyses of social norms and practical reason can make use of more than one model of fairness and justice. The Smithian approach does clearly have some advantages, including a greater versatility of application and the avoidance of any impasse related to the effect of substantial economic and social policy on the size and composition of the population. What is, however, worth noting in the context of the present argument is the extent to which one approach (based on the idea of an as-if legal contract) has come to dominate contemporary moral and political philosophy.

The limitation does not, of course, arise from the use of a legal analogy in general (of which the analogy with a legal contract is only a special case). Indeed, even Smith's model of the impartial spectator can be compared, as I have just commented, with legal models of arbitration. The problem arises from the tendency to get fixed on some very specific legal analogies, which then come to dominate moral and political thinking in that area. I am not arguing, I emphasize (to prevent a misunderstanding), against the use of legal analogies in general.

K. *Conclusion*

I do not summarize what I have tried to discuss, but attempt to place some of the issues in focus.

First, norms both (1) influence, and (2) are influenced by, the law. While I had a little bit to say on the impact of norms and values on laws and rules, the bulk of this essay has been concerned with investigating the influences that work in the converse direction – from laws and legal thinking to norms and normative thinking.

Second, in dealing with both norms and laws, there is an inescapable need to consider the demands of eradicating poverty – understood in an adequately broad way, as deprivation of economic, political, social, medical, and other enabling conditions that allow us to lead minimally acceptable lives. The conceptualization of human rights over an appropriately wide domain can greatly help to broaden the perspective on poverty.

Third, while legal concepts can be of much use in moral and political thinking in several different ways, nevertheless in many cases the influence of legal analogy and legal thinking has been to narrow the breadth and range of ethical and political reasoning. The legal analogies invoked have often been quite unequal to the demands of the moral or political exercise.

Fourth, while the basic idea of a right has extensive legal associations, normative concepts of rights cannot be adequately understood as some kind of surrogate legal rights. The powerful use of notions of rights of men and women championed by Tom Paine or Mary Wollstonecraft cannot be dismissed as "nonsense" or "nonsense on stilts," in the way Bentham, the legal fundamentalist, tended to treat the claims of nonlegal – or "natural" – rights. The dismissal of human rights as being conceptually confounded often follows the Benthamite route and suffers from the same limitations.

Fifth, normative rights cannot even be adequately understood as potential legal rights in waiting, and the analogy with legal rights, which has been so influential in critiques of the idea of human rights, may well have muddied the waters. The significance of human rights need not lie only in their being putative proposals for legislation and institutionalization. They have their own domain of importance and of effectiveness.

Sixth, another source of difficulty in understanding the discipline of human rights has been the tendency to insist that correlate duties must take the form of "perfect obligations" (as they typically would be if the rights in question had been legal rights in the Anglo-American tradition). Immanuel Kant's distinction between "perfect" and "imperfect" obligations is particularly important here. The duties associated with human rights often take the form of imperfect rather than perfect obligations.

Seventh, the legal concept of contracts has had a profound influence on contemporary moral and political philosophy, well illustrated by John Rawls's contractarian theory of "justice as fairness," along with other contractarian expositions presented by Harsanyi, Buchanan and others.[32] This is a powerful line of investigation, but it is also quite limited because of the rather narrow reach of the contractarian methodology. The problems include that of requiring an exact congruence of the negotiating group, the affected group, and the evaluating group. This group fixity makes it an awkward tool of analysis for many economic and social issues (where the size or composition of the population may be – directly or indirectly – influenced).

Eighth, the contractarian approach also makes it difficult to consider the claims of justice across borders. Even though national considerations of justice can be supplemented by international negotiation (in the lines proposed by Rawls in *The Law of Peoples*), this approach takes inadequate note of the plurality of groups to which any person belongs. Relations between two different persons are not invariably addressed through their respective nations, since there are many other connections, associations, and jointness that link people together. Global justice cannot be seen merely as international justice.

Ninth, an important way of incorporating the impartiality needed for the analysis of justice is to use Smith's approach of "an impartial spectator," rather

---

[32] *See supra* notes 17–19.

than the contract-based approach used by Kant, Rawls, and many others. This approach, which can be seen in terms of an analogy with fair arbitration as opposed to fair negotiation, avoids, I have argued, some of the problems that arise with the contractarian line of reasoning.

Finally, the limitations of being tied to very specific legal analogies (to the exclusion of other types of arguments) must not be seen as a claim that legal analogies are, in general, unhelpful in normative thinking. The point at issue, rather, is the danger of being imprisoned within the narrow limits of some very specific legal analogues, neglecting the use not only of other lines of normative reasoning, but also of other legal analogies. There is a need to transcend this limitation, which I believe has already extracted a heavy price.

References

Abbott Laboratories v. Gardner. 1967. 387 U.S. 136.

Abrams, Kathryn. 1999. "Some Realism about Electoralism: Rethinking Judicial Campaign Finance." *Southern California Law Review,* 72: 505.

Act of Feb. 5, 1867. Ch. 28, 14 Stat. 385.

Act of March 3, 1875. Ch. 137, §1, 18 Stat. 470.

Act of May 8, 1792. Ch. 36, § 2, 1 Stat. 275.

Act of Sept. 29, 1789. Ch. 21. § 2, 1 Stat. 93.

Act to Provide for the Administration of the United States Courts, and for Other Purposes. 1939. Ch. 501, § 306, 53 Stat. 1223.

Adams, Willi Paul. 1980. *The First American Constitutions.* Trans. Rita Kimber and Robert Kimber. Chapel Hill: University of North Carolina Press.

Adarand Constructors, Inc. v. Pena. 1995. 515 U.S. 200.

Adler v. Board of Education. 1952. 342 U.S. 485.

Air Courier Conference v. American Postal Workers Union. 1991. 498 U.S. 517.

Alabama Public Service Commission v. Southern Railway Company. 1951. 341 U.S. 341.

Alden v. Maine. 1999. 527 U.S. 706.

Alesina, Alberto, and Eliana La Ferrara. 2000. "Participation in Heterogeneous Communities." *Quarterly Journal of Economics,* 115: 847.

Alfange, Dean. 1993. "*Marbury v. Madison* and Original Understandings of Judicial Review: In Defense of Traditional Wisdom." *Supreme Court Review,* 1993: 329.

Allen v. Wright. 1984. 468 U.S. 737.

Alley, Robert S. 1996. *Without a Prayer.* Amherst, N.Y.: Prometheus Books.

Allison, Scott T., and Norbert L. Kerr. 1994. "Group Correspondence Biases and the Provision of Public Goods." *Journal of Personality and Social Psychology,* 66: 688.

American Bar Association. 1997. *An Independent Judiciary: Report of the ABA Commission on Separation of Powers and Judicial Independence.*

1998. Model Code of Judicial Conduct Canon.

Ammon, Harry. 1973. *The Genet Mission.* New York: Norton.

Ankenbrandt v. Richards. 1992. 504 U.S. 689.

Anti-Drug Abuse Act of 1986. Pub. L. No. 99-570, 100 Stat. 3207.

Appiah, Anthony K., and Amy Gutman. 1996. *Color Consciousness: The Political Morality of Race.* Princeton, N.J.: Princeton University Press.

Aristotle. *The Politics*. Rev. ed. R.F. Stalley, trans. Ernest Barker, 1995. New York: Oxford University Press.

Arnold, Richard S. 1996. "Money, or the Relations of the Judicial Branch with the Other Two Branches, Legislative and Executive." *St. Louis University Law Journal*, 40: 19.

Arrow, Kenneth. 1951. "Alternative Approaches to the Theory of Choice in Risk-Taking Situations." *Econometrica*, 19: 404.

    1963. *Individual Values and Social Choice*. New York: Wiley.

Ashenfelter, Orley, Theodore Eisenberg, and Stewart J. Schwab. 1995. "Politics and the Judiciary: The Influence of Judicial Background on Case Outcomes." *Journal of Legal Studies*, 24: 257.

Aspin, Larry. 1999. "Trends in Judicial Retention Elections, 1964–1998." *Judicature*, 83: 79.

Association of Data Processing Service Organizations v. Camp. 1970. 397 U.S. 150.

Aubert, Vilhelm. 1967. "Some Social Functions of Legislation." *Acta Sociologica*, 10: 98.

Axelrod, Robert M. 1984. *The Evolution of Cooperation*. New York: Basic Books.

Ayres, Ian, and Robert Gertner. 1989. "Filling Gaps in Incomplete Contracts: An Economic Theory of Default Rules." *Yale Law Journal*, 99: 87.

Bank of the United States v. Planters' Bank of Georgia. 1824. 22 U.S. (9 Wheat.) 904.

Banning, Lance. 1978. *The Jeffersonian Persuasion*. Ithaca, N.Y.: Cornell University Press.

Barr, Jeffrey N., and Thomas E. Willging. 1993. "Decentralized Self-Regulation, Accountability, and Judicial Independence under the Federal Judicial Conduct and Disability Act of 1980." *University of Pennsylvania Law Review*, 142: 25.

Barrow, Deborah J., et al. 1996. *The Federal Judiciary and Institutional Change*. Ann Arbor: University of Michigan Press.

Bartlett, Kate. 1990. "Feminist Legal Methods." *Harvard Law Review*, 103: 829.

Bator, Paul M. 1963. "Finality in Criminal Law and Federal Habeas Corpus for State Prisoners." *Harvard Law Review*, 76: 441.

Becker, Gary S. 1974. "A Theory of Social Interactions." *Journal of Political Economy*, 82: 1063.

    1991. Enlarged edition. *A Treatise on the Family*. Cambridge, Mass.: Harvard University Press.

    1996. *Accounting for Tastes*. Cambridge, Mass.: Harvard University Press.

Becker, Gary S., and Kevin M. Murphy. 1988. "The Family and the State." *Journal of Law and Economics*, 31: 1.

Benkler, Yochai. 2000. "From Consumers to Users: Shifting the Deeper Structures of Regulation." *Federal Communications Law Journal*, 52: 561.

Bentham, Jeremy. 1789. *An Introduction to the Principles of Morals and Legislation*. London: Payne.

Berg, Joyce, John Dickhaut, and Kevin McCabe. 1995. "Trust, Reciprocity, and Social History." *Games and Economic Behavior*, 10: 122.

Bergstrom, Theodore, Lawrence Blume, and Hal Varian. 1986. "On the Private Provision of Public Goods." *Journal of Public Economics*, 29: 25.

Berle, Adolph, and Gardiner Means. 1932. *The Modern Corporation and Private Property*. New York: Macmillan.

Bermant, Gordon, and Russell R. Wheeler. 1995. "Federal Judges and the Judicial Branch: Their Independence and Accountability." *Mercer Law Review*, 46: 835.

Bernstein, Lisa. 1992. "Opting Out of the Legal System: Extralegal Contractual Relations in the Diamond Industry." *Journal of Legal Studies*, 21: 115.

——— 1996. "Merchant Law in a Merchant Court: Rethinking the Code's Search for Immanent Business Norms." *University of Pennsylvania Law Review*, 144: 1765.

Bickel, Alexander. 1962. *The Least Dangerous Branch: The Supreme Court at the Bar of Politics*. Indianapolis: Bobbs-Merrill.

Black, Donald. 1976. *The Behavior of Law*. New York: Academic Press.

Blackstone, William. 1765, 1979. *Commentaries on the Laws of England*. Volume 1. Chicago: University of Chicago Press.

Blair, Margaret M. 1995. *Ownership and Control: Rethinking Corporate Governance for the Twenty-First Century*. Washington, D.C.: Brookings Institute.

Blair, Margaret M., and Lynn A. Stout. 2001. "Trust, Trustworthiness, and the Behavioral Foundations of Corporate Law." *University of Pennsylvania Law Review*, 149: 1735.

Blakely v. Washington. 2004. 542 U.S. 296.

Bloch, Susan Low. 1989. "The Early Role of the Attorney General in Our Constitutional Scheme: In the Beginning There Was Pragmatism." *Duke Law Journal*, 1989: 561.

Board of Trustees v. Garrett. 2001. 531 U.S. 356.

Booth, William James. 1993. *Households: On the Moral Architecture of the Economy*. Ithaca, N.Y.: Cornell University Press.

Bowles, Samuel. 1998. "Endogenous Preferences: The Cultural Consequences of Markets and Other Economic Institutions." *Journal of Economic Literature*, 36: 75.

——— 2004. *Microeconomics: Behavior, Institutions, and Evolution*. Princeton, N.J.: Princeton University Press.

Bowsher v. Synar. 1986. 478 U.S. 714.

Boyd, Robert, and Peter J. Richerson. 1985. *Culture and the Evolutionary Process*. Chicago: University of Chicago Press.

Brandon, Peter David. 2001. "State Intervention in Imperfect Families." *Rationality and Society*, 13: 285.

Brecht v. Abrahamson. 1993. 507 U.S. 619.

Bromley, Daniel W., and David Feeny, eds. 1992. *Making the Commons Work: Theory, Practice, and Policy*. San Francisco, Calif.: ICS Press.

Brown v. Allen. 1953. 344 U.S. 443.

Brown v. Board of Education. 1954. 347 U.S. 483.

Brown v. Board of Education. 1955. 349 U.S. 294.

Brown, Elizabeth Gaspar. 1964. *British Statutes in American Law 1776–1836*. Ann Arbor: University of Michigan Law School.

Brown-Kruse, Jamie, and David Hummels. 1993. "Gender Effects in Laboratory Public Goods Contribution: Do Individuals Put Their Money Where Their Mouth Is?" *Journal of Economic Behavior and Organization*, 22: 255.

Buchanan, James M. 1954a. "Social Choice, Democracy and Free Markets." *Journal of Political Economy*, 62: 114.

——— 1954b. "Individual Choice in Voting and the Market." *Journal of Political Economy*, 62: 334.

1975. *The Limits of Liberty: Between Anarchy and Leviathan.* Chicago: University of Chicago Press.

Buchanan, James M., and Gordon Tullock. 1962. *The Calculus of Consent: Logical Foundations of Constitutional Democracy.* Ann Arbor: University of Michigan Press.

Burbank, Stephen B. 1982a. "The Rules Enabling Act of 1934." *University of Pennsylvania Law Review,* 130: 1015.

1982b. "Procedural Rulemaking under the Judicial Councils Reform and Judicial Conduct and Disability Act of 1980." *University of Pennsylvania Law Review,* 131: 283.

1987. "Politics and Progress in Implementing the Federal Judicial Discipline Act." *Judicature,* 71: 13.

1999. "The Architecture of Judicial Independence." *Southern California Law Review,* 72: 315.

Burford v. Sun Oil Company. 1943. 319 U.S. 315.

Bush v. Gore. 2000. 531 U.S. 98.

Cabranes, Josè. 1993. Address at the University of Puerto Rico Law School. In "Cabranes Rips Sentencing Rules." *Legal Times,* April 11, p. 17.

Cadsby, Charles Bram, and Elizabeth Maynes. 1998. "Choosing between a Socially Efficient and a Free-riding Equilibrium: Nurses Versus Economics and Business Students." *Journal of Economic Behavior and Organization,* 37: 183.

Camerer, Colin F. 1997. "Progress in Behavioral Game Theory." *Journal of Economic Perspectives,* 11: 167.

1998. "Bounded Rationality in Individual Decision Making." *Experimental Economics,* 1: 163.

2003. *Behavioral Game Theory: Experiments in Strategic Interaction.* Princeton, N.J.: Princeton University Press.

Camerer, Colin, and Richard H. Thaler. 1995. "Anomalies: Ultimatums, Dictators and Manners." *Journal of Economic Perspectives,* 9: 209.

Cárdenas, Juan-Camilo. 2000. "Rural Institutions, Poverty and Cooperation: Learning from Experiments and Conjoint Analysis in the Field." Ph.D. diss., University of Massachusetts.

2003. "Real Wealth and Experimental Cooperation: Experiments in the Field Lab." *Journal of Development Economics,* 70: 263.

Cárdenas, Juan-Camilo, T. K. Ahn, and Elinor Ostrom. 2004. "Communication and Co-operation in a Common-Pool Resource Dilemma: A Field Experiment." In Steffen Huck, ed., *Advances in Understanding Strategic Behaviour: Game Theory, Experiments, and Bounded Rationality: Essays in Honour of Werner Güth.* New York: Palgrave MacMillan.

Cárdenas, Juan-Camilo, and Jeffrey Carpenter. 2005. "Experiments and Economic Development: Lessons from Field Labs in the Developing World." Working Paper. Bogota, Colombia: Universidad de Los Andes.

Cárdenas, Juan-Camilo, John K. Stranlund, and Cleve E. Willis. 2000. "Local Environmental Control and Institutional Crowding-out." *World Development,* 28: 1719.

Carpenter, William S. 1918. *Judicial Tenure in the United States.* New Haven, Conn.: Yale University Press.

Carrington, Paul D. 1998. "Judicial Independence and Democratic Accountability in Highest State Courts." *Law and Contemporary Problems*, 61: 79.

Cason, Timothy, and Vai-Lam Mui. 1997. "A Laboratory Study of Group Polarisation in the Team Dictator Game." *Economic Journal*, 107: 1465.

Casper, Gerhard. 1997. "The Judiciary Act of 1789 and Judicial Independence." In *Separating Power: Essays on the Founding Period*. Cambridge, Mass.: Harvard University Press.

Catanzariti, John, ed. 1995. *The Papers of Thomas Jefferson*. Volume 26. Princeton: Princeton University Press.

Champagne, Anthony, and Judith Haydel. 1993. *Judicial Reform in the States*. Lanham, Md: University Press of America.

Chemerinsky, Erwin. 1999. 3rd edition. *Federal Jurisdiction*. Gaithersburg, Md: Aspen Law and Business.

Cherokee Nation v. Georgia. 1831. 30 U.S. (5 Pet.) 1.

Chicago & Grant Trunk Railway Company v. Wellman. 1892. 143 U.S. 339.

Chicago & Southern Air Lines v. Waterman Steamship Corp. 1948. 333 U.S. 103.

Chisolm v. Georgia. 1793. 2 U.S. (2 Dall.) 419.

Chisom v. Edwards. 1988. 839 F.2d 1056.

Chisom v. Roemer. 1991. 501 U.S. 380.

Christenson, Caryn, and Ann Abbott. 2000. "Team Medical Decision Making." In Gretchen Chapman and Frank Sonnenberg, eds., *Decision Making in Health Care*. Cambridge: Cambridge University Press.

Cicero. *De Legibus*.

City of Los Angeles v. Lyons. 1983. 461 U.S. 95.

City of Richmond v. J. A. Croson Co. 1989. 488 U.S. 469.

City of Santa Barbara v. Adamson. 1980. 610 P.2d 436.

Civil Justice Reform Act of 1990. Pub. L. No. 101-650, 104 Stat. 5089.

Clark, Charles E., et al. 1947. 2nd edition. *Handbook of the Law of Code Pleading*. St. Paul, Minn.: West Publishing Company.

Clark, Homer H. 1988. 2nd edition. *The Law of Domestic Relations in the United States*. St. Paul, Minn.: West Publishing Company.

Clinton v. City of New York. 1998. 524 U.S. 417.

Coase, Ronald H. 1959. "The Federal Communications Commission." *Journal of Law and Economics*. 2: 1.

Cohen, Mark A. 1991. "Explaining Judicial Behavior or What's 'Unconstitutional' about the Sentencing Commission?" *Journal of Law, Economics and Organization*, 7: 183.

    1992. "The Motives of Judges: Empirical Evidence from Antitrust Sentencing." *International Review of Law and Economics*, 12: 13.

Coleman v. Thompson. 1991. 501 U.S. 722.

Coleman, James S. 1990. *Foundations of Social Theory*. Cambridge, Mass.: Belknap Press of Harvard University Press.

Colorado River Water Conservation District v. United States. 1976. 424 U.S. 800.

Commercial Trust Company v. Miller. 1923. 262 U.S. 51.

Commodity Futures Trading Commission v. Schor. 1986. 478 U.S. 833.

Cooter, Robert D. 1996. "Decentralized Law for a Complex Economy: The Structural Approach to Adjudicating the New Law Merchant." *University of Pennsylvania Law Review*, 144: 1643.

1998a. "Models of Morality in Law and Economics: Self-Control and Self-Improvement for the 'Bad Man' of Holmes." *Boston University Law Review*, 78: 903.

1998b. "Expressive Law and Economics." *Journal of Legal Studies*, 27: 585.

Corn-Revere, Robert. 2002. "Broadband Internet Access Debate Heightened by Agencies, Courts." *The First Amendment and the Media*. <http://www.mediainstitute.org/ONLINE/FAM2002/BCTV_B.html>.

County of Allegheny v. Frank Mashuda Company. 1959. 360 U.S. 185.

Cox, Archibald. 1996. "The Independence of the Judiciary: History and Purposes." *University of Dayton Law Review*, 21: 566.

Cox, James C., Daniel Friedman, and S. Gjerstad. 2004. "A Tractable Model of Reciprocity and Fairness." Working Paper. Tucson, Ariz.: University of Arizona, Department of Economics.

Crawford, Sue E. S., and Elinor Ostrom. 2005. "A Grammar of Institutions." In Elinor Ostrom, ed., *Understanding Institutional Diversity*, 137–74. Princeton, N.J.: Princeton University Press.

Crowell v. Benson. 1932. 285 U.S. 22.

Currie, David P. 1984. "Sovereign Immunity and Suits Against Government Officers." *Supreme Court Review*, 1984: 149.

1998. "Separating Judicial Power." *Law and Contemporary Problems*, 61: 7.

Dagan, Hanoch, and Michael A. Heller. 2001. "The Liberal Commons." *Yale Law Journal*, 110: 549.

Darwin, Charles. 1871. *The Descent of Man, and Selection in Relation to Sex*. New York: D. Appleton & Co.

Dauer, Manning J. 1953. *The Adams Federalists*. Baltimore: Johns Hopkins Press.

Davidson, Paul. 1991. "Is Probability Theory Relevant for Uncertainty? A Post Keynesian Perspective." *Journal of Economic Perspectives*, 5: 129.

Davis v. Bandemer. 1986. 478 U.S. 109.

Davis, Douglas D., and Charles A. Holt. 1993. *Experimental Economics*. Princeton, N.J.: Princeton University Press.

Dawes, Robyn M., and Richard H. Thaler. 1988. "Anomalies: Cooperation." *Journal of Economic Perspectives*, 2: 187.

Dawes, Robyn M., et al. 1990. "Cooperation for the Benefit of Us – Not Me, or My Conscience." In Jane J. Mansbridge, ed., *Beyond Self-Interest*. Chicago: University of Chicago Press.

Dawkins, Richard. 1976. *The Selfish Gene*. New York: Oxford University Press.

DeFunis v. Odegaard. 1974. 416 U.S. 312.

Demsetz, Harold. 1967. "Toward a Theory of Property Rights." *American Economic Review*, 57: 347.

de Quervain, Dominique J.-F., et al. 2004. "The Neural Basis of Altruistic Punishment." *Science*, 305: 1254.

District of Columbia Court of Appeals v. Feldman. 1983. 460 U.S. 462.

Dreyfuss, Rochelle Cooper. 1990. "Specialized Adjudication." *Brigham Young University Law Review*, 1990: 377.

Dworkin, Ronald. 1977. *Taking Rights Seriously*. Cambridge, Mass.: Harvard University Press.

Dyas v. Lockhart. 1983. 705 F.2d 993.

Edelman v. Jordan. 1974. 415 U.S. 651.

Edwards, Harry T. 1983–84. "The Role of a Judge in Modern Society: Some Reflections on Current Practice in Federal Appellate Adjudication." *Cleveland State Law Review*, 32: 385.

———. 1984. "Judicial Review of Deregulation." *Northern Kentucky Law Review*, 11: 229.

———. 1985. "Public Misperceptions Concerning the 'Politics' of Judging: Dispelling Some Myths About the D.C. Circuit." *University of Colorado Law Review*, 56: 619.

———. 1991. "The Judicial Function and the Elusive Goal of Principled Decisionmaking." *Wisconsin Law Review*, 1991: 837.

———. 1992. "The Growing Disjunction Between Legal Education and the Legal Profession." *Michigan Law Review*, 91: 34.

———. 1995. "To Err Is Human, But Not Always Harmless: When Should Legal Error Be Tolerated?" *New York University Law Review*, 70: 1167.

———. 1998. "Collegiality and Decision Making on the D.C. Circuit." *Virginia Law Review*, 84: 1335.

———. 2002a. "Race and the Judiciary." *Yale Law and Policy Review*, 20: 325.

———. 2002b. "Reflections (On Law Review, Legal Education, Law Practice, and My Alma Mater)." *Michigan Law Review*, 100: 1999.

———. 2003. "The Effects of Collegiality on Judicial Decision Making." *University of Pennsylvania Law Review*, 151: 1639.

Elkins, Stanley, and Eric McKitrick. 1993. *The Age of Federalism*. New York: Oxford University Press.

Ellickson, Robert C. 1991. *Order Without Law: How Neighbors Settle Disputes*. Cambridge, Mass.: Harvard University Press.

———. 1993. "Property in Land." *Yale Law Journal*, 102: 1394.

———. 2001. "The Evolution of Social Norms: A Perspective from the Legal Academy." In Michael Hechter and Karl-Dieter Opp, eds., *Social Norms*. New York: Russell Sage Foundation.

Ellickson, Robert C., and Charles DiA. Thorland. 1995. "Ancient Land Law: Mesopotamia, Egypt, Israel." *Chicago-Kent Law Review*, 71: 321.

Elliot, Jonathon. 1836. 2nd edition. *The Debates in the Several State Conventions*. Volume 4. Photo reprint, 1987. Salem, N.H.: Ayer Company, Publishers, Inc.

Ellis, Richard E. 1971. *The Jeffersonian Crisis: Courts and Politics in the Young Republic*. New York: Oxford University Press.

Engel v. Vitale. 1962. 370 U.S. 421.

England v. Louisiana State Board of Medical Examiners. 1964. 375 U.S. 411.

Ervin, Sam. 1970. "Separation of Powers: Judicial Independence." *Law and Contemporary Problems*, 35: 108.

Evers v. Dwyer. 1958. 358 U.S. 202.

Ex parte Burrus. 1890. 136 U.S. 586.

Ex parte Lange. 1873. 85 U.S. (18 Wall.) 163.

Ex parte McCardle. 1868. 74 U.S. (7 Wall.) 506.

Ex parte Merryman. 1861. 17 F. Cas. 144.

Ex parte Milligan. 1866. 71 U.S. (4 Wall.) 2.

Ex parte Siebold. 1879. 100 U.S. 371.

Ex parte Yerger. 1868. 75 U.S. (8 Wall.) 85.

Ex parte Young. 1908. 209 U.S. 123.

Fair Housing Act. 2000. 42 U.S.C. §3603.

Fairman, Charles. 1971. *The Oliver Wendell Holmes Devise: History of the Supreme Court of the United States: Reconstruction and Reunion, 1864–88*. Volume 6. New York: MacMillan.

Falk, Armin, Ernst Fehr, and Urs Fischbacher. 2000. "Appropriating the Commons: A Theoretical Explanation." Working Paper No. 55. University of Zurich, Institute for Empirical Research in Economics.

Fallon, Richard H., et al. 1996. 4th edition. *Hart & Wechsler's The Federal Courts and the Federal System*. Westbury, N.Y.: Foundation Press.

Fay v. Noia. 1963. 372 U.S. 391.

Federal Judicial Center. 1994. *Planning for the Future: Results of a 1992 Federal Judicial Center Survey of United States Judges*. Washington: Federal Judicial Center.

Federal Prison Population: Present and Future Trends, Hearings Before the Subcommittee on Intellectual Property and Judicial Administration of the House Committee on the Judiciary. 1993. 103d Cong. 15.

Fehr, Ernst, and Urs Fischbacher. 2004. "Third-Party Punishment and Social Norms." *Evolution and Human Behavior*, 25: 63.

Fehr, Ernst, and Jean-Robert Tyran. 1997. "Institutions and Reciprocal Fairness." *Nordic Journal of Political Economy*, 23: 133.

Fenster, Mark. 1999. "Community by Covenant, Process, and Design: Cohousing and the Contemporary Common Interest Community." *Journal of Land Use and Environmental Law*, 15: 3.

Ferejohn, John. 1999. "Independent Judges, Dependent Judiciary: Explaining Judicial Independence." *Southern California Law Review*, 72: 353.

Ferejohn, John, and Larry D. Kramer. 2002. "Independent Judges, Dependent Judiciary: Institutionalizing Judicial Restraint." *New York University Law Review*, 77: 962.

Fishback, Price, and Shawn Kantor. 2000. *A Prelude to the Welfare State: The Origins of Workers' Compensation*. Chicago: University of Chicago Press.

Fitzpatrick v. Bitzer. 1976. 427 U.S. 445.

Fitzpatrick, John C., ed. 1940. *The Writings of George Washington*. Volume 33. Washington, D.C.: U.S. Government Printing Office.

Flagg, Barbara. 1993. "'Was Blind But Now I See': White Race Consciousness and the Requirement of Discriminatory Intent." *Michigan Law Review*, 91: 953.

Flast v. Cohen. 1968. 392 U.S. 83.

Fleming, James, et al. 2001. 5th edition. *Civil Procedure*. New York: Foundation Press.

Fletcher v. Peck. 1810. 10 U.S. (6 Cranch) 87.

Fletcher, William A. 1983. "A Historical Interpretation of the Eleventh Amendment: A Narrow Construction of an Affirmative Grant of Jurisdiction Rather than a Prohibition Against Jurisdiction." *Stanford Law Review*, 35: 1033.

Florida Prepaid Postsecondary Education Expense Board v. College Savings Bank. 1999. 527 U.S. 627.

Ford, Paul Leicester, ed. 1896. *The Writings of Thomas Jefferson*. Volume 7. New York: G. P. Putnam's Sons.

    1897. *The Writings of Thomas Jefferson*. Volume 8. New York: G. P. Putnam's Sons.

Fortunato, Stephen J. 1999. "On a Judge's Duty to Speak Extrajudicially: Rethinking the Strategy of Silence." *Georgetown Journal of Legal Ethics*, 12: 679.

Frank, Robert H., Thomas Gilovich, and Dennis T. Regan. 1993. "Does Studying Economics Inhibit Cooperation?" *Journal of Economic Perspectives*, 7: 159.

Freedman, Eric M. 2000. "Milestones in Habeas Corpus: Part III: *Brown v. Allen*: The Habeas Corpus Revolution that Wasn't." *Alabama Law Review*, 51: 1541.

Friedenthal, Jack H., et al. 1999. 3rd edition. *Civil Procedure*. St. Paul, Minn.: West Group.

Friedman, Barry. 1998a. "The History of the Countermajoritarian Difficulty, Part One: The Road to Judicial Supremacy." *New York University Law Review*, 73: 333.

1998b. "'Things Forgotten' in the Debate over Judicial Independence." *Georgia State University Law Review*, 12: 737.

Friedman, Lawrence. 1997. "*Brown* in Context." In Austin Sarat, ed., *Race, Law, and Culture: Reflections on* Brown v. Board of Education. New York: Oxford University Press.

1999. "Taking Law and Society Seriously." *Chicago-Kent Law Review*, 74: 529.

2002. *American Law in the Twentieth Century*. New Haven, Conn.: Yale University Press.

2005. 3rd edition. *A History of American Law*. New York: Simon & Schuster.

Frohlich, Norman, Joe Oppenheimer, and Anja Kurki. 2004. "Modeling Other-Regarding Preferences and an Experimental Test." *Public Choice*, 119: 91.

Geyh, Charles Gardner, and Emily Field Van Tassel. 1998. "The Independence of the Judicial Branch in the New Republic." *Chicago-Kent Law Review*, 74: 31.

Gibbons, John J. 1983. "The Eleventh Amendment and State Sovereign Immunity: A Reinterpretation." *Columbia Law Review*, 83: 1889.

Gibson, Clark, Margaret McKean, and Elinor Ostrom, eds. 2000. *People and Forests: Communities, Institutions, and Governance*. Cambridge, Mass.: M.I.T. Press.

Gibson, James, Gregory A. Caldeira, and Lester Kenyatta Spence. 2003. "The Supreme Court and the U.S. Presidential Election of 2000: Wounds, Self-Inflicted or Otherwise?" *British Journal of Political Science*, 33: 535.

Gilbert, Stirling Price. 1946. *A Georgia Lawyer: His Observations and Public Service*. Athens: University of Georgia Press.

Gilligan, Carol. 1982. *In a Different Voice: Psychological Theory and Women's Development*. Cambridge, Mass.: Harvard University Press.

Gilson, Ronald. 2001. "Globalizing Corporate Governance: Convergence of Form or Function." *American Journal of Comparative Law*, 49: 329.

Ginsburg, Ruth Bader. 1998. "Reflections on Way Paving Jewish Justices and Jewish Women." *Touro Law Review*, 14: 283.

Gintis, Herbert. 2000. "Beyond *Homo Economicus*: Evidence from Experimental Economics." *Ecological Economics*, 35: 311.

Glendon, Mary Ann. 1981. *The New Family and the New Property*. Toronto: Butterworths.

Glick, Henry R. 1971. *Supreme Courts in State Politics: An Investigation of the Judicial Role*. New York: Basic Books.

Goffman, Erving. 1961. *Asylums: Essays on the Social Situation of Mental Patients and Other Inmates*. Garden City, N.Y.: Anchor Books.

Goldstein, Leslie Friedman. 1997. "State Resistance to Authority in Federal Unions: The Early United States (1790–1860) and the European Community (1958–94)." *Studies in American Political Development*, 11: 149.

Goldwater v. Carter. 1979. 444 U.S. 996.

Gottschall, Jon. 1983. "Carter's Judicial Appointments: The Influence of Affirmative Action and Merit Selection on Voting on the U.S. Court of Appeals." *Judicature*, 67: 165.

Granfinanciera, S. A. v. Nordberg. 1989. 492 U.S. 33.

Green v. Mansour. 1985. 474 U.S. 64.

Grodin, Joseph. 1988. "Developing a Consensus of Constraint: A Judge's Perspective on Judicial Retention Elections." *Southern California Law Review*, 61: 1969.

Gully v. First National Bank. 1936. 299 U.S. 109.

Gunther, Gerald. 1984. "Congressional Power to Curtail Federal Court Jurisdiction: An Opinionated Guide to the Ongoing Debate." *Stanford Law Review*, 36: 895.

    1994. *Learned Hand: The Man and the Judge.* New York: Knopf.

Güth, Werner, and Reinhard Tietz. 1990. "Ultimatum Bargaining Behavior: A Survey and Comparison of Experimental Results." *Journal of Economic Psychology*, 11: 417.

Haddock, David D., and Daniel D. Polsby. 1996. "Family As a Rational Classification." *Washington University Law Quarterly*, 74: 15.

Hadley, Janet. 1996. *Abortion: Between Freedom and Necessity.* Philadelphia: Temple University Press.

Hager, Philip. 1986. "Kaus Urges Reelection of Embattled Court Justices." *L.A. Times.* Sept. 28, p. A23.

Hall, Ford W. 1951. "The Common Law: An Account of Its Reception in the United States." *Vanderbilt Law Review*, 4: 791.

Hamilton, Alexander. *The Federalist.* Jacob E. Cooke, ed., 1961. Cambridge, Mass.: Belknap Press of Harvard University Press.

Hammer v. Dagenhart. 1918. 247 U.S. 251.

Hammerstein, Peter, ed. 2003. *Genetic and Cultural Evolution of Cooperation.* Cambridge, Mass.: M.I.T. Press.

Hans v. Louisiana. 1890. 134 U.S. 1.

Hansmann, Henry. 1996. *The Ownership of Enterprise.* Cambridge, Mass.: Belknap Press of Harvard University Press.

Hanson, Jon D., and Douglas A. Kysar. 1999. "Taking Behavioralism Seriously: The Problem of Market Manipulation." *New York University Law Review*, 74: 630.

Hardin, Garrett. 1968. "The Tragedy of the Commons." *Science* 162: 1243.

Harrison, Glenn W., and John A. List. 2004. "Field Experiments." *Journal of Economic Literature*, 42: 1009.

Harsanyi, John. 1976. *Essays in Ethics, Social Behaviour and Scientific Explanation.* Dordrecht: Reidel.

Harvard Law Review Association. 1993. "Developments in the Law: Legal Responses to Domestic Violence." *Harvard Law Review*, 106: 1498.

    1966. Note. "Litigation Between Husband and Wife." *Harvard Law Review*, 79: 1650.

Haskins, George Lee, and Herbert A. Johnson. 1981. *The Oliver Wendell Holmes Devise: History of the Supreme Court of the United States: Foundations of Power: John Marshall, 1801–15.* Paul A. Freund, ed. Volume 2. New York: MacMillan.

Hastings v. Judicial Conference of the United States. 1984. 593 F. Supp. 1371.

Hawrylyshn, Oli. 1976. "The Value of Household Services: A Survey of Empirical Estimates." *Review of Income & Wealth*, 22: 101.

Hayburn's Case. 1792. 2 U.S. (2 Dall.) 409.

Hayek, Friedrich H. 1952. *The Sensory Order: An Inquiry into the Foundations of Theoretical Psychology*. Chicago: University of Chicago Press.

   1973. *Law, Legislation and Liberty*. Chicago: University of Chicago Press.

Heise, Michael. 2004. "Litigated Learning and the Limits of Law." *Vanderbilt Law Review*, 57: 2417.

   2005. "*Brown v. Board of Education*, Footnote 11, and Multidisciplinarity." *Cornell Law Review*, 90: 279.

Heller, Michael A. 1998. "The Tragedy of the Anticommons: Property in the Transition from Marx to Markets." *Harvard Law Review*, 111: 621.

Helvering v. Davis. 1937. 301 U.S. 619.

Henkin, Louis. 1976. "Is There a 'Political Question' Doctrine?" *Yale Law Journal*, 85: 597.

Henrich, Joseph. 2000. "Does Culture Matter in Economic Behavior? Ultimatum Game Bargaining Among the Machiguenga of the Peruvian Amazon." *American Economic Review*, 90: 973.

Henrich, Joseph R., et al. 2001. "In Search of *Homo Economicus*: Behavioral Experiments in 15 Small-Scale Societies." *American Economic Review*, 91: 73.

Hines, N. William. 1966. "Real Property Joint Tenancies: Law, Fact, and Fancy." *Iowa Law Review*, 51: 582.

Hirshleifer, Jack. 1999. "There Are Many Evolutionary Pathways to Cooperation." *Journal of Bioeconomics*, 1: 73.

Hirschman, Albert. 1985. "Against Parsimony: Three Easy Ways of Complicating Some Categories of Economic Discourse." *Economics and Philosophy*, 1: 7.

Ho Ah Kow v. Nunan. 1879. 12 F. Cas. 252.

Hoffer, Peter Charles, and N. E. H. Hull. 1984. *Impeachment in America, 1635–1805*. New Haven, Conn.: Yale University Press.

Hoffman, Elizabeth, Kevin McCabe, and Vernon L. Smith. 1996. "Social Distance and Other-Regarding Behavior in Dictator Games." *American Economic Review*, 86: 653.

   1999. "Social Distance and Other-Regarding Behavior in Dictator Games: Reply." *American Economic Review*, 89: 340.

Hofstra Law Review Association. 1997. "Symposium on Judicial Independence." *Hofstra Law Review*, 25: 703.

Honig v. Doe. 1988. 484 U.S. 305.

Horowitz, Donald. 2000. *The Deadly Ethnic Riot*. Berkeley, Calif.: University of California Press.

Humphrey's Executor v. United States. 1935. 295 U.S. 602.

Hutchins, Edwin. 1995. *Cognition in the Wild*. Cambridge, Mass.: M.I.T. Press.

Hutto v. Finney. 1978. 437 U.S. 678.

Hylton v. United States. 1796. 3 U.S. (3 Dall.) 171.

Idaho v. Couer d'Alene Tribe. 1997. 521 U.S. 261.

Ifill, Sherrilyn. 1997. "Judging the Judges: Racial Diversity, Impartiality and Representation on State Trial Courts." *Boston College Law Review*, 39: 95.

   2000. "Racial Diversity on the Bench: Beyond Role Models and Public Confidence." *Washington & Lee Law Review*, 57: 405.

Illegal Immigration Reform and Immigrant Responsibility Act of 1996. Pub. L. No. 104-208, 110 Stat. 3009–3546.

Immigration and Naturalization Service v. Chadha. 1983. 462 U.S. 919.

In re Certain Complaints. 1986. 783 F.2d 1488.

"Inquiry Clears Chief D.C. Judge of Steering Cases of Clinton Friends." 2001. *Commercial Appeal*, Feb. 27.

Isaac, R. Mark, et al. 1985. "Public Goods Provision in an Experimental Environment." *Journal of Public Economics*, 26: 51.

Isaac, R. Mark, and James M. Walker. 1988a. "Group Size Effects in Public Goods Provision: The Voluntary Contributions Mechanism." *Quarterly Journal of Economics*, 103: 179.

　　1988b. "Communication and Free-Riding Behavior: The Voluntary Contribution Mechanism." *Economic Inquiry*, 26: 585.

Isaac, R. Mark, James Walker, and Arlington Williams. 1994. "Group Size and the Voluntary Provision of Public Goods: Experimental Evidence Utilizing Large Groups." *Journal of Public Economics*, 54: 1.

Jackson, Robert. 1971. Article. *New York Times.* Dec. 9, p. 26.

Jacobs, Clyde E. 1972. *The Eleventh Amendment and Sovereign Immunity.* Westport, Conn.: Greenwood Press.

Jay, Stewart. 1997. *Most Humble Servants: The Advisory Role of Early Judges.* New Haven, Conn.: Yale University Press.

Jefferson, Thomas. 1813. Letter to Isaac McPherson. In H. A. Washington, ed., *The Writings of Thomas Jefferson.* Volume 6. New York: H. W. Derby, 1861.

Jensen, Michael C., and William H. Meckling. 1976. "Theory of the Firm: Managerial Behavior, Agency Costs, and Ownership Structure." *Journal of Financial Economics*, 3: 305.

Jessup, Dwight Wiley. 1987. *Reaction and Accommodation: The United States Supreme Court and Political Conflict, 1809–1835.* New York: Garland.

Johnson v. De Grandy. 1994. 512 U.S. 997.

Johnson v. Zerbst. 1938. 304 U.S. 458.

Jolls, Christine, Cass R. Sunstein, and Richard Thaler. 1998. "A Behavioral Approach to Law and Economics." *Stanford Law Review*, 50: 1471.

"Judges Scrap Rule Used in Hubbell, Trie Cases." 2000. *Commercial Appeal*, Feb. 3.

Judicial Conference of the United States. 1995. Long Range Plan for the Federal Courts.

Judicial Councils Reform and Judicial Conduct and Disability Act. 1980. Pub. L. No. 96-458, 94 Stat. 2035.

Judiciary Act of 1789.Ch. 20, § 11, 1 Stat. 73.

Kahan, Dan M. 1996. "What Do Alternative Sanctions Mean?" *University of Chicago Law Review*, 63: 591.

　　1997. "Social Influence, Social Meaning, and Deterrence." *Virginia Law Review*, 83: 349.

Kahneman, Daniel, et al. 1998. "Shared Outrage and Erratic Awards: The Psychology of Punitive Damages." *Journal of Risk and Uncertainty*, 16: 49.

Kahneman, Daniel, Jack L. Knetsch, and Richard H. Thaler. 1986. "Fairness as a Constraint on Profit Seeking: Entitlements in the Market." *American Economic Review*, 76: 728.

Kaiser Steel Corp. v. W. S. Ranch Company. 1968. 391 U.S. 593.

Kammen, Michael. 1986. *A Machine that Would Go of Itself: The Constitution in American Culture.* New York: Knopf.

Kant, Immanuel. 1788, 1956. *Critique of Practical Reason.* Trans. L. W. Beck. Indianapolis: Bobbs-Merrill.

Karst, Kenneth. 1980. "The Freedom of Intimate Association." *Yale Law Journal*, 89: 624.

Keeney v. Tamayo-Reyes. 1992. 504 U.S. 1.

Kilgrow v. Kilgrow. 1958. 107 So. 2d 885.

Kimel v. Florida Board of Regents. 2000. 528 U.S. 62.

Klerman, Daniel. 1999. "Nonpromotion and Judicial Independence." *Southern California Law Review*, 72: 455.

Kluger, Richard. 1976. *Simple Justice.* New York: Knopf.

Knight, Frank H. 1921. *Risk, Uncertainty and Profit.* New York: Houghton Mifflin Co.

Koch, Adrienne. 1950. *Jefferson and Madison: The Great Collaboration.* New York: Knopf.

Kollock, Peter. 1998. "Transforming Social Dilemmas: Group Identity and Co-Operation." In Peter A. Danielson, ed., *Modeling Rationality, Morality, and Evolution.* New York: Oxford University Press.

Kornhauser, Lewis A., and Lawrence G. Sager. 1986. "Unpacking the Court." *Yale Law Journal*, 96: 82.

Korobkin, Russell. 2003. "Bounded Rationality, Standard Form Contracts, and Unconscionability." *University of Chicago Law Review*, 70: 1203.

Korobkin, Russell B., and Thomas S. Ulen. 2000. "Law and Behavioral Science: Removing the Rationality Assumption from Law and Economics." *California Law Review*, 88: 1051.

Kozinski, Alex. 1998. "The Many Faces of Judicial Independence." *Georgia State University Law Review*, 14: 861.

Kramer, Larry D. 1990. *Report of the Federal Courts Study Committee.*

 1992. "The Lawmaking Power of the Federal Courts." *Pace Law Review*, 12: 263.

 1999. "Madison's Audience." *Harvard Law Review*, 112: 611.

 2000. "Putting the Politics Back into the Political Safeguards of Federalism." *Columbia Law Review*, 100: 215.

 2001. "The Supreme Court, 2000 Term – Foreword: We the Court." *Harvard Law Review*, 115: 4.

Kruman, Marc W. 1997. *Between Authority and Liberty: State Constitution Making in Revolutionary America.* Chapel Hill, N.C.: University of North Carolina Press.

Kurtz, Stephen G. 1957. *The Presidency of John Adams.* Philadelphia: University of Pennsylvania Press.

Laird v. Tatum. 1972. 408 U.S. 1.

Lawler, Edward, and Jeongkoo Yoon. 1996. "Commitment in Exchange Relations: Test of a Theory of Relational Cohesion." *American Sociological Review*, 61: 89.

Lochner v. New York. 1905. 198 U.S. 45.

Ledyard, John O. 1995. "Public Goods: A Survey of Experimental Research." In John Kagel and Alvin Roth, eds., *Handbook of Experimental Economics.* Princeton, N.J.: Princeton University Press.

Lempert, Richard, and Joseph Sanders. 1986. *An Invitation to Law and Social Science.* New York: Longman.

Lessig, Lawrence. 1995. "The Regulation of Social Meaning." *University of Chicago Law Review*, 62: 943.

    2001. *The Future of Ideas: The Fate of the Commons in a Connected World*. New York: Random House.

Leuchtenberg, William. 1995. *The Supreme Court Reborn*. New York: Oxford University Press.

Levmore, Saul. 1995. "Love It or Leave It: Property Rules, Liability Rules, and Exclusivity of Remedies in Partnership and Marriage." *Law and Contemporary Problems*, 58: 221.

Lewis, Evelyn Alicia. 1994. "Struggling with Quicksand: The Ins and Outs of Cotenant Possession, Value Liability and a Call for Default Rule Reform." *Wisconsin Law Review*, 1994: 331.

Lieberman, David. 1999. "Media Giants' Net Change: Major Companies Establish Strong Foothold Online." *USA Today*. Dec. 14, p. B2.

Liljeberg v. Health Services Acquisition Corporation. 1988. 486 U.S. 847.

Lillich, Richard B. 1960. "The Chase Impeachment." *American Journal of Legal History*, 4: 49.

Liner v. Jafco, Inc. 1964. 375 U.S. 301.

Llewellyn, Karl N. 1950. "Remarks on the Theory of Appellate Decision and the Rules or Canons About How Statutes Are to Be Construed." *Vanderbilt Law Review*, 3: 395.

Longaker, Richard P. 1956. "Andrew Jackson and the Judiciary." *Political Science Quarterly*, 71: 341.

Lord v. Veazie. 1850. 49 U.S. (8 How.) 251.

Louisiana Power & Light Company v. City of Thibodaux. 1959. 360 U.S. 25.

Louisville & Nashville Railroad Company v. Mottley. 1908. 211 U.S. 149.

Loving v. Virginia. 1967. 388 U.S. 1.

Lujan v. Defenders of Wildlife. 1992. 504 U.S. 555.

Luna, Erik. 2000. "Transparent Policing." *Iowa Law Review*, 85: 1107.

Lundberg, Shelly, and Robert A. Pollak. 1996. "Bargaining and Distribution in Marriage." *Journal of Economic Perspectives*, 10: 139.

Luther v. Borden. 1849. 48 U.S. (7 How.) 1.

Madison, James. 1788. Letter to Thomas Jefferson, October 17, 1788. In Robert A. Rutland et al., eds., 1978. *The Papers of James Madison*. Volume 11. Chicago: University of Chicago Press.

    Notes of Debates in the Federal Convention of 1787. Indexed edition, 1984. Athens, Ohio: Ohio University Press.

    .*Writings*. Jack N. Rakove, ed., 1999. New York: Library of America.

Malone, Dumas. 1970. *Jefferson the President: First Term, 1801–1805*. Boston: Little, Brown.

Manuel, Frank E., and Fritzie Manuel. 1979. *Utopian Thought in the Western World*. New York: Free Press.

Marbury v. Madison. 1803. 5 U.S. (1 Cranch) 137.

Marcus, Maeva, ed. 1988. *The Documentary History of the Supreme Court of the United States, 1789–1800: The Justices on the Circuit*. Volume 2. New York: Columbia University Press.

Markovits, Inga. 1996. "Children of a Lesser God: GDR Lawyers in Post-Socialist Germany." *Michigan Law Review*, 94: 2270.

Marwell, Gerald, and Ruth E. Ames. 1981. "Economists Free Ride, Does Anyone Else?: Experiments on the Provision of Public Goods, IV." *Journal of Public Economics*, 15: 295.

McAdams, Richard H. 1997. "The Origin, Development, and Regulation of Norms." *Michigan Law Review*, 96: 338.

      2000. "A Focal Point Theory of Expressive Law." *Virginia Law Review*, 86: 1649.

      2001. "Signaling Discount Rates: Law, Norms, and Economic Methodology." *Yale Law Journal*, 110: 625.

McBryde v. Committee to Review Circuit Council Conduct & Disability Orders. 1999. 83 F. Supp. 2d 135.

McCabe, Kevin A., and Vernon L. Smith. 2003. "Strategic Analysis in Games: What Information Do Players Use?" In Elinor Ostrom and James Walker, eds., *Trust and Reciprocity: Interdisciplinary Lessons from Experimental Research*. New York: Russell Sage Foundation.

McCleskey v. Zant. 1991. 499 U.S. 467.

McCullagh, Declan. 1998. "Knifing the Baby." *Wired News*. <http://wired-vig.wired.com/news/politics/0,1283,16082,00.html>.

McCulloch v. Maryland. 1819. 17 U.S. (4 Wheat.) 316.

McFadden, Daniel. 2001. "Economic Choices." *The American Economic Review*, 91: 351.

McGinnis, Michael D. 1986. "Issue Linkage and the Evolution of International Cooperation." *Journal of Conflict Resolution*, 30: 141.

McGuire v. McGuire. 1953. 59 N.W.2d 336.

McKay, Robert B. 1956. "'With All Deliberate Speed': A Study of School Desegregation." *New York University Law Review*, 31: 991.

McKean, Margaret A. 1992. "Success on the Commons: Comparative Examination of Institutions for Common Property Resource Management." *Journal of Theoretical Politics*, 4: 247.

Meese, III, Edwin. 1987. "The Law of the Constitution." *Tulane Law Review*, 61: 979.

Merrill, Thomas W. 1998. "Property and the Right to Exclude." *Nebraska Law Review*, 77: 730.

Merryman, John Henry. 1985. 2nd edition. *The Civil Law Tradition*. Stanford, Calif.: Stanford University Press.

Mertes, Kate. 1988. *The English Noble Household, 1250–1600: Good Governance and Politic Rule*. New York: Blackwell.

Milgrom, Paul, and John Roberts. 1992. *Economics, Organization and Management*. Englewood Cliffs, N.J.: Prentice-Hall.

Miller v. Miller. 1889. 42 N.W. 641.

Miller v. Miller. 1948. 30 N.W.2d 509.

Miller, Geoffrey P., and Lori S. Singer. 1999. "Norm Enforcement in a Noncooperative Setting." Unpublished manuscript.

Milliken v. Bradley. 1977. 433 U.S. 267.

Minnesota Statutes, 2002.

Minow, Martha. 1992. "Stripped Down Like a Runner or Enriched by Experience: Bias and Impartiality of Judges and Jurors." *William & Mary Law Review*, 33: 1201.

Minow, Martha, and Elizabeth V. Spelman. 1988. "Passion for Justice." *Cardozo Law Review*, 10: 37.

Miranda v. Arizona. 1966. 384 U.S. 436.

Missouri v. Holland. 1920. 252 U.S. 416.

Mitchell, Thomas W. 2001. "From Reconstruction to Deconstruction: Undermining Black Landownership, Political Independence, and Community Through Partition Sales of Tenancies in Common." *Northwestern University Law Review*, 95: 505.

Monaghan, Henry P. 1973. "Constitutional Adjudication: The Who and When." *Yale Law Journal*, 82: 1363.

*Moore v. City of East Cleveland.*1977. 431 U.S. 494.

Moore v. Dempsey. 1923. 261 U.S. 86.

Morone v. Morone. 1980. 413 N.E. 2d 1154.

Mullenix, Linda S. 1991. "Hope Over Experience: Mandatory Informal Discovery and the Politics of Rulemaking." *North Carolina Law Review*, 69: 795.

    1992. "The Counter-Reformation in Procedural Justice." *Minnesota Law Review*, 77: 375.

    1995. "Judicial Power and the Rules Enabling Act." *Mercer Law Review*, 46: 733.

Murchison, Brian C. 2000. "Law, Belief, and *Bildung*: The Education of Harry Edwards." *Hofstra Law Review*, 29: 127.

Myers v. United States. 1926. 272 U.S. 52.

National Commission on Judicial Discipline and Removal. 1993a. Hearings of the National Commission on Judicial Discipline and Removal.

    1993b. Executive Summary to the Report of the National Commission on Judicial Discipline and Removal.

National Commission on Judicial Discipline and Removal Act. 1990. Pub. L. No. 101-650, §§ 409–410, 104 Stat. 5124, 28 U.S.C. § 372(c).

National Research Council. 2002. *The Drama of the Commons.* Elinor Ostrom et al., eds. Washington, D.C.: National Academy Press.

Naughton, John. 1999. *A Brief History of the Future: The Origins of the Internet.* London: Weidenfeld & Nicolson.

Neely, Jr., Mark E. 1991. *The Fate of Liberty.* New York: Oxford University Press.

Nelken, David. 1996. "The Judges and Political Corruption in Italy." *Journal of Law and Society*, 23: 95.

New Orleans Public Service, Inc. v. Council of the City of New Orleans. 1989. 491 U.S. 350.

New York Times. Dec. 9, 1971.

Nichol, Gene R. 1987. "Ripeness and the Constitution." *University of Chicago Law Review*, 54: 153.

Nixon v. United States. 1993. 506 U.S. 224.

Nollan v. California Coastal Commission. 1987. 483 U.S. 825.

Nolo Press. 2000. "Living Together: A Legal Guide for Unmarried Couples." <http://www.nolo.com/>.

Norris-LaGuardia Act. 2002. 29 U.S.C. §§ 101–105.

North, Douglass C. 1981. *Structure and Change in Economic History.* New York: Norton.

    1990. *Institutions, Institutional Change and Economic Performance.* Cambridge, U.K., New York: Cambridge University Press.

Northern Pipeline Construction Company v. Marathon Pipe Line Company. 1982. 458 U.S. 50.

Northwestern University School of Law. 2003. "Symposium: Empirical Legal Realism: A New Social Scientific Assessment of Law and Human Behavior." *Northwestern University Law Review*, 97: 1075.

Nowak, Martin A., et al. 2000. "Fairness Versus Reason in the Ultimatum Game." *Science*, 289: 1773.

O'Brien v. Brown. 1972. 409 U.S. 1.

Ockenfels, Axel, and Joachim Weinmann. 1999. "Types and Patterns: An Experimental East-West-German Comparison of Cooperation and Solidarity." *Journal of Public Economics*, 71: 275.

Oetjen v. Central Leather Company. 1918. 246 U.S. 297.

Ohio Bureau of Employment Services v. Hodory. 1977. 431 U.S. 471.

Okin, Susan Moller. 1989. *Justice, Gender, and the Family.* New York: Basic Books.

Okin, Susan Moller et al. 1999. *Is Multiculturalism Bad for Women?* Princeton, N.J.: Princeton University Press.

Olsen, Frances E. 1985. "The Myth of State Intervention in the Family." *University of Michigan Journal of Law Reform*, 18: 835.

Olson, Mancur. 1965. *The Logic of Collective Action: Public Goods and the Theory of Groups.* Cambridge, Mass.: Harvard University Press.

Orbell, John M., Alphons J. C. van de Kragt, and Robyn M. Dawes. 1988. "Explaining Discussion-Induced Cooperation." *Journal of Personality and Social Psychology*, 54: 811.

Ortmann, Andreas, and Lisa K. Tichy. 1999. "Gender Differences in the Laboratory: Evidence from Prisoner's Dilemma Games." *Journal of Economic Behavior and Organization*, 39: 327.

Osborn v. Bank of the United States. 1824. 22 U.S. (9 Wheat.) 738.

O'Shea v. Littleton. 1974. 414 U.S. 488.

Ostrom, Elinor. 1990. *Governing the Commons: The Evolution of Institutions for Collective Action.* New York: Cambridge University Press.

1998. "A Behavioral Approach to the Rational Choice Theory of Collective Action." *American Political Science Review*, 92: 1.

1999. "Coping with Tragedies of the Commons." *Annual Review of Political Science*, 2: 493.

2000. "Collective Action and the Evolution of Social Norms." *Journal of Economic Perspectives*, 14: 137.

2001. "Reformulating the Commons." In Joanna Burger, et al., eds., *Protecting the Commons: A Framework for Resource Management in the Americas*, 17–41. Washington, D.C.: Island Press.

Ostrom, Elinor, Roy Gardner, and James Walker. 1994. *Rules, Games, and Common-Pool Resources.* Ann Arbor: University of Michigan Press.

Pacific States Telephone & Telegraph Company v. Oregon. 1912. 223 U.S. 118.

Parden v. Terminal Railway. 1964. 377 U.S. 184.

Parfit, Derek. 1984. *Reasons and Persons.* Oxford: Clarendon Press.

Pennell v. City of San Jose. 1988. 485 U.S. 1.

Pennhurst State School and Hospital v. Halderman. 1984. 465 U.S. 89.

Pennsylvania v. Union Gas Company. 1989. 491 U.S. 1.

Penry v. Lynaugh. 1989. 492 U.S. 302.

People v. Wheeler. 1973. 106 Cal. Rptr. 260.

Perez v. Brownell. 1958. 356 U.S. 44.

Pfander, James E. 1998. "History and State Suability: An 'Explanatory' Account of the Eleventh Amendment." *Cornell Law Review*, 83: 1269.

Plato. 1968. *The Republic*. Allan David Bloom, ed. New York: Basic Books.

Plaut v. Spendthrift Farm, Inc. 1995. 514 U.S. 211.

Plessy v. Ferguson. 1896. 163 U.S. 537.

Pollak, Robert A. 1985. "A Transaction Cost Approach to Families and Households." *Journal of Economic Literature*, 23: 581.

Pollock v. Farmers' Loan & Trust Co. 1895. 158 U.S. 601.

Posner, Eric A. 1996. "Law, Economics, and Inefficient Norms." *University of Pennsylvania Law Review*, 144: 1697.

    2000. *Law and Social Norms*. Cambridge, Mass.: Harvard University Press.

Posner, Richard A. 1996. *The Federal Courts*. Cambridge, Mass.: Harvard University Press.

    2003. 6th edition. *Economic Analysis of Law*. New York: Aspen Publishers.

Prison Litigation Reform Act. 2002. 18 U.S.C. § 3626(e)(2).

Putnam, Robert D. 1988. "Diplomacy and Domestic Politics: The Logic of Two-Level Games." *International Organization*, 42: 427.

    1993. *Making Democracy Work: Civic Traditions in Modern Italy*. Princeton, N.J.: Princeton University Press.

Quackenbush v. Allstate Insurance Company. 1996. 517 U.S. 706.

Quah, Euston. 1993. *Economics and Home Production: Theory and Measurement*. Aldershot, England: Avebury.

Quern v. Jordan. 1979. 440 U.S. 332.

Radin, Margaret Jane. 1987. "Market-Inalienability." *Harvard Law Review*, 100: 1849.

Railroad Commission v. Pullman Company. 1940. 312 U.S. 496.

Rakove, Jack N. 1996. *Original Meanings*. New York: A. A. Knopf.

Raphael, D. D. 1975. "The Impartial Spectator." In Andrew S. Skinner and Thomas Wilson, eds., *Essays on Adam Smith*. Oxford: Clarendon Press.

Ravitch, Frank S. 1999. *School Prayer and Discrimination*. Boston: Northeastern University Press.

Rawls, John. 1958. "Justice as Fairness." *Philosophical Review*, 67: 164.

    1971. *A Theory of Justice*. Cambridge, Mass.: Belknap Press of Harvard University Press.

    1993. *Political Liberalism*. New York: Columbia University Press.

    1999. *The Law of Peoples*. Cambridge, Mass.: Harvard University Press.

Redish, Martin H. 1984. "Judicial Review and the 'Political Question.' " *Northwestern University Law Review*, 79: 1031.

Reed, David P. et al. 1998. "Active Networking in End-to-End Arguments." <http://web.mit.edu/saltzer/www/publications/endtoend/ANe2ecomment.html>.

Reid, John. 2001. "Controlling the Law: Jeremiah Smith, William Plumer, and the Politics of Law in the Early Republic: New Hampshire, 1791–1816." Unpublished manuscript.

Resnik, Judith. 1988. "On the Bias: Feminist Reconsideration of the Aspirations for Our Judges." *Southern California Law Review*, 61: 1877.

    1999. "Judicial Independence and Article III: Too Little and Too Much." *Southern California Law Review*, 72: 657.

Reston, James. 1954. Article. *New York Times*. May 18, p. 14.

Rheinstein, Max, ed. 1954. *Max Weber on Law in Economy and Society*. Cambridge, Mass.: Harvard University Press.

Rizzo v. Goode. 1976. 423 U.S. 362.

Roe v. Wade. 1973. 410 U.S. 113.

Romano, Roberta, ed. 1993. *Foundations of Corporate Law*. New York: Oxford University Press.

Rooker v. Fiduciary Trust Company. 1923. 263 U.S. 413.

Rose v. Lundy. 1982. 455 U.S. 509.

Rosenberg, Gerald. 1991. *The Hollow Hope: Can Courts Bring about Social Change?* Chicago: University of Chicago Press.

Ross, Lee, and Andrew Ward. 1996. "Naïve Realism in Everyday Life: Implications for Social Conflict and Misunderstanding." In T. Brown, et al., eds., *Values and Knowledge*. Mahwah, N.J.: Lawrence Erlbaum Associates.

Roth, Alvin E. 1995. "Bargaining Experiments." In John H. Kagel and Alvin E. Roth, eds., *The Handbook of Experimental Economics*, 253–348. Princeton, N.J.: Princeton University Press.

Rothschild, Emma. 2001. *Economic Sentiments: Adam Smith, Condorcet, and the Enlightenment*. Cambridge, Mass.: Harvard University Press.

Ruger, Jennifer Prah. 1998. "Aristotelian Justice and Health Policy: Capability and Incompletely Theorized Agreements." Ph.D. diss., Harvard University.

Rules Enabling Act. 1934. Pub. L. No. 73-415, 48 Stat. 1064.

Saenz v. Roe. 1999. 526 U.S. 489.

Sager, Lawrence Gene. 1978. "Fair Measure: The Legal Status of Underenforced Constitutional Norms." *Harvard Law Review*, 91: 1212.

——— 1993. "Justice in Plain Clothes: Reflections on the Thinness of Constitutional Law." *Northwestern University Law Review*, 88: 410.

Sally, David. 1995. "Conversation and Cooperation in Social Dilemmas: A Meta-Analysis of Experiments from 1958 to 1992." *Rationality and Society*, 7: 58.

——— 2001. "On Sympathy and Games." *Journal of Economic Behavior and Organization*, 44: 1.

Saltzer, J. H. et al. 1981. "End-to-End Arguments in System Design." <http://web.mit.edu/saltzer/www/publications/endtoend/endtoend.pdf>.

Samuelson, Paul A. 1969. "Classical and Neoclassical Theory." In Robert W. Clower, ed., *Monetary Theory*. Harmondsworth: Penguin.

Sanders v. United States. 1963. 373 U.S. 1.

Saphire, Richard B., and Michael E. Solimine. 1988. "Shoring Up Article III: Legislative Court Doctrine in the Post *CFTC v. Schor* Era." *Boston University Law Review*, 68: 85.

Scheb II, John M., and William Lyons. 2000. "The Myth of Legality and Public Evaluation of the Supreme Court." *Social Science Quarterly*, 81: 928.

Schechter Poultry Corp. v. United States. 1935. 295 U.S. 495.

Schkade, David, et al. 2000. "Deliberating About Dollars: The Severity Shift." *Columbia Law Review*, 100: 1139.

Schlesinger v. Reservists Committee to Stop the War. 1974. 418 U.S. 208.

Schneider, Carl E., and Margaret F. Brinig. 2000. 2nd edition. *An Invitation to Family Law*. St. Paul, Minn.: West Group.

Schultz, Marjorie Maguire. 1982. "Contractual Ordering of Marriage: A New Model for State Policy." *California Law Review*, 70: 204.

Scott, Elizabeth S. 2000. "Social Norms and the Legal Regulation of Marriage." *Virginia Law Review*, 86: 1901.

Seminole Tribe v. Florida. 1996. 517 U.S. 44.

Sen, Amartya K. 1970. *Collective Choice and Social Welfare*. San Francisco: Holden-Day.

    1977. "Rational Fools: A Critique of the Behavioral Foundations of Economic Theory." *Philosophy and Public Affairs*, 6: 317.

    1980. "Equality of What?" In S. McMurrin, ed., *Tanner Lectures on Human Values*. Cambridge: Cambridge University Press.

    1982. "Rights and Agency." *Philosophy and Public Affairs*, 11: 3.

    1990. "Justice: Means versus Freedoms." *Philosophy and Public Affairs*, 19: 111.

    1992. *Inequality Reexamined*. Cambridge, Mass.: Harvard University Press.

    1999a. *Development as Freedom*. New York: Knopf.

    1999b. *Reason before Identity*. Oxford: Oxford University Press.

    1999c. "The Possibility of Social Choice." *American Economic Review*, 89: 349.

    2000a. "Consequential Evaluation and Practical Reason." *Journal of Philosophy*, 97: 477.

    2000b. "Global Doubts." *Harvard Magazine*, Sept.–Oct., p. 68.

    2000c. "Other People." *New Republic*, Dec. 12, pp. 23–30.

    2006. *Identity and Violence: The Illusion of Destiny*. New York: Norton.

Sentencing Reform Act of 1984, Pub. L. No. 98-473, 98 Stat. 1987.

Sharp, James Roger. 1993. *American Politics in the Early Republic*. New Haven, Conn.: Yale University Press.

Shiffrin, Seana Valentine. 2005. "What Is Really Wrong with Compelled Association?" *Northwestern University Law Review*, 99: 839.

Sierra Club v. Morton. 1972. 405 U.S. 727.

Silbaugh, Katharine. 1996. "Turning Labor Into Love: Housework and the Law." *Northwestern University Law Review*, 91: 1.

Sisk, Gregory C. et al. 1998. "Charting the Influences on the Judicial Mind: An Empirical Study of Judicial Reasoning." *New York University Law Review*, 73: 1377.

Sisk, Gregory C., and Michael Heise. 2005. "Judges and Ideology: Public and Academic Debates About Statistical Measures." *Northwestern University Law Review*, 99: 743.

Skinner, B. F. 1948, 1976. *Walden Two*. New York: Macmillan.

Slack, John M. 1979. "Commentary, Funding the Federal Judiciary." *West Virginia Law Review*, 82: 1.

Smith, Adam. 1776. *An Inquiry into the Nature and Causes of the Wealth of Nations*. 1976. Oxford: Clarendon Press.

    1790. *The Theory of Moral Sentiments*. D. D. Raphael and A. L. Macfie, eds., 1976. Oxford: Clarendon Press.

Smith, Michael D. 1983. *Race versus Robe: The Dilemma of Black Judges*. Port Washington, N.Y.: Associated Faculty Press.

Smith, Vernon, L. 1994 "Economics in the Laboratory." *Journal of Economic Perspectives*, 8: 113.

Sober, Elliott, and David Sloan Wilson. 1998. *Unto Others: The Evolution and Psychology of Unselfish Behavior*. Cambridge, Mass.: Harvard University Press.

South Dakota v. Dole. 1987. 483 U.S. 203.

Spohn, Cassia. 1990. "The Sentencing Decisions of Black and White Judges: Expected and Unexpected Similarities." *Law & Society Review*, 24: 1197.

State Farm Fire & Casualty Company v. Tashire. 1967. 386 U.S. 523.

Steffensmeier, Darrell, and Chester L. Britt. 2001. "Judges' Race and Judicial Decision Making: Do Black Judges Sentence Differently? *Social Science Quarterly*, 82: 749.

Stern, Robert L., et al. 1993. 7th edition. *Supreme Court Practice*. Washington, D.C.: Bureau of National Affairs.

Steward Machine Company v. Davis. 1937. 301 U.S. 548.

Stoebuck, William, Dale A. Whitman, and Roger A. Cunningham. 2000. 3rd edition. *The Law of Property*. St. Paul, Minn.: West Group.

Stone v. Powell. 1976. 428 U.S. 465.

Stout, Lynn A. 2002. "Judges as Altruistic Hierarchs." *William & Mary Law Review*, 43: 1605.

　　2003. "On the Proper Motives of Corporate Directors (Or, Why You Don't Want to Invite *Homo Economicus* to Join Your Board)." *Delaware Journal of Corporate Law*, 28: 1.

Strawbridge v. Curtiss. 1806. 7 U.S. (3 Cranch) 267.

Stuart v. Laird. 1803. 5 U.S. (1 Cranch) 299.

Stumpf, Harry P. 1998. *American Judicial Politics*. Upper Saddle River, N.J.: Prentice Hall.

Stumpf, Harry P. and John H. Culver. 1992. *The Politics of State Courts*. New York: Longman.

Sugarman, David. 2002. "The Pinochet Precedent and the 'Garzón Effect': On Catalysts, Contestation and Loose Ends." *Amicus Curiae*, 42: 10.

Sumner v. Mata. 1982. 455 U.S. 591.

Sunderland, Edson R. 1934. "The Grant of Rule-Making Power to the Supreme Court of the United States." *Michigan Law Review*, 32: 1116.

Sunstein, Cass R. 1988. "Standing and the Privatization of Public Law." *Columbia Law Review*, 88: 1432.

　　1996a. "Social Norms and Social Roles." *Columbia Law Review*, 96: 903.

　　1996b. "On the Expressive Function of Law." *University of Pennsylvania Law Review*, 144: 2021.

　　2003. *Why Societies Need Dissent*. Cambridge: Harvard University Press.

Sunstein, Cass R., et al. 1988. "Assessing Punitive Damages." *Yale Law Journal*, 107: 2071.

　　2000. "Do People Want Optimal Deterrence?" *Journal of Legal Studies*, 29: 237.

　　2002a. "Predictably Incoherent Judgments." *Stanford Law Review*, 54: 1153.

　　2002b. *Punitive Damages: How Juries Decide*. Chicago: University of Chicago Press.

　　2004. "Ideological Voting on Federal Courts of Appeals: A Preliminary Investigation." *Virginia Law Review*, 90: 301.

Swartzbaugh v. Sampson. 1936. 54 P.2d 73.

Swisher, Carl Brent. 1935. *Roger B. Taney*. New York: Macmillan Co.

Syrett, Harold C., ed. 1969. *The Papers of Alexander Hamilton: June 1793–January 1794*. Volume 15. New York: Columbia University Press.

Tacha, Deanell Reece. 1995. "Independence of the Judiciary for the Third Century." *Mercer Law Review*, 46: 645.

Taylor & Marshall v. Beckham. 1900. 178 U.S. 548.

Teague v. Lane. 1989. 489 U.S. 288.

Terlinden v. Ames. 1902. 184 U.S. 270.

Thomas v. Union Carbide Agricultural Products Company. 1985. 473 U.S. 568.

Times Film Corp. v. City of Chicago. 1961. 365 U.S. 43.

Toilet Goods Association v. Gardner. 1967. 387 U.S. 158.

Tolman, Edgar Bronson. 1936. "Historical Beginnings of Procedural Reform Movement in This Country – Principles to Be Observed in Making Rules." *American Bar Association Journal*, 22: 783.

Townsend v. Sain. 1963. 372 U.S. 293.

Tribe, Laurence H. 2000. 3rd edition. *American Constitutional Law.* Volume 1. New York: Foundation Press.

Trop v. Dulles. 1958. 356 U.S. 86.

Troxel v. Granville. 2000. 530 U.S. 57.

Tversky, Amos, and Daniel Kahneman. 1987. "Rational Choice and the Framing of Decisions." In Robin Hogarth and Melvin Reder, eds., *Rational Choice.* Chicago: University of Chicago Press.

Twenty-first Century Department of Justice Appropriations Authorization Act. 2002. Pub. L. No. 107–273, 116 Stat. 1758.

Uhlman, Thomas M. 1978. "Black Elite Decision Making: The Case of Trial Judges." *American Journal of Political Science*, 22: 884.

United States v. Belmont. 1937. 301 U.S. 324.

United States v. Booker. 2005. 125 S.Ct. 738.

United States v. Curtiss-Wright Export Corp. 1936. 299 U.S. 304.

United States v. Johnson. 1943. 319 U.S. 302.

United States v. Lopez. 1995. 514 U.S. 549.

United States v. Morrison. 2000. 529 U.S. 598.

United States v. Richardson. 1974. 418 U.S. 166.

United States v. Robin. 1977. 553 F.2d 8.

United States v. Sandoval. 1913. 231 U.S. 28.

United States v. Students Challenging Regulatory Agency Procedures. 1973. 412 U.S. 669.

United States Census Bureau. 1996. *Statistical Abstract of the United States.* Washington, D.C.: U.S. Department of Commerce, Economics, and Statistics Administration, Bureau of the Census.

    1999. *Statistical Abstract of the United States.* Washington, D.C.: U.S. Department of Commerce, Economics, and Statistics Administration, Bureau of the Census.

United States Constitution.

University of Chicago. 1998. "Symposium: Social Norms, Social Meaning, and the Economic Analysis of Law." *Journal of Legal Studies*, 27: 537.

University of Pennsylvania. 1996. "Symposium: Law, Economics, and Norms." *University of Pennsylvania Law Review*, 144: 1643.

    2001. "Symposium: Norms and Corporate Law." *University of Pennsylvania Law Review*, 149: 1607.

Van Tassel, Emily Field. 1993. *Why Judges Resign: Influences on Federal Judicial Service, 1789–1992.* Washington, D.C.: Federal Judiciary History Office, Federal Judicial Center.

Village of Belle Terre v. Boraas. 1974. 416 U.S. 1.

Vining, Joseph. 1978. *Legal Identity: The Coming of Age of Public Law.* New Haven, Conn.: Yale University Press.

Virginia Law Review Association. 2002. "Symposium: The Legal Construction of Norms." *Virginia Law Review*, 86: 1577.

Wainwright v. Sykes. 1977. 433 U.S. 72.

Waley v. Johnston. 1942. 316 U.S. 101.

Walker, Thomas G., & Deborah J. Barrow. 1985. "The Diversification of the Federal Bench: Policy and Process Ramifications." *Journal of Politics*, 47: 596.

Warren, Charles. 1926. Revised edition. *The Supreme Court in United States History: 1789–1835.* Volume 1. Littleton, Colo.: F. B. Rothman.

Warth v. Seldin. 1975. 422 U.S. 490.

Washington, Linn. 1994. *Black Judges on Justice.* New York: New Press.

Wax, Amy L. 1998. "Bargaining in the Shadow of the Market: Is There a Future for Egalitarian Marriage?" *Virginia Law Review*, 84: 509.

Wayner, Peter. 2000. *Free For All: How Linux and the Free Software Movement Undercut the High-Tech Titans.* New York: Harper Business.

Wechsler, Herbert. 1961. *Principles, Politics, and Fundamental Law.* Cambridge, Mass.: Harvard University Press.

Weinstein, Mira. 1998. "Who Still Has a Choice?" *National NOW Times.* Washington, D.C.: National Organization for Women.

Weisselberg, Charles D. 1990. "Evidentiary Hearings in Habeas Corpus Cases." *Brigham Young University Law Review*, 1990: 131.

Welch, Susan et al. 1988. "Do Black Judges Make a Difference?" *American Journal of Political Science*, 32: 126.

Welch v. Texas Department of Highways and Public Transportation. 1987. 483 U.S. 468.

Whitebread, Charles H., and Christopher Slobogin. 1993. 3rd edition. *Criminal Procedure.* Westbury, N.Y.: Foundation Press.

Whittington, Keith E. 1998. "Dismantling the Modern State?: The Changing Structural Foundations of Federalism." *Hastings Constitutional Law Quarterly*, 25: 483.

    1999. *Constitutional Construction: Divided Powers and Constitutional Meaning.* Cambridge, Mass.: Harvard University Press.

Williams, Susan. 2002. "Religion, Politics, and Feminist Epistemology: A Comment on the Uses and Abuses of Morality in Public Discourse." *Indiana Law Journal*, 77: 267.

Williamson County Regional Planning Commission v. Hamilton Bank. 1985. 473 U.S. 172.

Williamson, Oliver. 1984. "Corporate Governance." *Yale Law Journal*, 93: 1197.

Wolfe, Alan. 1998. *One Nation, After All.* New York: Viking.

Wood, Gordon S. 1998. *The Creation of the American Republic 1776–1787.* Chapel Hill, N.C.: Published for the Institute of Early American History and Culture at Williamsburg, Virginia, by University of North Carolina Press.

Worcester v. Georgia. 1832. 31 U.S. (6 Pet.) 515.

Wright, Bruce. 1987. *Black Robes, White Justice.* Seacaucus, N.J.: L. Stuart.

Wright, Charles Alan. 1994. 5th edition. *Law of Federal Courts.* St. Paul, Minn.: West Publishing Company.

Wright, Charles Alan, and Kenneth W. Graham, Jr. 1977. *Federal Practice and Procedure.* Volume 21. St. Paul, Minn.: West Group.

Wright, Charles Alan, et al. 1988. *Federal Practice and Procedure.* Volume 17A. St. Paul, Minn.: West Publishing Company.

Wright, Robert. 1994. *The Moral Animal: The New Science of Evolutionary Psychology*. New York: Pantheon Books.

Yackle, Larry W. 1983. "The Exhaustion Doctrine in Federal Habeas Corpus: An Argument for a Return to First Principles." *Ohio State Law Journal*, 44: 393.

Yamagishi, Toshio. 1986. "The Structural Goal/Expectation Theory of Cooperation in Social Dilemmas." *Advances in Group Processes*, 3: 51.

Yeazell, Stephen C. 1987. *From Medieval Group Litigation to the Modern Class Action*. New Haven, Conn.: Yale University Press.

Younger v. Harris. 1971. 401 U.S. 37.

Zablocki, Benjamin. 1980. *Alienation and Charisma: A Study of Contemporary American Communes*. New York: Free Press.

Zelder, Martin. 1993. "The Economic Analysis of the Effect of No-Fault Divorce Law on the Divorce Rate." *Harvard Journal of Law and Public Policy*, 16: 241.

Zelmer, Jennifer. 2003. "Linear Public Goods Experiments: A Meta-Analysis." *Experimental Economics*, 6: 299.

Index